Fairbairn and the Origins of Object Relations

Edited by
JAMES S. GROTSTEIN
DONALD B. RINSLEY

Free Association Books/London
FAB *'an association in which the free development of*
each is the condition of the free development of all'

THE GUILFORD PRESS
New York   London

Published in Great Britain in 1994 by
Free Association Books Ltd
26 Freegrove Road
London N7 9RQ

Published in the United States in 1994 by
The Guilford Press
A Division of Guilford Publications, Inc.
72 Spring Street, New York, NY 10012

Printed in the United States of America

This book is printed on acid-free paper.

Last digit is print number: 9   8   7   6   5   4   3   2   1

A British CIP catalogue record for this book is available from
the British Library.
ISBN 1-85343-340-3

Library of Congress Cataloging-in-Publication Data
Fairbairn and the origins of object relations / edited by James S.
   Grotstein and Donald B. Rinsley.
      p.   cm.
   Includes bibliographical references and index.
   ISBN 0-89862-135-6
   1. Object relations (Psychoanalysis)   2. Fairbairn, W. Ronald D.
(William Ronald Dodds)   3. Object relations (Psychoanalysis)—
History.   I. Grotstein, James S.   II. Rinsley, Donald B.
BF175.5.O24F35 1994
155.2—dc 20   93-21211
                                                                   CIP

FAIRBAIRN AND THE ORIGINS
OF OBJECT RELATIONS

I am deeply indebted to the late Donald B. Rinsley for having asked me to join him as coeditor of this book, and am profoundly saddened at his untimely loss during the opening stages of our work. I hope he would have appreciated the final result. This work is dedicated to him, with the hope that it will honor his memory as well as Fairbairn's.

—JAMES S. GROTSTEIN

Contributors

ELEANORE M. ARMSTRONG-PERLMAN, M.A., T.Q.A.P. (Tavistock Qualification in Adult Psychotherapy), is a psychoanalytic psychotherapist in private practice.

W. RONALD D. FAIRBAIRN,* M.D., was a practicing psychoanalyst in Edinburgh and a member of the British Psycho-Analytical Society.

JAMES S. GROTSTEIN, M.D., is Clinical Professor of Psychiatry at the UCLA School of Medicine; Training and Supervising Analyst at the Los Angeles Psychoanalytic Institute and the Psychoanalytic Center of California, Los Angeles; and in the private practice of psychoanalysis.

VICTORIA HAMILTON, Ph.D., is Supervising and Training Analyst at the Institute of Contemporary Psychoanalysis, Los Angeles, and a member of the Association for Child Psychoanalysis (United States) and the Association of Child Psychotherapy (United Kingdom).

JUDITH M. HUGHES, Ph.D., is Professor of History at the University of California, San Diego, and Clinical Associate at the San Diego Psychoanalytic Institute.

OTTO F. KERNBERG, M.D., is Associate Chairman and Medical Director, The New York Hospital–Cornell Medical Center, Westchester Division; Professor of Psychiatry, Cornell University Medical College; and Training and Supervising Analyst, Columbia University Center for Psychoanalytic Training and Research.

STEPHEN A. MITCHELL, Ph.D., is Training and Supervising Analyst at the William Alanson White Institute and Faculty Member at the New York University Postdoctoral Program.

*Deceased

vii

ARNOLD H. MODELL, M.D., is Clinical Professor of Psychiatry at Harvard Medical School and Training and Supervising Analyst at the Boston Psychoanalytic Institute.

THOMAS H. OGDEN, M.D., is Co-Director of the Center for the Advanced Study of the Psychoses; Faculty Member at the San Francisco Psychoanalytic Institute; and Supervising and Training Analyst at the Psychoanalytic Institute of Northern California.

JOHN PADEL, M.R.C.Psych., is in private practice and was formerly Deputy to the Director of the London Clinic of Psycho-Analysis, Senior Tutor at the Institute of Psychiatry, and Honorary Consultant at the Tavistock Institute of Human Relations.

DONALD B. RINSLEY,* M.D., F.R.S.H., was Senior Faculty Member in Adult and Child Psychiatry at the Menninger School of Psychiatry and Associate Chief for Education, Psychiatry Service, Colmery–O'Neil Veterans Administration Medical Center, Topeka, Kansas.

MICHAEL ROBBINS, M.D., is Assistant Clinical Professor of Psychiatry, Harvard Medical School at McLean Hospital; Attending Psychiatrist at McLean Hospital; and a member of the Boston Psychoanalytic Society.

RICHARD L. RUBENS, Ph.D., is Faculty Member and Supervisor of Psychotherapy at the William Alanson White Institute; Adjunct Associate Professor in the Clinical Psychology Department of Teachers College, Columbia University; Faculty Member and Supervisor at the National Institute for the Psychotherapies; and in private practice.

JOHN D. SUTHERLAND,* M.D., was Training and Supervising Analyst for the British Psycho-Analytical Society; formerly Director of the Tavistock Clinic; and at one time Editor of the *International Journal of Psycho-Analysis*.

NEVILLE SYMINGTON, B.Sc., D.C.P., is a member of the British Psycho-Analytical Society, the Australian Psychoanalytical Society, and the Australian Psychological Society.

Acknowledgments

We wish to thank many individuals, organizations, and publishers for their gracious cooperation in helping this book to be published. I should like to express my own gratitude as well as that of the late Donald B. Rinsley to the Scottish Institute of Human Relations, especially to Mrs. Mona MacDonald, for their painstaking efforts and generosity in placing at my disposal so much of Fairbairn's memorabilia—particularly his "minor" contributions, which were published long ago and were not easily accessible otherwise. Mrs. Elinor Burtle, Fairbairn's daughter, has placed invaluable memorabilia at my disposal, including Fairbairn's correspondence and private notes on published and unpublished manuscripts and lectures; these, taken together, have been of profound importance in my learning how he came to develop his ideas. Unfortunately, space limitations prohibit a full itemization of them, but they subtlely occupy a great portion of my contributions to this volume. Nevertheless, it is hard to convey my thrill in experiencing his vitality in the immediacy of the creative presence evoked by these memorabilia. My regret is that I am unable to convey them at this time to the reader. Their richness deserves another volume, which I already have in mind to undertake.

In addition, I wish to thank the Scottish Association of Analytical Psychotherapists and the Scottish Division, Psychotherapy Section of the Royal College of Psychiatrists, for their joint sponsorship with the Scottish Institute of Human Relations of the W. Ronald D. Fairbairn Centennial Conference in Edinburgh, September 14–16, 1989. The conference provided significant inspiration for, contributions to, and input into this volume.

I am indebted to Dr. Glen Gabbard, medical director of the Menninger Hospital and the Menninger Foundation, for placing at our disposal copies of the late Harry Guntrip's unpublished autobiographical writings. I wish also to acknowledge my debt to Mrs. Marian Fairbairn and the Fairbairn family for their permission to republish Fairbairn's "Synopsis of an Object-Relations Theory of the Personality" (*International Journal of Psycho-Analysis*, 1963, 44, 224–225). A special acknowledgment is owed to the late Dr. John D. ("Jock") Sutherland for all his generosity, as well as intimate information about his long experience with Fairbairn.

I wish to acknowledge our gratitude to the *British Journal of Psychotherapy* for permission to adapt John Padel's "Narcissism—A Fairbairnian View" (1986, 3, 256–264); the *International Journal of Psycho-Analysis* for permission to republish Fairbairn's "Synopsis of an Object-Relations Theory of the Personality" (1963, 44, 224–225) and Thomas H. Ogden's "The Concept of Internal Object Relations" (1983, 64, 227–241); Jason Aronson, Inc., Publishers, for permission to republish Otto F. Kernberg's "Fairbairn's Theory and Challenge" (pp. 57–84), from his book *Internal World and External Reality* (1980); Analytic Press and Mrs. Charlotte Rinsley for permission to republish Donald B. Rinsley's "A Reconsideration of Fairbairn's 'Original Object' and 'Original Ego' in Relation to Borderline and Other Self Disorders" (pp. 219–232), from *The Borderline Patient: Emerging Concepts in Diagnosis, Psychodynamics, and Treatment*, Vol. 1 (1987), edited by James S. Grotstein, Marion F. Solomon, and Joan A. Lang; the University of California Press and the Regents of the University of California for permission to republish Judith M. Hughes's "Fairbairn's Revision of Libido Theory: The Case of Harry Guntrip" (pp. 95–117), from her book *Reshaping the Psychoanalytic Domain: The Work of Melanie Klein, W. R. D. Fairbairn, and D. W. Winnicott* (1989); *Contemporary Psychoanalysis* for permission to republish Stephen A. Mitchell's "The Origin and Nature of the 'Object' in the Theories of Klein and Fairbairn" (1981, 17[3], 374–398); the *American Journal of Psychoanalysis* for permission to adapt Michael Robbins's "A Fairbairnian Object Relations Perspective on Self Psychology" (1992, 52[3], 247–263); and Free Association Books for permission to republish John D. Sutherland's "Fairbairn's Achievement" (pp. 162–177) and to adapt his "Fairbairn's Main Papers" (pp. 179–181), from his book *Fairbairn's Journey into the Interior* (1989).[1]

I am indebted yet to others: my secretaries Shelley Turski and Yun Pak for their tireless efforts in preparing the manuscripts; Margaret

[1] I should note that in order to retain the style and flavor of the original publications, the republished material in this volume has been left essentially unaltered. Punctuation, capitalization, British spelling and usage in contributions that were originally published in Great Britain, reference style, and so forth are all as they were in the original papers.

Johnson, the librarian for the Los Angeles Psychoanalytic Society/Institute Library, and Lee Freeling, the librarian for the Reiss Davis Child Development Center, for their diligence and generosity in helping me with innumerable references; and to my wife, Susan, for her patience, encouragement, and help.

I cannot close the acknowledgments without a special acknowledgment of debt and gratitude to Dr. Ivan McGuire, who introduced the ideas of Fairbairn to many of us in Los Angeles and who, for many years, was his staunchest advocate.

JAMES S. GROTSTEIN

Contents

IV. FAIRBAIRN'S CONTRIBUTIONS TO UNDERSTANDING DISORDERS OF THE SELF

FAIRBAIRN AND THE ORIGINS
OF OBJECT RELATIONS

PART I

Introduction

1

Editors' Introduction

JAMES S. GROTSTEIN
DONALD B. RINSLEY

William Ronald Dodds Fairbairn has stood the test of time as one of the most original and important contributors to psychoanalysis in this century. Although eclipsed by the larger stars of Melanie Klein and Donald Winnicott, he nevertheless has finally emerged in his own right as a pivotal psychoanalytic thinker. Current research in infant development and child abuse, as well as in the primitive mental disorders such as borderline personality and narcissism, is increasingly taking notice of his invaluable concepts. It is now over 50 years since Fairbairn published his first major theoretical paper, "Schizoid Factors in the Personality" (1940), and the present volume is a tribute to his continuing impact on the development of object relations theory in psychoanalysis.

Fairbairn's name, like Freud's ("joy" in German), describes an important aspect of his contributions—that of acknowledging "fairness" to the child at a time when such a view could not be taken for granted. At the same time, his name represents the acknowledgment of the sense of a "blessing" offered to the "fair" child ("bairn").

His style of writing reveals a man who was highly sensitive, educated, philosophical, logical, and religious—one who had studied Latin and employed its arcane and cumbersome mode in his punctilious, complex, and highly structured sentences, which added all the more rigor to his reasoning. He was shy and uncharismatic, but revealed an inner flame of passion over the near-heretical views he offered to a psychoanalytic public that was unable, with a few outstanding exceptions, to comprehend their importance.

Isolated in Edinburgh, Fairbairn had few colleagues with whom he could share his ideas on an ongoing conversational basis. More importantly, he lacked the opportunity to obtain proper psychoanalytic training (including training analysis, supervisions, and disciplined reading of psychoanalytic works), although he read Freud and his followers on his own (Sutherland, 1989).

Yet, despite this stark and solitary existence, Fairbairn became the "voice of the North" in British psychoanalysis. He can be considered, along with Ian Suttie, the founder of the school and concept of "object relations" as it has come to be known, with allowances made for the earlier adumbrations of Freud and Abraham and the contributions of Klein. (The "object relations" taught and practiced by the British independent group should be distinguished from the Kleinian concept of "internal objects." In our chapters in this volume, Ogden, Mitchell, and I [J. S. G.] discuss at length the comparisons between Fairbairn's "object relatedness" and "endopsychic structure" on the one hand, and Klein's "internal objects" on the other.)

Fairbairn had begun to question some of Freud's most fundamental concepts during the hegemony of "orthodox" analysis, with its emphasis on the id and on the primacy of the instinctual drives. The rise of the school of ego psychology, principally in the United States, was in part a reaction to the same overemphasis on the id that Fairbairn protested. Fairbairn's lack of awareness of the object-related (relational) aspect of American ego psychology is a subject that Rinsley, Kernberg, Robbins, and Rubens discuss in their contributions. It is also a subject that I addressed personally to the late Harry Guntrip when I invited him to Los Angeles for a series of lectures, and that bore fruit in his subsequent work. I believe I succeeded in convincing Guntrip that ego psychology champions the idea of "adaptation," and that adaptation constitutes a *relational* theory, one in which there is an indivisible bond between infant and mother. Today we would speak in terms of "attunement," "mutuality," "reciprocity," and "intersubjectivity." What was to become clearer over time was that Fairbairn (and other members of the independent school) played a critical role in the theoretical development of British psychoanalysis, similar to the contributions of Erik Erikson to North American psychoanalysis.

Throughout his career, Fairbairn inaugurated a series of pivotal changes in psychoanalytic theory, many of which have been documented and critiqued by the contributors in this volume. His most central contributions can be summarized as follows:

1. He was the first to formulate a true object-related (relational) nature of the self (Sutherland, 1963, 1965, 1980, and Chapter 2, this volume; Guntrip, 1961, 1963, 1968, 1971, 1975; Mitchell, Chapter 5, this volume; Ogden, Chapter 6, this volume; Rubens, 1984 and Chapter 8,

this volume). In so doing, he stated that primary, nonpathological relationships are really *interpersonal* and not, like their pathological equivalents, internalized.

2. He helped to establish the psychoanalytic conception of infantile *dependence*, in contrast to primary autoerotic infantile *sexuality*, thus formulating the principles of infantile innocence and entitlement that anticipated the work of Bowlby on attachment.

3. His conception of endopsychic structure depicted the psyche as a closed system of egos and internalized objects, for which splitting and repression function as defensive operations. For Fairbairn, endopsychic structure was the indicator and subsequent cause of pathology (Mitchell, Chapter 5, this volume; Rubens, 1984 and Chapter 8, this volume).

4. He discovered the existentialist domain of schizoid isolation and withdrawal, which has had important ramifications for the treatment of traumatic, symbiotic, borderline, and narcissistic personality disorders.

FAIRBAIRN'S OBJECT-RELATIONAL THEORY OF THE SELF

Fairbairn believed that normal human relationships are fundamentally interpersonal. In this sense he differentiated between "interpersonal relationships" and "object relationships." A nonpathological relationship with a real person, he maintained, does not require internalization because the interpersonal interaction is inherently satisfying. In contrast, an intolerably ambivalent relationship results in a splitting of one's attitude about the person, such that the *rejected* part of that person is transformed into the status of an "internal object."[1] Thus, the shadow of object relations falls upon interpersonal relations and inexorably constrains them.

In Fairbairn's object-relational view, then, it is the *external* person who is the disappointing object. Pathological relationships are characterized by "object relatedness" in terms of their need to adapt to or comply with a disappointing real-life situation by internalizing the very badness of the needed (but rejecting) person. Indeed, the more unsatisfying an object (e.g., mother, father) has been in actual reality, the more a child is compelled to internalize it. Specifically, the child takes in those images of the mother or father that cause fear or shame. An important consequence of Fairbairn's theory is that all identifications are either defen-

---

[1]He subsequently modified this position when he allowed for the internalization of the *ideal* object to offset the badness of the other internalized objects. Yet here too, the ideal object is constrained in its internal role as the obligatory moderator of absolute badness to produce relative badness.

sive or pathological—a provocative but infrequently commented-on conception, and one that I address later.

The idea of "object relations" had been in the psychoanalytic literature ever since Freud discovered the instinctual drive theory and designated the "object" as both the target and facilitator of discharge. As a term in the psychoanalytic lexicon, "object" has been the cause of considerable confusion—and revision. When employed by Freud as contents of the unconscious, "objects" represented a sanitization of bygone demonology and even of alchemy, in the sense of eerie, transformed imagos of the inner world. Fairbairn, however, deferred to the contemporary usage of the term "object," which confused external persons and internal images, rather than the more experientially accurate "phantoms" or "chimerae," which, strictly speaking, are neither "selves" nor "objects." (See Chapter 6, of this volume, for a further discussion of this topic.)

Although for Fairbairn the term "object" persisted to connote actual human beings, an important distinction must be made between the concepts of "object" and "person." Fairbairn, confusingly, used "object" in two senses—as an *external* person and as an *internalized* (distorted) version of that person—but assigned the former sense to the interpersonal realm, and the latter sense to the pathological arena of object relations. Harry Guntrip (1975), one of Fairbairn's foremost expositors, failed to understand this difference, erroneously asserting that Fairbairn had discovered a "psychology of *personology*" (interpersonal), rather than a psychology of object relations.

Yet despite his dual usage of the term, Fairbairn viewed "objects" within a *relational* perspective—one that ran counter to Freud's (1905) conception of libido by assigning it instead to the ego drives and their pursuit of self-survival. Freud's (1914) "On Narcissism: An Introduction" and his (1917) "Mourning and Melancholia," however, are works dominated by an object (internal)-related orientation that Fairbairn could sanguinely endorse. But he did not seem to emphasize these contributions. He also failed to acknowledge the courageous efforts of Ian Suttie (1935), whose *The Origins of Love and Hate*, endorsed by the anthropologist Ashley Montagu, had fundamentally challenged the then-dominant school of "orthodox" analysis. Nor was Fairbairn conversant with the object relations ideas of the Hungarian school (Ferenczi and Hermann in particular), which was to find later expression in England through Balint and Bowlby. Similarly, he was unaware of the contributions of Harry Stack Sullivan and his interpersonal school, as Greenberg and Mitchell (1983) have stated. It is ironic, therefore, that the recent contributions of Heinz Kohut, which bear such a striking resemblance to those of Fairbairn, never refer to Fairbairn's work. The same irony unfortunately applies to Winnicott, who never acknowledged Fairbairn's anticipations of his work along several avenues.

Yet Fairbairn did acknowledge the work of Melanie Klein and her idea of internal objects, although he conceptualized them differently. Whereas she pictured a primitive internal world, created by the infant's phantasmal transformation of external objects using its own instinctual palette, Fairbairn opted for the opposite—a transformation of the infant's instinctual world through impingement or neglect by external persons, the transformation being an accommodation of *necessity* in order to survive in the closed system of the family. One of our contributors, Michael Robbins, has commented on this in a previous publication (Robbins, 1980) and has provided a fresh consideration of this issue for this volume. Following Abraham (1924) and Freud, Fairbairn portrayed "object relatedness" as the intimate conjunction of instinctual experience with the corresponding external object (person).

Freud and Klein created an infant psychology based on a "purified pleasure ego" that banishes, through splitting-off and projecting, contradictory self-experiences. In contrast, Fairbairn stressed the infant's need to create, at the expense of his own pleasurable ego, the myth of the "purified pleasuring mother"—by introjecting and identifying with her unpleasuring aspects. By postulating the obverse of classical and Kleinian theory, he helped us understand the well-known conundrum that the worse one's internal objects are experienced to be, the less one is able to leave them!

Fairbairn's ideas, which are clearly at variance with both traditional and Kleinian psychoanalysis, entitle him to be considered the founder of a distinctive branch of object relations theory. In this schema, there are four levels of object relations:

1. Internal object relations (Freud, Klein), which emphasize an internal world wherein "objects" are the instinctual transformations of the projecting subject.
2. Endopsychic structure (Fairbairn), which stresses the obligatory internalization (and alteration) of unsatisfying external objects (persons); that is, the internal objects reflect images of the needed but unsatisfying external person, modified (exaggerated and/or transformed) by the subject's capacity for phantasy.
3. Interpersonal relations (Sullivan) or "personology" (Guntrip), a psychology based on mishaps between the infant and mother, which anticipates self psychology.
4. The object-representational world of ego psychology.

These differences are discussed at greater length in the text of this book.

Fairbairn remained on the border between "person" and "object," emphasizing the idea of the former but cloaking it in the terms of the latter. In this sense, "object" designated an internal phantom whose exaggerations and distortions stem from unconscious mechanisms—a view held to an even stronger degree (at the expense of the concepts of "person" and "interpersonal") by Freud, Abraham, and Klein. To the extent that for Fairbairn the emphasis was on the "person" and on the "interpersonal," and on how the *breakdown* of the latter relationship inevitably results in "object relations" (endopsychic structure), he indeed was—and remains—unique.

INFANTILE DEPENDENCY

The infant is not oral because he is autoerotic; he is oral because he seeks a breast.—W. R. D. FAIRBAIRN

One of Fairbairn's first major challenges to contemporaneous Freudian thought was to the primacy and separateness of libido. Classical psychoanalytic metapsychology had emphasized autoeroticism as the key to infantile *sexuality.* Fairbairn, however, eschewed the notion that the drives are disconnected from the ego and from objects. He asserted that the ego is "object-seeking, not discharging," and that egos and objects are embraced in "dynamic relationships," which libido inseparably energizes.

Following in the footsteps of the Hungarian school of object relations and of Ian Suttie (1935) in Britain, Fairbairn continued the principle of genetic continuity (Isaacs, 1952) that had been adumbrated by Abraham (1924). This principle stressed the genetic importance and primacy of the *oral* stages of development, as well as the successive pregenital stages. Fairbairn (1941, 1943a, 1943b) suggested that infantile dependency undergoes an epigenesis, not merely to genitality, but through a transitional phase to the mature dependency of adulthood—a conception that Kohut (1984) was later to espouse.

He also embraced the idea of the separateness of the infant from birth—one that had already appeared in Klein's work and that challenged the classical notion of primary narcissism (Fairbairn, 1940). This concept of primary separateness was a seminal idea that helped the object relations school prepare the way for the modern conception of attachment theory and the indivisibility of the mother–infant bond. By elevating the mother to a primary importance (and assigning the father to a more subordinate role), it relegated the shibbolethic Oedipus complex to a constituent role of developmental succession.

When one reads psychoanalytic literature today, one is impressed by the extent to which the object relations views of Fairbairn pervade current classical psychoanalytic theory, especially with regard to the importance of the object (and selfobject) at the expense of the drives, and the importance of infantile (nurturing) dependency over Oedipal sexuality.

Dependency has now become the central issue in psychoanalytic theory and technique. In Fairbairn's terms, the issue is how to allow infantile dependency to emerge into mature (mutual) dependency, or what we would now call "interdependency." It is to Fairbairn's original influence that Bowlby's concepts of bonding and attachment owe some measure of their current popularity—especially as they have been translated into such contemporary terms as "mutuality," "interactionality," and "intersubjectivity," which are central to a new understanding of the analyst–patient relationship. Yet it is important to note that it was mainly Klein who, while trying to remain Freudian, eschewed Freud's idea of "infantile"[2] sexuality and opted instead for a breast–mouth relationship based on the ego or survival instincts rather than on the libidinal instincts.

What was at issue was a crucial paradigmatic change in culture and in psychoanalytic emphasis. Psychoanalytic theory was conjoined to the *Zeitgeist* of European logical positivism *and* of German Romanticism: The former informed psychoanalysis as a biology-derived science, and the latter informed its emphasis on the preternatural powers of Mother Nature and her instinctual forces, which, in the male-dominated and paternalistic spirit of the times, became translated into demonic sex drives. These forbidden sex drives were in turn linked with the quest for the mother's body, and with that for the father's body only by derivation. The sanctity–profanity associated with the inescapable lust for the mother's body became the issue of "infantile sexuality," the Oedipus complex, and the predominance of the pleasure principle. Klein (and the Hungarians) made the first break with tradition by de-emphasizing this hegemony in favor of the importance of the maternal breast–infant relationship.

Whereas Klein succeeded in illuminating the importance of the mother for the infant, she nevertheless continued the orthodox/classical tradition of the metaphor of the "demonic infant," *her* emphasis being on infantile *omnipotence* rather than infantile sexuality. It was here where Fairbairn (following Suttie) diverged, espousing that the infant should "be treated as a person in his own right," and thus establishing infantile innocence and entitlement as legitimate necessities for infant survival as a self. In so doing he discovered the premoral stage of infant development—one that was extraterritorial to the vicissitudes of instinctual drives and responsive to the nurturing environment (a subject to be addressed later by Winnicott, 1954, and Stern, 1985).

[2]I have placed "infantile" in quotes to note that Freud's concept of "infantile" applies more to toddlers and children. It was Klein, inspired by Abraham, who first enfranchised the truly infantile infant with mental life—that is, allowed for it to escape the anonymity of primary narcissistic mindlessness to which orthodox and classical analysis successively had committed it.

Winnicott followed Fairbairn with even greater enthusiasm for the positive aspects of infant entitlement, which he was to call "primary creativity." With it was also namelessly born the concept of "infantile innocence" (Grotstein, 1994a, 1994b), which was to free the infant from the ancient tradition of demonic signification. The orthodox/classical rejection of Klein may have been due in part to the patriarchal–matriarchal debate, whereas the classical *and* Kleinian differences from the hatred of the independent school may been partially due to the parent–child hierarchy. To put it succinctly, Freud championed the father, Klein the mother, and Fairbairn and Winnicott the child.

Fairbairn, like Winnicott, was essentially a "Kleinian revisionist," however. His ideas were based as much on her work as on Freud's, if not more so. His innovation was his greater emphasis on the *psychological importance* of the external nurturing person and of that person's failures. Thus Klein informed all his work, although perhaps not deeply enough since he was untrained in her theories, as Padel (Chapter 16, this volume) states. Perhaps he can be likened to Erik Erikson in the latter's modification of Freud in terms of social issues (as I have mentioned earlier and as Kernberg notes in his contribution), or to Wilfred Bion, the first Kleinian to place the external world in a Kleinian metapsychological perspective with his concepts of the "container" and the "contained," which modify the Kleinian conception of projective identification.

Fairbairn was critical of instinctual drive theory, but as many of our contributors demonstrate, he never completely abandoned it. In his attempt at a dependency-informed pragmatism about human relations, he shied away from Darwinism, biology, and innate aggression. Had he been informed by Hegel, as had Lacan, he might have said that the infant "desires the object's desire." What constitutes, then, the infant's *need* for the object—Fairbairn's answer to the Kleinian metaphor of breast milk? Recognition? Meaningfulness? Authentication? Mirroring? Safety? He settles for only one response—being treated as a person in his own right.

ENDOPSYCHIC STRUCTURE AND THE SCHIZOID CONDITION

Perhaps Fairbairn's most innovative ideas are those concerning endopsychic structure and the schizoid condition that subtends it. Essentially, Fairbairn created a psychoanalytic metapsychology based upon the splitting of the ego and its objects. According to Fairbairn, this splitting occurs in the earliest instance of dependent neediness (the oral sucking phase), when the infant's love is rejected; this triggers a severing of the original object into an accepting object and a rejecting one, as well as a corresponding split in the infant's own ego to conform to these new split objects, which then become internalized separately.

The schizoid condition constitutes man's fate, insofar as splitting inheres as an inevitable consequence of human experience. The very establishment of endopsychic structure is an archival testimony to archaic moments of critical disappointments. I use the term "disappointment" in its literal sense—when the original (all-good) object fails to keep its "appointment" when critically needed. Strictly speaking, then, no individual can escape being slightly "pathological," although this is a point that is debated by some of our contributors.

In identifying the schizoid personality, Fairbairn was emphasizing the experience of alienation, anticipating Winnicott's (1952, 1958, 1965, 1971) "false self" and Laing's (1960) "divided self." His was the first deficiency theory in psychoanalysis since Freud's (1911) concept of "decathexis." His belief that pathology as the result of deficit (based on environmental factors) was antecedent to conflict (based on instinctual drive excesses) distinguished him from both Freud and Klein. Yet Fairbairn's shift of emphasis from Freud's and Klein's melancholic paradigm, which led him to formulate the truly *withdrawn* personality, seems ultimately to be but a detour from theirs. Though they stressed that pathology results from the infant's sense of guilt and persecutory anxiety at hating (or causing harm to) the object, Fairbairn's schizoid infant believes that his *love* is bad because it has not been validated. The infant, in attributing the mother's rejection to his *a priori* badness, comes to believe that his love is inherently destructive (ruthlessly predatory). This schizoid process can readily be witnessed in infant research videotapes in which, after unsuccessful bonding or malattunement, the infant can be observed to give up, withdraw, and become detached (Murray, 1991; Trevarthen, 1991). The schizoid process seems also to become associated with the cases of psychological infantile autism that have been or are now being treated in psychoanalysis and psychoanalytic psychotherapy (Grotstein, 1993).

The phenomenon of the schizoid personality as an entity in its own right *and* as a universal personality characteristic escaped most psychoanalysts and mental health workers in Fairbairn's day, and failed to inspire an existential trend within psychoanalysis generally. But Fairbairn's concepts of splitting the ego and objects, of endopsychic structure, and of the moral defense of the superego offer a unique angle on the formation of the internal world, with enormous clinical implications in particular for victims of trauma (especially victims of child abuse and sufferers from multiple personality disorder). His understanding of schizoid withdrawal led to the definition of the narcissistic and borderline personality disorders.

In his papers "The War Neuroses—Their Nature and Significance" (1943a) and "The Repression and the Return of Bad Objects (with Special Reference to the 'War Neuroses')" (1943b), Fairbairn uncovered the "symbiotic personality" disorder in individuals who experienced the traumata of abrupt wartime separation and battle stress.

Although Klein relied on the inherent destructiveness of the death instinct to account for most psychopathology, positing that the infant unconsciously believes that his *hatred* is the irreducible element of its badness, Fairbairn maintained that the presence (or absence) of maternal love at the earlier oral (preambivalent) stage of sucking puts the infant at risk for believing that *love* is bad and dangerous, thereby instigating defensive schizoid withdrawal. He accorded the aspect of putative badness to the infant's depressive position where the experience of willful aggression (the stage of biting) can be owned.

Thus, one of Fairbairn's most unique contributions is a theory that is "premoral" and "preambivalent," and that attributes pathology not to destructiveness or hatred but to the failure of the capacity to love and to be considered a person in his own right.

THE DUAL-TRACK HYPOTHESIS

Relational analysis, of which Fairbairn can be considered a founder, has often been accused of "being in collusion with the patient" at the expense of allowing the patient to reown his own sense of self and the responsibility for it. In Fairbairn's deficit psychology, the schizoid and depressive positions are constrained by his predilection for "tragic man," whereas in Klein's theory of melancholia, the paranoid–schizoid and depressive positions are constrained by her adherence to "guilty man." Yet in Fairbairn's brief clinical notes in which he alluded to his interventions—and in Guntrip's (1975) account of his analysis with Fairbairn—one gets the impression that Fairbairn may have been moving toward a "dual-track" perspective, which we would today call a dialectic between "guilty man" and "tragic man."

To his credit, Fairbairn exemplifies this balanced view in his conception of endopsychic structure—especially in terms of how he conceives that the infant/patient seems to have surrendered his sense of self to the authority of the bad object, or at least believes that he does! Whereas Fairbairn was possibly attempting to rescue the psychoanalytic infant from the purgatory into which doctrinaire libido theory had cast him, he was not unaware of the dangers of its obverse—the "tabula rasa" paradigm, whose Skinnerian simplicity left the infant without an unconscious. Today, by employing a "dual-track" and semiotic theory, we are able to theorize more sanguinely that the infant *believes* that his inner nature (drives and feelings) has harmed the object, but also that the infant is, to a degree, very much at the mercy of outside forces or fate. It is critical that any psychoanalytic theory that purports to clarify the complexity of the human condition balance these two perspectives (inner and outer) constantly (Grotstein, 1994c).

CONCLUSION

It is our hope that the reader will emerge from this book well informed on Fairbairn. To do so, we recommend that this book be considered a complement to Sutherland's (1989) *Fairbairn's Journey into the Interior,* which portrays Fairbairn's life, his family, his times, and his creative struggles. But Sutherland's and our own efforts are no replacement for Fairbairn's (1952) main work, *Psychoanalytic Studies of the Personality,* which includes most of his important papers.

Fairbairn's brilliance shines throughout this volume. Each author's contribution offers a holographic miniature of the totality of his work. Many aspects of his theoretical and clinical contributions are discussed, illuminated, questioned, and restated along updated lines.

There are also criticisms of some of Fairbairn's shortcomings. Behind these exhortations may lie a disappointment (but not disillusionment) that this solitary, insufficiently recognized analyst *almost* succeeded in becoming acknowledged as one of the foremost thinkers of 20th-century psychoanalysis. His deserved acclaim was eclipsed by timing (analysts were not ready yet for his innovations), by politics (see the introduction to Chapter 7 of this volume for a brief explanation), and by the absoluteness as well as the unfinished and incomplete nature of some of his formulations (e.g., he rejected libido theory and yet retained it as a term in his lexicon of endopsychic structure). In this book, we hope to stimulate the reader's interest in and appreciation of a remarkably innovative man who might have become a castaway of history, had he not been rescued by a small band of advocates (principally Sutherland and Guntrip), by a timely resurgence of interest in infant development research, and by a changing atmosphere in psychoanalysis generally.

In closing this introduction, we quote directly from Fairbairn himself:

> I consider that the term 'analysis' as a description of psycho-analytic treatment is really a misnomer, and that *the chief aim of psycho-analytic treatment is to promote a maximum 'synthesis' of the structures into which the original ego has been split, in the setting of a therapeutic*

relationship with the analyst. Involved in the achievement of this aim are two further aims, viz. (a) a maximum reduction of persisting infantile dependence, and (b) a maximum reduction of that hatred of the libidinal object which, according to my theory, is ultimately responsible for the original splitting of the ego. Such aims, together with an aim to be mentioned, are, in my opinion, the chief aims of psycho-analytic treatment. The resistance on the part of the patient to the achievement of these aims is, of course, colossal; for he has a vested interest in maintaining the early split of his internalized object, upon which, according to my theory, the split of his ego depends, and which represents a defence against the dilemma of ambivalence. In addition, he has a vested interest in keeping his aggression internalized for the protection of his external libidinal object—with the result that his libidinal cathexis is correspondingly internalized. Implied in these various manifestations of resistance on the part of the patient is a further defensive aim which I have now come to regard as *the greatest of all sources of resistance— viz. the maintenance of the patient's internal world as a closed system.* In terms of the theory of the mental constitution which I have proposed, the maintenance of such a closed system involves the perpetuation of the relationships prevailing between the various ego structures and their respective internal objects, as well as between one another; and, since the nature of these relationships is the ultimate source of both symptoms and deviations of character, *it becomes still another aim of psychoanalytic treatment to effect breaches of the closed system which constitutes the patient's inner world, and thus to make this world accessible to the influence of the outer reality.* (Fairbairn, 1958, p. 380; emphasis in original)

REFERENCES

Abraham, K. (1924). A short study of the development of the libido. In *Selected Papers on Psycho-Analysis*. London: Hogarth Press, 1949, pp. 418–501.

Fairbairn, W. R. D. (1940). Schizoid factors in the personality. In *Psychoanalytic Studies of the Personality*. London: Tavistock, 1952, pp. 3–27.

Fairbairn, W. R. D. (1941). A revised psychopathology of the psychoses and psychoneuroses. In *Psychoanalytic Studies of the Personality*. London: Tavistock, 1952, pp. 28–58.

Fairbairn, W. R. D. (1943a). The war neuroses—their nature and significance. In *Psychoanalytic Studies of the Personality*. London: Tavistock, 1952, pp. 256–287.

Fairbairn, W. R. D. (1943b). The repression and the return of bad objects (with special reference to the 'war neuroses'). *British Journal of Medical Psychology*, 19, 327–341.

Fairbairn, W. R. D. (1952). *Psychoanalytic Studies of the Personality*. London: Tavistock.

Fairbairn, W. R. D. (1958). On the nature and aims of psycho-analytic treatment. *International Journal of Psycho-Analysis*, 39(5), 374–385.
Freud, S. (1905). Three essays on a theory of sexuality. *Standard Edition*, 7, 125–145.
Freud, S. (1911). Psycho-analytic notes on an autobiographical account of a case of paranoia (dementia paranoides). *Standard Edition*, 12, 3–84.
Freud, S. (1914). On narcissism: An introduction. *Standard Edition*, 14, 67–104.
Freud, S. (1917). Mourning and melancholia. *Standard Edition*, 14, 237-260.
Greenberg, J. R., & Mitchell, S. A. (1983). *Object Relations in Psychoanalytic Theory*. Cambridge, MA: Harvard University Press.
Grotstein, J. S. (Issue Ed.). (1993). Prologue to *Fear of Fusion*. *Psychoanalytic Inquiry*, 13(1), 1–8.
Grotstein, J. S. (1994a). Why Oedipus and not Christ?: The importance of innocence, original sin, and human sacrifice in psychoanalytic theory and practice. I. A selected re-reading of the myth of Oedipus and Christ. Manuscript in preparation.
Grotstein, J. S. (1994b). Why Oedipus and not Christ?: The importance of innocence, original sin, and human sacrifice in psychoanalytic theory and practice. II. The transference/countertransference neurosis psychosis and their consummate expression in the crucifixion, the Pieta, and "therapeutic exorcism." Manuscript in preparation.
Grotstein, J. S. (1994c). The dual-track theorem: A newer paradigm for psychoanalytic theory and technique. Manuscript in preparation.
Guntrip, H. (1961). *Personality Structure and Human Interaction*. London: Hogarth Press.
Guntrip, H. (1963). Psychodynamic theory and the problem of psychotherapy. *British Journal of Medical Psychology*, 36, 161–172.
Guntrip, H. (1968). *Schizoid Phenomena, Object-Relations and the Self*. London: Hogarth Press.
Guntrip, H. (1971). *Psychoanalytic Theory, Therapy, and the Self*. New York: Basic Books.
Guntrip, H. (1975). My experience of analysis with Fairbairn and Winnicott (How complete a result does psycho-analytic therapy achieve?). *International Review of Psycho-Analysis*, 2, 145–156.
Isaacs, S. (1952). The nature and function of phantasy. In M. Klein, P. Heiman, S. Isaacs, & J. Riviere, eds., *Developments in Psycho-Analysis*. London: Hogarth Press, pp. 67–121.
Kohut, H. (1984). *How Does Analysis Cure?*, A. Goldberg, ed. Chicago: University of Chicago Press.
Laing, R. D. (1960). *The Divided Self*. London: Tavistock.
Murray, L. (1991, June 29). A prospective study of the impact of maternal depression on infant development. Paper and videotape presented at "The Psychic Life of the Infant: Origins of Human Identity," conference sponsored by the University of Massachusetts at Amherst.
Robbins, M. (1980). Current controversy in object relations theory as outgrowth of a schism between Klein and Fairbairn. *International Journal of Psycho-Analysis*, 61, 477–492.

Rubens, R. L. (1984). The meaning of structure in Fairbairn. *International Review of Psycho-Analysis, 11*, 429–440.
Stern, D. (1985). *The Interpersonal World of the Infant.* New York: Basic Books.
Sutherland, J. D. (1963). Object-relations theory and the conceptual model of psychoanalysis. *British Journal of Medical Psychology, 36*, 109–124.
Sutherland, J. D. (1965). W. R. D. Fairbairn: Obituary. *International Journal of Psycho-Analysis, 46*, 245–247.
Sutherland, J. D. (1980). The British object relations theorists: Balint, Winnicott, Fairbairn, Guntrip. *Journal of the American Psychoanalytic Association, 28*, 829–860.
Sutherland, J. (1989). *Fairbairn's Journey into the Interior.* London: Free Association Books.
Suttie, I. (1935). *The Origins of Love and Hate.* New York: Matrix House, 1952.
Trevarthen, C. (1991, June 29). The other in the infant mind. Paper and videotape presented at "The Psychic Life of the Infant: Origins of Human Identity," conference sponsored by the University of Massachusetts at Amherst.
Winnicott, D. W. (1952). Psychoses and child care. In *Collected Papers: Through Pediatrics to Psycho-Analysis.* New York: Basic Books, 1958, pp. 219–228.
Winnicott, D. W. (1954). The depressive position in normal emotional development. In *Collected Papers: Through Pediatrics to Psycho-Analysis.* New York: Basic Books, 1958, pp. 262–277.
Winnicott, D. W. (1958). *Collected Papers: Through Pediatrics to Psycho-Analysis.* New York: Basic Books.
Winnicott, D. W. (1965). *The Maturational Processes and the Facilitating Environment: Studies in the Theory of Emotional Development.* New York: International Universities Press.
Winnicott, D. W. (1971). *Playing and Reality.* London: Tavistock.

2

Fairbairn's Achievement

JOHN D. SUTHERLAND

When I ask myself what the significance is of Fairbairn's contribution to psychoanalysis, my answer will strike most analysts as making grandiose claims. I believe, nevertheless, it is entirely accurate to say that he was the first to propose in a systematic manner the Copernican change of founding the psychoanalytic theory of human personality on the experiences within social relationships instead of on the discharge of instinctual tensions originating solely within the individual. In short, he replaced the closed-system standpoint of nineteenth-century science with the open-system concepts that were evolved by the middle of the present century to account for the development of living organisms, in which the contribution of the environment has to be considered at all times.

His viewpoint is receiving increasingly sympathetic and careful appraisal. Here I wish to stress that his specific theories about the structuring of the personality will certainly be amended, but such advances will be made by the adoption of his basic assumptions.

In judging the importance of his work, it is appropriate to comment first on his challenge to the fundamental assumptions upon which Freud's classical theories were based and which he retained until his death. Having asserted the vicissitudes in the personal relationships between the infant, his mother, and his family, as the primary consideration for the development of the personality instead of the instincts, there was, of

From *Fairbairn's Journey into the Interior* (pp. 162–177) by John D. Sutherland, 1989, London: Free Association Books. Copyright 1989 by John D. Sutherland. Reprinted by permission of the author and publisher.

course, no question of the instinctive endowment being ignored. The issue was how the interaction of the innate factors and the environment was conceived. Fairbairn was highly critical of the way in which instinctive energies were reified, one could almost say deified, in early psychoanalytic theory. Guntrip, following on this lead, has been interpreted as dispensing with 'the instincts', and at times he can give this impression. Like Fairbairn, however, he was in no way a naïve thinker. What they both felt strongly about, and it was this aspect of Fairbairn's writings that attracted Guntrip in the first instance, was that the concept of 'drives', the motivating forces originating in the instincts, was being used to create a quite inadequate picture of human nature.

The danger they reacted to was the insidious dehumanization of man with no adequate account of his nature at the personal level. With Guntrip's background as a clergyman it was easy to 'explain away' his arguments, though these were put forcefully. (It was not so widely known that Fairbairn had started out to become a clergyman and had retained an active membership of the Church, otherwise he, too, might have had an even less serious reception.)

The accepted theory of the instincts had, therefore, to be questioned as an appropriate foundation for the understanding of the conflicts underlying the presenting problems. Though that was naturally of the first importance, there were also dangers from its influence on social and cultural values. The pleasure accompanying the satisfactions of instinctive needs did not lose its importance; it was essential in selecting maintaining relatedness. When pleasure-seeking became the foremost motive, however, this was the result of a deterioration in the essential relationships, a failure in the attainment of the capacity for rich and mutual relations with others in which the individuality of the other provides a deeper satisfaction than the use of him or her to provide gratification. The unfortunate consequences of adopting Freud's instinct theory as making gratification the aim could be seen when the writings of social philosophers like Herbert Marcuse (1953) and Norman O. Brown (1929) were taken to justify sexual indulgence as something with little or no restraint—for 'kicks', as the saying went. Fairbairn was not concerned with moral values here. The biological importance of his views stemmed from his conviction that the family is the crucial agency in the development of healthy, creative individuals. For it to fulfill this function, sexuality is an essential component in the maintenance of the optimal relationship between the parents and between them and their children.

Both Fairbairn and Guntrip were trained in philosophy. In their book, *Ego and Instinct* (1970), the social scientist/philosopher Daniel Yankelovich and the philosopher William Barrett gave a highly pertinent critique of psychoanalytic theory. While neither was a practising analyst, both were well informed and deeply convinced of the importance of psycho-analysis for the human sciences in general. Their concern was to further its acceptance and development by getting its basic assumptions right, for in their view no science can progress unless this is done, and they thought those of psychoanalysis were wrong. Despite a great deal of dis-cussion with a group of distinguished analysts in Boston in the USA, they make no reference to Fairbairn, presumably because his book was not made known to them. (Elizabeth Zetzel, a leading figure of the psycho-analytical establishment in the Boston area, may have contributed to this neglect. In an article on 'Recent British approaches to problems of early mental development' (1955) she treated Fairbairn's views as an ingenious intellectual exercise, without seeing the fundamental challenge that his powerful clinical data had forced upon him.) I have always felt this was a great pity, because these thinkers reached conclusions closely similar to his and so might have added to the impact of all of them. They pro-pose as a fundamentally required step the replacement of the 'id' by one of 'developmentals'. These are the dynamic structures that are formed when instinctive activity interacts with critical experience at specific stages in the life cycle. Their concepts derive from a wide consideration of human development, social, cultural and biological, and their arguments add up to conclusions which cannot be ignored, the more so when placed along-side those reached by Fairbairn twenty-five years earlier. Nevertheless, their line of thought has had little effect upon psychoanalysis. The re-sponse to their book reassured me that the reluctant recognition of Fair-bairn's views could not be justified by the commonly expressed super-ficial reasons.

The issue that they and the 'object-relations' theorists had introduced has been a preoccupying one amongst analysts for the last fifty years. In an admirably critical and comprehensive account of its history, Greenberg and Mitchell (1983) have described this dialectic as showing the progres-sive encroachments of the object-relationships viewpoint into the drive theory. These challenges have been met by a succession of accommoda-tions made by tenacious analytic thinkers which bring out the increasing strain of defending an untenable position. In their constructive critique of the psychoanalytic view of human nature, Yankelovich and Barrett describe a similar process with which they draw a parallel in the devel-opment of astronomy, with the constant addition of epicycles to the tradi-tional scheme of the solar system.

As an evaluation of Fairbairn's views, I believe that of Greenberg and Mitchell is quite unusual in its scope and penetrative accuracy. They note that the abstractness of his language can mislead the reader into thinking that, in his stress on libido as object-seeking rather than pleasure-seek-ing, these are somewhat Talmudic and arcane distinctions. What Fairbairn is suggesting, according to them, is really a fundamentally different view of human motivation, meaning and values. The orientation of the infant to others is there from the very beginning because the infant has adaptive genic roots for his biological survival. Moreover, this urge to seek and maintain interaction with others is characteristic of adults at all stages of life.

Development begins in the total dependence of the infant, at which stage a security is normally established that lays the foundation for the later transformations towards the normal personality. Fairbairn's views of the transitional stage between this infantile dependency and maturity are not spelled out, and this is a weak feature of his developmental theory, though this lack is easily remedied from the wealth of data on childhood and adolescence. He does stress, however, that the earliest structuring from the experience in relationships forms a basic pattern which shapes the future patterns of relationships.

Clearly Fairbairn has left much that needs to be expanded, and what he ended with points to tasks for a more complete theory of the self as fashioned from relationships. His primary text, so to speak, is that the individual from the very start has to be loved for himself by the unconditional loving care of (at first) the mother. This loving care has then to be continued by the father as well, and adapted within the family to the specific behavioral stages brought about by maturation and the cultural environment. In all development and in maturity, persons have to be in satisfying relationships for their own survival together with that of their groups.

Assumptions about the infant not having any ego or self at the start contributed to the long period in which the self was scarcely mentioned. Freud's 'Ich' had the significance of the personal self until, as Bettelheim (1983) suggested, the absorption in instinct theory led to it being replaced the impersonal 'ego'. When Hartmann found it necessary to postulate an autonomous ego, he described the self as the separate structure that was cathected in narcissism. He did not elaborate the concept of the self, however, because of his inability to free himself from the traditional drive energies, even though he realized these were making a theoretical impasse.

If we take Fairbairn's basic statement we have clearly got to conceptualize a potential structure, operating as a whole, that only becomes functional, in the effective way for which it is designed, through certain experience with the mother, the father and the wider society. It 'seeks' to become the organizing agent of a conscious 'person' who remains aware of the continuity of his past with his present and of the future as immanent, and with a unique sense of himself as having an identity in relationship with other persons.

As mentioned earlier, Fairbairn accepted that 'self' is a more appropriate term in most of his considerations, since it refers to the whole from which sub-selves are spilt off. The ego is useful for the central self, that is, the dominant part of the self that incorporates the main purposes and goals of the individual in his relationships with the outer world and with which consciousness is usually associated.

Along with his humanistic and philosophical background, the understanding of the personality for Fairbairn had to be firmly based upon its evolution, that is, its biological roots. A modern image of man must illumine his essential properties, and for this I find Chein's (1972) definition invaluable. I have already referred to this but it will bear repetition. 'The essential psychological human quality is, thus, one of commitment to a developing and continuing set of unending, interacting, interdependent, and mutually modifying long-range enterprises' (Chein, 1972, p. 289). When we start with a modern biological outlook, we depart from Freud, for whom the science available allowed only the Newtonian base with its emphasis on the second law of thermodynamics. Chein concludes that man's motivation is a unique development. As a living organism, man is removed from the closed systems characterized by entropy, and this focus has to be replaced by a commitment to accomplish something—even if only the survival of his family in the environment.

As an open system, the living organism is 'negentropic', a feature maintained by its perpetual incorporation of energy. All organisms are created from other organisms. (For a modern perspective on evolution I am indebted to Jantsch (1980) and Jantsch and Waddington (1976).) They are wholes which cannot be made from the aggregation of parts. Their constant exchanges with the environment mean that constant transformations are proceeding, despite which they maintain their own characteristic form by a process of self-regulation. What is essential in these continuous self-renewals and self-expressions are the self-bounding processes rather than the changing structures. While evolution has led to many subsystems in the organism which maintain an equilibrium or steady state, this 'homoeostasis' does not obtain for the organism as a whole. At this level, equilibrium means death, because of the ending of the never-ceasing interaction with the environment in which processes of self-transformation and self-maintenance constitute life. As Sir Julian Huxley said, our perspective for man must be *sub specie evolutionis* rather than *sub specie aeternitatis*.

In the lower levels of the evolutionary scale the form of the animal along with its behavioral repertoire is directly determined by the genic inheritance. Thus, given that the dinosaurs lay their eggs in places that provide the appropriate environment, and with some early protection against external dangers, the embryo can emerge and fend for itself. An 'organizing principle' within the fertilized egg provides for successful maturation under these conditions. Life can be lived in an action mode with learning restricted to the limited skills required to feed, to fight and to mate. Evolutionary development does not greatly require increased adaptive capacities as long as the environment provides what is needed. Their huge physical bulk could evolve along with a relatively small brain being adequate for perceptual–motor learning and the co-ordination of all the bodily parts by the organizing principle its nervous system carried. Clearly this organizing principle is of the greatest importance, since it embodies the management of the life process as a whole. In the lower animals we can conceive of it carrying out this function on the basis of an affective field which controls the fitting together of sentient experiences from bodily and environmental changes according as the overall state is within the range of what feels 'right' or not 'painful'. Innate patterns for finding the objects required for survival can be transmitted by the genic inheritance, as they are in the human infant in 'desiring' and seeking the breast. In an unchanging environment little need for complex information storage arises. Any threat to its autonomy is a threat to life and so is reacted to ferociously and the individual and the species group survive.

When man is reached, an extremely complex behavioural equipment has been evolved. In brief, he has become a social person who survives not only by adaptation to, but largely by the creation of, his environment. Social animals survive by the evolution of innate mechanisms to keep them together, thereby gaining protection against predators and facilitating the rearing of the young. The common mode of achieving this grouping is by innate mechanisms creating attachment to dominant members. With the enormously increased psychological resources and creative capabilities required to cope with life in human communities, there has been an evolutionary development in which these are maximized by each individual acquiring a high level of autonomous creativity. The innate equipment for each has to provide for such development and the relatively huge cortex in man's brain emerges to meet it. As well as the behavioural systems providing for basic actions, there is now a great range of behavioural properties required for community living, especially for the amount of activity that has to be shared if optimal creativity is to be achieved. Relationships are mediated by holistic features in each human being, the essential character of which we describe as 'becoming a person'. The individual becomes aware of having a self and, moreover, a self which can transcend itself in order to observe and appraise its inner processes and its position in the world. When this subjectivity can be shared an enormous facilitation occurs for co-operative action in joint plans and purposes. *Homo sapiens* has emerged with all his unique characteristics. Added to the innate equipment that provides for the specific behaviour survival requires, there is now much behaviour that has innate components sufficiently influential to ensure its emergence, although not such as to restrict too narrowly the fit with the environment. The adaptive behaviour is then given a final pattern by training within the family and its society. Thus, what has been evolved in the genic inheritance is not the complete structural basis for the required behaviour, but a 'potential' for it, as in the acquisition of language.

The notion of inherited potential was thought by many biologists until recent years to be a somewhat vitalistic notion. Critical evidence came from the Cambridge ethologist W. H. Thorpe (1963) in the 1950s when he and his colleagues showed that while the basic song units in chaffinches were inherited the young birds could not perform the adult song unless they heard this from the adults. The possession of the song as shared by all members of the species is critical for survival. Learning from experience provided by the parents or adults had thus entered the process of evolution. With the mammals, prolonged parental care has become a necessity for dependent young. In man this care becomes loving care, and powerful love feelings have evolved as the great means of creating and maintaining the most vital human relationships, those in the family and in the group. (In connection with this outline see also Artiss, 1985.)

Yankelovich and Barrett quote from Cantril's study of functional uniformities in widely different cultures which suggest a list of innate potentials in the individual for behaviour at the human or personal level. The potential has to be realized within a specific culture, and in this way great variation exists in specific characteristics such as in languages. Language plays an essential part in many other acquisitions in which a rich range of communication amongst adults and between parents and children is required, while its symbolic function underpins creativity and the extremely flexible use in the development of tools and shared skills. Other innate potentials seem to be the attaining of food and shelter, getting security in a territorial and emotional sense, a need for ordering the data from environment, the need to seek new experiences, for procreation and safeguarding the future, the capacity to make choices, to experience a sense of the individual's own value to himself and others, and the need for a system of values and beliefs to which he can be committed and even sacrifice himself.

All these potentials, when realized, have to be fitted together and in an overall way that is managed by an autonomous self. As Angyal (1965) put it, it is paradoxical that this autonomy can only be attained within the heteronomy of being raised in, and belonging to, the community. In short, optimizing creativity in the individual can be achieved with a simultaneous bonding of the self to the group. This list is not quoted to be a comprehensive one of essential capacities, but to bring out how the highly complex task facing the individual in his development towards being a mature member of the community can be seen from an evolutionary standpoint. These attainments are all expressions of what we mean by becoming a person, that is, of having a mature self. Without these innate potentials and their development within the group to which persons will belong, or enough of them in sufficient measure, and without the integration or cohesive functioning that only a whole can offer, the individual cannot become a person.

Several specific capacities have been listed, but the critical feature has been left, namely, how the 'person' is formed as an essential unity. To put these capacities together in various ways does not add up to being a person. Indeed, to learn to fulfill most of them, the individual has to be a person in the first instance, for it is the sense of autonomous agency that determines the learning. Moreover, much learning, for example language, needs a shared subjectivity between mother and child. (See Stern, 1985.) An intensely dynamic potential power in the self is thus what motivates the sustained purposiveness of the individual to contribute to the well-being of himself and the group.

The answer to how the whole is formed can be given as the simple one that it is there from the start, a view adopted by Lichtenstein (1977). All organisms are wholes, and they create other wholes for survival. Fairbairn long felt critical of the atomism of so much analytic theorizing. He himself found no difficulty in assuming the existence of 'wholes'. That the infant gives the strong impression of being a whole 'person' from a very early stage is certainly vouchsafed by all parents and most infant–mother research workers. Kohut (1971) quotes the way adults react instinctively to babies as persons and treat them as such, usually with expressions to indicate their pleasure in responding to this quality, as strong evidence in favour of a whole self being actively present. It is not difficult to conceive of this potential being present in the innate endowment and giving rise to the 'expectation' to be treated in this way; and this does not only occur at the infant stage. The person at all stages of the life cycle resents not meeting this response from others, with intensities of feeling covering the whole range of aggression.

To return to Fairbairn, it is very much this trend of thought that can be seen in his conception of a unified self that is an autonomous potential, at first, and which is then suffused with a sense of of being a person in proportion as the mother's loving care is assimilated. It can also be inferred that frustrations that interfere with this autonomous development are reacted to as with the animal fighting for its life, for the self is the living centre of the individual.

Since being a person, that is, having a self that is autonomous yet preserving its autonomy or identity by means of its matrix of relationships, is the essential resource for effective enjoyable and satisfying living, the nature and development of the self is the paramount issue for general psychology as well as psychoanalysis. For the latter, the immediate concern is the role of the self in psychopathology. Fairbairn attributes all psychopathology to the splitting of the self in early experience, and Melanie Klein also adopted this position.

Winnicott's therapeutic studies, together with the observation of mothers and babies in his paediatric work, fully supported Fairbairn's assertion of the primacy of personal relationships for the development of the self. He spelled out the mother's empathic responsiveness as establishing a positive attitude to others and to the outer world. This attitude characterized the child's 'true self' in contrast with the conforming self that emerged to maintain the relationship with mother on her terms if not allowed enough scope to express his own. Bowlby (1980) has amply confirmed by his careful research studies the psychological necessities in the mother–child relationship. His theory of attachment stresses, so far, the conditions for the essential development of the self rather than the nature of the processes of the latter. He fully recognizes the complex developments involved in that process, a research area now receiving the attention of psychoanalytically trained workers. (See Stern, 1985.)

Clinical data suggest that, while the mother's initial influence establishes security or otherwise in the sense of being a person, the interaction with the father seems to be essential in the realization of the full autonomous potential. Winnicott (1971) referred to 'male and female elements' needing to be combined, and Fairbairn mentioned the need for a father. It would thus seem that while Fairbairn came to view the Oedipus situation in its relationship with infantile sexuality as a social situation and not a fundamental one for development as Freud had portrayed, there is another dimension to the importance of the relationship with the father in the maturation of the self. Indeed, Fairbairn's symptom can be seen as an attempt to bring back to life the father he had destroyed in phantasy, a need greatly increased when the imago of the castrating mother was revived by his wife's negative attitude to his work.

While it was the formation of splits in the self that formed the start of Fairbairn's line of thought, the defensive reactions against this situation suggest that the original self has retained a holistic dynamic within which these incompatible demands are dealt with, either by repression or by finding some substitute mode of satisfying the need. The structuring of these internal relations is much more complex than is apparent at first sight. Some of the internal objects have a relatively separate structure which is recognized as such, for example Freud's super-ego. The variety of objects and their topology seems to be quite large. Thus, Fairbairn regards dreaming not as wish-fulfilment but as the spontaneous 'imaginative' playing out of relations amongst them. The person, in short, emerges as a cast of characters, each related to a specific kind of object. These systems of self–object relationships have constant dynamic effects on each other and are also in perceptual contact with the other world, so that when it presents a situation that fits what an inner split self is seeking, then the latter can become activated to the point of taking overall control of the self. We see here the mode of action in compulsive relationships when the activation is intense.

  These subsystems, like the self as a whole, do not require to borrow energy from separate 'drives'. They operate in the quite different way that systems under cybernetic control do. The strength of the drive exhibited is governed by what is switched on by inner releasing mechanisms. The power of the whole self to manage behaviour with optimal adaptiveness is thus the resultant of the integrity of the whole self against the pressure from sub-selves, and these two sets of forces vary according to the past history of the person and the nature of the external environment to which behaviour is being directed. The outer world is frequently the main releaser of action, but more important are the internal goals and imagos embodied within the self, again with varying 'distances' from the central self. All of these carry a dynamic of internal origin into the world to mould it, even with considerable coercion, to attain its goals.

  With a sub-self becoming dominant, it is difficult to specify where the 'autonomy' of the self is then located. Even under strong compulsions, there is usually an awareness of the situation of being 'possessed', as though the observing self remains intact though powerless to exert enough control over it.

  The compelling power of subsystems is not confined to instinctive action from sexual or aggressive arousal. Though less dramatic, it seemed that Fairbairn's ideal self could separate itself from these pressures and retain its own motivation in the sustaining of his creative work. Freud met this problem when he discussed the ego ideal and when he puts civilization into an adversarial relationship with the autonomy of the self. His position is a complex one. On the one hand, he felt the individual has to accept tiresome constraints, yet he observed that with the development of the ideals shared by the group, the individual acquires an identity for his self that he defends against any threat. Furthermore, he does this with a ferocity that has to be conceived as coming from an elemental force, one he linked with his postulation of the death instinct. In short, if we adopt a theory of aggression as a reaction to danger, then threats to the autonomy of the self readily suggest the origin of hate; and its relative permanence follows from structured internal threats.

A comprehensive theory of the self will have to fill in the areas that are largely left out of consideration by Fairbairn. The whole of Fairbairn's transitional phase can be seen as occupied with the final structuring of the self under the influence of the realization of the various potential aspects, such as those listed by Yankelovich and Barrett. In this development, Erikson's contributions (Erikson, 1959) at once seem to fill in the gap, with the epigenetic phases presumably deriving from the maturation of developmental potentials in the experiences which each culture seeks to provide at the appropriate period. Fairbairn gave a theory of the basic structuring that arises from the experiences in the earliest stages of mismatch between the child's needs and the parental responses. The schizoid split has a far-reaching influence because of the early highly formative stage in which it operates. Subsequent stages, for example the phallic–masculine–gender complex, can be more restricted in the disturbance they engender when the schizoid position has been free of deprivation. This freedom from inner constraints is especially important when the investment of the self becomes so much focused in the deep satisfaction of using special talents, for example in the acquisition of knowledge and evolving specific goals for the self. The split-off internalized objects can have a great range in the degree to which they deform development, and here we note whole areas in which much more research is needed. When mention was made of Fairbairn's relationship with his father, it seemed as though his father, at least as a sexual figure, had remained very much separated within his self, though very much present despite his repression.

When we take an evolutionary perspective for the development of the self as a fundamental characteristic structure, then the understanding of the dynamic of the ego ideal becomes much more plausible than that offered by classical theory. Thus in his Introduction to Chasseguet-Smirgel's study of *The Ego Ideal* (1985), Lasch adopts her account, with all the richness of her observations of its development. Her basic assumptions, however, are strikingly rooted in a closed-system perspective from which all the commitments of man are seen to stem from his fear of death and a longing to re-establish a sense of primal unity with the natural order of things. Evolution, in contrast, can be seen as providing man with powerful innate potentials enabling him to strive purposefully, and not as a passive victim of chance and necessity, to alter this natural order. The prospect of death, moreover, is surely altered when it is seen as a planned necessity for the 'progress' of life that evolution appears to embody. The Socratic injunction to examine one's life can thus focus on what has been given to life by the individual.

Jantsch, in his view of the role of evolution, brings in the relevance of myths in man's awareness of his condition. For him, the striving after the 'steady state' of an imagined perfection is reflected in the myth of

Sisyphus. The evolutionary perspective on the other hand sees him as Prometheus. From our consideration of the self the vultures would then perhaps represent the deep hate over the frustrations of his autonomy—or the death instinct for Melanie Klein. It seemed to me that Fairbairn was always far more profoundly motivated by the 'developmentals' in Cantril's list than by a longing to return to the 'perfection' of the intra-uterine state. If evolution has a thrust in it 'to evoke', it is not too fanci-ful to imagine that man, or a proportion of men, get something of it within their nature. Hitherto his religions may have been one of its main expres-sions. Now he has to find ways in which selves in their groups do not need to eat each other, as the lower forms of life did, for survival. The development in social animals of the submissive action when a fight for domination has ended, exemplifies evolutionary possibilities.

Fairbairn's emphasis on relationships started in his suffering from bad ones. His potential for an ideal self seized on Christianity as a means of realizing it. He then discovered, as Freud did, that only more knowl-edge of the self would in the long run sustain him towards his goals.

In the formation of commitments, the internal object may occupy a very different position in that it may be suffused in its influence by an assimilation into the central ego. We get a strong impression that Freud was internalized in this was following upon the similar internalization of Christ. The situation is then extremely complex when what was the bad mother becomes the adopted model after a change in her attitude from castration to active encouragement of a masculine autonomy. I am re-minded here of Freud when puzzled to account for an instinctual demand being 'tamed' when brought into the ego. His solution was to seek help from 'the Witch Metapsychology' and I wonder if it was his 'bad mother' who unconsciously prompted this suggestion (Freud, 1937, p. 225). Fair-bairn recognized the therapeutic problem here because of the deeper hate being overlain by so much gratitude that was felt later for the support of the realization of his masculine ideals. When he referred at various points to the intense resistance aroused by the therapeutic process, this seems to centre on the fear for self-structures that have become so important. In these later internalizations, there is also the problem of the relation be-tween the parents being internalized, as when he felt in later adolescence he was in a secret collusion with his mother against his father. This enact-ment of the interparental conflicts within the self, with parts identified with each parent, is extremely common, highly destructive and highly resistant to exposure because of the threat to the integration of the self.

In this rather personal version of where I believe Fairbairn would have continued his journey, a particular area is outlined, because I be-lieve that the whole tenor of his work was steadily moving to the conceptualizing of the self. It was, after all, where he started, as Ernest Jones commented. Guntrip, his close student, moved openly in this direction and Fairbairn was not in any way out of sympathy. Klein's contribution can also be seen as heading in this direction, though I believe with Fairbairn that her theoretical progress was hampered by her adherence to the drive theory, especially in relation to aggression. But when a powerful ideal has been formed, with its inherently committed urges to sustained action, then the anchorage in the outer world keeps the interference of conflicting inner relations to a minimum. Fairbairn was struck by this feature, which Kris (1953) described in the artist, whose chaotic life in many areas was nevertheless not allowed to interfere with the creation of his object.

What is the significance of this approach for treatment? The main implication is what Melanie Klein and her group have expounded so clearly, that is, the need to focus on the inter-subjective process which underlines the transference phenomena. Fairbairn made a minor change to permit the analysand to see him if desired. I doubt whether this is of much importance. The psychoanalyst wants to get to the deepest layers of conflict, and for this purpose the classical method and setting have most to commend them. It is the perspective which the analyst brings to what is presented to him that is of the greatest importance. A consequence of being in practice for a very long time is that one sees several analysands who felt dissatisfied with what they had achieved in previous analysis, often many years earlier. I have been greatly impressed in these cases by the importance of exposing the internal object-relationships that get concealed within the central self and some of its activities. A particular constellation I have met is one in which a highly successful individual has become threatened with the sabotage of his success by, for instance, taking risks with actions that would bring public humiliation, and indeed succeeding at times. Dealing with these problems as related to impulses out of control had not produced appreciable change. What did prove effective in several cases was the exposure of the sadistic attack on the central self, identified with the mother, as a vengeful retaliation for early hostility from the mother to the masculine/sexual self identified with a despised father. A great deal of work in almost all of these cases had to go into the reparation of a deeply repressed destroyed mother who was later idealized. Correspondingly, the father had to be brought back into a state that corresponded with his good aspects. The best results seemed to follow when the self was felt to have brought both parents back internally into a good relationship. The great resistance was prominently related to a fear of going mad over the disintegration of the self or of committing suicide as a way out of the primitive hate for the mother's rejection of the autonomy of the self in becoming 'its true self'.

30 I. *Introduction*

One feature of working at the primitive levels of the development of the self is the impact on the analyst. What happened to Fairbairn has been described, and sadly with no help he could not work through this situation. For myself, I certainly experienced a good deal of unconscious turmoil from the recognition of much of the analysands' secret selves in myself. This point brings me to a Winnicott's accusing Fairbaim of 'knocking Freud'.

Greenberg and Mitchell are quite puzzled by this savage attack. The personalizing of this remark around Freud has to be noted, for what Fairbairn was challenging was not Freud, but his libido theory. Towards the person Freud, along with his work, Fairbairn's admiration and respect were reverential. Greenberg and Mitchell note most carefully that in contrast, Winnicott 'adopts' a version of Freud's theories that is quite at odds with what Freud postulated. In his intellectual work, Fairbairn is responsive all the time to Freud's views and his recasting of some of his assumptions is in no sense a destructive act directed at Freud. Freud was therefore an intellectual father who had been so profoundly admired that Fairbairn 'metabolized' him into his own self. His ideal object became his ego ideal, that is, a less concretely personalized structuring. This seems to be quite a distinct process from internalization of an idol and which persists largely in this form. Winnicott was well known as having a pronounced maternal character and he expressed a disappointment in the relationship with his father, whose busy life had prevented the close contact Winnicott would have liked. In *Playing and Reality* (1971, pp. 72 ff.) he describes a session with a middle-aged man in which he said to this patient: 'I am listening to a girl talking about penis envy.' This remark had a pronounced effect on the patient, but it also set up a deep personal experience that Winnicott needed to live through in the next few months to arrive at the understanding he reached about male and female. It felt to me that the incident had really disturbed Winnicott's envy and hate of his father, feelings in a secret self which he projected into Fairbairn in his attack. Greenberg and Mitchell clearly recognized his attack as quite irrational, in view of the closely related nature of his contribution with Fairbairn's.

In this connection, I have suspected that Kohut had a similar experience in the early stages of his work. There is no question of the value of Kohut's contributions in expanding the concept of the self with his rich descriptions, and I am very much in agreement with his eventual position of coming out boldly against the retention of the drive theory. What disturbed me is his lack of specific recognition of the work of others, a characteristic that Greenberg and Mitchell comment upon. His work has become adopted in a flood of enthusiasm in which the contribution of others is completely lost. Thus in a recent review of his work by Cooper

(1988), Kohut is credited with discovering the capacity for transference and its actual prominence in narcissistic patients, and other authors have noted *his* concepts of tragic versus Guilty Man, the perversions as products of deteriorated relationships, or of the Oedipus complex as a social derivative and not a basic aetiological issue. All of these ideas are expressed in the very words that Fairbairn used fifty years ago to describe his schizoid patients; he also commented on their omnipotence, though this was often concealed. Fairbairn, in turn, when he claimed the unusual readiness of these patients to form transferences, was drawing on Melanie Klein's description of its manifestations in severely disordered personalities. It has been noted by several analysts that Kohut's preoccupations have been a focus for many years amongst analysts, for example Harry Stack Sullivan, Winnicott and Michael Balint. Due accord should, of course, be given to those who introduce innovating thinking, but I am less concerned with the neglect of Fairbairn's contribution than with the avoidance of issues that can confront analysts with a threat to their work self.

I have a strong impression that Kohut read Fairbairn (I have been informed his work was talked about in the Institute of which Kohut was a member), but I do not imagine he was simply plagiarizing. It seems to me much more likely that his interest was deeply aroused, and he then split it off, because it was for him unconsciously disturbing and concerning lest it obtrude in a way that might invoke criticism from the establishment, to whose views he was for many years inordinately sensitive. What has almost convinced me in my belief is a passage very early on in *The Analysis of the Self* (1971, p. 14). He describes a particular defence against the dangerous regressive potential in the narcissistic personality which results in what is referred to as the *schizoid personality* (Kohut's italics), though he says it is not found in the analysable narcissistic disturbances. Such individuals have learned to distance themselves from others to avoid narcissistic injury. He then continues: '*In opposition to his explanation it might be claimed that the retreat of these persons from human closeness is caused by their inability to love and is noticeable by their conviction that they will be treated unempathically, coldly or with hostility*' (my italics). He claims this is incorrect, because many schizoid patients are capable of meaningful contact with others—a rather jejune remark for someone of Kohut's standing. I do not know of any writer other than Fairbairn who asserted that the schizoid personality had been made specifically afraid to love by the experience of rejection, and Greenberg and Mitchell describe this particular view as one of Fairbairn's most innovative ideas. If Kohut's interest was unconsciously aroused in it as something to be developed, it points to a difficulty in taking and giving that Fairbairn described as prominent in schizoid personalities. Fairbairn further suggested omnipotence and grandiosity as reactions to this form of deep insecurity, and to the covering over by these traits of the deep hatred for the early deprivation.

I do not make these observations lightly or disparagingly. For me their value is to draw attention to reactions in one's own self as one becomes immersed in the earliest phases of its development. Fairbairn's own disturbance, as well as Winnicott's, illustrates this possibility, which may account for some of the resistance to its close study.

Any borrowing, even if repressed, has had a valuable outcome in the way Kohut has developed his ideas in much more detail than Fairbairn did. Perhaps, too, much of what has been reacted to negatively in Kohut's work might well be overcome by the adoption of some of Fairbairn's rigorous and uncompromising statements of the basic assumptions that psychoanalysis must build upon. Fairbairn, I am certain, would have greatly welcomed Kohut's work with generous approval.

I am grateful to Professor Henry Walton for drawing my attention to a passage in *The Dean's December* (1982) where Saul Bellow gives his thoughts about the contemporary human scene in an interchange between the Dean and his wife, who was enraged by her mother's death. The Dean is reflective and says:

> It's the position of autonomy and detachment, a kind of sovereignty we're all schooled in. The sovereignty of atoms—that is, of human beings who see themselves as atoms of intelligent separateness. But all that has been said over and over. Like, how schizoid the modern personality is. The atrophy of feelings. The whole bit. There's what's-his-name—Fairbairn. And Jung before him comparing the civilized psyche to a tapeworm. Identical segments, on and on. Crazy and also boring, forever and ever. This goes back to the first axiom of nihilism—the highest values losing their value. (p. 259)

Such acknowledgement from one of our greatest contemporary writers seemed an appropriate finish.

REFERENCES

Angyal, A. (1965). *Neurosis and Treatment.* New York: Wiley.
Artiss, K. L. (1985). *Therapeutic Studies.* Rockville, MD: Psychiatric Books.
Bellow, S. (1982). *The Dean's December.* New York: Penguin.
Bettelheim, B. (1983). *Freud and Man's Soul.* New York: Knopf.
Bowlby, J. (1980). *Attachment and Loss.* London: Hogarth Press.
Brown, N. O. (1929). *Life against Death.* Middletown, CN: Wesleyan University Press.

Chasseguet-Smirgel, J. (1985). *The Ego Ideal.* London: Free Association Books.
Chein, I. (1972). *The Science of Behavior and the Image of Man.* New York: Basic Books.
Cooper, A. M. (1988). Review of *How Does Analysis Cure? Journal of the American Psychoanalytic Association, 36,* 175–179.
Erikson, E. (1959). *Identity and the Life Cycle.* New York: International Universities Press.
Freud, S. (1937). Analysis terminable and interminable. *Standard Edition, 23,* 209–253.
Greenberg, J. R., & Mitchell, S. A. (1983). *Object Relations in Psychoanalytic Theory.* Cambridge, MA: Harvard University Press.
Jantsch, E. (1980). *The Self-Organizing Universe.* Oxford: Pergamon Press.
Jantsch, E., & Waddington, C., eds. (1976). *Evolution and Consciousness.* Reading, MA: Addison-Wesley.
Kohut, H. (1971). *The Analysis of the Self.* New York: International Universities Press.
Kris, E. (1953). *Psychoanalytic Explorations in Art.* London: Allen & Unwin.
Lasch, C. (1985). Introduction. In J. Chasseguet-Smirgel, *The Ego Ideal.* London: Free Association Books.
Lichtenstein, H. (1977). *The Dilemma of Human Identity.* New York: Jason Aronson.
Marcuse, H. (1953). *Eros and Civilization.* Boston: Beacon.
Stern, D. N. (1985). *The Interpersonal World of the Infant.* New York: Basic Books.
Winnicott, D. W. (1971). *Playing and Reality.* London: Tavistock.
Yankelovich, D., & Barrett, W. (1970). *Ego and Instinct.* New York: Random House.
Zetzel, E. (1955). Recent British approaches to problems of early mental development. *Journal of the American Psychoanalytic Association, 3,* 534–543.

3

Synopsis of an Object-Relations Theory of the Personality

W. RONALD D. FAIRBAIRN

In response to many requests I have prepared the following brief synopsis of the theoretical views I have expounded over the last twenty years. (See bibliography.)

(1) An ego is present from birth.

(2) Libido is a function of the ego.

(3) There is no death instinct; and aggression is a reaction to frustration or deprivation.

(4) Since libido is a function of the ego and aggression is a reaction to frustration or deprivation, there is no such thing as an 'id'.

(5) The ego, and therefore libido, is fundamentally object-seeking.

(6) The earliest and original form of anxiety, as experienced by the child, is separation-anxiety.

(7) Internalization of the object is a defensive measure originally adopted by the child to deal with his original object (the mother and her breast) in so far as it is unsatisfying.

(8) Internalization of the object is not just a product of a phantasy of incorporating the object orally, but is a distinct psychological process.

(9) Two aspects of the internalized object, viz. its exciting and its frustrating aspects, are split off from the main core of the object and repressed by the ego.

From the *International Journal of Psycho-Analysis*, 1963, *44*, 224–225. Copyright 1963 by W. Ronald D. Fairbairn. Reprinted by permission of Mrs. Marian Fairbairn, the Fairbairn family, and the publisher.

(10) Thus there come to be constituted two repressed internal objects, viz. the exciting (or libidinal) object and the rejecting (or antilibidinal) object.
(11) The main core of the internalized object, which is not repressed, is described as the ideal object or ego-ideal.
(12) Owing to the fact that the exciting (libidinal) and rejecting (antilibidinal) objects are both cathected by the original ego, these objects carry into repression with them parts of the ego by which they are cathected, leaving the central core of the ego (central ego) unrepressed, but acting as the agent of repression.
(13) The resulting internal situation is one in which the original ego is split into three egos—a central (conscious) ego attached to the ideal object (ego-ideal), a repressed libidinal ego attached to the exciting (or libidinal) object, and a repressed antilibidinal ego attached to the rejecting (or antilibidinal) object.
(14) This internal situation represents a basic schizoid position which is more fundamental than the depressive position described by Melanie Klein.
(15) The antilibidinal ego, in virtue of its attachment to the rejecting (antilibidinal) object, adopts an uncompromisingly hostile attitude to the libidinal ego, and thus has the effect of powerfully reinforcing the repression of the libidinal ego by the central ego.
(16) What Freud described as the 'superego' is really a complex structure comprising (*a*) the ideal object or ego-ideal, (*b*) the antilibidinal ego, and (*c*) the rejecting (or antilibidinal) object.
(17) These considerations form the basis of a theory of the personality conceived in terms of object-relations, in contrast to one conceived in terms of instincts and their vicissitudes.

BIBLIOGRAPHY

Fairbairn, W. R. D. (1952a). *Psycho-Analytic Studies of the Personality.* (London: Tavistock; New York: Basic Books [1954].)
——— (1952b). 'Theoretical and Experimental Aspects of Psycho-Analysis.' *Brit. J. Med. Psychol.*, 25.
——— (1954). 'Observations on the Nature of Hysterical States.' *Brit. J. Med. Psychol.*, 27.
——— (1955). 'Observations in Defence of the Obeject-Relations Theory of the Personality.' *Brit. J. Med. Psychol.*, 28.
——— (1956a). 'A Critical Evaluation of Certain Psycho-Analytical Concepts.' *Brit. J. Philos. Sci.*, 7.

———— (1956b). 'Considerations arising out of the Schreber Case.' *Brit. J. Med. Psychol.*, **29**.

———— (1957). 'Freud, the Psycho-Analytical Method and Mental Health.' *Brit. J. Med. Psychol.*, **30**.

———— (1958). 'On the Nature and Aims of Psycho-Analytical Treatment.' *Int. J. Psycho-Anal.*, **39**.

Guntrip, H. (1961). *Personality Structure and Human Interaction.* (London: Hogarth.)

PART II

Theoretical Overview

Section A

Fairbairn and
Object Relations Theory

4

Fairbairn's Theory and Challenge

OTTO F. KERNBERG

Among the psychoanalytic theoreticians who have made object relations theory a major focus of their work, W. Ronald D. Fairbairn stands out because of his consistent effort to formulate a developmental model based upon the internalization of object relations, and also to establish a comprehensive object relations theory which would replace traditional metapsychology, particularly instinct theory.

In spite of his geographic isolation in Edinburgh, Fairbairn's ideas were intensively debated in the British psychoanalytic community. The originality of his clinical contributions regarding schizoid personalities and the relation between schizoid processes and hysterical dissociation, as well as his frontal attacks on Freud's dual-instinct theory made his work controversial, controversy further complicated by Melanie Klein's influence on him and by his radical rejection of the death-instinct theory. Indeed, fortunately for us, because he and the Kleinian group used similar terminology to cover very different concepts and because he revised some of his ideas, Fairbairn was several times prompted to restate his basic contributions. These overviews (1949, 1951, 1963) present an integrated and consistent viewpoint with broad theoretical and clinical implications.

Fairbairn remained relatively unknown to the American psychoanalytic community and the non-English speaking psychoanalytic societies throughout the nineteen-forties and fifties. It was Guntrip's book *Personality Structure and Human Interaction* (1961) with its detailed

From *Internal World and External Reality* (pp. 57–84) by Otto F. Kernberg, 1980, New York: Jason Aronson. Copyright 1980 by Otto F. Kernberg. Reprinted by permission of the author and publisher.

exposition of Fairbairn's views and almost fervent defense of these views against various criticisms which had been raised about them that made Fairbairn's views more widely known both in Great Britain and the United States. In fact, Guntrip's analysis of Fairbairn's work includes not only a detailed review of his major contributions, but an explicit outline of Fairbairn's theoretical system, its origins and relations to other formulations, and a passionate yet lucid support of Fairbairn's views. To this day, Guntrip's presentation of Fairbairn's theories is the most comprehensive we have.

In my opinion, however, Guntrip's presentation suffers from important shortcomings. He seems to me to have uncritically idealized Fairbairn's theories and at the same time to have subtly distorted them. Chiefly by means of emphasis, Guntrip makes it appear that Fairbairn is supporting Guntrip's own theoretical biases. In addition, Guntrip, by sharply attacking instinct theory and metapsychology, stretches Fairbairn's critique to accommodate his own views.

For example, Fairbairn stressed that libido was intrinsically object-seeking, and that the pleasure connected with good object relations corresponded to the "reality principle" in its most profound sense (in contrast to a "pleasure principle" unrelated to reality). But Guntrip implied that for Fairbairn the pleasurable aspects of satisfactory object relations were a consequence of them and not a primary motive for the libidinal approach to objects. Also, Guntrip fails to mention that Fairbairn adhered closely to classical psychoanalytic technique. Fairbairn proposed that, in addition to the analysis of the transference, the qualities of the personal relationship between the analyst and the patient were a crucial therapeutic factor in bringing about therapeutic change, but this view did not imply a retreat from a systematic analysis of the transference. Guntrip's blurring of the distinction between psychoanalytic and psychotherapeutic technique does not correspond to Fairbairn's clear delimitation of psychoanalytic treatment. Also, in order to highlight his own battle cry against traditional metapsychology, Guntrip fails to explore a number of significant theoretical issues wherein Fairbairn's thinking was potentially congruous with Freud's genetic and structural viewpoints and even with formulations of contemporary ego psychology regarding energic deployments in early development.

It is true that Fairbairn was inclined to emphasize his areas of disagreements with Freud, but this trend is softened by his thoughtful and profound understanding and acknowledgment of Freud's theoretical and clinical contributions, particularly Freud's clarification of neurotic psychopathology and his development of psychoanalytic technique as a basic psychological research instrument. In this regard, one might say that

Guntrip, while idealizing Fairbairn, also places greater stress on what, from a less partisan viewpoint, may appear the more problematic aspects of Fairbairn's contributions.

Furthermore, in his effort to replace traditional metapsychology by a "complete object relations theory of the personality," Guntrip (1961), although he reviews Fairbairn's theories in great detail, is much less systematic in reviewing his clinical contributions, such as the characteristics of the schizoid personality and of various types of psychopathology. Guntrip thereby significantly impoverishes the impression one gets of Fairbairn's contributions (this is particularly regrettable since the space given over to Fairbairn in Guntrip's book exceeds the length of Fairbairn's own theoretical statements).

The impression that Guntrip's summary of Fairbairn does not do justice to the richness of Fairbairn's thinking is supported by an article Guntrip wrote (1975) in which he describes his own psychoanalysis with Fairbairn (and subsequently with Winnicott). He criticizes Fairbairn for not deviating from standard technique and candidly admits that he selected Fairbairn as his analyst in the first place because he thought Fairbairn agreed with his own thinking and there would hence be no problem with theoretical discussions (!). While it would ordinarily not be appropriate to evaluate one man's personal motives for writing about another man's work, Guntrip's inclusion in his discussion of Fairbairn of his personal analysis with him (Guntrip wrote his book while he was being analyzed by Fairbairn) seems to me to justify the conclusion that Guntrip's idealization of Fairbairn was not devoid of significant ambivalence, an ambivalence that is reflected in his summary of Fairbairn's work. Glatzer and Evans (1977) and Anzieu et al. (1977) have also written about Guntrip vis-à-vis Fairbairn and Winnicott.

Sutherland's (1963, 1965, 1979) reviews of Fairbairn's work and Wisdom's (1962, 1963, 1971) comparative studies of the contributions of Fairbairn and Melanie Klein are also basically sympathetic, yet—in contrast to Guntrip—not uncritically partisan. In spite of the brevity of Sutherland's and Wisdom's articles, they jointly convey a more comprehensive idea of Fairbairn's basic contributions to psychoanalysis, in my opinion, than the reader is left with after an exhausting study of Guntrip's book.

Because some of Fairbairn's ideas have contributed to my own thinking and because I suspect they are not as well known as they might be and in order to correct certain impressions left by Guntrip, I am offering a summary and critique of Fairbairn's contributions—including what others have said about his theory—and describing how his work relates to contemporary ego psychology.

FAIRBAIRN'S CONTRIBUTIONS

Basic Theory: Schizoid Position

Fairbairn's core contributions include two clinical (1931 and 1936) and four theoretical papers (1941, 1943, 1944—with a 1951 addendum—and 1946). All these papers are included in Fairbairn's book (1954a), in addition to other clinical and miscellaneous papers and two of the overviews (1949, 1951) previously mentioned. Although several of Fairbairn's later publications (1954b, 1955, 1957, 1958, 1963) further clarified his theoretical thinking, and add significant clinical information in the process, in my opinion, the main body of his work lies in the earlier theoretical papers and in the clinical paper of 1931. This latter demonstrates the subtlety and acuity of Fairbairn's clinical understanding, his highly sophisticated treatment of an enormously difficult and complicated case.

Although Fairbairn possessed a truly elegant style of writing, it is not easy to extract his theory from a reading of his papers. Fairbairn himself, in his introduction (1954a, p. ix), explains why: ". . . this series of papers represents, *not the elaboration of an already established point of view, but the progressive development of a line of thought*. In other words, the series embodies the actual working out of a point of view, step by step" (emphasis in original). The raw material came from Fairbairn's consulting room; the point of view that emerged came from his analysis of clinical data—especially of dreams and transference phenomena.

In analyzing his patients' dreams, Fairbairn paid particular attention to the symbolic meanings attached to all the persons—real and fantastic, including various images of the same person and of the dreamer himself—in these dreams. He found in these "personifications" a remarkably stable organization.

Fairbairn at first saw personifications of objects (what I would call object representations) and the related personifications of aspects of the ego (or self) in dreams as the expression of intersystemic conflict, with each personification standing for the superego, the id, or the ego. Gradually, however, he reached the conclusion that the most precise and clinically most relevant formulation to account for these characteristics of dreams was a conception of the patient's ego as divided into a preconscious or conscious ego that related to a conscious or preconscious idealized internal object, in contrast to two repressed, unconscious, subsidiary ego segments that related to a prohibitive or rejecting "antilibidinal" object, and an exciting, gratifying "libidinal" object. All personifications in dreams could be sorted into representatives of these three self and object series.

Fairbairn proposed that this universal characteristic of dreams reflected a "schizoid" operation, namely, a splitting of the ego in the service of defense, with a consonant splitting of a fundamental, core object that was libidinally invested and yet frustrating at the same time. The frustrating aspect of the object was repressed as a "bad internal object" (the antilibidinal object) and the exciting aspect of the object as the unavailable repressed libidinal object. The segments of the ego relating to these two split-off and repressed aspects of the object constituted the "antilibidinal ego" and the "libidinal ego." (Fairbairn originally designated the antilibidinal ego as the "internal saboteur," but replaced this term later.)

Fairbairn described clinical connections between these universally "schizoid" tendencies of dreams and the unconscious meaning of hysterical conversion symptoms, dissociative episodes, and multiple personalities.

In contrast to these personifications which reflected the latent meaning of hysterical symptoms, the patient's conscious and preconscious ego was devoid of both primitive libidinal aspirations of a sexual and pregenital kind, and of the identifications with sadistic prohibitions and needs reflected by the antilibidinal ego in relating to the antilibidinal object. This relatively impoverished "central" ego was related, in turn, to an "ideal object" reflecting the remnants of those internalized aspects of the external object that were shorn of the split-off, frustrating, and exciting aspects of it.

In the transference, Fairbairn now perceived the gradual enactment of a sequence of internalized object relations, beginning with the initial relation of the conscious "central" ego to the analyst as an "ideal" object. This initial relationship was tenaciously maintained by the patient in order to avoid the eruption of the bad internal object and the corresponding unconscious need for a submissive, clinging, masochistic dependency on a sadistic, persecutory object projected onto the analyst (the relation between the antilibidinal object and the antilibidinal ego); beyond that relationship, patients tried to avoid the even more threatening activation of the libidinal ego in relating to the libidinal object. To the obvious question, why would the activation of the libidinal object–libidinal ego relationship appear as dangerous? (other than because of superego or "antilibidinal object plus antilibidinal ego" prohibitions), Fairbairn developed clinical and theoretical answers which stemmed from his study of patients with schizoid personalities.

Fairbairn was struck by the similarity between the chronically detached, withdrawn, emotionally apparently superficial attitude of schizoid patients and the central ego attitude of hysterical patients during periods of depersonalization and dissociative states, and also the impoverishment of the dominant ego segment of patients with multiple personalities. He was particularly impressed by what seemed to him a fascinating continuum in the psychopathology of hysteria and that of schizoid personalities. In fact, it was the intensive psychoanalytic study of patients with schizoid personalities that led him to formulate answers to the general questions of the origin of splitting processes within the ego, the causes and mechanisms involved in the splitting of internalized objects, the nature of the conflicts involved, and the primary and secondary defensive operations characteristic of various types of psychopathology.

The finding that careful analysis of superego pathology in schizoid patients often did not lead to resolving unconscious guilt, but to a worsening of the patients' detachment in the transference led Fairbairn to search for causes of this active process of detachment and ego splitting, and to conflicts that predated the Oedipus complex and the consolidation of the superego. He regularly found that schizoid personalities, in attempting to withdraw within the transference, were defending against a dreaded activation of a basic relationship in the transference characterized by a libidinal investment of the analyst experienced as a preoedipal, particularly oral, mother. This libidinal investment seemed a major threat to these patients, a threat derived from the fear that their love of the object would be devastatingly destructive to the object.

In analyzing this fear, Fairbairn found a typical constellation of feelings and fantasies, in essence reflecting the patient's conviction that mother could not love him, that his own love for mother had exhausting, emptying-out qualities which were destructive to her and at the same time threatened the patient with a fundamental feeling of futility, a sense of depletion related to the wasting of his own love without a receptive, responsive object. These patients' experience of deprivation had the effect not only of intensifying their oral needs but also of imparting an aggressive quality to such needs. By the same token, the patient's frustration derived from his perception of mother's lack of love made the patient experience his own love as demanding and aggressive. Therefore, the patient had to withdraw, not only because of the sense of futility and fear over the aggressive qualities of his own love, but also because of the projectively motivated feeling that mother's lack of response indicated her aggression toward him.

For all these reasons, the patient had to maintain a carefully guarded isolation and detachment in the transference, thus protecting the remaining "ideal" relationship with the analyst (the relation between the residual, "central" ego and the ideal object), while dissociating all his love and hate in the split-off, repressed relations of segments of his ego (self) to bad and exciting inner objects.

Fairbairn linked the chronic subjective experience of artificiality and of emotional detachment of schizoid personalities with these patients' attitude of omnipotence, objective isolation and detachment, and marked preoccupation with inner reality. He interpreted schizoid patients' "intro-version" as a replacement of the relation with the external object by rela-tions with their internal ones. He described schizoid over-valuation of intellectual pursuits as an expression of detachment and a displacement from repressed internal object relations to the intellectual sphere: he saw in this development the schizoid basis of subsequent complicating obses-sive intellectualization linked to anal conflicts. Schizoid omnipotence reflected the patient's secret superiority over external objects—particu-larly the analyst—derived from the patient's sense of control and manipu-lation of his internal world, and his related sense of freedom and inde-pendence from the external world. Schizoid patients also developed the capacity for carrying out superficial social roles, thus protecting from the invasion of libidinal demands both residual object relations in reality and the secrecy of the patient's internal world.

Fairbairn concluded that, because of a deep fear that their needs to love and be loved would be frustrated, schizoid individuals unconsciously struggle against a true investment of others and regress to and/or are fix-ated at an essentially receptive, demanding stage of object relations in which they experience themselves as only on the taking side and care-fully avoid having to give of themselves. Giving becomes equivalent to being emptied out, a catastrophic reminder of the sense of depletion de-rived from libidinal investment not responded to.

A regression in relating from persons to "part objects," such as the surge to gratify sexual impulses, particularly perverse sexual needs in replacement of adult geniality, is another schizoid process Fairbairn de-scribes. Efforts to avoid "giving" may reinforce the need to repress all affects to avoid affective investment. In order to avoid a sense of loss, the patient may curtail his links with his own artistic products, stifle his cre-ativity, and take active measures to drive away those who potentially threaten him with love (thus triggering the danger of the destructive effects of the patient's own love).

Fairbairn saw schizoid patients' sense of being wasted, their sense of unreality, their intense self-consciousness and constant self-observation as consequences of the impoverishment of their central ego by excessive splitting. He also observed that, as an effect of the libidinal withdrawing from external objects, further splitting processes occurred; the end point of ego impoverishment reflected not simply a deficit state but an active ongoing defensive process.

The study of transference developments of schizoid patients provided Fairbairn with evidence that there was an active "de-emotionalization" of object relations resulting in the patients' characteristic detachment in the relations with external objects, side by side with an intense preoccupation with internal reality. This internal reality seemed to consist of the same split-off and repressed object relations that Fairbairn had already found in hysterical pathology and as a universal characteristic in dreams.

Like others of that era, Fairbairn occasionally uses *self* as equivalent to *ego*, but mostly refers to *ego aspects* or *ego fragments* to describe what we call self-representations. And, as already mentioned, he uses *internal objects* or *personifications* for what we would call object representations. It was the variety of personifications appearing in a patient's dreams that contributed to Fairbairn's dissatisfaction with Freud's tripartite structure of the mind and to propose the existence of other functional units.

The final synopsis of his point of view, occupying less than a page of the *International Journal of Psycho-Analysis* (1963, p. 224), facilitates the presentation of a brief outline of his object relations theory. He starts off succinctly: An ego, he says, "is present from birth. Libido is a function of the ego. There is no death instinct; and aggression is a reaction to frustration or deprivation." Hence, he adds, "there is no such thing as an 'id.' The ego, and therefore libido, is fundamentally object-seeking." This ego present at birth is a "pristine" ego, that is, a whole ego which has as a key function the libidinal search for infantile dependence on a gratifying object. Erotogenic zones are not themselves primary determinants of libidinal aims but only channels mediating the primary object-seeking aims of the ego. Libido, therefore, in contrast to Freud's assumption that it originally follows the pleasure principle (or is "primarily pleasure seeking") is essentially reality oriented and fulfills the reality principle in promoting attachment to the earliest objects, first, mother's breast, and later, mother as a total person. In fact, in Fairbairn's thinking, an excessive dependence on the breast as a "part object" may signal the deterioration of the relation to mother as a total object and its regressive replacement by a part-object relation.

Insofar as Fairbairn rejects aggression as an instinct, he comes close to the culturalists; but insofar as he stresses the importance of "endopsychic structures," that is, of an internal world of object relations, as the central focus of analytic work, he is very far from directly equating the intrapsychic with the interpersonal, prevalent in culturalists' approaches. In presenting an instinct theory centering exclusively upon (an object-seeking) libido and rejecting aggression as an instinct, Fairbairn would seem to come close to Jung, a correspondence strengthened by Fairbairn's focus on introversion and the schizoid personality's replacement of external by internal, fantastic object relations. However, for Fairbairn, introversion is determined by a defensive withdrawal from threatening object relations and not by constitution, and clinically he is totally identified with a Freudian model of psychoanalytic psychopathology, diagnosis, and treatment technique. In a sharply critical yet elegant reply to Abenheimer's (1955) Jungian critique of his writings, Fairbairn (1955) clarifies that, for him, internal objects are not simply "images," but endopsychic structures. They are not, therefore, "inborn" images. He also states that, in contrast to Jung, he agrees with Freud "in regarding aggression as incapable of being resolved into libido"; and although he rejects Freud's dual-instinct theory, he continues "to accept Freud's view that libido and aggression constitute the two primary dynamic factors in mental life" (1955, p. 145).

I would here raise a question about rejecting aggression as an instinct. Fairbairn stresses the importance of conceiving the ego as a dynamic structure, that is, a structure that energizes, primarily, object relations and, secondarily, the intrapsychic function of internalized objects. He also underlines the importance of conceiving of structure and function as two aspects of the same dynamic whole. While I see this as an eminently reasonable suggestion, Fairbairn creates an artificial dichotomy between inborn dispositions to certain behaviors and external experiences as originating other behaviors; he then arbitrarily assigns libido to the inborn disposition (to object relations), while equally arbitrarily assigning aggression to the effects of frustrating object relations. One cannot, however, escape the conclusion that what frustrating object relations evoke are inborn behavioral dispositions to aggression and corresponding painful affect states. Similarly, it is the presence of a gratifying object that evokes inborn capabilities for pleasurable affects and behavior dispositions toward attachment to objects. Thus, aggressive behavior reflects an inborn disposition activated by certain experiences with objects, and the same complementarity of inborn disposition and experiences with objects obtains for libido as well. In Fairbairn's thinking, it is the pleasurable experience at the breast that immediately activates the libidinal attachment of the pristine ego. I find arbitrary the assignment to libido of a primary instinctive quality, while aggression is denied that quality.

Given the history of the development of Fairbairn's ideas, and the influence of Kleinian thinking on his developmental model, it may well be that Fairbairn, in an effort to differentiate his views from those of Melanie Klein (1952a, b), stressed the difference with her in terms of his concept of aggression, while maintaining her telescoping of early development into the first few months of life, with all the problems and internal contradictions that implied.

The earliest and original form of anxiety, Fairbairn suggests, is separation anxiety, activated when frustrations, including, basically, temporary separations from mother occur. These frustrations bring about the internalization of the object and also the development of ambivalence toward it. As Fairbairn himself puts it, "Two aspects of the internalized object, viz. its exciting and its frustrating aspects, are split off from the main core of the object and repressed by the ego" (1963, p. 224). Fairbairn calls the exciting, gratifying aspects of the libidinal object and the frustrating, rejecting, prohibiting aspect the antilibidinal object. "Thus," he continues, "there come to be constituted two repressed internal objects, viz. the exciting (or libidinal) and the rejecting (or antilibidinal) object." He describes the main core of the internalized object, which is not repressed, as the ideal object or ego ideal. The resulting internal situation represents the basic schizoid position, antedating, in Fairbairn's view, the depressive position Melanie Klein describes.

All three ego structures as well as their respective internal objects have energic properties. Because the libidinal and antilibidinal objects are "cathected by the original ego, these objects carry into repression with them parts of the ego by which they are cathected," leaving the central ego unrepressed, "but acting as the agent of repression." Hence, "the original ego is split into three egos—a central (conscious) ego attached to the ideal object (ego-ideal), a repressed libidinal ego attached to the exciting (or libidinal) object, and a repressed antilibidinal ego attached to the rejecting (or antilibidinal) object" (1963, p. 224). This tripartite structure differs from Freud's in that, not only is there no id, but all three structures are fundamentally ego structures, so that Freud's ego represents only one segment of the original pristine ego.

Following Freud, Fairbairn considered anxiety the most direct symptom of unconscious intrapsychic conflict. It was aggression directed by the antilibidinal ego against the libidinal ego that transformed pleasurable excitement into painful anxiety. Fairbairn thus came close to Freud's first theory of anxiety—the assumption that anxiety reflected dammed-up libido (or rather, dammed-up libidinal needs reflecting the repressed relation between libidinal ego and libidinal object). In agreeing with Freud that oedipal conflicts were central in the psychopathology of hysteria, he explained the origin of oedipal conflicts, however, as derived from the earliest struggle with the ambivalently loved and needed mother of the earliest oral period of development.

In the light of his analysis of the relationship between oedipal conflicts and intrapsychic structures, Fairbairn saw his endopsychic structures as constituted by successive fusions and condensations of internalized objects and corresponding ego segments from successive stages of development. He was aware that the organization of all internalized object relations that he proposed remained remarkably close to Freud's tripartite structure. Fairbairn stated, however, that Freud's superego included not only Fairbairn's antilibidinal ego and antilibidinal object, but also Fairbairn's ideal object, and that it corresponded to a later and more complex stage of development than the psychic structures based upon schizoid processes in the preoedipal period. He also objected, on principle, to the analogy of his "tripartite" structure with Freud's: in contrast to Freud, Fairbairn, as previously mentioned, considered all three structures as representing *ego* structures, and as provided with energic functions derived from the libidinal investments in all three of them.

Fairbairn thus conceives of endopsychic structures as not rigid, impersonal, frozen molds but actively maintained and dynamically interacting object-relations-determined. He differentiates the establishment of the schizoid position, and the related consolidation of endopsychic structures, from the pathological fixation at this stage of development reflected by schizoid factors in the personality—which he considers quite universal—and from the schizoid personality proper (the prototypical psychopathology of the schizoid position).

Fairbairn conceptualized penis envy, castration anxiety, and genital longings for both parents in the positive and negative oedipal situation as an expression of deterioration of the object relations to the parents resulting from the repression of major affective libidinal needs. In other words, Fairbairn considered the longing for genital relations with the oedipal objects and the corresponding fears and prohibitions a consequence of the regression from total, integrated, to part-object relations with the oedipal parents. He defined adult, mature heterosexual relations as total-object relations which permit mutual dependency and the expression of libidinal needs through predominantly, but not exclusively, genital channels. For Fairbairn, the various erotogenic zones represented not the origin of libidinal stimuli but the channels available for expression of libidinal needs directed to objects. He (1955) defined anal and phallic conflicts not in terms of libidinal stages, but as particular "techniques" activated in a sequence directed primarily by the nature of interactions and conflicts with parental objects as the child moves from infantile dependence to mature independence.

It is difficult to clearly relate Fairbairn's thinking to that of Melanie Klein, in spite—or because—of their attaching different meanings to the same terms. Klein (1946), under the influence of Fairbairn's contributions to the understanding of schizoid personality characteristics and defenses, decided to rename the earliest stage of development the "paranoid–schizoid position," rather than "paranoid position," and she agreed with Fairbairn in that this position predated the development of the depressive position. Klein also agreed with the particular emphasis Fairbairn laid on the inherent relation between hysteria and schizophrenia. She strongly disagreed, however, with Fairbairn's revision of the theory of mental structure and instincts, with his view that only the bad object is internalized, and with his underrating of the role aggression and hate play from the beginning of life. Fairbairn originally proposed that only bad object relations induced internalized and splitting mechanisms. A gradual shift away from this early view led him to his final proposal that the original internalization is that of the actually experienced mother as a consequence of the infant's efforts to deal with the unavoidably frustrating aspects of this first love object.

Other clinical differences between the two British theorists derived from these theoretical differences: Klein's stress on the need to systematically analyze the positive and negative transference from a position of technical neutrality contrasts with Fairbairn's assumption that the reality aspects of the analyst's personality are the most important therapeutic factor. Fairbairn criticized Klein's overemphasis on aggression, and Kleinian authors think that Fairbairn (as well as Balint and Winnicott) underemphasized the importance of aggression, particularly regarding severe and early psychopathology.

Fairbairn formulated the specific danger situations characteristic of the schizoid and the depressive positions. The most devastating and basic experiences were those of ego fragmentation, of loss of a sense of oneness, and a conviction of futility (characteristic of the schizoid position) under the impact of the fear of the destructiveness of one's love. The principal danger of the depressive position, he proposed—here agreeing with Klein—was the devastating loneliness he derived from the loss of the loved object destroyed by one's own aggression.

In exploring the unconscious guilt feelings generally characteristic of superego functioning and the abnormally intense expression of guilt in depression, in particular, Fairbairn differed from Freud. He called the defense of the superego a "moral defence." It reflected an effort to maintain the good object relation with bad objects by reinforcing the internalization of the split-off, bad (frustrating and exciting) object. In depression, this reinforced internalization was an effort to transform the "unconditional badness" of the object into a "conditional" one, that is, the development of the fantasy that it was the child's own badness that brought about frustration or attack from the good object. Hence, the sadistic self-accusations of the depressed patient reflected not only the object's aggression directed against the ego, but the antilibidinal ego's effort to protect the good relation with the ideal object by attacking the libidinal ego as if it were bad, as having caused the frustration from the object.

The theoretical consequences of this explanation of the schizoid and depressive positions led Fairbairn to increasingly stress the primary nature of libidinal relations, the secondary nature of aggression as derived from frustration of the infant's libidinal needs by mother, and the primarily object-directed quality of libidio. On the clinical side, however, Fairbairn stressed the crucial importance of internalized bad objects and bad object relations and the need to interpretively resolve the defensive function of the activation in the transference of the central ego-ideal object relation. Only the full activation of the bad internalized object (in both its frustrating and gratifying aspects) in the transference permitted the reduction of splitting of the endopsychic structure and an increase in the depth and scope of the central ego so that it could develop fully satisfactory libidinal relations with external objects.

Fairbairn felt that, because Freud had developed his structural model, particularly his concept of the superego, under the influence of his study of mourning and melancholia, he had overestimated both the importance of aggression in psychopathology and the conflicts between later stages of the superego and the ego, and had neglected the underlying characteristics of schizoid developments. Nevertheless, Fairbairn acknowledged repeatedly that it was Freud's description of the superego as an internalized structure having the capacity for repressive action and reflecting the internalization of the parental images of the oedipal conflict that had first stimulated Fairbairn to formulate endopsychic structure in terms of internalized object relations. Fairbairn felt that he had taken a step that evolved from Freud's structural theory.

Internalized Object Relations in Psychopathology

Fairbairn also explored the relation between the characteristics of the schizoid personality and other psychopathological conditions, particularly narcissism, repetition compulsion, negative therapeutic reaction, and the relation between the dynamics of schizoid and depressive psychopathology.

While he described hysterical psychopathology as the prototype of all psychopathology, illustrating the dynamic organization of endopsychic structure based upon schizoid processes (that is, splitting of an original, pristine ego into three subsidiary ones with their respective internalized object relations), Fairbairn considered the schizoid personality proper a most severe type of psychopathology. In the schizoid personality, a self-perpetuating splitting of the central ego occurred as a consequence and expression of extremely severe fears of any libidinal object relationship. The schizoid personality is characterized by an impoverished central ego relating to objects mostly stripped of their aggressive and libidinal characteristics, a general impoverishment of the affective capabilities of the central ego, and a withdrawal into an internal world of fantasy which permits the gratification of libidinal and aggressive needs intrapsychically and is reflected in detachment, secrecy, and subtle superiority in the relation with external objects. This condition represented, for Fairbairn, a highly pathological fixation at or regression to the basic intrapsychic organization elaborated into a specific clinical syndrome. In the transference, the schizoid patient's detachment from the analyst, his withdrawal into fantasies drained of emotion, the sense of emptiness and futility the patient conveys about himself and also induces in the analyst, have to be explored as a very active consequence of defensive splitting of the patient's total emotional relation with the analyst. Split-off segments of that relation emerge in dissociated emotional experiences, in the activation of fleeting, nonintegrated, nonverbal aspects of the patient's behavior, in displacements toward other objects, and in the patient's dreams. The analysis of all this material permits the gradual transformation of the initial "ideal," friendly but distant relation to the analyst.

In a broad sense, Fairbairn differentiated a psychopathology of "infantile dependence" (both of the early oral and the late oral stage), namely, the schizoid and depressive positions, from the psychopathology of the "quasi-independent" or "transitional" stage of development of later childhood, characterized by various ways of dealing with internal and external objects that included what he called the phobic, hysterical, paranoid, and obsessive "techniques." The final stage of development, following the infantile dependent and the transitional one, was the stage of "mature dependence," characterized by whole object relations and genital primacy. At one point, Fairbairn (1941, p. 28) explicitly defines his term *primary identification* "to signify the cathexis of an object which has not yet been differentiated (or has been only partly differentiated) from himself by the cathecting subject." I find it hard to reconcile this statement with the repeated affirmation that a pristine (that is, integrated and therefore differentiated) ego exists from birth on, and that a search for object relations exists when there is not yet any differentiation between the ego (or self) and the object.

Fairbairn criticized Abraham's (1924) effort to devise an organized scheme of psychopathology on the basis of fixation and/or regression to certain stages of libidinal development. He agreed with Abraham's description of the first two stages of development—the earliest oral stage characterized by sucking and the later oral stage characterized by biting. He rejected, however, Abraham's relating subsequent developmental stages to various types of psychopathology. Fairbairn suggested that the major neurotic syndromes—phobic neurosis, hysteria, obsession, and paranoid personality—reflected alternative methods of dealing with the same intrapsychic conflicts that gave rise to the schizoid and depressive positions.

Fairbairn saw the development of masochistic tendencies as a key manifestation of the activation of previously split-off bad internalized object relations in the transference. In the masochistic relation there is a desperate attempt not only to activate the relation between the antilibidinal ego and the antilibidinal object (a relation which, in itself, illustrates the libidinal ties between these two endopsychic structures) but also to modify the antilibidinal object and to transform its hatred into love. In a general sense, the desperate search for libidinal gratification on the part of the libidinal ego in relating to the libidinal object is condensed with the activation of the bad object relation in order to bring about the gradual mitigation of the latter and its consolidation with the good one in the same relationship.

According to Fairbairn, the child takes onto himself the badness of his frustrating, persecuting objects and also internalizes his good objects, which then combine in assuming a superego role. In explaining the internalizing of the bad object, he remarks, "It is better to be a sinner in a world ruled by God than to live in a world ruled by the Devil" (1943, p. 66). Paraphrasing this, in light of his concept of the "conditionally bad object," we might say that the Devil is internalized in an effort to transform him into an irate God, and later condensed with the ideal God in order to maintain the hope for an eventual redemption in God's world. This hope lies hidden in the activation of masochistic object relations in the transference.

Masochistic needs thus reflected, for Fairbairn, a key phase in the resolution of pathological schizoid states, and he saw the need to reactivate these split-off and repressed object relations as the basic explanation of repetition compulsion as well. In fact, Fairbairn stressed that the psychoanalytic resolution of unconscious guilt feelings might, if anything, bring about an intensification of the patient's resistances and of negative therapeutic reactions because the patient then would be faced with coming to terms with his libidinal attachment to bad, ambivalently loved objects. Fairbairn also linked the masochistic components of hysteria with underlying schizoid features.

Fairbairn pointed to the internal relationships of hypomanic, psychopathic, and narcissistic defenses against deeply repressed, denied, and split-off dependent needs. He stressed the connections between schizoid psychopathology, narcissistic features, and psychopathic tendencies, but he did not actually differentiate narcissistic pathology or clarify to what extent the psychopathic personality reflected complicating developments within an essentially schizoid psychopathology. Although he gives a comparative description of the defenses (he calls them techniques) characteristic of hysterical, phobic, obsessive, and paranoid psychopathology, Fairbairn had relatively little to say about these various types of "transitional" psychopathology and conveys the impression that his outline is essentially an answer to Abraham's schema of psychopathology. In this connection, it is of interest to note how little Fairbairn has to say about the psychoses, particularly schizophrenia. This stems, I suspect, from his tendency to remain close to the clinical base.

Psychoanalytic Technique

Fairbairn has written little on psychoanalytic technique. He maintained a standard technique during most of his professional years and rejected the abandonment of both the historical and genetic approach of the existential and the culturalist psychoanalytic approaches (he explicitly rejected the interpretation in the "here and now" *only*). He stressed the importance of the interpretation of resistances, the central nature of the interpretation of the transference, but expressed his concern that a combination of technical neutrality plus interpretations in terms of what he called "impulse psychology" only (in contrast to interpretation in terms of the reactivation of repressed object relations) might convey to the patient an excessive distance on the part of the analyst (1957). There is some irony in the protest Guntrip (1975) expressed at Fairbairn's adherence to classical psychoanalytic technique—implying distance and lack of personal involvement—in contrast to Guntrip's experience with his second analyst, Winnicott. In my opinion, Guntrip's criticism here speaks for Fairbairn.

Fairbairn stressed however, that therapeutic effects do not derive only from the analyst's interpretations—particularly from the interpretations of the transference—but also, and fundamentally, from the analyst's capacity to provide, by means of his real interest and concern, the necessary counterbalance to the activation of bad repressed object relations in the transference.

Later in his professional life, Fairbairn (1958) raised questions regarding the validity of the requirement that the patient should lie on a couch with the analyst out of view. Although he did not favor the face-to-face interviews advocated by the Sullivanians, he eventually adopted an arrangement in which, while patient and analyst were not ordinarily looking at one another, they were sitting within each other's potential field of vision. He stressed that the relationship of the patient to the analyst was the decisive therapeutic factor upon which the other therapeutic factors—insight, recall of infantile memories, and catharsis—rested.

Fairbairn saw as the primary aim of psychoanalytic treatment to bring about a synthesis of the personality by reducing "that triple splitting of the pristine ego which occurs to some degree in every individual, but in some individuals to a greater degree than others" (1958, p. 380). He considered the chief resistance to change as stemming from the unconscious effort to maintain the internal world of object relations as a "closed system," within which, in subtle expressions in fantasies and dreams, in symptoms and avoided relations with external objects, the patient attempts to maintain the libidinal ties between the split-off and repressed bad objects and their corresponding split-off and repressed parts of the ego.

CRITIQUE

In 1953, Winnicott and Khan in an extensive review of Fairbairn's book, criticized sharply—and, in my opinion, appropriately—Fairbairn's claims that his theory supplants that of Freud. The strong need, whatever its origin, to differentiate his theoretical formulations from Freud's has done poor service to Fairbairn's presentation of his theories and created what seems to me, in agreement with Winnicott and Khan, a largely unnecessary polemic atmosphere around Fairbairn's work. Guntrip's enthusiastic, uncritical, and distorting presentation of Fairbairn's views, to which I have already referred, has only exacerbated this tendency.

Winnicott and Khan (1953) pointed out that Fairbairn cannot consistently maintain a view in which the infant is always a separate entity, seeking an object that is distinct and yet emerges from within the infant's own entity. They agreed with Fairbairn's stress that at the root of the schizoid personality is the infant's failure to feel that the mother loves him in his own right, but pointed to the difficulty of finding out whether Fairbairn considers this the mother's failure or the result of the child's projection onto her of his own hate. They suggested that, in contrast to Fairbairn's own statement to the contrary, there is much in his book to indicate that it is the child's projection onto mother of his own hate that is importantly involved.

Winnicott and Khan (p. 331) also criticized the hopelessness of trying to correlate Fairbairn's statements with Klein's, "since Klein's work has been set down with great clarity, and Fairbairn's discoveries seemed to run criss-cross with those of Klein."

Another of their major criticisms derives from the problem created by Fairbairn's assumption that a primary identification with the object is compatible with a primary conception of an independent object. They state (p. 332): "Now if the object is not differentiated it cannot operate as an object. What Fairbairn is referring to then is an infant with needs, but with no 'mechanism' by which to implement them, an infant with needs not 'seeking' an object, but seeking detension, libido seeking satisfaction, instinct tension seeking a return to a state of rest or un-excitement; which brings us back to Freud." They feel that "Fairbairn's clinical intuitive sense brings him all the way while his theory gets bogged down a few miles in the rear."

Balint (1956a, b), in agreement with Winnicott and Khan's views, affirms the need for a consideration of pure pleasure-seeking along with the central importance of object relations. Zetzel (1955) also criticizes Fairbairn's underemphasis of the importance of aggression, and points to the similarity of Balint's and Fairbairn's position in this regard. Wisdom (1962, 1963, 1971), in comparing Fairbairn's and Klein's approaches, has probably clarified more than anybody else where implicit areas of agreement and disagreement lie, particularly regarding their concepts of introjection and projection, the psychopathology of hysteria and depression, and some of the philosophical implications of their work.

Sutherland (1963, 1965, 1979) has introduced important modifications into Fairbairn's model which have permitted him to establish bridges between Fairbairn's thinking and certain aspects of an ego psychology approach. Sutherland reintroduces the concept of instincts into Fairbairn's clinical observations by pointing to the ethological studies on attachment and to Bowlby's (1969) work, and by connecting Fairbairn's endopsychic structures with a concept of split-off affect states.

Sutherland (1963) made an important addition to the concept of the division of the pristine ego into substructures, stressing that each of them contains "a) a part of the ego, b) the object that characterizes the related relationships, and c) the affects of the latter." Sutherland stressed that the split-off ego structures of Fairbairn's model should be conceived as (p. 115)

> interrelated dynamic psychological systems, constantly in active relationship with each other and with the outer world. Each structure has a great complexity and depth into which is built its history. The particular experiences of the person will contribute many subsystems which could, for instance, be precipitates of repressed relations at the oral, anal or phallic phases of classical theory; but there is a tendency for these constituent subsystems to group or to assume a hierarchical order around the image of one person, even if only loosely. The first manifestation of a bad object relationship in the course of analysis may therefore center around one or other of these subsystems, but as the analysis proceeds all the components come to the surface.

Sutherland also focuses on the potential relations between Erikson's (1950) developmental model and Fairbairn's approach.

Referring to Fairbairn's technical approach, Sutherland stresses that "the repressed not only returns, but it tends to return to the representative of the more comprehensive relationship from which it was originally split off." Sutherland (1979) points out that, for Fairbairn, "impulses" are related to reality from the start, and the pleasure principle is an accompaniment of relationships with objects in reality and a guide to them.

Sutherland (1979) considers the self—his term for Fairbairn's ego—an overall system integrated by subsystems represented by the split-off self components described by Fairbairn, and suggests that the self may be considered "a supraordinate structure of great flexibility and perhaps in the nature of a 'field force,' its primary function [being] the container of motives from all the subsystems which have differentiated from it. Subsystems such as the behavioral systems of the ethologists, or the higher level organizations we call the subegos and internal objects all fall within its influence." He goes on to suggest that the value of the "self," conceptualized as "the overall dynamic structural matrix," is that "we can give underpinning to the personal level of action as 'I' and yet allow for the self to be dominated at different times and in different situations by any of its subsystems such as the superego, the antilibidinal ego, the exciting object, etc. etc."

By focusing on the intimate connection between object and self-structures in intrapsychic subsystems, Sutherland approaches, I think, Jacobson's concept of the build-up of internalized object relations in terms of self- and object representations. This relation of Fairbairn's to Jacobson's thinking can also be considered in Sutherland's stress on the affect components of internalized object relations. It is a paradox that Fairbairn, so vehemently in protest against Freud's instinct theory, consistently uses terms such as libidinal and aggressive cathexes or investment to refer to the dynamic qualities of endopsychic structures. In fact, to consider such libidinal and aggressive investments of self- and object representations as affective investments, and to consider these investments as the basic drive derivatives indissolubly linked to self- and object representations, offer a new perspective to the relation between ego psychology and object relations theory. Fairbairn, writing his central theoretical papers in the nineteen-forties, tended to ignore the writings of contemporary ego psychologists, particularly those in the United States. Jacobson's paper, "The Self and the Object World" was published in 1954, and it was only in 1963 that Sutherland's reformulation of Fairbairn's statements on endopsychic structures permitted this relationship between Fairbairn and Jacobson to become apparent.

I agree with Sutherland (1979) that Fairbairn emerges as the theoretically most profound, consistent, and provocative writer of the British "middle group," including here particularly Balint, Winnicott, and Guntrip. Fairbairn was able to transform into a theoretical statement what analysts had long sensed before—and after—him, namely, that in all clinical situations we never find pure drives, but always an activation of affects reflecting such drives in the context of internalized object relations reenacted in the transference. I think Fairbairn was right in feeling that this concept was already implicit in Freud and required just one step further for fundamental reexploration of metapsychology; but I totally disagree with his assumption that this view requires an abandonment of Freud's metapsychology.

Our current knowledge about inborn motor, perceptive, and affective patterns which mature rapidly in the first few weeks and months of life and are reflected in early attachment behavior confirms, I believe—in agreement with Sutherland—Fairbairn's concept that libido is always object-seeking and does not exist independently from object-seeking. However, this statement also ignores the contemporary instinct theory that instincts are the hierarchical organization of inborn behavior patterns under the influence of the environment. In psychological terms, pleasurable, rewarding early object relations develop into an organized drive—or supraordinate motivational system, for which the concept of libido seems to me adequate and convincing in the light of Freud's theory of the continuity between early and later object-related instinctual aims.

Fairbairn's observation that libido emerges in the context of object relations and cannot be observed outside that context is perfectly consistent with my concept of the organization of libidinal drive throughout development (1976, Chapter 3). By the same token, while Fairbairn is correct, it seems to me, in observing that aggression emerges as a response to frustration, he, as well as many behaviorists and culturalists, neglects the fact that there are inborn affective, perceptual, and behavior patterns that activate aggressive behavior, thus contributing for aggression the same maturational and developmental conditions as for libido.

Aggression as a drive is the supraordinate integration of aggressively invested object-relations into an overall hierarchically supraordinate motivational system. This concept of aggression is in fact clinically in harmony both with Fairbairn's stress on the crucial importance of the activation of aggressive internalized object relations in the transference, and with Sutherland's (1979) warning against simplistic deficit theories of psychopathology that neglect the enormous importance of dissociated envy and aggression in early development.

Regarding the relation between Fairbairn's model and ego psychology object relations theory, it seems to me that an impressive contribution of Fairbairn's theory resides in his proposal, at least ten years before the related work of Jacobson (1964) and of Mahler (1972), that the internal world of object relations starts out as a dyadic, internalized relation between a self-component and an object component, what we would now call a self-representation and an object representation. In fact, I think the structural units of self- and object representations linked by determined affect dispositions, first described by Fairbairn and then elaborated by Sutherland, are the basic constituents of the id or dynamic unconscious. I have never understood why Fairbairn felt that such a concept of the id (the repressed exciting object and the libidinal ego related to it) is necessarily in contradiction to Freud's concept of the id. It is true that Fairbairn was not alone in assuming such an incompatibility; a good many traditional ego psychologists in this country, particularly Rapaport, would probably agree on the mutual incompatibility of these two models.

However, I think that Jacobson's and Mahler's developmental concepts, and beyond that, Hartmann's (1939) elaboration of the concept of an original ego–id matrix that predates the id as a discrete, organized system, points to the compatibility of Freud's and Fairbairn's model in this area. Fairbairn's protest against the relation between his tripartite model and that of Freud is weak not only in terms of his ignoring Hartmann's concept (in harmony with Freud's) of a primary undifferentiated ego–id. Fairbairn, in defining Freud's superego in terms of his own endopsychic structures, fails to note that in the thinking of contemporary ego psychology not all guiding value systems are incorporated in the superego, and, insofar as the superego reflects the infantile, sadistically infiltrated, childhood-derived morality that is essentially repressed and irrational, it corresponds much more closely to Fairbairn's antilibidinal object and antilibidinal ego than to his "ego-ideal."

In short, I see Fairbairn as having alerted us to the fact that, in contrast to the older concept of the id as a "reservoir" of "impulses," all three systems, ego, superego, and id, originate from the organization of internalized object relations, and I consider this concept compatible with the contemporary ego psychology approach that maintains Freud's structural theory and his dual-instinct theory linked to a developmental model centering on internalized object relations.

Fairbairn, in following Melanie Klein, ignored or neglected the lack of differentiation between self- and object representations that characterizes earliest development. Fairbairn, therefore, failed to consider early developmental stages that predate the differentiated self- and object components of his "schizoid position," which he saw as the fundamental endopsychic structure, as the earliest intrapsychic structural development. In contrast, Jacobson and Mahler's concept of earliest experience as reflecting a fused self–object representation—the original, undifferentiated, libidinally invested mother–infant dyad out of which both the internal world of object relations and the conception of the self gradually emerge—is, it seems to me, a better way of formulating the gradual origin of subjective awareness derived from intrasystemic early conflicts and of the conscious-self concept as related to the dynamic underpinning of the tripartite system.

A major problem with Fairbairn's theory of endopsychic structure is similar to that of the Kleinian approach: the telescoping of all developments into an assumed extremely early sequence of schizoid and depressive "positions," thus neglecting the important connections between structural developments in the preoedipal stages of life and the consolidation of the tripartite structure under the influence of oedipal conflicts. Both Klein and Fairbairn had important contributions to make to the understanding of the connections between preoedipal and oedipal conflicts, but, because of the strange telescoping of development into the earliest months of life, both missed the boat. Winnicott avoided this collapse of early developmental stages. He assumed an earliest stage of undifferentiation (predating self and object differentiation) and described the pathology of early differentiation as related to excessive intrusion or impingement by mother with the subsequent consolidation of a "false self." Winnicott, however, did not formulate a fully integrated developmental model. The schizoid dynamics described by Fairbairn and Winnicott—as well as, presumably, Klein's paranoid–schizoid operations—would correspond, broadly, to Mahler's period of separation–individuation, with Fairbairn's schizoid defenses probably ranging from early differentiation to the rapprochement stage.

One more problem derived from Fairbairn's collapse of early development is his failure to differentiate splitting from repression proper. While I agree with his idea of the continuity of early splitting mechanisms, the later dissociative ego defenses leading to hysterical dissociative states and, finally, repression proper, there are developmental tranformations involved in these increasingly complex processes that Fairbairn misses completely. Particularly striking is his failure to mention the clinical differences between splitting mechanisms and repressive mechanisms in adult patients.

And yet, Fairbairn's concept of "dynamic structures" in referring to the stable organization of internalized object relations constitutes a potentially powerful link between the early ego substructures that enter into self- and object representations and the tripartite structure and the emerging self. Although Fairbairn himself—wrongly, I believe—thought that his viewpoint was in opposition to the dual-instinct theory, he rightly objected to the mystical and mechanical, impersonal qualities of instinct as reflected in the concept of a death instinct and the general use of aggression as conceptualized by Klein.

While starting out with Klein's description of multiple internal objects in his formulations, Fairbairn transcended her lack of structural thinking, the "free floating" internal objects in her theories, and he also brought back the real relation with mother, which was strongly underemphasized in the pseudobiological orientation of the Kleinian school.

The gradual integration of the self-components of early internalized object relations permits the concept of an emerging self that does not stem from impersonal instincts per se but from the organization of the self-representations, part of a world of internal object relations which is activated in the context of activation of inborn instinctive patterns and gradually leads to the simultaneous organization of drives and internalized object relations to form the tripartite structure. Bowlby, who originally developed his formulations under the influence of the British middle group, traced the organization of drives from primary inborn attachment behavior. However, he grossly neglected the organizing importance of intrapsychic structures reflecting object relations enacted under the impact of loving and hating affect states. My own efforts to integrate Bowlby's and Fairbairn's findings with the more recent and sophisticated developmental models of Jacobson and Mahler seem to me to do justice to clinical psychoanalytic findings, and to relate naturally the psychoanalytic concept of the self and the object world to the structural properties of the psychic apparatus.

Fairbairn's consistent stress on the link between particular self- and object components as dynamic units (in the context of what I would prefer, in agreement with Sutherland, to describe as an affective investment of such units) represents the earliest effort to link with metapsychology the clinical observation that we never see pure drives but always object relations under the effect of drive derivatives. Fairbairn's stress on considering endopsychic structure both a structure and an energy system seems to me, in the light of contemporary biological thinking as well as clinical evidence, a more sophisticated basis for updating psychoanalytic metapsychology than the numerous efforts to altogether eliminate energy concepts from psychoanalytic thinking because older, "hydraulic" energy models no longer seem satisfactory.

REFERENCES

Abenheimer, K. M. (1955). Critical observations on Fairbairn's theory of object relations. *British Journal of Medical Psychology*. 28: 29–41.
Abraham, K. (1924). A short study of the development of the libido, viewed in the light of mental disorders. In: *Selected Papers on Psycho-Analysis*. New York: Basic Books, 1953, pp. 418–501.
Anzieu, D., Pontalis, J. B. & Rosolato, G. (1977). A propos du texte de Guntrip. In: *Mémoires: Nouvelle Revue de Psychanalyse*. 15: 29–37. Paris: Gallimard.
Balint, M. (1956a). Criticism of Fairbairn's generalisation about object relations. *British Journal of the Philosophy of Science*. 7: 323–327.
——— (1956b). Pleasure, object and libido: Some reflexions on Fairbairn's modi-

fications of psychoanalytic theory. *British Journal of Medical Psychology.* 29: 162–167.

Bowlby, J. (1969). *Attachment & Loss, Vol. I: Attachment.* New York: Basic Books.

Erikson, E. H. (1950). Growth and crises of the healthy personality. In: *Identity and the Life Cycle.* New York: International Universities Press, 1959, pp. 50–100.

Fairbairn, W. R. D. (1931). Features in the analysis of a patient with a physical genital abnormality. In: *An Object-Relations Theory of the Personality.* New York: Basic Books, 1954, pp. 197–222.

—— (1936). The effect of a king's death upon patients undergoing analysis. *International Journal of Psycho-Analysis.* 17(3): 278–284.

—— (1940). Schizoid factors in the personality. In: *An Object-Relations Theory of the Personality.* New York: Basic Books, 1954, pp. 3–27.

—— (1941). A revised psychopathology of the psychoses and psychoneuroses. In: *An Object-Relations Theory of the Personality.* New York: Basic Books, 1954, pp. 28–58.

—— (1943). The repression and the return of bad objects (with special reference to the 'war neuroses'). In: *An Object-Relations Theory of the Personality.* New York: Basic Books, 1954, pp. 59–81.

—— (1944). Endopsychic structure considered in terms of object-relationships, with an addendum (1951). In: *An Object-Relations Theory of the Personality.* New York: Basic Books, 1954, pp. 82–156.

—— (1946). Object-relationships and dynamic structure. In: *An Object-Relations Theory of the Personality.* New York: Basic Books, 1954, pp. 137–151.

—— (1949). Steps in the development of an object-relations theory of the personality. *British Journal of Medical Psychology.* 22: 26–31.

—— (1951). A synopsis of the development of the author's views regarding the structure of the personality. In: *An Object-Relations Theory of the Personality.* New York: Basic Books, 1954, pp. 162–179.

—— (1954a). *An Object-Relations Theory of the Personality.* New York: Basic Books.

—— (1954b). Observations on the nature of hysterical states. *British Journal of Medical Psychology.* 27: 105–125.

—— (1955). Observations in defence of the object-relations theory of the personality. *British Journal of Medical Psychology.* 28: 144–156.

—— (1957). Freud, the psycho-analytical method and mental health. *British Journal of Medical Psychology.* 30: 53–62.

—— (1958). On the nature and aims of psycho-analytic treatment. *International Journal of Psycho-Analysis.* 39: 374–385.

—— (1963). Synopsis of an object-relations theory of the personality. *International Journal of Psycho-Analysis.* 44: 224–255.

Glatzer, H. & Evans, W. N. (1977). On Guntrip's analysis with Fairbairn and Winnicott. *International Journal of Psychoanalytic Psychotherapy.* 6: 81–98.

Guntrip, H. (1961). *Personality Structure and Human Interaction.* New York: International Universities Press.

——— (1975). My experience of analysis with Fairbairn and Winnicott. *International Review of Psycho-Analysis.* 2: 145-156.

Hartmann, H. (1939). *Ego Psychology and the Problem of Adaptation.* New York: International Universities Press, 1958.

Jacobson, E. (1954). The self and the object world. *Psychoanalytic Study of the Child.* 9: 75-127. New York: International Universities Press.

Jacobson, E. (1964). *The Self and the Object World.* New York: International Universities Press.

Kernberg, O. (1976). *Object Relations Theory and Clinical Psychoanalysis.* New York: Jason Aronson.

Klein, M. (1946). Notes on some schizoid mechanisms. In: *Developments in Psycho-Analysis*, Eds. M. Klein, P. Heimann, S. Isaacs, & J. Riviere. London: Hogarth Press, 1952, pp. 292-320.

——— (1952a). Discussion of the mutual influences in the development of ego and id. *Psychoanalytic Study of the Child.* 7: 51-68. New York: International Universities Press.

——— (1952b). Some theoretical conclusions regarding the emotional life of the infant. In: *Developments in Psycho-Analysis*, Eds. M. Klein, P. Heimann, S. Isaacs, & J. Riviere. London: Hogarth Press, pp. 198-236.

Mahler, M. S. (1972). On the first three subphases of the separation–individuation process. *International Journal of Psycho-Analysis.* 53: 333-338.

Sutherland, J. D. (1963). Object-relations theory and the conceptual model of psychoanalysis. *British Journal of Medical Psychology.* 36: 109-124.

——— (1965). Obituary: W. R. D. Fairbairn. *International Journal of Psycho-Analysis.* 46: 245-247.

——— (1979). The British object relation theorists: Balint, Winnicott, Fairbairn, and Guntrip. Presented at a scientific meeting of the Association for Psychoanalytic Medicine, May. Unpublished.

Winnicott, D. W. & Khan, M. M. R. (1953). Book review of *Psycho-Analytic Studies of the Personality* by W. R. D. Fairbairn. *International Journal of Psycho-Analysis.* 34: 329-333.

Wisdom, J. O. (1962). Comparison and development of the psycho-analytical theories of melancholia. *International Journal of Psycho-Analysis.* 43: 113-132.

——— (1963). Fairbairn's contribution on object-relationships, splitting, and ego structure. *British Journal of Medical Psychology.* 36: 145-159.

——— (1971). Freud and Melanie Klein: Psychology, Ontology, and Weltanschauung. In: *Psychoanalysis and Philosophy*, Eds. C. Hanly & M. Lazerowitz. New York: International Universities Press, pp. 327-362.

Zetzel, E. (1955). Recent British approaches to problems of early mental development. *Journal of the American Psychoanalytic Association*, 3, 534-543.

5

The Origin and Nature of the "Object" in the Theories of Klein and Fairbairn

> But of late I have been increasingly able to catch, if I listen
> attentively, the sound of the sobs which I had the strength to
> control in my father's presence, and which broke out only when I
> found myself alone with Mamma. Actually, their echo has never
> ceased: it is only because life is now growing more and more quiet
> round about me that I hear them afresh, like those convent bells
> which are so effectively drowned during the day by the noises of
> the streets that one would suppose them to have been stopped for
> ever, until they sound out again through the silent evening air.
>   *Swann's Way*, M. PROUST

Object relations theory has become one of the *ubiquitous* phrases within
contemporary psychoanalytic literature. It is used variously to refer to:
theorists who have departed from the classical tradition, like Klein and
Fairbairn; theorists who have remained within the tradition yet stretched
its boundaries, like Mahler, Jacobson and Kernberg; as well as to all those
who acknowledge the importance that other people play in personality
development. Within this spread of meaning and amid the controversies

From *Contemporary Psychoanalysis*, 1981, *17*(3), 374–398. Copyright 1981 by the William
Alanson White Institute. Reprinted by permission of the author and publisher.

among dedicated proponents and denigrating detractors, the term "object relations theory" loses much of its significance. In fact, with its current wave of popularity, object relations theory threatens to degenerate into a tired psychoanalytic cliche, becoming for psychoanalysis what existentialism was for philosophy during the 1950's and 1960's—an innovative and powerful theoretical framework which became, in its ever widening application, thinned to simplistic truisms.

Melanie Klein and W. R. D. Fairbairn have been two of the most significant theorists within psychoanalysis during the past 50 years. Traces of their influence are discernible in almost every area of contemporary psychoanalytic theory and practice. Yet, because of the politics and polemics surrounding "object relations theory" as a movement, there has been little critical and balanced appraisal of their contributions and a tendency to blur together their very different and highly distinct theoretical systems. The theories developed by Klein and Fairbairn are complex, incomplete and often internally inconsistent. Since much of the discussion of their work tends either to glorify or dismiss it, the richness of their thought is often lost. The purpose of this paper is to contribute to the explication of Klein's and Fairbairn's concepts, and their differentiation from each other, through a detailed examination of their views concerning the origins and nature of "objects," a concept which occupies a central place within both systems.[1]

"Object" was the term chosen by Freud to designate the target of the drives, the "other," real or imaginary, toward whom the drive is directed. Although other persons are clearly central to many of Freud's clinical concepts, the "object" is the least intrinsic, most "accidental" feature within his formulations concerning the nature of the drives. The specific "source," "aim," and "impetus" are all *a priori*, inherent aspects of drive; the particular object is serendipitously tacked on through experience. All of the most important psychic processes are produced by excesses or deficiencies of gratification; the object is merely the vehicle through which gratification is either obtained or denied. In Freud's system, primary narcissism, in which all libido is directed towards the ego, is the earliest developmental stage, *before* libido is directed towards objects apart from the ego itself. This reflects the temporally secondary nature of objects within classical theory.

Although he never employed the term "internal object" as such,

---

[1]This paper concerns itself explicitly with Klein and Fairbairn, not with "Kleinian" theory as a whole, which, particularly in the work of Bion and Meltzer, has extended *a segment* of Klein's formulations in a speculative, extremely philosophical direction, nor with Guntrip's "extensions" of Fairbairn's formulations which, in my view, fundamentally alter the thrust of Fairbairn's vision.

Freud, from the beginning of his work, had described clinical phenomena involving internal "voices," images, parental values, etc. These were drawn together theoretically with the introduction of the concept of the super-ego in 1923. The super-ego, product of the internalization at the conclusion of the oedipal period of images and aspects of the parents, generally serves as the ego's ally in controlling the intensity of oedipal desires and conflicts. It functions as an internal presence with structural properties—the child fantasizes and imagines these values and images of the parents within his psyche, and these in turn aid the ego in the channeling of drive energies. Thus, for Freud, external objects, and the super-ego as an "internal object," serve similar functions; they are vehicles for drive gratification and regulation.

THE "OBJECT" IN KLEIN'S SYSTEM

Klein further developed the notion of internal objects, and this was central in the expanded role of objects in her own and Fairbairn's work. In her early papers she had described more and more complex phantasies[2] in young children concerning their mothers' "insides." The latter were believed to contain all varieties of substances, organs, babies, etc. During the late 1920's, Klein began to write of parallel phantasies which the child develops concerning his *own* insides, a place similar to his mother's interior, also populated by body parts, substances, people, etc. In contrast to Freud's super-ego concept, Klein suggests that these phantasies of internal presences begin in the first months of life. As development proceeds, Klein suggests, representations of *all* experiences and relations with significant others also become internalized, in an effort to preserve and protect them. This complex set of internalized object relations is established, and phantasies and anxieties concerning the state of one's internal object world become the underlying basis, Klein was later to claim, for one's behavior, moods, and sense of self.

Klein conceives of the drives as more tightly bound to objects, both internal and external, than did Freud, and hence she rejected the notion of "primary narcissism." The infant, Klein argued, has a much deeper and more immediate relation to others than previous psychoanalytic theory has credited him with (1932, p. 33). This rejection of the concept of "primary narcissism" was no mere theoretical refinement. Narcissism

[2]The Kleinian school has adopted the spelling *ph*antasy to differentiate the pervasive and largely unconscious mental processes referred to by Klein from *f*antasy in Freud and others which generally refers to more circumscribed, largely substitutive, and usually conscious processes. I have employed this same usage.

had been applied, within classical psychoanalysis, as an explanatory concept with regard to many clinical phenomena, ranging from tics (Ferenczi 1921) to schizophrenia (Freud, 1914), and as a tool for understanding rigid resistances within the psychoanalytic situation itself (Abraham 1919). Klein and her collaborators took issue with these explanations. They argued that seemingly narcissistic manifestations like tics (Klein 1925), schizophrenia (Klein 1960) and extreme resistances in analysis (Riviere 1936) are not objectless states (i.e., with only the ego as object), but reflect intense relations to *internal* objects. For Klein, the content and nature of relations with objects, both real people in the outside world and phantasized images of others imagined as internal presences, are *the* crucial determinant of most important psychical processes, both normal and pathological. She argued that Freud's "narcissistic libido" reflects not a cathexis of the ego itself, but of internal objects, and thus replaced Freud's distinction between narcissistic libido and object libido with the distinction between relations to internal vs. relations to external objects.

Where does the content of the patient's images, perceptions and phantasies of objects, external and internal, come from? Klein devotes considerable effort to this question, and there has been much controversy concerning her resulting formulations. Her critics (e.g., Guntrip 1971) accuse Klein of depicting the objects of human passion as phantasmagoric, solipsistic creations, with no necessary connection to the outside world. Her adherents dismiss these criticisms, pointing to Klein's frequent mention of the importance of real others. But the controversy remains unresolved. It derives from the fact that Klein actually developed several quite different formulations concerning the origins of objects, all highly innovative. One or another of these explanations dominates her writing at any particular time, while the others recede into the background. At some points she attempts to integrate some of them with each other, but only incompletely and suggestively. In this respect Klein's creative style is similar to Freud's; both seemed more interested in generating new concepts than in integrating new ideas with earlier ones. Much of the unnecessary controversy surrounding Klein's contributions stems from efforts by her disciples, and her detractors, to present her views as if they were comprehensive and internally consistent. I will try to avoid this unnecessary distortion by considering each formulation in turn.

In the most prevalent and widely known of Klein's formulations concerning the origin of objects she suggests that objects are inherent in, and thereby created out of the drives themselves, independent of real others in the external world; ". . . the child's earliest reality is wholly phantastic" (1930, p. 238). In this formulation, Klein argues that perceptions of real others are merely a scaffolding for projections of the child's innate object images. How is this possible? How can the child know of others and the outside world before he encounters them in experience? At various places in her writing, Klein proposes different explanations concerning the generation of inherent internal objects. One explanation involves a novel approach to understanding the nature of desire itself. This is implicit in Klein's writings throughout, and was finally argued explicitly by S. Isaacs (1952). Isaacs suggests that desire implies an object of that desire; desire is always *desire for something*. Implicit in the experience of wanting is some image, some phantasy of the conditions leading to the gratification of the wanting. In Freudian metapsychology, the drives are uninformed about the nature of objects and reality, about potential vehicles for their gratification; this objectlessness (apart from the ego itself) persists until objects are thrust upon the infant and become associatively linked with drive gratification. For Klein, the drives possess, by virtue of their very nature as desire, inherent *a priori* images of the outside world, which are sought for gratification, either in love or destruction.

Klein bases her presupposition of inherent images and the knowledge of objects separate from and prior to experience on certain more speculative passages in Freud's own work, where he posits a phylogenetic inheritance containing specific memory traces and images. This line of thought, revealing Jung's influence, is developed most fully in *Totem and Taboo* (1913), at the peak of Jung's impact on Freudian theory, and is a minor theme appearing now and again in Freud's later writing. Klein's use of this concept is much broader and more systematic. She argues the existence not just of specific phylogenetic memory traces and images, but of an inherent, broad set of images and phantasied activities such as: breasts, penises, the womb, babies, perfection, poison, explosions, conflagrations, etc. The earliest object relations of the child are relations with images of body parts, which operate, Klein suggests, as "universal mechanisms" (1932, p. 195 f.n.), without the child necessarily having experienced the actual organs in reality. Only later do the child's images of objects take on aspects of the real objects they represent in the world. It is towards these *a priori* images that the child's drives are directed, both lovingly and hatefully, and they serve as a substratum and scaffolding onto which later experiences accrue. In her later writing, Klein further extended the principle of *a priori* knowledge and images of objects to whole objects as well. She wrote, ". . . the infant has an innate unconscious awareness of the existence of the mother . . . this instinctual knowledge is the basis for the infant's primal relation to his mother" (1957, p. 248).

A second explanation accounting for inherent, phantastic early objects involves the earliest channeling of the death instinct, which, Klein argues, *must* take place if the infant is to survive. Klein, following Freud, felt that the infant is threatened by destruction from within immediately following birth. Freud had suggested that Eros, or the life instinct, inter-venes and rechannels the death instinct. He proposed two mechanisms for this rescue operation—most of the destructiveness is turned outward into aggression towards others; some remains as primary erotogenic masochism. Klein proposes a third mechanism—an additional part of the death instinct is deflected or projected (she varies her language in differ-ent accounts) onto the external world. Thus, Eros actually *creates an image* of an external object, projects part of the death instinct into it, and redi-rects the remainder of the destructiveness outward towards this new cre-ated object. To preclude the experience of a world populated solely by bad objects, a portion of the life instincts likewise is projected, *creating a good object*, towards which love is then directed. The nature of the good objects, like the bad objects, is determined by the child's own motiva-tions, as he generates a "belief in the existence of kindly and helpful fig-ures—a belief which is founded upon the efficacy of his libido" (1932, p. 260). Thus, in this view, the first objects of the drives are created out of the drives themselves; their content is derived from the content of the child's own impulses which are now experienced as directed towards him by an external object. "By projection, by turning around libido and aggres-sion and imbuing these objects with them, the infant's object relations come about. This is the process which underlies the cathexis of objects" (1952, p. 58). This view of the child's earliest objects as actually creations of his own drives was developed by Klein in her earliest papers to ac-count for the harsh, primitive, punishing super-ego figures which she discovered accompanying early oedipal phantasies in the first years of life.[3] This explanation seemed to account for the fact that the child imagines punishments whose content matches his own aggressive phantasies. The child lives in dread of his objects destroying, burning, mutilating and poisoning him, because these activities dominate his own phantasies towards them, and therefore constitute the substance of his projections onto them. Thus, in the child's psychic economy, as with the "Lord High Executioner," the punishment always fits the crime (1928, p. 203). The world of the child, both internal and external, is populated by creatures whose nature is a reflection of the child's own motivations. "External reality is mainly a mirror of the child's own instinctual life . . . peopled

[3]Klein's derivation of the content of the super-ego differed from that originally posited by Freud in 1923, when he derived the super-ego from internalizations of features from the actual parents. Perhaps because Freud was so sparing in crediting Klein with any important contributions, she seems to have been particularly pleased to see Freud adapt her view later in *Civilizations and Its Discontents,* where he sug-gests that much of the content of the super-ego derives from the child's own aggres-sion turned inwards.

in the child's imagination with objects who are expected to treat the child in precisely the same sadistic manner as the child is impelled to treat the objects" (1930, p. 251). The child's fear of his early objects is proportional to the degree of his own aggressive impulses, and the specific nature of these objects in his phantasies is particular to his own instinctual makeup. ". . . each child develops parental imagoes that are peculiar to itself" (1933, p. 270).

A third explanation for the existence of inherent, phantastic early objects was introduced by Klein in 1946. Now she suggested that the first experience of objects, internal and external, grows out of perceptual misinterpretation. Klein proposes that the experience by the child of the workings of the death instinct within is *perceived* as an attack by something foreign, apart from any specific mechanism of projection *per se*. The death instinct is "felt as fear of annihilation and takes the form of fear of persecution . . . (it) attaches itself at once to an object . . . or rather *it is experienced as the fear of an object*" (1946, p. 4) (emphasis added). The nature of the child's experience itself, Klein suggests, leads him to construe the existence of objects. She did not limit this formulation to the experience of the death instinct, but also suggests that in the experience by the child of any frustration of bodily needs, the physical sensations, the tension and discomfort, are experienced as foreign bodies, or as attacks produced by foreign bodies. In a later paper she suggests that pleasurable sensations such as comfort and security as well are "felt to come from good forces" (1952a, p. 49). Riviere later extended this approach to feelings of rage, suggesting that the tensions constituting the experience of rage are experienced as bad internal objects. She also suggests that the child naturally personalizes all frustrations into a presumption of a depriving other. "Internal privation and need are always *felt* as external frustration" (Riviere, 1936a, p. 46).[4]

At other points in her work, Klein suggests a very different approach to understanding the origin of objects, in which both perceptions of real, external others and images of internal objects derive from the child's experience with real others in the outside world. The full development of this line of thought emerged in the mid-1930's, with the publication of Klein's views on the depressive position. Here, the theory of the internal origins of early objects recedes into the background, and Klein posits the view that the real others in the infant's external world are constantly internalized, established as internal objects, and projected out onto

---

[4]Racker (1968) was to further extend this approach in his depiction of the "primary paranoid situation" to the point of eliminating projected aggression altogether in the establishment of initial bad objects.

external figures once again. Klein does not seem to consider such inter-nalization to be a defense mechanism *per se*, but rather a mode of relat-ing to the outside world. "The ego is constantly absorbing into itself the whole external world" (1935, p. 286). Internal objects are established corresponding to real external others, as "doubles." Not just people, but all experiences and situations are internalized. The child's internal world ". . . consists of innumerable objects taken into the ego, corresponding partly to the multitude of varying aspects, good and bad, in which the parents appeared to the child's unconscious mind . . . they also represent all the real people who are continually being internalized" (1940, p. 330–1). This view of objects, particularly internal objects, as constituted from the beginning by perceptions of real others was elaborated by several of Klein's collaborators. Riviere notes that the term "introjection" is best not re-stricted to a defense mechanism, that it "operates continually from the first dawning perception of something external to me" (1936a, p. 51). Heimann (1952) further extends the range of this process of internaliza-tion, seemingly making it synonymous with perception in general. "When the ego receives stimuli from outside, it absorbs them and makes them part of itself, it introjects them" (p. 125).[5]

If objects derive both from internal and external sources, how do images arising from these different sources intersect and join? Klein ap-proaches this tricky problem of the blending of object images in several different ways; it is not apparent how these different formulations con-cerning synthesis can themselves be reconciled with each other.

One combinatory approach suggested by Klein involves a simple tem-poral sequence. Early objects are internally derived, largely generated out of the child's numerous and varied sadistic impulses. Therefore, they tend to be essentially harsh and punitive. Later images of the real parents are internalized; these are at first largely kind and benevolent imagoes, "magic helpers." Klein proposes a layering process, in which the harsh "inner super-ego" is overlaid by the kinder parental imagoes. Gradually, over time, the early objects are transformed, softened by the images of the real parents. The closer the content of internal objects comes to real objects, Klein suggests, the less the pathology (1932, p. 217). Real objects pro-vide a crucial ameliorative function. For example, Klein suggests that the only child, like all children, has hateful relations with "bad" sibling ob-jects, whom he phantasizes destroying inside mother's womb and from whom he fears retaliation. Yet, unlike children with brothers and sisters the only child is deprived of the "opportunity of developing a positive

[5]The differences between the establishment of internal objects and simple mem-ory, the recording of experience, become blurred here.

relation to them in reality" (1932, p. 74). Thus, although they play a temporally secondary role, real objects provide a crucial vehicle for the transformation of the earliest, phantastic objects into less frightening, more realistic representations of other people.

A second formulation concerning the blending of internally-derived and externally-derived objects posits a more immediate mix. At points Klein suggests that early objects derive essentially from real external figures, but that they are distorted through the child's projections of his own impulses onto them. These early images are "constructed on the basis of the real oedipus objects and the stamp of the pre-genital instinctual impulses." Thus, around a kernel of real perception is elaborated a mirror image of the child's own motives. These object images contain features of the real mother and father, but grossly distorted, resulting in figures of an "incredible or phantastic character" (1933, p. 268).

A third approach to the problem of blending posits a more fluid mechanism of perpetual cycles of projection and introjection. Early internal objects of a harsh and phantastic nature are constantly being projected onto the external world. Perceptions of real objects in the external world blend in with the projected images. A subsequent reinternalization takes place in which the resulting internal objects are partially transformed by the perceptions of real objects. Klein (1932) suggests that the early establishment of harsh super-ego figures actually stimulates object relations in the real world, as the child seeks out allies and sources of reassurance which in turn, transform his internal objects.

> In the early stages the projection of his terrifying imagos into the external world turns that world into a place of danger and his objects into enemies; while the simultaneous introjection of real objects who are in fact well-disposed to him works in the opposite direction and lessens the force of his fear of the terrifying imagos. Viewed in this light, super-ego formation, object-relations and adaption to reality are the result of an interaction between the projection of the individual's sadistic impulses and the introjection of his objects (1932, p. 209).

This process also forms the basis for the repetition compulsion, which involves a constant attempt to establish external danger situations to represent central, internal anxieties (1932, p. 70). To the extent to which one can perceive discrepancies between internally-derived anticipations and reality, to allow something new to happen, the internal world is transformed accordingly, and the cycle of projection and introjection has a positive, progressive direction. To the extent to which one finds confirmation in reality for internally-derived anticipations, or is able to induce others to play the anticipated roles,[6] the bad internal objects are simply reinforced, and the cycle has a negative, regressive direction.

In Klein's system, relations with objects occupy center-stage. Both phantastic images of others as internal and external presences as well as experience with others in the external world play dominant roles in the child's emotional life from the very beginning. Relations with internal objects constitute, for Klein, the very fabric of the self. However, Klein does not provide a unified theory concerning the origins and nature of objects. She developed several highly innovative formulations concerning inherent, *a priori* origins of objects, a comprehensive view of object images and internal objects as deriving from the absorption of real experience with others, and several possible mechanisms for the blending of these products.

Klein's formulations stressing the *a priori* and phantastic origin of objects were developed prior to 1934, during the period in which aggression was her major focus, while the view stressing the synthesis of object images out of absorptions of experience with real others was developed during the period in which depressive anxiety and reparation were her major focus. This is not happenstance. While Klein's focus was on aggression, it was bad or hateful objects which she was most concerned with. Her papers on depressive anxiety, on the other hand, focus more on the good objects and their feared destruction. Klein has a tendency to see bad objects as internally derived (projectively), i.e. from the child's own drives, and good objects as derived largely from external others (introjectively). Unfortunately, each of her formulations is postulated as a universal mechanism for the origin of objects; therefore, this distinction becomes blurred, resulting in what seem to be incongruent and, perhaps, incompatible concepts. Klein's tendency to view bad objects as created internally and good objects as absorbed from the outside stems from the conceptual proximity of her work to classical instinct theory. Klein, as Freud, sees the source of difficulties in living as arising from internal, constitutional sources; real others in Klein's writing serve to ameliorate anxiety arising from internal origins. Klein minimizes the pathogenic significance of parental anxiety, ambivalence and character pathology. Fairbairn, in reaction to this omission in Klein's work, makes parental deprivation the *exclusive* cause of psychopathology.

[6]In these depictions of the structuring of relations with others on the basis of characteristic anxietysituations, and in her brief mention of the role of anticipation and the induction of others to play desired roles, Klein is venturing into the kind of approach Sullivan emphasized in his study of interpersonal relations (cf. Klein 1936, p. 115).

The cumulative impression of Klein's formulations concerning the origin and nature of objects is that of an incomplete patchwork. Her contributions consist of a rich but loosely organized set of ideas and approaches, which tend to be juxtaposed to, rather than fully integrated with, each other.

THE "OBJECT" IN FAIRBAIRN'S SYSTEM

Fairbairn came to intellectual maturity in a climate dominated by Klein's extensions and elaborations of Freud's theory. His early papers are written in a distinctively Kleinian mode with extensive use of her concept of internal objects. Although in his later work Fairbairn retains much of Klein's language, the meaning he attributes to these terms has changed. Fairbairn retained the terms "objects" and "internal objects," yet his conceptualization of the origin and nature of objects is quite different from Klein's; these differences reflect Fairbairn's more radical rejection of classical drive theory as well as other fundamental divergences between the Kleinian and Fairbairnian systems.

At the center of Fairbairn's broad and varied contributions lies his critique and reformulation of the psychoanalytic theory of motivation— the drive theory. The basic motivational unit within drive theory is the impulse. Impulses are derivatives of drive tension, and provide the energy which fuels all activities of the psychic apparatus.[7] Fairbairn pointed out that although Freud's later work stressed the functioning of the ego and the super-ego, the more social dimensions of the personality, and although Klein's work has elaborated a complex theory of internal objects, the source of motivational energy for both classical and Kleinian theory remained the instinctual impulse. The psychology of the ego and its objects had been superimposed upon the earlier psychology of impulses. Fairbairn argued that the basic assumptions upon which the drive theory rests are anachronistic (derived from 19th century Newtonian physics) and misleading, and, in the broadest sense, he saw his work as entailing a ". . . reintegration of Freud's views on the basis of a differing set of underlying scientific principles" (1946, p. 149). The first step in this reintegration was the "recasting and reorientation of the libido theory" (1941, p. 28).

Within Freud's system, the most salient and most constant characteristic of the functioning of the psychic apparatus is its propulsion towards tension-reduction, otherwise known as the pleasure principle.

---

[7]Descriptions of classical drive theory in this paper refer to drive theory at the time Fairbairn was writing and do not reflect subsequent changes in Freudian thinking.

The ultimate goal of all impulses is the satisfaction accompanying the reduction of bodily tension, experienced as pleasure.[8] Impulses become directed toward objects (other than the ego itself) only when objects present themselves and prove useful in reducing tension. Fairbairn focused his disagreement with drive theory on the proposition that libido is not pleasure-seeking, but object-seeking. This principle can be understood as an extension of Klein's emendations of drive theory. We have noted that Klein argued that objects are not added onto impulses secondarily through experience, but are built into the impulses from the start, *a priori*. For Klein, however, as for Freud, the fundamental aim of the impulse is still satisfaction—the object is a means toward that end. Fairbairn explicitly reverses this means/end relationship. He argues that the object is not only built into the impulses from the start, but that the main characteristic of libidinal energy is its object-seeking quality. Pleasure is not the end goal of the impulse, but a means to its real end, relations with others.

What is the nature of the "objects" towards which the libido is striving? In classical drive theory the object facilitates the attainment of the ultimate aim of the impulse which is satisfaction. Just about anything can become the object of an instinctual impulse—another person, a body part of another person, a part of the subject's own body, a piece of the inanimate world, etc.—contingent solely on having been associatively linked with the reduction of the tension of the impulse. "Natural objects," for Fairbairn, objects which the libido seeks prior to any deprivation, are simply other people. Fairbairn, as Sullivan, felt that there is a naturally unfolding, maturational sequence of needs for various kinds of relatedness with others, from infantile dependence to the mature intimacy of adult love. If relations with others were non-problematic, if satisfying contacts could be established and maintained, psychology would consist simply of the study of the individual's relations with other people. However, Fairbairn felt that this is not the case with modern man. Relations with others, particularly the earliest needs of infantile dependence on maternal figures, become unsatisfying, "bad." Fairbairn suggests that one large factor in this general deprivation has been the interference which civilization has caused in the mother–infant bond. With other animals, the young are in direct, physical contact with mothers for as long as their physical helplessness and dependency require. With humans, with the numerous other domestic, economic and social claims on the mother, this intense and unbroken contact is seldom possible. The consequence of what

---

[8]Freud (1924) revised this conception in his later work to regard pleasure not as the consequence of a simple reduction of tension, but as the consequence of a particular rhythm of increases and decreases in tension, but he never revised his basic metapsychology accordingly.

Fairbairn regards as this unnatural separation is that early relations with objects becomes "bad," or depriving. It becomes too painful to long for and depend on an object which is physically or emotionally absent a good deal of the time. Therefore, the child establishes internal objects inside himself, which act as substitutes and solutions for unsatisfying relationships with real external objects. These objects are wholly compensatory, unnatural and not dictated by the biological object-seeking nature of libido (1941, p. 40). The greater the degree of interference and deprivation in relations with its "natural" objects, real people, the greater the need for the ego to establish relations with internal objects. Thus, for Fairbairn, while psychology is the "study of the relations of the individual to his objects," psychopathology is the "study of the relations of the ego to its internalized objects" (1941, p. 60).

Under what circumstances and through what processes are internal objects established? Fairbairn's view of the *nature* of internal objects remained fixed throughout. They are compensatory substitutes for unsatisfactory relations with real others. His account of the specific motives and circumstances leading up to the establishment of these compensatory structures varies, however. In each of his major theoretical papers (1941, 1943, 1944) as well as in a review of his theory in 1951, he presents a somewhat different solution to this problem. They are not wholly incompatible with each other, nor are they easily integratable. Each has its own theoretical weakness and rough spots, and none seems wholly satisfactory.

In 1941, Fairbairn speaks of the internalization of objects simply as the result of the general incorporative tendencies in the early oral period. He alludes to a general internalization of both good and bad objects during the early months of life, in response to frustrations in external relations with others. The ". . . incorporation of the object . . . is the process whereby the individual attempts to deal with frustrations in oral relationships" (p. 34). If the child runs into later difficulties in his relations with others, he returns to these early incorporated objects and regressively reactivates his relations with them. In this approach to the process of internalization, Fairbairn is still clearly greatly influenced by drive theory, particularly as elaborated by Klein. The infant is seen as by nature incorporative, which is a property of his oral attitude towards the world. He takes in because that is his nature, as dictated by his biological equipment. ". . . the early urge to incorporate is essentially a libidinal urge" (p. 48). Fairbairn adds the stipulation that the taking in is preceded by frustration, departing from Klein's more fluid view that *all* experiences with objects eventually become internalized. However, at this point Fairbairn still roots internalization in the biological properties of orality.

In 1943 Fairbairn offers a second view of the circumstances surrounding the first internalization, shifting the motivational focus away from oral incorporation towards motives more purely concerned with object relations and defense. In this account, Fairbairn stresses the extent to which parents who are emotionally absent, intrusive or chaotic and inconsistent pose a considerable dilemma for the child. He cannot do without them, yet living in a world in which one's parents, the constituents of one's entire interpersonal world, are unavailable or arbitrary is unbearably painful. Therefore, according to Fairbairn, the first in a series of internalizations, repressions and splits takes place, based on the necessity for preserving the illusion of the goodness of the parents as real figures in the outside world. The child separates and internalizes the bad aspects of the parents—it is not they who are bad, it is he. The badness is inside him; if he were different, their love would be forthcoming. Every child needs to feel that his parents understand the world, are just and dependable. If he doesn't experience them in these ways, he transfers the problem into himself. He takes upon himself the "burden of the badness" (1943, p. 65). The "badness," the undesirable qualities of the parents, i.e. the depression, the disorganization, the sadism, are now in him. These "bad" features become bad objects, with whom the ego identifies (through primary identification). The child has purchased outer security at the price of sacrificing internal security. Another feature of this initial internalization process is the perpetuation of the fantasy of omnipotent control. When the child experiences the "badness" as outside, in the real parents, he feels painfully unable to make any impact at all. If the "badness" is inside him, he preserves the hope of omnipotent control over it.

A secondary process of internalization follows the initial internalization of the "bad" aspects of the parents which Fairbairn terms the "moral defense." This involves the establishment of "good" internal objects. As a consequence of the initial internalization, Fairbairn reasoned, the child feels himself to be irreversibly and unconditionally bad. He is unloved, not because of any constriction or difficulty in the mother, but because he himself is bad, unlovable. The moral defense involves the internalization of good and ideal aspects of the parent to create the possibility of internal goodness. The identification with the good objects serves as a defense against the badness the child feels as a result of the initial internalization. He is now morally and conditionally bad, rather than libidinally and unconditionally bad. The experience of the child is now that he *has been* bad and undeserving of the parents' love, but that he can be good, through identification with his good objects. One sees this kind of internal logic again and again in clinical work with patients who constantly place grandiose and perfectionistic demands upon themselves, who have, in classical language, a harsh and demanding superego. Fairbairn argues that the self-accusations and perfectionistic strivings are not fundamentally punishments for fantasied crimes and instinctual gratifications, as they are viewed within the classical model. They result from the double process of internalization comprising the moral defense, in which the child protects himself from the core feeling of helplessness and despair at the lack of relatedness with the parent. First, he internalizes the badness—it is not they who are bad, but he. Second, he internalizes a good object—(composed of actual, admired qualities or values of the parent)—if only he can live up to his perfectionistic strivings, his parents will be available and love him.

The two basic approaches to internalization which Fairbairn had presented up until this point are contradictory. The original 1941 approach, with its Kleinian emphasis on the innate oral incorporative tendencies in the child, suggested that an early internalization of both good and bad objects takes place in the earliest months of life. The 1943–4 approach, with its stress on the defensive and purely object-relational aspects of internalization suggested that the first objects internalized are bad objects, enabling the child to preserve the illusion of good relatedness to the real mother and protect her from intense libidinal and aggressive affects. The good object is internalized only secondarily through the "moral defense." In 1951 Fairbairn attempted to reconcile these two views. He presents a synthetic view enabling him to have both good and bad objects internalized from the beginning, and yet to define internalization as a defensive phenomenon. What he argued was that the first internalization is of an original "pre-ambivalent object," the earliest experience of the mother, in which the child has not yet fully separated the gratifying and ungratifying features. The motive for this internalization, Fairbairn stresses, is frustration—the object is internalized *because* it is not wholly gratifying. If it were, no internalization would be necessary. Although the object is internalized through an oral incorporative response to frustration, it soon becomes employed by the ego in its struggle to maintain good object relations. Fairbairn reasoned that the ego becomes ambivalent about this originally pre-ambivalent object. In an effort to control it, it splits it into gratifying and ungratifying aspects, and then splits the ungratifying aspects further into exciting and rejecting components.

This solution reflects Fairbairn's characteristic tendency to become absorbed in schematic, intricate theoretical constructs which drift away from their clinical and developmental referents. The revision works within its own terms, but it is not clear what those terms mean. As Winnicott and Khan (1953) point out in their review of Fairbairn's work, this solution simply creates more problems than it solves. First, if the original "pre-

ambivalent object" is internalized because it is in "some measure gratifying and some measure ungratifying," what is meant by ambivalence? If
the child has been able to distinguish experientially between gratifying
and ungratifying aspects, is not this ambivalence? If this *is* the case, why
would it be necessary to internalize the whole object? Second, what is
the process through which the ego would develop ambivalence toward
an already internalized object? Unless Fairbairn is implying a much more
fluid relationship between real objects and internal objects than he usually presupposes, this process seems impossible to grasp. Third, if the ideal
object is already internalized as a facet of the original pre-ambivalent
object, what becomes of the moral defense? What of Fairbairn's argument that identification with good internal objects serves as a distraction
from and bulwark against internalized bad objects? The neatness of the
1951 revision is contrived, and Fairbairn's attempt to synthesize his 1941
Kleinian-influenced view with his 1943–4 purely object relations approach
doesn't work. Further, it seems unnecessary. The latter approach, in its
stress on internalization as a defensive protection of the relationship with
the parents, in which bad objects are internalized first, followed by good
objects as part of a secondary "moral defense," seems to be his most compelling view, and the one most consistent with the general thrust of his
theoretical innovations.

THE "OBJECT" FOR KLEIN
AND FAIRBAIRN COMPARED

The major movement in the history of psychoanalytic ideas over the past
40 years has been a shift in emphasis from drives and their transformations to relations with others.[9] Most broadly put, this shift rests on the
premise that the major motivational thrust within human experience and
the major determinant of the patterning of personality and psychopathology is not the search for pleasure through drive gratification, but the
establishment and maintenance of relations with others, real and imaginary, past and present. Klein and Fairbairn have played key roles in this
larger movement. Klein served as a transitional figure, straddling Freudian drive theory and relational concepts; Fairbairn formulated one of the

[9]J. Greenberg and I will publish a critical history of this shift, including a fuller
treatment of the systems of Klein and Fairbairn under the title *Theories of Object
Relations: A Critique*, Cambridge: Harvard University Press, in press. [Editors' note:
This book was subsequently published as *Object Relations in Psychoanalytic Theory*
by Greenberg and Mitchell, 1983.]

purest and most comprehensive theories of object relations, and his work offers, together with the interpersonal theory of H. S. Sullivan, the most thorough-going and systematic alternative to classical drive theory.

The concept of the psychic "object" occupies a central place in the theoretical systems devised by Klein and Fairbairn, and it is the increased significance attributed by each theorist to the "object" that underlies their departures from classical Freudian metapsychology. Both Klein and Fairbairn describe relations both with real others and with fantasies of internal presences. As we have seen, these descriptions and accounts vary considerably, even within their own work. Klein offered several different approaches to understanding the origins of objects, both from internal sources as well as from the child's earliest experiences with real others. Fairbairn's view of the origins and nature of "natural objects" remained constant throughout, but he continually revised his views concerning the earliest establishment of internal objects. Despite the shifts and variability in understanding the origins and nature of "objects" taken by Klein and Fairbairn, there are consistent and fundamental differences between them with respect to their analysis of object relations, as well as with respect to their larger vision of human experience. These differences stem, partially, from Klein's transformation of, yet allegiance to, classical drive theory, and Fairbairn's abandonment of the concept of drive altogether.

For Klein, the internal object world is a natural, inevitable and continual accompaniment of all experience. Internal objects are established at the beginning of psychological life, and they become the major content of phantasy. The internal object world for Klein is the source of both life's greatest horrors and its deepest comforts. In Klein's vision of emotional health and analytic cure, internal objects play a central role. Health is constituted by a particular constellation of internal object relations, in which, with the resolution of the depressive position, the "whole object" is established and ambivalence contained. Thus, even in health, internal object relations parallel and underlie relations with real others in the external world.

For Fairbairn, internal objects are neither primary nor inevitable (theoretically). They are compensatory substitutes for unsatisfactory relations with real, external objects, the "natural," primary objects of libido. For Fairbairn, relations with internal objects are inherently masochistic. Bad internal objects are persistent tempters and persecutors, while good internal objects do not offer real gratification, but merely a refuge from relations with bad objects. In Fairbairn's vision of emotional health and analytic cure, internal objects are abolished altogether. The ego's attachment to internal objects is relinquished, and the energy bound up in internal object relations is made available to the central ego for relationships with real others in the outside world.[10] Whereas in Klein's view, phantasied relations with internal objects constitute the bedrock of *all* experience, for Fairbairn such relations represent a secondary retreat from disturbances in relations with real people, toward whom man is more fundamentally directed.

Klein and Fairbairn differ not only in their views concerning the *function* of internal objects, but concerning their *content* as well. For Klein, objects tend to have *universal* features. In many of her theoretical statements she stresses the *a priori* origins of object images as: part of a phylogenetic inheritance built into the experience of desire itself, construed from early sensations, or derived from the drives through projections. Although different in terms of frequency and severity, the content of these objects is the same for everyone—good and bad breasts, good and bad penises, babies, united parental couples. Klein also stresses the importance of real people in the child's life; however, here too it is the universal features of these real objects that are most important—their anatomical characteristics as representatives of the human species, their durability in the face of phantasied attacks against them, their inevitable mixture of gratifying and depriving features. Within Klein's system, the *dramatis personae* within the external and internal object worlds are standard. Although in her case illustrations Klein occasionally mentions some more personal or characterological feature of the parents (a mother's depression, lack of warmth, dislike for the child), these features never appear in Klein's formulations concerning internal object relations, where the cast of characters is always composed of universal images.

For Fairbairn, the content of internal objects derives completely from real, external objects, fragmented and recombined, to be sure, but always deriving from the child's experiences of his actual parents. The categories into which internal object relations are organized are uniform. "Bad" objects, for Fairbairn, are emotionally unavailable for the satisfaction of the child's dependency needs. Bad objects are split into exciting vs. rejecting components. Nevertheless, the content of these categories, the constituents of internal object relations in Fairbairn's system, are the personal features of the parents: the particular kind of promise and hope which the mother seemed to offer, the specific form of rejection displayed by the father, the parents' idiosyncratic ideals and values, etc.

A final major area bearing on the nature and function of objects in which Fairbairn and Klein differ is in their view of the ultimate source of

[10]Perhaps the greatest weakness of Fairbairn's system is his failure to account for the residues of good object relations and the structuralization of the self on the basis of healthy identifications. For Fairbairn, all internal object relations derive from frustration and are, by definition, pathological.

pathology or suffering in human experience. For Klein, the root of evil lies in the heart of man himself, in the instincts, particularly the death instinct and its derivative, aggression. The great dilemma for the child in both the paranoid–schizoid position and the depressive position is the safe discharge of his aggression. The earliest anxiety for the child is persecutory; he experiences the threat of his own demise as the victim of his own projected aggression. For Fairbairn, on the other hand, the root of psychopathology and human suffering is maternal deprivation. Ideally perfect mothering results in a whole, non-fragmented ego, with its full libidinal potential available for relations with actual, external objects. Inadequate parenting poses grave threats to the integrity of the ego. The central anxiety for Fairbairn involves the protection of the tie to the object in the face of deprivation, and all psychopathology is understood as deriving from the ego's self-fragmentation in the service of protecting that tie and controlling its ungratifying aspects. The difference in their views of the ultimate source of evil is reflected in the different meanings of the term "bad object" in the theories of Klein and Fairbairn. For Klein, the "badness" of an object, whether internal or external, refers to malevolence, deriving ultimately from the child's own inherent destructiveness, projected onto others. By contrast, "badness" for Fairbairn means unsatisfying, depriving (1944, p. 111). The "bad object" is the one which frustrates the object seeking of the libido by its absence and unresponsiveness. For Klein, "bad objects" are reflections, creations derived from the child's own inherent and spontaneous destructiveness. For Fairbairn, "bad objects" are aspects of the parents which make them unavailable to him, and frustrate his inherent longing for contact and relation.

CONCLUSION: TOWARD SYNTHESIS

In their understanding of the origins of human suffering Klein and Fairbairn stand in polar relation to one another; in this respect, they reflect a more general tendency inherent in psychoanalytic theory towards extreme positions on the issue of the causation and accountability for psychopathology. In his original theory of infantile seduction, Freud viewed the neurotic as an innocent childhood victim of adult molestation. Freud saw adult neurosis as incubating since early childhood, its seeds sowed by the precocious arousal of sexuality in the child. Having discovered the apochryphal nature of these retrospective accounts, Freud concluded that the problem was not in the parents but in the sexual quality and intensity of the child's own wishes. Infantile innocence was a universal ruse—the child's own incestuous desires and murderousness were the cause of the neurosis; the role of the actual parents in the etiology of neurosis was minimized. Klein represents the farthest swing of the pendulum in this direction. For Klein, the seeds of neurosis lie in the child's inherent longings and violence. It is the child's own greed, envy, jealousy and murderousness which create early anxiety situations and generate "bad" internal objects with pathogenic properties. Other people are potential, if not always successful, ameliorating factors; human caretakers, within Klein's formulations, are important in many respects, but they play no discernible role in generating "bad" internal objects and causing psychopathology. The position developed on this issue by Fairbairn constitutes a polar over-reaction to Klein's original extreme position: for Fairbairn, neurosis derives from parental failure. The child's needs are potentially satisfiable; parental inadequacy intensifies them and produces a secondary, problematic rage. This "excess" need and rage necessitates the internalization of "bad" objects and a consequent pathogenic ego-splitting. In Fairbairn's system, and even more so in Guntrip's extensions, the parents become universal villains, the child the passive victim. In Fairbairn's work, the essential innocence of the child has been reinstated.[11] The choice between a view of the child and hence the adult neurotic as either victim or villain has been perpetuated in the systems devised by Klein and Fairbairn. This choice is an unnecessarily limiting product of the preoccupation with blame, absolution and a medical model approach to difficulties in living.

The most productive development of the work established by Klein and Fairbairn requires a dialectical synthesis of a more interactional nature. It is my hope that this explication and differentiation of Klein's and Fairbairn's views concerning the origin and nature of objects will serve as a prolegomena to such a synthesis. From this point of view, difficulties in living can be regarded as universal, and developing out of the interaction between unfulfillable childhood desires and longings and the necessarily human imperfections of parental caretakers. Klein's formulations of infantile greed and envy can be applied without the presupposition of inherent aggression arising within the child. The infant's actual helplessness and lack of a stable sense of time and space lend a quality of great intensity and urgency to its needs, making any deprivation very painful and reactive rage and hatefulness unavoidable. The formulations supplied by Fairbairn concerning the internalization of inevitable parental difficulties and character pathology based upon the child's active allegiance and earliest object ties can be applied without the unilateral

[11]This battle is being currently argued in the dialogue between Kernberg and Kohut concerning the origins of pathological narcissism in either constitutional aggression or failures in parental empathy respectively. (Cf. Robbins (1980) for a study of the origins of the Kohut/Kernberg controversy in what he characterizes as the "schism" between Klein and Fairbairn.)

assignation of blame onto the parents and the treatment of the child as passive victim. All caretakers, by virtue of their humanity, inevitably fail their children, each in their own particular way. Thus, internal object relations, concerning both "bad" and "good" objects are generated out of both the intensity of infantile passions as well as parental character pathology. An approach to both the child and the parent based on *accountability without blame* is necessary, making possible a more balanced view of the origins of neurosis in the interaction between the parents' difficulties in living and the child's infantile needs, immature understanding of the nature of reality, and primitive loyalties.

REFERENCES

Abraham, K. (1919) A particular form of neurotic resistance against the psychoanalytic method. In *The Evolution of Psychoanalytic Technique*. M. Bergmann and F. Hartman, eds. New York: Basic Books, 1976.

Fairbairn, W. R. D. (1941) A revised psychopathology of the psychoses and psychoneuroses. In *An Object-Relations Theory of the Personality*. New York: Basic Books, 1954.

Fairbairn, W. R. D. (1943) The repression and the return of bad objects (with special reference to the 'war neuroses'). In *An Object-Relations Theory of the Personality*. New York: Basic Books, 1954.

Fairbairn, W. R. D. (1944) Endopsychic structure considered in terms of object-relationships. In *An Object-Relations Theory of the Personality*. New York: Basic Books, 1954.

Fairbairn, W. R. D. (1946) Object-relationships and dynamic structure. In *An Object-Relations Theory of the Personality*. New York: Basic Books, 1954.

Fairbairn, W. R. D. (1951) Addendum. In *An Object-Relations Theory of the Personality*. New York: Basic Books, 1954.

Ferenczi, S. (1921) Psychoanalytic observation on tic. In *Further Contributions to the Theory and Technique of Psycho-Analysis*. London: Hogarth, 1926.

Freud, S. (1913) Totem and taboo. *Standard Edition*, 13.

Freud, S. (1914) On narcissism. *Standard Edition*, 14.

Freud, S. (1924) The economic problem of masochism. *Standard Edition*, 19.

Guntrip, H. (1971) *Psychoanalytic Theory, Therapy, and the Self*. New York: Basic Books.

Heimann, P. (1952) Certain functions of introjection and projection in early infancy. In *Developments in Psycho-Analysis*. M. Klein, P. Heimann, S. Isaacs, J. Riviere, eds. London: Hogarth, 1952.

Isaacs, S. (1952) The nature and function of phantasy. In *Developments in Psycho-Analysis*. M. Klein, P. Heimann, S. Isaacs, J. Riviere, eds. London: Hogarth, 1932.

Klein, M. (1925) A contribution to the psychogenesis of tics. In *Contributions to Psycho-Analysis*. New York: McGraw-Hill, 1964.

Klein, M. (1928) Early stages of the oedipus conflict. In *Contributions to Psycho-Analysis*. New York: McGraw-Hill, 1964.

Klein, M. (1930) The importance of symbol-formation in the development of the ego. In *Contributions to Psycho-Analysis*. New York: McGraw-Hill, 1964.

Klein, M. (1932). *The Psycho-Analysis of Children*. London: Hogarth.

Klein, M. (1933) The early development of conscience in the child. In *Developments in Psycho-Analysis*. M. Klein, P. Heimann, S. Isaacs, J. Riviere, eds. London: Hogarth, 1952.

Klein, M. (1935) A contribution to the psychogenesis of manic–depressive states. In *Contributions to Psycho-Analysis*. New York: McGraw-Hill. 1964.

Klein, M. (1936) Love, guilt and reparation. In *Love, Hate and Reparation*. M. Klein and J. Riviere, eds. New York: Norton, 1964.

Klein, M. (1940) Mourning and its relation to manic–depressive states. In *Contributions to Psycho-Analysis*. New York: McGraw-Hill, 1964.

Klein, M. (1946) Notes on some schizoid mechanisms. In *Envy and Gratitude and Other Works*. London: Hogarth, 1975.

Klein, M. (1952) The mutual influences in the development of ego and id. In *Envy and Gratitude and Other Works*. London: Hogarth, 1975.

Klein, M. (1952a) The origins of transference. In *Envy and Gratitude and Other Works*. London: Hogarth, 1975.

Klein, M. (1957) Our adult world and its roots in infancy. In *Envy and Gratitude and Other Works*. London: Hogarth, 1975.

Klein, M. (1960) A note on depression in the schizophrenic. In *Envy and Gratitude and Other Works*. London: Hogarth, 1975.

Racker, H. (1968) *Transference and Countertransference*. New York: International Universities Press.

Riviere, J. (1936) A contribution to the analysis of the negative therapeutic reaction. *International Journal of Psycho-Analysis*, 17: 304–320.

Riviere, J. (1936a) On the genesis of psychical conflict in earliest infancy. In *Developments in Psycho-Analysis*. M. Klein, P. Heimann, S. Isaacs, J. Riviere, eds. London: Hogarth, 1952.

Robbins, M. (1980) Current controversy in object relations theory as outgrowth of a schism between Klein and Fairbairn. *International Journal of Psycho-Analysis*, 61: 477–492.

Winnicott, D. and Khan, M. (1953) Review in *International Journal of Psycho-Analysis*, 34: 329–333.

6

The Concept of Internal
Object Relations

THOMAS H. OGDEN

Object relations theory, although often erroneously thought to be an exclusively interpersonal theory that diverts attention from the unconscious, is in fact fundamentally a theory of unconscious internal[1] object relations in dynamic interplay with current interpersonal experience. The analysis of internal object relations centres upon the exploration of the relationship between internal objects and the ways in which the patient resists altering these unconscious internal object relations in the face of current experience. Classical theory does not include a concept of internal objects. Instead there are related and in part overlapping concepts of memory traces, mental representations of self and object, introjects, identifications, and psychic structures.

It is the thesis of the present paper that the 'internalization' of an object relationship necessarily involves a splitting of the ego[2] into parts that

[1]In this paper, the term *internal* will be used to refer not to a geographic locale, but to an intrapersonal event (i.e. an event involving a single personality system) as opposed to an interpersonal interaction involving two or more different people.

[2]The term *ego* will be used to refer to an aspect of personality capable of generating conscious and unconscious psychological meanings including perceptual meanings, cognitive meanings, emotional meanings, etc. As development proceeds, this aspect of personality becomes increasingly capable not only of organizing and link-

From the *International Journal of Psycho-Analysis*, 1983, 64, 227–241. Copyright 1983 by Thomas H. Ogden. Reprinted by permission of the author and publisher.

when repressed constitute internal objects which stand in a particular unconscious relationship to one another. This internal relationship is shaped
by the nature of the original object relationship, but does not by any means
bear a one-to-one correspondence with it, and is in addition potentially
modifiable by subsequent experience. The internal object relationship may
be later re-externalized by means of projection and projective identification in an interpersonal setting thus generating the transference and
countertransference phenomena of analysis and all other interpersonal interactions.

It will further be proposed that internal objects be thought of as
dynamically unconscious suborganizations of the ego capable of generating meaning and experience, i.e. capable of thought, feeling and perception. These suborganizations stand in unconscious relationships to one
another and include (1) self-suborganizations of ego, i.e. aspects of the
ego in which the person more fully experiences his ideas and feelings as
his own, and (2) object suborganizations of ego through which meanings are generated in a mode based upon an identification of an aspect of
the ego with the object. This identification with the object is so thorough
that one's original sense of self is almost entirely lost. This conception of
internal object relations goes well beyond the classical notion of self and
object mental representations (cf. Hartmann, 1964; Jacobson, 1964;
Sandler & Rosenblatt, 1962). What is being proposed here is the idea
that the ego is split into parts each capable of generating experience and
that some of these subdivisions of ego generate experience in a mode
modelled after one's sense of an object in an early object relationship while
others generate experience in a mode that remains fixed in a pattern congruent with one's experience of oneself in the same early object relationship. The two parts of the ego remain linked and when repressed constitute an unconscious internal object relationship.

This conceptualization of internal object relations is an outgrowth
of the work of Freud, Abraham, Melanie Klein, Fairbairn, Winnicott and
Bion. Although there are significant theoretical differences amongst this
group of analysts, the concept of internal objects has been handled by
each of them in such a way as to lay the groundwork for the next in what
together constitutes in my view the central line of thought or object relations theory. The contribution of each of these analysts to the concept of
internal object relationships will be discussed. On the basis of the mutually enhancing contributions of these analysts, an integrated conception
of the nature of internal object relations will be presented. It will then be

---

ing individual meanings in the process of thinking, remembering, loving, hating,
etc., but also of regulating to some extent the relationship between suborganizations of ego that have been split off from the original whole.

shown how an understanding of the clinical phenomena of transference, countertransference and resistance is enriched when viewed from the perspective of the theory of internal objects proposed in this paper.

THE DEVELOPMENT OF AN OBJECT RELATIONS THEORY OF INTERNAL OBJECTS

Freud neither used the term *internal objects* nor did he generate a conceptualization equivalent to that which will be discussed as an object relations conception of internal objects. In *The Interpretation of Dreams* (1900), he referred to unconscious memory traces and implied that they had the power to perpetuate the feelings involved in the forgotten early experience, to attract attention to themselves in the course of dream and symptom formation and to press for conscious expression, dream representation and symbolic representation in symptomatic behavior and character pathology. In 1914, Freud introduced the idea that unconscious fantasies about objects may under certain circumstances take the place of actual relationships with people.

In 'Mourning and melancholia' (1917), identification is focused on as the means by which one not only remembers, but in part emotionally replaces, a lost external object with an aspect of oneself that has been modelled after the lost external object. Freud described how in melancholia a relationship with an external object is 'transformed . . . into a cleavage between the critical activity of the ego and the ego as altered by identification' (p. 249). In other words, an external relationship is replaced by an internal one that involves an interplay of two *active* aspects of the person that have resulted from a splitting of the ego.

In 1923, Freud extended the notion of identification to include not only a modelling of oneself after the external object, but as in the case of superego formation, a process by which the functions of the external object are instated within the psyche. Freud (1940a) at the end of his life summarized his theory of structure formation by which a new active agency is generated: 'A portion of the external world has, at least partially, been abandoned as an object and has instead, by identification, been taken into the ego and thus become an integral part of the internal world. This new psychical agency continues to carry on the functions which have hitherto been perfomed by the people [the abandoned objects] in the external world: it observes the ego, gives it orders, judges it and threatens it with punishments, exactly like the parents whose place it has taken' (p. 205). Freud is in this line of thought proposing a model wherein an external object is 'by identification . . . taken into the ego'. He goes on to explain that taking the object into the ego involves establishing 'a new psychical agency', i.e. an aspect of personality that has the capacity to carry on functions in the internal world than have previously been performed in the external world by the object. This new agency stands in relation to the ego and can perceive, think, respond and initiate activity. Further, it has its own system of motivations: 'it observes the ego, gives it orders, judges it and threatens it with punishments'. Freud is here describing a normal developmental sequence wherein the child, in the context of his relations with external objects, establishes a suborganization of ego that has the capacity for independent motivation and carries on an object relationship with other aspects of the ego.

Freud's 'Fetishism' (1972) and 'Splitting of the ego in the process of defence' (1940b) papers invoke the concept of a split in the ego[3] to recount for the way in which one can know and not know at the same time. In other words, the ego can be defensively divided so as to operate on the basis of different types of understanding of reality. This represents both a clarification of the process of ego splitting involved in superego formation and an extension of the idea to account for internal division within the personality other than that involved in superego formation.

Freud's concept of psychic structures or 'agencies' operating in an 'internal world' that is developed in the context of one's early relations with external objects constitutes the theoretical framework within which all succeeding contributions to object-relations theory were developed. Karl Abraham's work played a pivotal role in the development of the object-relations branch of psychoanalytic theory and in particular provided the foundation upon which both Klein and Fairbairn developed their ideas. Working within the framework of Freud's sexual instinct theory, Abraham (1924) placed more importance than did Freud on the role of the object in libidinal development and placed more emphasis on the place of unconscious fantasy in psychological life. Abraham's division of early development into pre-ambivalent, ambivalent and post-ambivalent phases was the forerunner of Klein's and Fairbairn's schizoid[4] and depressive levels of early psychological organization. Inherent in Abraham's conception of different forms of ambivalence toward objects was the notion of a variety of forms of psychological conflict over the experience of self–object differentiation.

While Abraham's contributions to object-relations theory consisted

---

[3]Bettelheim (1981) has pointed out that 'ego' is an incorrect translation of '*das Ich*' which is more accurately translated as 'the I'. The phrase 'splitting of the I' better captures the notion of a subdivision of the person's capacity to think perceive and create experience than does the more impersonal term, 'splitting of the ego'.

[4]Klein initially used the term *paranoid position,* but under the influence of Fairbairn's work, adopted the term *paranoid–schizoid position* in 1952 (Klein, 1975, p. 2n).

largely in his shift of emphasis within the conceptual framework provided by Freud, Melanie Klein (1975), by making the role of unconscious internal object relationships primary, introduced a new perspective from which to organize clinical and metapsychological thinking. Klein (1946, 1958) conceived of the infant at birth as functioning with a primitive, loosely organized, but whole ego in relation to an object that is experienced as whole. Under the pressure of the intolerable anxiety of impending annihilation produced by the death instinct, the infant defensively attempts to distance himself from his sense of his own destructiveness by splitting both the ego and the object into more manageable (because separate) good and bad facets of object-related experience. Stated in less mechanical terms, the infant simplifies, makes more manageable, an unmanageably complicated relationship with the mother (including the coexistence of hating and loving feelings felt toward and experienced from the mother) by treating the relationship as if it were many relationships between unmistakably loving and unmistakably malevolent conceptions of self and object. These aspects of the infant's relationship with the object are kept separate by means of protective and introjective fantasies. The infant's splitting of his experience of his relationships with objects allows him to create a psychological sanctuary (safe from hostile and destructive feelings) within which he can safely feed, safely take in what he needs from his mother.

This theory of early development established a conception of psychological life based upon an internal organization derived from the relationship of split-off aspects of the ego to associated internal objects. There are considerable shortcomings in Klein's theory of internal object relations. Most fundamentally, Klein is not clear whether she views internal object relations as fantasies or as relationships between active agencies capable of feeling, thinking, perceiving, etc. In fact, she says both and often mixes the two by formulating clinical phenomena in terms of relationships between an active agency and a thought (cf. Mackay, 1981). This involves a confusion of levels of abstraction analogous to saying that a thought is contained in a neuron.

The fallacy of establishing direct relations between active agencies and ideas permeates Klein's writing. For example, in describing the development of early psychological life, Klein writes, 'The splitting off of persecutory figures which go to form part of the unconscious is bound up with splitting off idealized figures as well. Idealized figures are developed to protect the ego against the terrifying ones' (1958, p 241). Classical analysts point out that the notion of idealized figures protecting the ego against terrifying ones is tantamount to proposing that there are internal friendly and hostile 'demons' operating within the mind. 'A multitude of minds is introduced into a single psychic apparatus . . . the person is being envisaged as a container of innumerable, independent micro-organizations that are also microdynamisms' (Schafer, 1968, p. 62). Kleinians have replied that these figures are not demons, but unconscious fantasies: 'Internal objects are not "objects" situated in the body or the psyche: like Freud [in his theory of the superego] Melanie Klein is describing unconscious phantasies which people have about what they contain' (Segal, 1964, p. 12). However, despite this clarification on the part of the Kleinians, it must be remembered that an unconscious fantasy (the product of 'fantasy-thinking', Isaacs, 1952, p. 108) is after all a thought as are the figures within the fantasy. If internal objects are thoughts as Segal and Isaacs conceptualize them to be, then they cannot themselves think, perceive or feel, nor can they protect or attack the ego. Even to the present, Kleinian theorists have not been able to disentangle themselves from the Scylla of demonology and the Charybdis or mixing incompatible levels of abstraction (i.e. active agencies and thoughts).

It was this Kleinian theory of internal object relations with its unsatisfactory mixture of fantasy and dynamism, together with Freud's theory of the origin of the superego that formed the background for Fairbairn's contributions to object-relations theory. Fairbairn (1940, 1944), like Klein, viewed the infantile ego as whole at birth and capable of relating to whole external objects. To the extent that the 'fit' between mother and infant is lacking, the infant experiences an intolerable feeling of disconnectedness and defends himself by means of splitting off the aspects of the ego which were felt to be unacceptable to the mother. These split-off portions of ego remain fixed in a relationship with the unsatisfactory aspects of the object. This part-object relationship (split-off ego in relation to an emotionally absent or rejecting object) is repressed in order to master the feelings involved and in an effort to change the object into a satisfactory object. The ego and frustrating object undergo further subdivisions along lines of cleavage determined by different affective qualities of the unsatisfactory object relationship. For example, the tantalizing qualities of the relationship and the rejecting qualities of the relationship become separated from one another in the infant's internal world. A significant aspect of the ego (the central ego) retains a relationship with the accepting and accepted qualities of the object (the 'good enough' mother [Winnicott, 1951] as opposed to the defensively idealized mother). The central ego is in part the conscious ego, but also includes dynamically unconscious facets, e.g. its defensive efforts to make itself unaware of the unsatisfactory aspects of object-related experience.

Fairbairn, although working within a Freudian psychoanalytic framework, was struggling against what he felt were shortcomings of both the Freudian and the Kleinian theories. Fairbairn (1946) pointed out that Freud conceived of the id as energy without structure (Freud, 1933) and

the ego as structure without energy. That is, the id was seen as 'instinctual cathexes seeking discharge—that in our view is all there is in the id'
(Freud, 1933, p. 74) while the ego was seen as organized into functions
but without its own source of energy. Fairbairn (1944, 1946) replaced
the Freudian dichotomy of ego and id, structure and energy, with a notion
of 'dynamic structures'. These dynamic structures are conceived of as
aspects of the mind capable of acting as independent agencies with their
own motivational systems. In energic terms one would say that they have
their own power source. In psychological terms, Fairbairn is saying that
these aspects of the person have the capacity to think and to wish according to their own system of generating meaning. According to this
theory, each bit of ego (aspect of the personality) defensively split off in
the course of development, functions as an entity in relation to internal
objects and in relation to other subdivisions of the ego.

   With regard to the important question of the theoretical status of
internal objects, Fairbairn states that 'in the interests of consistency, I must
now draw the logical conclusion of my theory of dynamic structure and
acknowledge that, since internal objects are structures, they must necessarily be, in some measure at least, dynamic. In drawing this conclusion
and making this acknowledgment, I shall not only be here following the
precedent of Freud, but also, it would seem, conforming to the demands
of such psychological facts as are revealed, e.g. in dreams and in the phenomena of paranoia . . . It must be recognized, however, that, in practice, it is very difficult to differentiate between the activity of internalized objects and the activity of the ego structures with which they are
associated; and, with a view to avoiding any appearance of demonology,
it seems wise to err, if anything, on the side of overweighting the activity
of the ego structures rather than otherwise. It remains true, nevertheless,
that under certain conditions internalized objects may acquire a dynamic
independence which cannot be ignored. It is doubtless in this direction
that we must look for an explanation of the fundamental animism of
human beings, which is none the less persistent under the surface . . .'
(1944, p. 132).

   Fairbairn's conclusion that not only ego suborganizations, but also
internal objects, must be considered 'in some measure at least' to be
dynamic structures, fully establishes the concept of internal object relations
between active semi-autonomous agencies within a single personality.

   It is evident from the above quotation that Fairbairn experienced some
hesitancy in drawing this conclusion, in large part because it seemed overly
close to Klein's formulations which he considered demonologic. There
are a number of incompletely thought-out aspects of Fairbairn's theory
which may have contributed to his misgivings about this facet of his thinking. In studying Fairbairn's work, one searches in vain for definitions of

the terms structure and dynamic. (One also is unable to find a definition of the concept of psychic structure in Freud's writing.) I infer from Fairbairn's use of the term structure that he is thinking of a stable set of ideas or mental representations. These conscious and unconscious ideas are consistent beliefs in terms of which one plans and measures one's behaviour and one's responses to new experience, but do not themselves think, respond, perceive, etc. It is the capacity for the latter forms of psychological activity (i.e. thinking, feeling, perceiving) that is the basis for the determination that an aspect of the personality is dynamic. When Fairbairn says that internal objects are not 'mere objects' but dynamic structures, he seems to mean that, at least in part, internal figures are not simply mental representations of objects, but are active agencies whose activity is perceived by itself and by other dynamic structures to have specific characteristics which are then organized and registered as stable mental representations. It is possible for there to be structure without dynamism (stable sets of ideas or convictions), but it is not possible for there to be dynamism without structure. For Fairbairn, the concept of id as energy reservoir is replaced by a notion of an unconscious set of ego and object structures each capable of psychological activity of varying degrees of primitivity.

It remains unclear in Fairbairn's thinking what relationship the concept of ego bears to the concept of dynamic internal objects. Can there be dynamic structure (e.g. an internal object) that is distinct from ego? This appears to be what Fairbairn is saying and, as will be discussed later, may be the reason for his hesitancy about fully acknowledging the dynamic nature of internal objects.

Donald Winnicott's major contribution to the development of a theory of internal object relations was his theory of multiple self-organizations functioning in relation to one another within the personality system. Winnicott (1951, 1952, 1954, 1960) envisioned the infant as born with the potential for unique individuality of personality (termed a True Self personality organization) which can develop in the context of a responsive holding environment provided by a good enough mother. However, when a mother substitutes something of herself for the infant's spontaneous gesture (e.g. her own anxiety over separateness for the infant's curious exploration), the infant experiences traumatic disruption of his developing sense of self. When such 'impingements' are a central feature of the early mother–child relationship, the infant will attempt to defend himself by developing a second (reactive) personality organization (the False Self organization). This False Self vigilantly monitors and adapts to the conscious and unconscious needs of the mother and in so doing provides a protective exterior behind which the True Self is afforded the privacy that it requires to maintain its integrity.

The False Self is not conceived of as malevolent; on the contrary it is a caretaker self (1954) that energetically 'manages' life so that an inner self might not experience the threat of annihilation resulting from excessive pressure on it to develop according to the internal logic of another person (the mother). The dread of annihilation experienced by the True Self results in a feeling of utter dependence on the False Self personality organization. This makes it extremely difficult for a person to diminish his reliance on this False Self mode of functioning despite an awareness of the emptiness of life that devolves from such functioning. Functioning in this mode can frequently lead to academic, vocational, and social success, but over time, the person increasingly experiences himself as bored, 'going through the motions', detached, mechanical, and lacking spontaneity (cf. Ogden, 1976).

The theoretical status of the object is not discussed by Winnicott, but his writing makes it clear that he treats internal objects as mental representations. Both Fairbairn's theory of dynamic structure and Winnicott's conception of the True and False Self represent steps in the development of an object-relations theory in which unconscious aspects of the person, each with the capacity to generate meanings according to its own patterns of linkage, engage in internal relationships with one another. Implicit in Fairbairn's and Winnicott's thinking is the idea that conceptualizing intrapsychic conflict as an unconscious fantasy of opposing internal forces does not adequately capture the way in which a person engaged in internal conflict is in fact feeling, thinking, perceiving, and behaving in two ways at once and is not simply imagining himself to be doing so. According to Fairbairn and Winnicott, it is more accurate to say that the person is behaving as two people at once than to say he is thinking about being two people at odds with one another.

With the unsettled issue of the theoretical status of internal objects in mind, a consideration of aspects of the work of Wilfred Bion becomes particularly pertinent. Bion at first described projective identification as an interpersonal process in which one finds oneself 'being manipulated so as to be playing a part, no matter how difficult to recognize, in somebody else's phantasy' (1952, p. 149). In the interpersonal setting, the person projectively identifying engages in an unconscious fantasy of ejecting an unwanted or endangered aspect of himself and of depositing that part of himself in another person in a controlling way. There is accompanying, real interpersonal pressure exerted on the 'recipient' of the projective identification that is unconsciously designed to coerce him into experiencing himself and behaving in a way that is congruent with the unconscious projective fantasy. Under optimal circumstances, the recipient 'contains' (Bion, 1962) or 'processes' (i.e. maturely handles) the evoked feelings and ideas, and thus makes available for re-internalization by the projector, a more manageable and integrable version of that which had been projected. (See Ogden, 1979, 1981, 1982b for more detailed discussions of projective identification.)

Bion (1957) later made clear that he viewed projective identification not only as an interpersonal process but as an intrapersonal process as well. This is a reasonable extension of theory if one conceives of the individual as composed of multiple personality suborganizations each capable of functioning semi-autonomously, and thus capable of processing one another's projective identifications. As can be seen from the foregoing discussion, this view of the personality system is an outgrowth of Klein's, Fairbairn's and Winnicott's contributions to object-relations theory.

For Bion (1956, 1957) projective identification involves the splitting of the personality (not simply a splitting of self-representations) and an ejection of the resulting suborganization into an internal object. The schizophrenic, due to an almost complete incapacity to tolerate reality, replaces perception with an extreme form of projective identification. By fragmenting his perceptual functions into isolated component parts and then projecting these functions (still experienced to some extent as self) into the object, the schizophrenic creates a type of internal object termed a 'bizarre object'. The object is then experienced as having life of its own: 'In the patient's phantasy the expelled particles of ego lead an independent and uncontrollable existence outside the personality, but either containing or contained by external objects' (1956, p. 39). An example given is the projection of the visual function into a gramophone (more accurately the psychological representation of the gramophone) thus producing a bizarre object that is felt to be capable of spying upon the patient. It is as if a part of the personality 'has become a thing' (1957, p. 48). This type of defensive fragmentation and projection of the mind into an object (representation) is the hallmark of the psychotic personality.

Bion stresses the role of fantasy in the process of generating bizarre objects. However, I feel that in so doing, he overlooks the way in which the process of fragmentation of the mental apparatus is more than a fantasy. I feel that one must understand the formation of bizarre objects as involving two different sorts of mental operations. One facet of the process is simply a fantasy—a gramophone is a mental representation that is imagined to be capable of perception. However, this fantasy is a thought generated by a part of the mind that has in fact been split off from the 'non-psychotic' mind and is actually functioning as an active, separate suborganization of the personality that experiences itself as a thing (cf. Ogden, 1980, 1982a). I would understand the gramophone image to be equivalent to a selfrepresentation of this aspect of the personality.

Grotstein (1980a,b, 1981) has built upon Bion's theory of the simultaneous functioning of psychotic and non-psychotic parts of the personality to construct a 'dual track model' of the mind in which experience is no longer conceived of as unitary, but as an overlapping of two or more separate experiences generated by autonomous suborganizations of the personality. Only through integration of various experiential perspectives is the illusion of unitary experience created, much as an integrated visual field with visual depth is achieved through an integration of slightly different visual images perceived by each eye. Grotstein's proposal represents an important rediscovery of Freud's most fundamental contribution to psychology. Freud proposed that we view the human mind as consisting of two facets, the conscious and the unconscious mind. Although these two aspects of mind function in different modes (primary and secondary process modes), they operate concurrently, and together contribute to the generation of experience that feels unitary to the subject. This sense of unity of experience is achieved despite the fact that the conscious and unconscious aspects of mind are operating semi-autonomously.

Before presenting an integration of the foregoing contributions to a theory of internal objects, I will briefly recapitulate the critical turning points in the development of this aspect of psychoanalytic theory. Melanie Klein was the first to establish a conception of an internal object world organized around internal object relationships consisting of an unconscious split-off aspect of ego in relation to an internal object. Her theory suffered from an unsatisfactory formulation of the theoretical status of internal objects which were conceived of as unconscious fantasies, but were at the same time thought of as capable of thinking, feeling, perceiving, and responding. Fairbairn clarified the matter by stating that neither objects nor object representations are internalized; rather, that which is internalized is an object relationship consisting of a split-off part of the ego in relation to an object which is itself, at least in part, a dynamic structure. The split-off aspect of the ego retains the capacity to function as an active psychological agency, albeit functioning in a primitive mode due to its relative isolation from other aspects of the developing personality. Fairbairn, although designating internal objects dynamic structures, did not explain how an internal object (presumably originally a thought) achieves its dynamism. Winnicott extended the notion of splitting of the ego to include subdivisions of the experience of self, but did not contribute to a clarification of the concept of internal objects.

Bion's theory of the pathological formation of bizarre objects provided an important insight into the formation of all internal objects. He envisioned a defensive splitting of the mind into parts that include active suborganizations of the mind which then experience themselves as having become things. Thus, the formation of a bizarre object is a process by which a suborganization of the mind engages in a specific object-related fantasy involving feelings of merger with, or entrapment by, the object.

On the basis of these contributions to object-relations theory, I shall now attempt to clarify the theoretical status of internal objects in a way that will facilitate clinical thinking with regard to various transference and resistance phenomena. An internal object relationship necessarily involves an interaction between two subdivisions of the personality each capable of serving as an active psychological agency. Otherwise one's theory must posit either (1) a direct relationship between non-equivalent levels of abstraction, e.g. the ego (a structure) in a relationship with an object representation (a thought), or (2) a relationship between two thoughts which would necessarily empower thoughts with the capacity to think. Freud's recognition of the fact that two active agencies are required for an internal object relationship is reflected in his theory of superego formation wherein the ego is conceived of as split into two active organizations which become involved in an internal relationship with one another.

Fairbairn's insight that it is object relationships and not objects that are internalized opened the way to thinking of both the self- and the object-components of the internal relationship as active agencies, 'dynamic structures'. The self-component was understood as a split-off aspect of the ego, thus accounting for its capacity to think, perceive, respond, etc. However, as stated above, although Fairbairn recognized that theoretical consistency demanded that the object-component of the internal object relationship also be considered a dynamic structure, he did not offer an explanation for the source of the dynamism of the internal object. Applying Bion's theory of the formation of pathological bizzare objects to the problem of the formation of internal objects in general, one can conceptualize internal objects as split-off aspects of the ego which have been 'projected into' mental representations of objects. That is, an aspect of ego is split off and becomes profoundly identified with an object representation. Since the ego suborganization is itself capable of generating meanings, its identifying with an object representation results in a shift in the way in which that aspect of the person thinks of himself. That which was originally an object representation becomes experientially equivalent to a self-representation of one of the split-off facets of ego.

In this light, I would suggest that the internalization of an object relationship be thought of as necessarily involving a dual subdivision of the ego. *Such a dual split would result in the formation of two new suborganizations of the ego, one identified with the self in the external object relationship and the other thoroughly identified with the object.* This formulation accounts for the dynamic nature of the internal object and also defines the relationship between the concept of ego and the concept of internal objects. In brief, internal objects are subdivisions of the ego that are heavily identified with an object representation while maintaining the capacities of the whole ego for thought, perception, feeling, etc.

It must be reiterated here that such a proposal goes no further in the direction of demonology than did Freud in describing the formation of the superego. The logical extension of Fairbairn's notion of dynamic structure is the idea that the ego is the only source of dynamism and that further dynamic structures are formed only by means of a subdivision of the ego. The dynamism of an internal object must in every case reflect the fact that an aspect of the ego has been split off and is at the core of the new structure. The fact that this structure (the internal object) is experienced as non-self is accounted for by means of its profound identification with the object. Internalization requiring a splitting of the ego occurs only in early development and as a result, the identification with the object is of a poorly differentiated nature, i.e. the experiential quality of the identification is one of 'becoming the object' as opposed to 'feeling like' the object. Adult 'internalizations' are built upon existing splits in the ego and do not involve the creation of new ones.

TRANSFERENCE, COUNTERTRANSFERENCE, AND PROJECTIVE IDENTIFICATION

From the perspective of the view of internal object relations presented above, transference and countertransference can now be understood as the interpersonal externalization ('actualization,' Ogden, 1980, 1982a) of an internal object relationship. Transference can be thought of as taking one of two forms depending on whether it is the role of the object or that of the self in the internal object relationship that is assigned to another person in the externalization process. When it is the role of the internal object that is projected, the patient experiences another person as he has unconsciously experienced that internal object (an unconscious split-off part of the ego identified with the object). In such a case, countertransference involves the therapist's unconsciously identifying with the aspect of the patient's ego identified with the object (Racker's 'complementary identification', 1957). Projective identification involves *in addition* an interpersonal pressure on the therapist to engage in an identification of this sort. The 'recipient' (e.g. the therapist) is coerced into seeing himself only as the object is represented in the internal object relationship. More accurately, there is an attempt to make the recipient's experience congruent with the way in which the internal object (aspect of the ego) *experiences itself* and perceives the self-component of the internal relationship. This is accompanied by an unconscious fantasy on the part of the subject of ejecting part of himself and entering into the object in a controlling way.

This form of externalization in which another person is treated as if he were the object-component of an internal object relationship is the psychological process that is generally referred to when we speak of transference. For example, a 20-year-old patient maintained a fearful, but defiant internal relationship in which one aspect of ego was locked in battle with another split-off aspect of ego that was identified with a bullying father representation. This patient was preoccupied with his anxiety concerning a particular male teacher whom he experienced as extremely intimidating. Nevertheless, the patient would struggle against unconscious wishes to undermine and 'show up' the teacher in class. Such a transference relationship (based on the externalization of the object-component of the internal relationship) became a projective identification as the patient began to imagine being able to 'push the buttons' of the teacher in an omnipotent way and would in reality provoke the teacher into a bullying stance.

The other of the two forms of transference described above involves the patient's experiencing another person (e.g. the therapist) the way the internal object (split-off portion of ego identified with the object) in a given internal object relationship experiences the aspect of the ego identified with self. The countertransference in this case consists of the therapist's identification with the self-component of the patient's internal object relationship (Racker's 'concordant identification'). Projective identification would in this case involve, in addition, an unconscious fantasy of projecting the self-component into the external object together with interpersonal pressure on the object for compliance with this fantasy, i.e. pressure on the external object to experience himself only as the internal object experiences the self in the internal object relationship.

The externalization of the self-component of an internal object relationship was exemplified by a psychotic adolescent who was continually tormented by intrusive obsessional thoughts, accusatory auditory hallucinations, and feelings that his mind was being controlled. He felt that he could not find a single moment of reprieve from these internal emotional assaults. The patient was seen in intensive individual psychotherapy in a long-term psychiatric hospital. In the course of this work, the patient's current experience came to be understood as an internal version of his experience of his relationship with his mother who had regularly, secretly observed him for hours at nursery school, had given him placebo medication for his 'nerves', and had tape recorded his dinner conversation and temper tantrums to play back to him for 'study' later. He had been sent to a family friend for 'therapy'. Following each session, the 'therapist' would report to the parents about what had transpired.

In the psychotherapy occurring during the patient's hospitalization, the patient subjected the therapist to a continual verbal and sensory barrage. In a relentless, loud, whiney, highly pressured tone of voice, he would make incessant demands of the therapist. When not gratified, the patient would call the therapist a string of mocking names that were repeated so often and so loudly that a fifty-minute session felt to the therapist like being subjected to the din of a jackhammer for hours. The therapist not only felt angry, but also experienced feelings of disorganization and utter helplessness that at times reached the point that he felt a panicky feeling that he was drowning. The patient described these sessions as 'negative mind control games', a term which referred to the idea that efforts at controlling his mind were 'jammed' and the jamming in turn had the effect of sending the mind control back to its source.

In this example, the self-component of an internal object relationship (in which the patient experienced himself as violently intruded upon by his mother) was projected into the therapist. The fantasy of negative mind control was accompanied by an interpersonal interaction that served to induce in the therapist the experience of the self in the internal object relationship. The fantasy, the interpersonal pressure, and the therapist's resonant response together constituted a projective identification.

The following is a second example of the type of transference involving the externalization of the self-component of the internal object relationship. Robert, a 20-year-old schizophrenic patient seen in intensive psychotherapy, unconsciously engaged in a painful internal object relationship in which he felt 'contaminated' by a mother who would insinuate herself into every facet of his body and mind. In an extended period of therapy, the patient refused to bathe and as time went on the therapist became preoccupied with the patient's odour which filled the office long after the patient had left. The therapist's office chair absorbed the patient's odour and became a symbol of the patient's entry into the therapist's life outside of the therapy hours. Thus, the therapist felt as if he himself had become inescapably suffused by the patient. In this case, the therapist had unwittingly been coerced into experiencing himself as the self-component of the internal relationship to the contaminating mother (an aspect of the patient's ego identified with this representation of the mother). (See Ogden, 1982a, for an in-depth discussion of this case.)

It is my experience that projective identification is a universal feature of the externalization of an internal object relationship, i.e. of transference. What is variable is the degree to which the external object is enlisted as a participant in the externalization of the internal object relationship. In other words, there is always a component of the therapist's response to the patient's transferences that represents an induced identification with an aspect of the patient's ego that is locked in a particular unconscious internal object relationship. This identification on the part of the therapist represents a form of understanding of the patient that can be acquired in no other way. In my opinion, it is not possible to analyse the transrerence without making oneself available to participate to some degree in this form of identification. However, it is by no means sufficient to have become a participant in the externalization of an internal relationship. One must, in addition, be able to understand that which one is experiencing as a reflection of a need on the part of the patient to reduce the therapist to the status of a surrogate for a part of the patient's ego. The therapist must himself be aware that the patient is selectively excluding all aspects of the therapist's personality that do not correspond to the features of the split-off ego with which the therapist is being identified. There is considerable psychological work involved in the therapist's consciously and unconsciously integrating the roles imposed upon him with his larger, more reality-based sense of himself (in particular his role as therapist).

RESISTANCE

From the perspective of the conception of internal objects proposed in this paper, resistance is understood in terms of the difficulty the patient has in giving up the pathological attachments involved in his unconscious internal object relationships. Fairbairn (1944, 1958) was the first to understand resistance in this way. He placed particular emphasis on the tie to the bad internal object. This tie is based on one's need to change the bad object into the kind of person one wishes the object were.

Fairbairn (1944) described two forms of attachment to the frustrating internal object. One type of tie to a bad internal object is the attachment of the craving self to the tantalizing object. The nature of this tie to the object is that of the addict for the addicting agent and is extremely difficult to relinquish. (See Ogden, 1974, for a description of a psychotherapy in which the central resistance was derived from this type of internal object tie.)

The second category of bond to a bad internal object described by Fairbairn is the tie of the wronged and spoiling self to the unloving, rejecting object. This often takes the form of a crusade to expose the unfairness of, coldness of, or other forms of wrong-doing on the part of the internal object.

Fairbairn (1940) presented graphic clinical data demonstrating the phenomenon of loyalty to the bad internal object that is fuelled by the unconscious conviction that a bad object is far preferable to no object at all. Fairbairn's thinking stems from the idea that a human being's sanity and survival depend on object-relatedness, and a person experiences the terror of impending annihilation when he feels that all external and internal object ties are being severed. Therefore, he clings desperately to any object tie (external or internal), even ones that are experienced as bad, when that is all that is available.

Fairbairn, because of his incomplete formulation of the nature of internal objects, focused exclusively on resistances derived from the experience of the self-component of the internal object relationship. As discussed earlier, Fairbairn only hesitantly accepted the idea that internal objects are dynamic structures and was not able to delineate the relationship between the concept of internal objects and the concept of ego. As a result, he restricted himself to studying ways in which the loyalty of the self to the internal object functions as a resistance to therapeutic work.

Other forms of resistance become recognizable from the perspective of a theory that more fully recognizes internal object relations as involving two active agencies each capable of generating experience. Not only does one encounter resistance stemming from the loyalty of the self to the bad object, one regularly encounters resistance based on the object's need for the self. This is not to introduce a conception of an inner world occupied by internal objects flying about one's mind on their own steam. From the perspective of the present paper, these internal objects are understood as aspects of the ego identified with objects, and as such can enter into a tormenting, tantalizing, humiliating, dependent or any other form of relatedness to other aspects of the ego. Freud himself used such words to describe the relationship of the superego to the ego. Resistance to giving up internal object ties can then be seen to stem both from those aspects of ego experienced as self and from the aspects of ego identified with objects. The latter set of resistances have not been nearly as well recognized nor elucidated.

Heretofore, almost exclusive focus has been placed on the experience of the self in relation to objects in internal object relations. This has been so largely because the object component has been conceptualized primarily as a mental representation (an idea), and therefore, it would not make sense to talk about the way in which a thought experiences a change in an internal object relationship. However, from the perspective of the object as suborganization of the ego, one is in a position to think about the following aspects of resistance stemming from the unwillingness of the object to relinquish its tie to other aspects of the ego involved in internal object relationships.

(1) The ego suborganization identified with the object is under constant pressure from the self-component of the relationship to be transformed into a good object. Such a transformation is strenuously resisted by the object-component because this type of massive shift in identity

would be experienced as an annihilation of an aspect of the ego.[5] The internal object relationship is vigorously defended from two directions: the self-component is unwilling to risk annihilation resulting from absence of object relatedness and instead strives to change the bad object into a good one; at the same time, the object-component fends off annihilation that would result from being transformed into a new entity (the good object). It is this latter motivation that accounts for the often encountered moment in therapy when the patient pleadingly looks at the therapist and says, 'I know that what I am doing is self-defeating, but to stop thinking and acting in that way would require that I become somebody else and I can't do that. I wouldn't recognize myself when I look in the mirror'.

In work with borderline and schizophrenic patients, this form of resistance often underlies the patient's intensely conflicted feelings about accepting the therapist's interpretations. Frequently the transference relationship in such circumstances involves an externalization of an internal object relationship of the following type: the analyst is experienced as the self-component of the internal relationship in which the self is intent on changing the object-component at the cost of annihilating that aspect of the patient. For example, a schizophrenic patient over many years of therapy would periodically become psychotic and profoundly regressed to the point of entering an almost totally mute, immobile state that would last for many months. These regressions occurred just as the patient began to 'get better'. 'Improvement' was experienced by the patient as literally becoming the therapist and in so doing losing himself entirely. Stubborn passivity evidenced by the patient at such points was an unconscious assertion that the therapist could not induce, seduce, manipulate, or coerce the patient into changing into the person that the therapist 'wanted' or 'needed' the patient to be. 'Getting better' meant being transformed into somebody else and no longer existing as the person he felt himself to be.

Interpretations are regularly experienced by schizophrenic and borderline patients as placing the patient in a terrible dilemma: to listen (in fantasy to 'take in') is to risk becoming changed into the therapist; not to listen (in fantasy to 'refuse to take in') is experienced as risking losing all connexion with the therapist and as a result floating off into absolute 'outer-space-like' isolation. Either way, the patient's existence is threatened. The danger of losing one's self as a result of being transformed into a 'good' object is the danger experienced by the object-component of the internal relationship; the risk of absolute isolation resulting from loss of the connexion with the internal object is the danger

[5]I am grateful to Dr. Michael Bader for discussing portions of his clinical work with me that have helped to illustrate this aspect of object-relations theory.

experienced by the self-component of the internal object relationship. It is as important for the object-component of ego in the internal relationship to resist being changed by the self-component as it is for the self-component to attempt to change the bad object into a good one.

(2) The suborganization of ego identified with the object experiences as much need for object relatedness as the self-component of the internal object relationship. The object-component frequently maintains internal object ties by means of attempting to exert control over its object (i.e. control over the self-component of the internal relationship). The object-component may taunt, shame, threaten, lord-over, or induce guilt in its object (the self-component of the internal relationship) in order to maintain connectedness with the self-component. These efforts at control over the self-component become greatly intensified when there is a danger of the bond being threatened, e.g. by a more mature form of relatedness to the therapist that would make this internal, more primitive form of relatedness less necessary.[6]

An obsessional patient in intensive psychotherapy would regularly disrupt her rare periods of genuinely self-analytic free association with 'outbreaks' of obsessional self-torment. For instance, while insightfully discussing an interchange with a boyfriend, she interrupted her train of thought to ruminate self-critically about her weight, a subject with which she was chronically preoccupied. As the ruminations continued she then became anxious that the therapist would terminate therapy because of her endless and fruitless obsessional thinking. The patient was at this point in therapy aware of the connexion between her self-torment and the way in which she had continually felt belittled and tormented by her mother. The patient's mother in addition to tirelessly pointing out her disdain for the patient, regularly threatened to send her away to live with relatives. (It must be emphasized that this was the patient's experience of her mother and it is this experience of the mother and not an objective depiction of the mother that is preserved in the internal object relationship.)

The internal object relationship upon which the transference was modelled consisted of a mutually dependent mother–child relationship in which the child was willing and eager to be masochistic if that would help solidify the tie to a sadistic mother who was felt to be always on the

---

[6]The unconscious self and object suborganizations of the ego are affected to some extent by current experience. Self suborganizations of the ego are influenced by experience, particularly as the current experience involves issues of goals, ambitions and autonomy. Object suborganizations are influenced by current relations with external objects, particularly with regard to issues of idealization, denigration, jealousy, envy, etc. One measure of psychological health is the degree to which internal object relations can be modified in the light of current experience.

verge of abandoning her. The internal object (suborganization of the ego) experienced the ability of other aspects of the patient to engage in free association in the therapeutic setting as dangerous evidence of an enhanced capacity of those other aspects of the ego to engage in a more mature form of relatedness to the therapist than had been previously possible. The fear of this more mature form of object tie resulted from the object's conviction that such relatedness would make the self-component of the internal object relationship less dependent on the object-component. In the clinical sequence described, the object (suborganization of ego) then redoubled its efforts at subjecting the masochistic self to sadistic torment in the form of guilt-inducing taunts about being overweight. There can be no mistaking that the nature of the ultimate threat made by the object-component is that of abandoning the self-component of the internal relationship. In the clinical sequence the threat of abandonment is projected onto the therapist and is experienced as a threat made by the therapist to abandon the patient if she does not behave as he demands.

In this clinical material, the resistance (the disruption of the free association) arose from the rear of giving up a particular internal object relationship. This fear is predominantly that of the object (ego suborganization) which upon sensing decreasing dependence on the part of the self-component, reintensified its efforts at control by raising the spectre of abandonment. In the context of an internal object relationship, any independent activity on the part of one party of the relationship is experienced as an impending dissolution of the relationship which is based on mutual dependence. From the perspective of the patient's unconscious psychic reality, it is as essential for the object-component of ego in an internal relationship to maintain its tie to the self-component as it is for the self-component to tirelessly pursue and attempt to hold onto the internal object.

(3) Envious feelings experienced by the object-component and directed at the self-component of an internal object relationship, constitute another type of internal object relatedness that can serve as the basis for resistance. Not infrequently we hear patients expressing envy toward others at points when it does not make immediate sense in terms of the patient's current situation. For example, a borderline patient who had been in intensive psychotherapy for four years was able for the first time in a decade to return to school and to relate to her second husband in a way that she was taking some pride in. She had abandoned her latency-aged children when she left her first husband fifteen years previously. In her current therapy meetings, in addition to discussing the enhanced feelings of self-worth, she reported having written an extremely angry letter to her children. As she talked about this, she said that she had been a much better mother to them than her own mother (who had committed

suicide when she was 10-years-old) had been to her. It became abundantly clear to the patient that she was feeling intensely envious of her children. From the point of view of the self in an internal object relationship with a deeply depressed, rejecting mother, envy is not a feeling one would expect at a time when the patient is experiencing enhanced self-esteem. However, from the point of view of the object (the patient's ego sub-organization identified with her mother), not only is control over the self-component threatened by enhanced feelings of self-esteem, the object also feels envious of the self for this newly acquired set of feelings. The object-component, in order to maintain a tie (based on control) over the self-component, wished to sap the feelings of well-being from its object (the self) and make those feelings its own. It is vitally important for the object to maintain connectedness with the self. Signs of diminished dependence on the part of the self will be enviously attacked as the object (suborgani-zation of ego) begins to fear being left behind.

Searles (1979) vividly describes similar clinical data in which the patient unconsciously functions as multiple people, one of whom may become jealous of the other. He gives detailed accounts of the way in which such internal splitting may be externalized as a countertransference experience in which one aspect of the therapist feels jealous of another aspect of himself that is currently felt to be more desirable to the patient. Searles (1979) concurs with Fairbairn that although such internal divi-sions are more apparent in borderline and schizoid individuals, 'it would take a bold man to claim that his ego was so perfectly integrated as to be incapable of revealing any evidence of splitting at the deepest levels, or that such evidence of splitting of the ego could in no circumstances declare itself at more superficial levels, even under conditions of extreme suffer-ing or hardship or deprivation' (Fairbairn, 1940, p. 8).

Searles focuses entirely on jealousy of the self for another aspect of self. The theoretical framework of the present paper allows us to supple-ment Searles' ideas with a way of thinking about types of resistance based on jealousy or envy of an internal object for the self.

SUMMARY

The development of the concept of internal object relations is traced through the work of Freud, Abraham, Klein, Fairbairn, Winnicott and Bion. I have proposed that the establishment of an internal object rela-tionship requires a dual splitting of the ego into a pair of dynamically unconscious suborganizations of personality, one identified with the self and the other with the object in the original early object relationship. These aspects of ego stand in a particular relationship to one another the nature of which is determined by the infant's subjective experience of the early relationship. Since both the self- and the object-component of the internal object relationship are aspects of the ego, each has the capacity to generate experience (e.g. to think, feel, and perceive) semi-autonomously and yet in relation to one another.

Resistance is understood as the difficulty a patient has in relinquishing pathological attachments involved in unconscious internal object relationships. The view of internal objects proposed in this paper brings into focus types of resistance heretofore only partially understood. These types of resistance are based on the need of the internal object (suborganization of ego) not to be changed by the self (suborganization of ego), the dependence of the internal object on the self, and the envy and jealousy of the internal object for the self-component of the internal object relationship.

REFERENCES

Abraham, K. (1924). A short study of the development of the libido, viewed in the light of mental disorders. In *Selected Papers on Psycho-Analysis*. London: Hogarth Press, 1949, pp. 418–501.

Bettelheim, B. (1981). Presentation at the San Francisco Psychoanalytic Institute, 10 November 1981.

Bion, W. R. (1952). Group dynamics: a review. In *Experiences in Groups*. New York: Basic Books, 1959, pp. 141–192.

——— (1956). Development of schizophrenic thought. In *Second Thoughts*. New York: Jason Aronson, 1967, pp. 36–42.

——— (1957). Differentiation of the psychotic from the non-psychotic personalities. In *Second Thoughts*. New York: Jason Aronson, 1967, pp. 43–64.

——— (1962). *Learning from Experience*. In *Seven Servants: Four Works by Wilfred R. Bion*. New York: Jason Aronson, 1977.

Fairbairn, W. R. D. (1940). Schizoid factors in the personality. In *Psychoanalytic Studies of the Personality*. London: Routledge and Kegan Paul, 1952, pp. 3–27.

——— (1944). Endopsychic structure considered in terms of object-relationships. In *Psychoanalytic Studies of the Personality*. London: Routledge and Kegan Paul, 1952, pp. 82–136.

——— (1946). Object-relationships and dynamic structure. In *Psychoanalytic Studies of the Personality*. London: Routledge and Kegan Paul, 1952, pp. 137–151.

——— (1958). On the nature and aims of the psycho-analytic treatment. *Int. J. Psychoanal.*, 39: 374–385.

Freud, S. (1900). The interpretation of dreams. *S.E. 4/5*.

——— (1914). On narcissism: An introduction. *S.E. 14*.

——— (1917). Mourning and melancholia. *S.E. 14*.

——— (1923). The ego and the id. *S.E. 19*.

——— (1927). Fetishism. *S.E.* 21.
——— (1933). New introductory lectures XXXI: The dissection of the personality. *S.E.* 22.
——— (1940a). An outline of psycho-analysis. *S.E.* 23.
——— (1940b). Splitting of the ego in the process of defence. *S.E.*, 23.
Grotstein, J. S. (1980a). The significance of Kleinian contributions to psychoanalysis I. Kleinian instinct theory. *Int. J. Psychoanal. Psychother.*, 8: 375–392.
——— (1980b). The significance of Kleinian contributions to psychoanalysis II. Freudian and Kleinian conceptions of early mental development. *Int. J. Psychoanal. Psychother.*, 8: 393–428.
——— (1981). *Splitting and Projective Identification.* New York: Jason Aronson.
Hartmann, H. (1964). *Essays on Ego Psychology.* New York: Int. Univ. Press.
Isaacs, S. (1952). The nature and function of phantasy. In *Developments in Psycho-Analysis*, ed. M. Klein, et al. London: Hogarth Press, 1952, pp. 67–121.
Jacobson, E. (1964). The *Self and the Object World.* New York: Int. Univ. Press.
Klein, M. (1946). Notes of some schizoid mechanisms. In *Envy and Gratitude and Other Works, 1946–63.* New York: Delacorte Press/Seymour Lawrence, 1975, pp. 1–24.
——— (1958). On the development of mental functioning. In *Envy and Gratitude and Other Works, 1946–63.* New York: Delacorte Press/Seymour Lawrence, 1975, pp. 236–246.
——— (1975). *Envy and Gratitude and Other Works, 1946–63.* New York: Delacorte Press/Seymour Lawrence.
Mackay, N. (1981). Melanie Klein's metapsychology: phenomenological and mechanistic perspectives. *Int. J. Psychoanal.*, 62: 187–198.
Ogden, T. H. (1974). A psychoanalytic psychotherapy of a patient with cerebral palsy: the relationship of aggression to self and body representations. *Int. J. Psychoanal. Psychother.*, 3: 419–433.
——— (1976). Psychological unevenness in the academically successful student. *Int. J. Psyhoanal. Psychother.*, 5: 437–448.
——— (1979). On projective identification. *Int. J. Psychoanal.*, 60: 357–373.
——— (1980). On the nature of schizophrenic conflict. *Int. J. Psychoanal.*, 61: 513–533.
——— (1981). Projective identification in psychiatric hospital treatment. *Bull. Menninger Clinic*, 45: 317–333.
——— (1982a). Treatment of the schizophrenic state of non-experience. In *Technical Factors in the Treatment of the Severely Disturbed Patient*, ed. L. B. Boyer & P. L. Giovacchini. New York: Jason Aronson, pp. 217–260.
——— (1982b). *Projective Identification and Psychotherapeutic Technique.* New York: Jason Aronson.
Racker, H. (1957). The meanings and uses of countertransference. *Psychoanal. Q.*, 26: 303–357.
Sandler, J. & Rosenblatt, B. (1962). The concept of the representational world. *Psychoanal. Study Child*, 17: 128–145.
Schafer, R. (1968). *Aspects of Internalization.* New York: Int. Univ. Press.
Searles, H. F. (1979). Jealousy involving an internal object. In *Advances in Psycho-*

therapy of the Borderline Patient, ed. J. LeBoit & A. Capponi. New York: Jason Aronson, pp. 347–404.

Segal, H. (1964). *Introduction to the Work of Melanie Klein.* London: Hogarth Press, 1978.

Winnicott, D. W. (1951). Transitional objects and transitional phenomena. In *Through Paediatrics to Psycho-Analysis.* New York: Basic Books, 1958, pp. 229–242.

———— (1952) Psychoses and child care. In *Through Paediatrics to Psycho-Analysis.* New York: Basic Books, 1958, pp. 219–228.

———— (1954). Metapsychological and clinical aspects of regression within the psycho-analytical set up. In *Through Paediatrics to Psycho-Analysis.* New York: Basic Books, 1958, pp. 278–294.

———— (1960). Ego distortion in terms of true and false self. In *Maturational Processes and the Facilitating Environment.* New York: Int. Univ. Press, 1965, pp. 140–152.

7

Notes on
Fairbairn's Metapsychology

JAMES S. GROTSTEIN

INTRODUCTION

Fairbairn is recognized by many as one of the founders of the British school of object relations[1] and one of the most significant theorists of his time. Yet his reputation was shadowed during his lifetime by those of his better-known contemporaries, most notably Melanie Klein and Donald Winnicott. His practice, located in Edinburgh, placed him at a great communicative disadvantage for profitable interchange with either of them (Sutherland, 1989). Moreover, his contributions were eclipsed further during the "time of the troubles" between the titans Melanie Klein and Anna Freud. Klein, immersed in her involvement with Anna Freud, ignored Fairbairn and seemingly dismissed him perfunctorily.

Fairbairn inaugurated a series of pivotal changes in psychoanalytic theory and understanding, particularly with respect to some of the contributions of Freud and Melanie Klein. Although he revered Freud, Fairbairn openly challenged his theories of the pleasure principle and of instinctual drives. (Indeed, it is largely because of Fairbairn that these two

[1]The British school of object relations now comprises the "middle" or "independent" group of the British Psychoanalytic Institute.

fundamental structures of psychoanalytic theory are in such jeopardy today.) Fairbairn's modification of Freud represented the championship of the infant and child, and their elevation to a new psychoanalytic status —that of "primal innocence." He, along with Klein and Winnicott, shifted the emphasis from infantile sexuality (autoeroticism) to infantile dependence (neediness), thereby establishing the primacy of the reality principle over the pleasure–unpleasure principle.

Although all of Fairbairn's contributions were emendations of Freud— his paper on the Schreber case, in which he emphasized the importance of the primal scene, clearly attests to his orthodox Freudian views (Fairbairn, 1956)—he owed even greater allegiance to Melanie Klein. Virtually all the contributors to the British object relations (independent) school[2] (including Suttie, Fairbairn, Winnicott, Balint, and others) although claiming to be midway between Klein and classical analysis—and therefore "independent"—took Klein's conception of infantile pre-oedipal positions and internal objects for granted. Their own individual contributions constituted a reality modification of Klein's "id mythology."[3]

As a "neo-Kleinian," Fairbairn helped to launch not only the object relations revolution, but also underlined its prime position of infant advocacy: that the infant is born innocent and is entitled to be treated as a person in his own right. He believed that the "original sin" legacy of the drives, espoused by Klein, is a mistaken conception, since libido is an inseparable part of the relationship between the infant and the needed object. One of Fairbairn's most significant discoveries is that of the premoral stage of infant development—one that he regarded as being both extraterritorial to the vicissitudes of instinctual drives, and immediately and realistically responsive to the nurturing environment (a subject to be addressed later by Winnicott, 1954, and Stern, 1985). Fairbairn maintained that there is no "instinctual sin" if the caretaking objects relate appropriately to the infant's needs; thus, the appearance of autoeroticism is evidence of an *unsatisfying* (external) object relationship. For Fairbairn, reality—with its hazards and disappointments—is primary.

Fairbairn's advocacy of children (which established innocence and entitlement as legitimate necessities for infant survival as a self), together with his modification of libido theory and belief in the primacy of the reality principle, constitutes the foundation of his relational model of psychoanalysis.

[2]I am thankful to Dr. Victoria Hamilton for reminding me that the British Institute had already been prepared for pre-Oedipality and consequently for Klein's contributions by Ernest Jones (see Stewart, 1979).

[3]This unfortunate terminology was sarcastically suggested by Rapaport (1959).

FAIRBAIRN'S CONCEPTION OF THE OBJECT
AND OF OBJECT RELATIONS

At the root of Fairbairn's theory is his concept of the object.[4] The idea of the object, particularly the *internalized* object, is critical to Fairbairn's understanding of schizoid personality, endopsychic structure, and the origins of psychopathology in object identification.

As Mitchell (Chapter 5, this volume) and Greenberg and Mitchell (1983) show, Fairbairn employed the term "object" in two ways: to refer to an external person *and* to an internalized (distorted) version of that person. In Fairbairn's scheme, objects, together with their dynamic relations with split-off egos, constitute the irreducible elements of the internal world, and their interrelationships (with egos and other objects) comprise its basic functioning. He believed that objects are principally internal because of the failure of their external counterparts (persons) to sustain a sufficiently satisfying interpersonal mutuality (Fairbairn, 1941, 1943a).

Once internalized, these endopsychic structures become a powerful, constraining entity that shapes all further external relationships. Indeed, they function in a manner almost identical to the impulsive and peremptory libidinal drives[5] of Freud's (1923) id. Furthermore, the infant/patient seems to maintain a tenacious loyalty to these structures, which mitigates against his abandoning them. The threat of a disjunction with endopsychic structures is a frequent cause of the negative therapeutic reaction in treatment.

Fairbairn (1943) believed that the infant does not need to internal-

---

[4]The term "object relations" has created considerable confusion in the history of psychoanalysis. As will become clearer as I proceed, Fairbairn's conception of object relations is not identical with that of Klein's but is complementary to it, insofar as he emphasizes the external person as a disappointing object, whereas Klein emphasizes the internal object as reflecting a mirroring of the infant's instinctual endowment channeling through the external person. Fairbairn's "objects" belong to a relational perspective that has been more clearly delineated than those of Klein have been, but Mitchell (Chapter 5, this volume) disagrees with the idea that Klein's objects are relational. Both their views derive from Freud and Abraham, however. The term "object representation," especially as used by ego psychologists, bears little connection with either Klein's or Fairbairn's "internal objects," as I hope to show later, although their concept of the "part-object representation" is somewhat more approximate. Also, Jacobson's (1964) "object images" and Kernberg's (1976) "split affect–selfobject representations" are attempts to reconcile this discrepancy (Grotstein, 1982, 1991b, 1991c, 1991d, in press).

[5]It would be of interest to know whether Fairbairn, were he alive today, would believe that "affects" should be considered similarly to "drives"—that is, as dynamic constituents of ego–object relationships.

ize a good object (or part-object), insofar as the object satisfies the infant's needs. A needed caretaker who is *un*trustworthy becomes dissociated into a rejected object that is internalized, along with a portion of the ego. Thus, to Fairbairn, internalization of objects is an adaptive mechanism whereby the helpless infant/child can, in phantasy, regain control over the traumatizing or depriving dependency situation.

He further elaborated on the adaptive aspects of internalization in his discussion of the "moral defense of the superego." Here the putative badness of the needed object is split off from the external object, internalized, and identified with in order to keep the external object ideal (Fairbairn, 1943a). This mechanism amounts to a "laundering" of the image of the object at one's own expense. The moral defense corresponds in many ways to Klein's (1945) concept of "idealization," and depends on the collusion of the ideal object.

Although Fairbairn does not elaborate on this point, he implies that the internalization of unaccepted objects can be *active* as well as *passive*. In clinical practice, we commonly observe passive–aggressive identifications with objects. Often such identification with the bad aspects of an object is aimed at "busting" a parent; it is an unconscious attempt to betray the parent to the authorities, who then rescue the child. One aspect of the active defense of internalization corresponds to Klein's (1940) concept of the "manic defense," where there is triumph, contempt, and control over the object and over the self dependent on this object. When this mechanism, and the object and ego involved in this defense, are internalized, we could say that a "depressive defense" is in operation.

Meanwhile, the internalized objects are reconstituted with corresponding parts of the original ego as endopsychic structures. A rejecting object (hereafter abbreviated as RO), in identification with an antilibidinal ego (AE), constitutes a primitive negating superego toward its opposite counterpart, the exciting object (EO), and its partner in identification, the libidinal ego (LE). Whereas topographically, both are repressed horizontally by the central ego (CE) in association with the ideal object (IO), the RO and AE secondarily repress the EO and LE vertically. Thus a maximum of repression (CE/IO in addition to RO/AE) is directed toward the needy LE in its relationship to its EO.

Fairbairn's internal objects reflect the infant's identification with the external object's psychopathology. Indeed, the formation of endopsychic structures is a defense against the psychic catastrophe of being without objects altogether. For Fairbairn, the external object (person) is recognized all too realistically from the beginning (as Stern, 1985, has clearly demonstrated in his infant research). The infant employs introjective phantasy to modify this realistic (but threatening) image to produce a more tolerable relationship. The infant accomplishes this, paradoxically, by maximizing his own internal badness in order to "launder" the external image of the parental object. Clinically, such internalization is accompanied by a deep sense of shame, guilt, and self-consciousness of being unblessed, unloved and unlovable, and vulnerable to criticism and even assault. A brief clinical vignette illustrates some of these points:

R. W. was a 43-year-old married business executive who entered analysis because of a lifelong depression and his schizoid way of relating. His behavior in analysis was characterized by frequent prolonged silences, which seemed more like self-consciousness than active resistance. He described himself as a cold, aloof person, and this characteristic seemed correct, both to his current wife and to me.

When he was born, his affluent mother and father immediately left him with a nanny and housekeepers while they took a 6-week vacation—a practice that was repeated 3 years later when his brother was born. He continued throughout his life to idealize his mother and attempt to get her love and approval—in vain. She always thought of him as ugly (even from birth), and he identified with this verdict while always seeking exciting, rejecting women.

His first wife was of this type, and they got along badly. After divorcing her he met and married a warm, loving woman, but he was concerned that she was not beautiful enough. This belief that she was ugly diminished considerably after I interpreted to him that she was the projective scapegoat of his feelings of ugliness, as he was for his mother—and that she (his second wife) was the split-off aspect, as well, of his "counteruglification" of his rejecting mother's image.

The patient reported a dream in which he had become frozen in a winter landscape holding onto his beautiful mother, who was encased in a piece of ice. He was afraid to leave his "ice mother" for fear that she would melt and he would then be left without anyone—and would fall into a "black hole"!

This case provides an illustration of Fairbairn's "moral defense" (1943a), the schizoid mechanism whereby the individual re-establishes the image of a pleasure-giving mother through idealization, but at the expense of introjecting and identifying with her pathology. The dream reveals the patient's beginning failure to maintain the moral defense—the unwavering loyalty that schizoids maintain toward their objects because leaving them is believed to be catastrophic. This particular patient unwittingly took LSD while drinking a glass of wine at a friend's home; as a result, he developed the belief that his whole family had died. Upon later analysis, he discovered he always knew that they were dead *to* him and *for* him (even though they both were still nominally alive), but he believed that he had to maintain the illusion of their being alive for him—at the expense of his own schizoid deadness.

In Fairbairn's main conception of object relations, internalization occurs when external objects are unsatisfying. Later, he allowed for the internalization of the accepted object. This ultimately becomes the IO, descended from the preambivalent object of the early oral phase. It is internalized so as to modify the absolute badness of the primarily unaccepted object, which, upon internalization, becomes the EO and the RO.

> From this point of view, ambivalence must be regarded as a state first arising in the original unsplit ego in relation to the *internalized* preambivalent object; and the motive determining the internalization of the pre-ambivalent object in the first instance will be provided by the fact that this object presents itself as in some measure unsatisfying as well as in some measure satisfying. The establishment of ambivalence, once this has been accomplished, leads to an internal situation in which the unsplit ego is confronted with an *internalized ambivalent object*. The next step envisaged is the splitting of this object, not into two objects (good and bad), but into *three* objects; and this result is attributed to action on the part of the ego whereby both the *over-exciting* and *over-frustrating* elements in the internal object are split off from it and repressed in such a way as to give rise to the *exciting object* and the *rejecting object*. . . . It follows from this conception that, when the exciting and rejecting objects are split off, there remains a *nucleus of the original object* shorn of its over-exciting and over-frustrating elements; and this nucleus then assumes the status of a desexualized and idealized object which is cathected and retained for itself by the central ego after it (the central ego) has divested itself of those parts of itself which cathect the exciting and rejecting objects, and which I have described respectively as 'the libidinal ego' and the 'internal saboteur.' (Fairbairn, 1951, pp. 178–179; emphasis in original)

This seemingly complex theoretical rearrangement helped Fairbairn to account for the "conditional badness" of the internalized objects (Fairbairn, 1943a, p. 66).[6] He altered his original conception so that the accepted object, once internalized, could modify the absolute badness of the originally internalized unaccepted object. Later he had to account for the existence of the IO as the original object from the preambivalent stage. The latter thus becomes split in three ways: Two portions of it become internalized as the RO and the EO, and the remaining one becomes the IO, which helps to keep the other two (with their attached egos) in re-

---

[6]Later in the chapter I discuss Fairbairn's conception of the transitional (neurotic) techniques, which are mechanisms for mediating defenses against the emergence of the dissociations of the self and the objects to which they are conjoined (i.e., against the "psychotic" anxieties of immature dependency). They include the paranoid, phobic, hysteric, and obsessive compulsive techniques.

pression. Ultimately, Fairbairn concluded that the ego's *relationships* with objects are what irreducibly undergo internalization.

Thus, Fairbairn ultimately distinguished between (1) the objects of external (interpersonal) relationships, which constitute the matrix of normal infantile dependency; and (2) objects (actually, part-objects) that are internalized and have a split (alienated, dissociated) relationship to the self. "Object" is a logical-positivistic and pseudoscientific term, which fails to capture the phenomenology of the internal world. It is my belief that "internal objects," whether Kleinian or Fairbairnian, are *third forms*— neither the external person from whom they were partially modeled, nor merely split-off parts of the self. They are in fact phantasmally altered, transformed montages that have been referred to across all the ages of mankind as "monsters," "demons," "ghosts," "witches," "angels," and so on. However, in Fairbairn's scheme internalized objects, these split-off aspects of self, form the template for the schizoid, narcissistic, borderline, and multiple personality disorders—and the general condition of "being schizoid."

FAIRBAIRN, THE EXISTENTIALIST

Fairbairn, in identifying the schizoid personality, described the experience of alienation. Yet the schizoid personality and the associated phenomena he elucidated did not inspire an existential trend within psychoanalysis generally, but were reconceptualized instead as the narcissistic, borderline, symbiotic, multiple, and dissociative personality disorders. Fairbairn's (1949) "premoral" and "preambivalent" theory stood in direct contrast to Freud's and Klein's psychologies, which were based upon the theory of melancholia. Fairbairn maintained that the psychopathology of hysteria in particular, and of the neuroses generally, involves the splitting of objects and of respective egos beginning in the early oral period, not as consequences of sexual guilt in the later Oedipal stage.

Fairbairn's conception of the alienation of the self is implicit in the formation of endopsychic structure, and the introjective identifications of the egos with their internalized alienated objects. Such alienation from one's sense of self has also been described by Lacan (1953) as *méconnaissance* or "misrecognition."

Fairbairn's Contributions to the Conception of Narcissism

Fairbairn (1940), as Robbins and Padel demonstrate in their contributions to this volume, deserves credit for launching the narcissistic–symbiotic revolution and, along with Klein and Winnicott, the borderline revolution as well. His description of the schizoid personality corresponds closely to the present concept of narcissistic personality disorder, just as his description of the schizoid state approximates our current understanding of the borderline. The symptomatology of inner grandiosity and of the exhibitionistic technique ("relating through showing" and "losing through giving"), which Fairbairn (1940) assigned to the schizoid personality, found its way virtually intact into Kohut's (1971, 1977, 1978, 1984) conception of the narcissist's need for the mirroring of his grandiosity and exhibitionism (Robbins, 1980 and Chapter 17, this volume). Throughout his work, Fairbairn challenged the classical ideal of development from infantile sexuality to genitality, advancing a concept based solely upon the maturation of the state of dependency on objects—from "immature dependence" through a "transitional state" to "mature dependence." Kohut (1984) also proffered this point, but once again without crediting Fairbairn.

More recently, Gabbard (1989) has distinguished between two aspects of the narcissistic personality—the "oblivious" and the "hypervigilant" subtypes. The oblivious subtype can be thought of as the more outgoing, hypomanic, yet unempathic type, whereas the hypervigilant subtype seems to correspond to the withdrawn, schizoid type.[7] Kohut and Kernberg have mainly emphasized the former, whereas Fairbairn emphasized the latter.

According to Symington (Chapter 11, this volume) Fairbairn believed that schizoids relate to their objects "autistically." That is, a schizoid dismantles the image of the external object, detaches its value and meaning, and then reattaches it to the self or a part of the self (masturbation), thereby enabling himself to relate to the self as if he *were* the object. Fairbairn (1940) characterized the narcissistic attitude of schizoids as omnipotent; isolated and detached; and preoccupied with inner reality. It would appear that Fairbairn's schizoid personality is a more withdrawn, isolated, and introspective form of the manic–depressive variant described by Kohut and Kernberg.

More recently, Kohut's followers have tried to respect the links between object relations theory and self psychology, as laid down by Fairbairn and Winnicott (Bacal, 1985, 1987, 1990a, 1990b; Brandchaft, 1986), but the authors point out that the concept of the selfobject transferences[8] remains the major difference between them, as well as one of Kohut's most important and unique discoveries.

---

[7]When one thinks of the narcissistic personality disorder in general, one usually thinks of the grandiose type, which would seem to correspond to the personality *trait* form of a hypomanic personality. The depressive and withdrawn forms of the narcissistic personality disorder repress or suppress their grandiosity and present outwardly as difficult or schizoid.

[8]Archaic merger, mirroring, idealizing, and twinships.

Kernberg's (1975, 1976, 1980, 1984; see also Chapter 4, this volume) conceptions of narcissism, on the other hand, avowedly incorporate many aspects of Fairbairn's endopsychic structure, and he so acknowl-
edges. In integrating Fairbairn's endopsychic structure and concepts of
splitting with Klein's concepts of splitting and Mahler's concept of sepa-
ration/individuation, he arrived at his own unique concept of narcissism.
     Although nosologically distinct from the narcissistic personality dis-
order, the symbiotic personality disorder was well defined (though not
so named) by Fairbairn, according to Johnson (1991). When Fairbairn
(1943b) examined the case histories of soldiers suffering from the war
neuroses, he discovered that in each case they suffered from the persistence of infantile dependent object relations, which predisposed them to
believe that they had been orally incorporated by their objects. The persistence of infantile dependence could be attributed, Fairbairn reasoned,
to an unusually severe separation anxiety that had been characterologically
masked by a pseudoindependence, the breakdown from which resulted
in the compulsion to return home and re-enter a primal identification with
significant objects. In their traumatic regression under stress, the soldiers
became "swallowed" by the object they desperately sought to "swallow,"
thereby producing the mutually interpenetrating image of a "Siamese
twinship" or symbiotic relationship.[9] Mahler (1968) was later to make
the symbiotic paradigm the centerpiece for her conception of the origins
of infant development.

The Pleasure–Unpleasure Principle versus
the Principle of Nurture and Safety

In challenging Freud's concept of the primacy and separateness of libido,[10]
Fairbairn recast libido from its role in sex to its role in nurture (Fairbairn,
1940, 1941, 1943a, 1943b, 1944), thus relegating the pleasure–unpleasure
principle to a secondary position and emphasizing the primacy of the
reality principle. Side by side with these ideas was his notion of the separateness of the infant from birth—an idea that had already appeared in
Klein's work and that challenged the classical notion of primary narcissism (Fairbairn, 1940). The idea of primary separateness was a seminal

[9]Klein (1946) would understand symbiosis as the result of the phantasy of projective identification, in which the projecting subject becomes confusingly enmeshed
with the object. Should the object be in collusion with this aim as well, then the phenomenon of folie à deux exists (Mason, 1985).
     [10]Today we might even free affect as well as libido from the notion of its being
separate, and allow for it to be an integral part of self and object.

idea, which helped the object relations school prepare the way for the modern conceptions of (1) attachment theory; (2) the importance of the principle of genetic continuity from infantile dependence to mature dependence[11]; and (3) the importance of "transitionalness"[12] between archaic infantile dependence and its successive stages.

Fairbairn, following in the footsteps of the Hungarian school of object relations and of Ian Suttie (1935) in Britain, continued the principle of genetic continuity (Isaacs, 1952) that had been adumbrated by Abraham (1924). This principle stressed the primacy of the oral stages of development, the successive pregenital stages, and also the importance of the mother–infant bond. Classical psychoanalytic metapsychology, long dominated by the primacy of libido theory—and, along with it, the predominant positions of the Oedipus complex, the father complex, and the organizing hegemony of the phallic stage—confused "sex," "genitality," and "libido." An offshoot of this emphasis was the underlying importance of autoeroticism as a subset of infantile sexuality in the classical developmental model, as opposed to infantile dependency in the object relations developmental model. Fairbairn (1941, 1943a, 1943b), however, suggested that infantile dependency undergoes an epigenesis, not merely to genitality, but through a transitional phase to the mature dependency of adulthood—a conception that Kohut (1984) was later to espouse, as noted above.

In abrogating the sexuality of Freud's (1905) libido theory (for the survival of the race), Fairbairn substituted in its stead Freud's (1910) erstwhile self-preservative ego libido theory. Freud first conceived of ego libido as narcissistic and associated aggressiveness with it. Freud did away with its separateness when he unified it with sexual libido in his paper on narcissism (1914). Fairbairn's and Klein's conception of libido differs from the orthodox/classical one, insofar as they postulate that libido is always object-seeking and object-directed, rather than autoerotically discharging. Freud (1914) did postulate that the libidinal instincts subserve the survival of the species, whereas the ego instincts subserve the survival of the individual. It is in this latter category that Fairbairn's and Klein's employment of libido fits.

These changes were to have a subtle and yet profound impact on classical psychoanalysis, especially on its conception of the importance of

[11]See Isaacs (1952) for the relationship between phantasy and the principle of genetic continuity in Klein's work.

[12]It is interesting and relevant to note that Fairbairn originated the concept of "transitionalness" (in terms of a "transitional phase" and "transitional techniques" of relating to objects) a decade before Winnicott spoke of "transitional objects" and "transitional phenomena." The latter referenced him on it.

infantile dependency versus Oedipal sexuality. Fairbairn, in particular, eschewed the idea that drives are not fundamentally linked to the ego and its objects. In stating that the ego was object-seeking, not discharging, he meant that egos and objects are embraced in libidinally dynamic relationships.

In reappraising Freud's theory of libido, and assigning it to the ego drives for self-survival, Fairbairn also modified his notion of "the repressed" and "the repressing" from the superego and ego repressing the id to the egos and objects. He revised the notion of the Oedipus complex: In his scheme, it is a post-infantile-dependency way station that condenses the four split egos and objects of infantile dependency (good mother, bad mother; good father, bad father—all with associated split egos) into one good parent and one bad parent. Most importantly, he repersonified psychic structure. He created a psychoanalytic metapsychology based upon the prime importance of splitting of the ego and its objects; in so doing, he uncovered the alienated self, who suffers because in the earliest instance of dependent neediness (the oral sucking phase) the very goodness of his love has been rejected.

Why is a realistically bad object internalized? Fairbairn's answer is unique yet obvious: "because the object is needed!" (1943a, p. 67). Thus, Fairbairn replaced Freud's pleasure principle with what might more appropriately be called the "safety principle"—a concept that was to be taken up by Sandler (1960) as the "background of safety"—or might just as well be called the "nurturing principle" (or "reality principle"). Fairbairn termed this developmental phenomenon the "schizoid position." The predominant affect of this position is futility, because one's very love (innocent neediness) is rejected. In the subsequent "depressive position," where biting (and therefore anger and aggression) are believed to be what made the objects bad, the predominant affect is despair, which is more hopeful than futility.[13]

Fairbairn strongly suggested that the infant must protect his view of his parents by absorbing their pathology. It is the reverse of Freud's "purified pleasure ego," in which the infant projects unpleasure and introjects pleasurable experiences. What is of importance here is that the infant must "repair" his image of the parents at his own expense (through idealizing them by becoming a "false self"), and thus must become the identified "owner" of bad objects that are now indistinguishable as "self." This is the moral defense of the superego and leads to the phenomenon of "scapegoating" (Searles, 1979; Brooks, 1985; Tuohy, 1987; Grotstein, 1994a).

---

[13]Fairbairn's and Klein's respective conceptions of the infantile developmental positions are compared later in the chapter.

Fairbairn's adaptive paradigm complements Freud's and Klein's concept that the infant must adapt to its instinctual drive irruptions. Fairbairn, however, supplied the "nurture" track of a dual-track (nature–nurture) conception. Yet his understanding of the need for the object and the necessity to "launder" it through introjection and splitting constitutes the most apposite paradigm yet proffered for child abuse, child molestation, post-traumatic stress disorder, and multiple personality disorder to date (Davies & Frawley, 1992).

Revision of the Oedipus Complex

Once Fairbairn was able to conceive of the primacy of infantile dependency (as did Klein), his conception of the Oedipus complex became contextualized accordingly. The classical conception highlights the importance of the Oedipal phase at the expense of the pre-Oedipal autoerotic phases. The infant in the autoerotic phases is capable of experiencing traumata, according to classical theory, but demonstrates a postponement of their effects—as later regressive elaborations of and from the Oedipus complex. Furthermore, the Oedipus complex is classically conceived of as a phallic/genital striving for the parent. When oral or anal elements are present, they are conceived of as regressive flights from the former.

Fairbairn never accepted the notion that aggression has a separate drive status; he thought instead that it arises defensively. Thus, his conception of the Oedipus complex and of the attainment of genital sexuality seems to be inadequate. He might have been well advised to have conceived of his two endopsychic units, the rejecting (aggressive) self (RO/AE) and the libidinal self (EO/LE), as future components of the genital self when they become integrated.

Fairbairn reasoned that splitting is the essential phenomenon of normal and pathological existence, and that the Oedipus complex represents, in part, a later edition of earlier splitting of both the maternal and paternal objects and their associated split egos (which have undergone a condensation from four parental splits into two splits—an accepting father and a rejecting mother for a girl, the reverse for a boy).

In essence, Fairbairn's conception of the Oedipal phase and complex differs from Freud's and Klein's insofar as he elevated dependency as the principal developmental line—one that proceeds from immature dependence through a transitional stage (the neurotic techniques) to mature dependence, a progression in which the Oedipal phase is merely another "technique" of relating to split objects and egos. In this regard, one may conclude that his conception is simplistic; yet its advantage is that it places

the Oedipal phase and complex in developmental succession from infantile dependency, as a necessary way station for helping to resolve the
splitting of egos and their respective objects. As such, it seems to occupy
his transitional phase of development (Fairbairn, 1941). In his conceptualization of the Oedipal phase as an outgrowth of the oral stages, he again
seemed to anticipate the work of Kohut (1977), who likewise believed
that the Oedipal *phase* is a normal way station for the independent development of the self and only becomes the Oedipus *complex* when Oedipal selfobjects fail the infant during that phase.

Primary Identification

One of Fairbairn's (1941, 1943a, 1943b, 1946) most intriguing conceptions is that of the relationship between infantile dependency and "primary identification"[14]—an obscure concept of Freud's (1921, 1923),
which the latter associated with but did not actually equate with primary
narcissism. Freud (1923) stated:

> . . . whatever the character's later capacity for resisting the influences of
> abandoned object-cathexes may turn out to be, the effects of the first
> identifications made in earliest childhood will be general and lasting. This
> leads us back to the origin of the ego ideal; for behind it there lies hidden
> an individual's first and most important identification, his identification
> with his father in his own personal prehistory.[15] This is apparently not
> in the first instance the consequence or outcome of an object-cathexis; *it
> is a direct and immediate identification and takes place earlier than any
> object-cathexis.* But the object-choices belonging to the first sexual period
> and relating to the father and mother seem normally to find their out-
> come in an identification of this kind, and would thus reinforce the pri-
> mary one. (p. 31; emphasis in original)

Fairbairn (1941) defined primary identification as follows:

> I employ the term *"primary identification"* . . . to signify the cathexis
> of an object which has not yet been differentiated from the cathecting
> subject. The unqualified term 'identification' is, of course, sometimes
> used in this sense; but it is more commonly used to signify the estab-
> lishment of a relationship based on non-differentiation with an object

[14]The concept of primary identification has also been elaborated by A. Balint
(1943) and myself (Grotstein, 1980a, 1991d).
[15]Freud offered a footnote to this passage: "Perhaps it would be safer to say
'with the parents' . . . " (p. 31).

which has already been differentiated in some measure at least. This latter process represents a revival of the type of relationship involved in primary identification, and should thus, strictly speaking, be described as a *"secondary identification."* (pp. 34–35; emphasis in original)[16]

And later (1943b), he stated:

The process in question [infantile dependence and separation anxiety] is that of *identification*—a process by virtue of which the individual fails to differentiate himself from, and thus spontaneously identifies himself emotionally with, those upon whom he emotionally depends. So intimate is the connection between identification and infantile dependence that, psychologically speaking, they must be treated as the same phenomenon. So far as we conceive of the mental state of the child before birth, we must regard it as characterized by a degree of primary identification so absolute as to preclude his entertaining any thought of differentiation from the maternal body, which constitutes his whole environment and the whole world of his experience. (p. 275; emphasis in original)[17]

Primary Identification, Primary Narcissism, and Object Relations

Fairbairn exhumed "primary identification" in order to translate "primary narcissism," a non-object-relationship concept, into an equivalent concept within which a primal object relationship could be envisioned. Freud (1914), when he conceived of the id's choice of the ego as its love object, hinted at this possibility of a primal object relationship. In Fairbairn's view, then, the fetus can be thought of as having a relationship to a primal object from whom, at the same time, it is not separated. Fairbairn then reasoned that primary identification and oral incorporation are two sides of the same coin, insofar as the latter is a phantasmal attempt to reinstate the former.[18] He also attributed the heightened experience of separation anxiety to the need for oral incorporation and the need to reinstate the illusion of primary identification. Kernberg (Chapter 4, this volume) takes issue with Fairbairn's conception that identification can

---

[16]This quotation is of importance in understanding Fairbairn's conception about the fundamentally pathological nature of identifications generally.

[17]The reader will note that Fairbairn's conception of the "object of primary identification" corresponds to his "preambivalent object."

[18]In other contributions I attempt to reconcile the ambiguity of primary separation and primary identification (narcissism) with the concept of the "Siamese twins," a personification of the dual-track notion (Grotstein, 1980a, 1981, 1994c).

precede object relations, for in emphasizing the omnipotent phantasy of oral incorporation, Fairbairn neglected the Kleinian notion of projective identification as the other means of omnipotently achieving phantasied "at-one-ness" with the object.

Moreover, by stressing the infantile need to reinstate the condition of primary identification as pathological, Fairbairn neglected its positive aspects. He only hinted at this when he spoke of the failure of the schizoid individual "to be treated as a person in his own right" (1940, p. 13), implying that the patient persists in infantile dependency relationships because of the *absence* of primary identification—a concept that was to be ignored and forgotten until it re-emerged as Winnicott's (1960a) "holding environment," Sandler's (1960) "background of safety," my own (Grotstein, 1980a) "background object (presence) of primary identification," and Ogden's (1986) "matrix." It also prefigures Kohut's (1984) concept of the narcissist's sense of entitlement. Perhaps what Fairbairn may have meant was that the infant (1) must experience primary identification and (2) must surrender it for the acceptance of himself as a subject who is separate and dependent on a person (external object). Thus, it might be conceivable that the legacies of good interpersonal relationships are internalized not as objects per se, as mentioned earlier, but as reinforcements for the "original object" (Rinsley, Chapter 15, this volume) of primary identification (Grotstein, 1980a, 1992c)—as background forces conveying a sense of blessing and birthright. By contrast, internalized bad objects conform and reinforce a corrupted, malignantly perverse, or absent background, with a consequent legacy of a curse.

Thus, we can see that primary identification is a sine qua non for normal individuation and separation; at the same time, when it becomes the object of regressive reinstatement, it is the hallmark of psychopathology. There appears to be a direct reciprocal relationship between the return of bad objects from repression (to be discussed next) and the quest for a reinstatement of an infantile dependent relationship based upon primary identification. Indeed, a relationship that has been inadequate in terms of *original* primary identification predisposes the infant all the more to internalize bad object relationships.

The Return of Bad Objects

Fairbairn's (1943a) conception of the return of bad objects as the true scenario of the traumatic return of the repressed represents one of the most important paradigmatic shifts in psychoanalysis. It is the subject of both Armstrong-Perlman's and Hamilton's clinical contributions to this volume. The classical conception of the repressed relied exclusively on the drives and affects. In my view, Fairbairn conceptualized internalized object relationships in the same way Freud regarded the id's peremptory instinctual drives. The contents of the repressed are split internal objects identified with their respective split egos (relationships)[19]; the contents of the forces of repression are, in part, also split internal objects and corresponding egos. Fairbairn maintained that the irruption and return of bad objects (and egos) into the ego are what constitute the traumatic state, not the irruption and return of libido (or of the death instinct). The "death instinct" is merely an appellation for bad objects, and their "dynamism" (activity) constitutes the repetition compulsion. Finally, Fairbairn believed that the possessor of bad internal objects feels guilty as well as ashamed (compromised, "cursed") for being identified with or containing them; traumata such as rape cause the victims to feel guilty (and ashamed) retrospectively because of the putative stigma that they signify—a lack of protection by good objects. Similarly, victims of war neuroses become demoralized by endangering, traumatizing external objects because they resonate with and reinvoke awareness of internalized bad objects, as Freud (1919, 1920) found from his own studies on war trauma.

Masterson and Rinsley (1975) employed some of these ideas in their conception of the heightened separation anxiety problems of borderline personality disorder. They conceived of a "RORU" and a "WORU," the former being the acronym for a "*r*ewarding *o*bject *r*elations *u*nit" and the latter of a "*w*ithdrawing *o*bject *r*elations *u*nit." The former is characterized by the collusive relationship of an overly dependent mother who rewards her child if the child remains an appendage of the mother; the latter represents the anger and withdrawal of the mother as the child chooses to separate and individuate.

The concept of the return of bad objects, along with Fairbairn's concept of primary identification and emphasis on the importance of splitting, offers an interesting paradigm for the currently highlighted phenomena of child abuse and molestation and their sequela, post-traumatic stress disorder (Brooks, 1985; Tuohy, 1987; Berman, 1974, 1981; Peebles, 1989; Davies & Frawley, 1992).

Demoniacal Possession

Fairbairn, who was steeped in religion and the notions of "angels" and "demons," failed to take the bold step of calling his "objects" by those

---

[19]Ogden (Chapter 6, this volume) suggests that Fairbairn explicates internal *objects* as the content of the repressed, but only hesitantly implies internalized object *relationships*.

terms. Yet at times he did make some references to the Devil.[20,21] In describing the symbolic "Satanic pact" the schizoid personality makes with the Devil, he used this phrase: "'Evil, be thou my good'" (1940, p. 27). Later he stated:

> "It is to the realm of these bad objects, I feel convinced, rather than to the realm of the super-ego that the ultimate origin of all psychopathological developments is to be traced; for it may be said for the psychoneurotic and psychotic patients that, if a True Mass is being celebrated in the chancel, a Black Mass is being celebrated in the crypt. (1943a, p. 70).

He also referred to Freud's (1923 [1922]) discussion of demoniacal possession in the Haitzmann case, and quoted Freud as follows:

> "Despite the somatic ideology of the era of 'exact' science, the demonological theory of these dark ages has in the long run justified itself. Cases of demoniacal possession correspond to the neuroses of the present day." This comment reflects the inadequacy of the classic conception that libido is primarily pleasure-seeking; for the whole point of a pact with the Devil lies in the fact that it involves a relationship with a bad object. (Fairbairn, 1943a, p. 71)

Fairbairn's portrayal of endopsychic structures belies their demoniacal nature, insofar as he dissociates the RO from the EO and the AE from the LE. When we see his endopsychic configuration as a totality, in other words, we too readily compare it with Freud's (1923) tripartite psychic apparatus. If, on the other hand, we picture the RO and EO as "Siamese twins," connected and yet paradoxically disconnected (rather than absolutely and cleanly split off from each other)—and the same for the LE and AE—then the full appearance of the Devil would be evident. The LE is haunted, not merely because of its fatal desire for the EO, but because the EO is also the RO. The same applies for the "Siamese twinship" between the LE and AE. The former's awareness that its "alter ego" has totally succumbed to the Devil's influence results in its abject demoralization and fatal hopelessness—as damned. In my own caseload, I have

---

[20]Actually, he even went out of his way to disavow any demonic categorization of his work, as in the following quotation: ". . . and, with a view to avoiding any appearance of demonology, it seems wise to err, if anything, on the side of overweighing the activity of the ego structures rather than otherwise" (Fairbairn, 1944, p. 132).

[21]I am indebted to Drs. Irving Rosen and Glen Gabbard for their help in understanding Fairbairn's references to demonology.

seen many patients who actually believed themselves to be "cursed" and even "possessed" by bad "demons," or even by the Devil himself (Grotstein, 1979a, 1979b, 1994a, 1994b).

It seems clear that Fairbairn had demoniacal possession in mind when he thought of the split-off egos' trance-like subservience to and worship of their intimidating bad objects. It appears that Fairbairn may have "laundered" the demons of yore and, following in Freud's logical-positivistic footsteps, maintained the word "object" but meant "demon" (or "witch," "monster," "angel," "ghost," "spirit," "presence," etc.). Could Freud have been one of Fairbairn's bad but exciting (as well as ideal) "objects," from whom his revolutionary deviations constituted an attempt to become released?

From the demonic perspective, it would appear that Freud's licentious id and instinctual drives correspond to Fairbairn's LE and to the EO and RO, plus the AE. Fairbairn had discovered that Hell *is* the endopsychic world and that becoming demonic is the result not of primary instinctual excess, as Freud had suggested, but rather of intolerable frustration and subsequent surrender to the hegemony of bad internal objects. Elsewhere, I refer to these and related phenomena as "the loss of innocence," and associate this loss with the development of the "feral child" syndrome as well as that of the "changeling" (Grotstein, 1994a).

Repression and the Release of Bad Objects

I should now like to reconcile the concept of demoniacal possession with Fairbairn's trenchant observation about the tenacious loyalty of the subject (CE) to his internalized bad objects and their relationships. Blomfield (1985) and I (Grotstein, 1994a) both invoke the concept of the "Faustian bargain" in order to comprehend this perverse loyalty. Freud (1923 [1922]) himself addressed it in the Haitzmann case, where the painter made a pact with the Devil in order to be reunited with his father. Blomfield, in linking parasitism, projective identification, and the Faustian bargain, states:

> Parasitism is commonly observed in everyday life and clinical practice. Psychoanalysts may perceive that one part of an analysand's psychic structure derives its energy parasitically from some 'other'—an aspect of the self or another individual. . . . Parasitism represents an evolutionary short-cut in the struggle of life against entropic decay and is a *Faustian bargain* at the most archaic level. (p. 309; emphasis in original)

When trauma is felt to be too severe, the victim enters into a state of projective identification with the enemy or with a phantasied personification of the horror, as if he has had to "die" a little (disappear as a self) in order to survive. This is tantamount to making a pact with the Devil, with the proviso of the foreclosure of the victim's soul and its innocence. The victim feels trapped forever in Hell and can never be released. The loyalty to these bad objects has occurred by default but is all the more binding, since the victim believes that he has foresworn his innocence and thus his right to salvation and release. It is as if Fairbairn based his conception of the endopsychic world on Dante's *Inferno*.

FAIRBAIRN VERSUS KLEIN: THE INTERNAL WORLD

In this section, I highlight some of the theoretical convergences and divergences between Fairbairn and Melanie Klein. Fairbairn's contributions were sometimes independent of and different from Klein's; at other times they were frequently parallel to, and generally complementary to, her views (Sutherland, 1989). Both emphasized the primacy of splitting, orality, internal objects, and infantile dependency. Padel (Chapter 16, this volume) believes that Fairbairn needed Klein's concept of projective identification in order to explain the exaggeration of the badness of internal objects.

Fairbairn remarked that Klein's concepts, like Freud's (except for the latter's earlier work on hysteria), were based upon the concept of melancholia rather than that of the splitting of the ego. I understand Fairbairn to mean by this that classical and Kleinian tenets are based upon the irreducible element of the instinctual drives as *unconscious intentionality and will* (unconscious determinism), which must inexorably account for the primal sense of "original sin." This concept of the irreducibility of the drives conveys a sense of savage infantile power, one that needs the taming influence of the parent. Fairbairn, who upheld the concept of infantile innocence—and with it the concept of normal infantile entitlement (Grotstein, 1991a, 1991b, 1991c, 1994a)—eschewed the existence of the death instinct and the legacy of potential evil, hatred, envy, destructiveness, and perverseness inherent in Klein's notion of "original sin," assigning these qualities to a bad environmental situation. If we employ the dual-track hypothesis (Grotstein, 1978, 1980a, 1994c), we can state that the infant is born with a sense of both innocence and potential guilt, and in this way reflects both Freud's and Klein's perspective. Freud's "scientific" explanation of instinctual drives (and thus the origin of unconscious phantasy) became reified by psychoanalysts as a concrete reality. But Freud—and Klein too—meant that the analyst does not know the cause of the infant's fantasies, but interprets to the patient how his infant aspect accounted for his experiences. From that point of view, the infant/patient "explains" all events from the personal perspective of both innocence and "original sin."

Schizoid Detachment (Dissociation) versus Paranoia

One of the most subtle but significant differences between Klein and Fairbairn is their differing emphasis on the use and deployment of the infant/patient's internal world.

Klein's internal objects are projectively introjected aspects of the self. Hers is a model based upon Freud's (1917) melancholic paradigm. In phantasy, the infant damages the object and incorporates it in the ego and superego, out of guilt (or preguilt in the form of persecutory anxiety). Fairbairn, on the other hand, believed that the object that has failed the infant must be internalized in the schizoid position, so as to "protect" the external object. The internalized objects then, in consort with their subsidiary egos, live an independent, autonomous, *detached* (schizoid, autistic), dissociated existence. This concept is the heartland of "being schizoid" and has rarely been addressed by other authors. Yet Klein did refer, at least on one occasion, to the dissociative (schizoid) kind of splitting described by Fairbairn:

> I . . . found that young children introject their parents—first of all the mother and her breast—in a phantastic way, and I was led to this conclusion by observing the terrifying character of some of their internalized objects. These extremely dangerous objects give rise, in early infancy, to conflict and anxiety within the ego; but under the stress of acute anxiety they, and other terrifying figures, are split off in a manner different from that by which the super-ego is formed, and are relegated to the deeper layers of the unconscious. The difference in these two ways of splitting . . . is that in the splitting-off of frightening figures the fusion seems to be in the ascendant; whereas super-ego formation is carried out with a predominance of fusion of the two instincts. (Klein, 1958, p. 241)[22]

Similarly, Winnicott (1971), in describing the differences among "fantasying," dreaming, and living, stated: "Dream[23] fits into object-relating in the real world in ways that are quite familiar, especially to psychoanalysts. By contrast, however, fantasying remains an isolated phenomenon, absorbing energy but not contributing-in either to dreaming or to living" (p. 26).

[22]I am indebted to Dr. Erna Osterweil for alerting me to this article.
[23]For "dream," I read Klein's (and Freud's) "phantasy."

Fairbairn's concept of splitting, which emphasized infantile helplessness and powerlessness rather than omnipotent willfulness, was closer to that of Janet (1889), in which the original ego and the original object *fall* into splits because of the lack of support of the object. Furthermore, Fairbairn, unlike Freud and Klein, but like Sullivan, American Freudians, and British object relationists, emphasized the prime importance of the nurturing influence of the mother and father. His views, which were to be paralleled by those of Winnicott, Bowlby, and Balint, have been reconfirmed by Stern (1985) and other observers of infant development, as well as by students of child abuse.

Symington (Chapter 11, this volume) draws attention to the similarity implied in Fairbairn's concept of the schizoid personality and Tustin's of the autistically encapsulated child, suggesting that there may be a developmental continuity between the latter and the former. Tustin herself (1981b, 1986) has drawn attention to two distinct types of psychotic children: the "encapsulated" type (which is isolated and withdrawn), and the "entangled" or "confusional" type (which is so needy of object contact that it becomes confused with its objects—extreme projective identification). Tustin believes that Klein's theories apply mainly to the entangled or confusional infant; the correlation of the encapsulated infant with Fairbairn's schizoid personality has had to await Symington's contribution, but it also corresponds to contributions by Marcelli (1983) and Ogden (1989), the former of whom postulates an "autistic position" and the latter an "autistic contiguous position," each of which describes schizoid phenomena.

In brief, Fairbairn, like Winnicott and others, schematized the role of reality in infant development, and conceptualized its role in forming the endopsychic situation in the internal world—when it goes awry, as Rubens (1984 and Chapter 8, this volume) points out.

Klein, even more than Freud, was solely focused on the importance of unconscious phantasy and its role in forming the internal world. Although she recognized external reality, she saw its importance in its power to select or invoke (I would say "release," in the ethological sense) phantasmal drive ensembles organized by instinct-based persecutory and/or depressive anxiety. Klein claimed that she did not ignore reality, but merely addressed the infant's reality in the same way as the infant does. Her theory of phantasy, which itself was an imaginative leap beyond Freud's, presupposed that the infant has at his disposal only the capacity of primary-process thinking and has to await the depressive position for the rudiments of secondary process to occur. This primary-process "thinking" is solipsistic and autochthonous (narcissistic): "Everything I perceive and experience has its origins in me! There is no world that is independent of me!" Klein's schizoid mechanisms, which include splitting, projective identification, magic omnipotent denial, and idealization, are the instruments of this primary process. They are elaborated in the "paranoid position," which Klein modified to "paranoid–schizoid position" in deference to Fairbairn.

Today, observers of infant development assure us that Klein was right in her emphatic insistence that the infant experiences himself as separate from the beginning, but was significantly wrong that the infant is dominated by primary process. Stern (1985) avers that the infant perceives external reality from the very beginning (thus affirming Fairbairn), and does possess the rudiments of secondary process; however, the infant does not possess the instruments of primary process until the second year of life—and therefore is incapable of phantasy until then.[24]

Fairbairn, on the other hand, emphasized the prime importance of the infant's awareness of his own reality vis-à-vis external objects (persons)—a view corroborated by infant development studies (Stern, 1985)—and believed that phantasies are secondary to this reality. Thus Klein and Fairbairn approached the same phenomena in similar but complementary terms, but emphasized opposite domains of experience (as Hughes points out, 1989 and Chapter 14, this volume). I think it more likely that Klein, Fairbairn, and Stern are all correct and that what is needed is a dual-track paradigm, as mentioned earlier—a "Siamese twinship," in which parallel, seemingly incompatible ideas can be simultaneously encompassed (Grotstein, 1980b, 1994c). Thus the infant can be thought of as able to experience parenting both realistically, according to Fairbairn's (and Stern's, 1985) conceptions, and phantasmally, according to Klein's. Fairbairn's zeal in object relatedness seems to be at the expense of the primacy and importance of constitutional (biological) considerations. To him, therefore, the life and death instincts are not primary, but rather are offshoots of object relatedness. Fairbairn at worst may have underestimated the power of innate potential destructiveness to be released by experience as an relentless and indomitable ensemble of raw power needing a mother's containment (Bion, 1962) to defuse. Fairbairn, like G. Klein, Thickstun, Goldblatt, and others, seems to have inaugurated a tendency toward a psychoanalytic metapsychology that is purely psychological, divorced from its biological template.

Another interesting series of studies that seems to support Fairbairn's point of view is that of Cramer (1982a, 1982b, 1984, 1985, 1986), Apprey (1987), and Cramer and Stern (1988). All these studies were conducted as longitudinal in-depth observations of infant–mother interactions, in

---

[24]This may be because Stern and other American infant developmentalists have been trained in the American school of ego psychology, and consequently may not acknowledge the difference between imagination and symbolization.

which the main variable consisted of mothers' unconscious phantasies of projective identification into their infants of their own unresolved infantile neuroses. In virtually every case, infant correspondence to the mothers' projective identifications were deemed significant as behavioral organizers. These findings do not refute Klein; they simply signify the need for an intersubjective revision of Kleinian thinking, one that Bion (1961) set out to achieve with his idea of the "container" and the "contained."

Though he failed to state this, it was to Klein that Fairbairn owed the conceptualization of the origin of the omnipotence of the schizoid's inner world (projective and introjective identification into the objects of the schizoid's own inherent omnipotence). When he stated that the schizoid-to-be infant believes that by giving love or feelings generally he *loses* bodily substance, and thus must consequently relate to his objects through the exhibitionistic technique of showing (imitating) rather than sharing and through the playing of roles, Fairbairn could have availed himself once again of Klein's conceptualizations of splitting and projective identification and of phantasies in general.

The Moral Defense: The Contrast between Fairbairn's and Klein's Use of Phantasy

There is one point at which Fairbairn's and Klein's conceptions significantly intersect, and that is the moral defense (defense of the superego). Although Klein and Fairbairn agreed about the importance of phantasy, they employed it from different perspectives. To Klein phantasy was primary; to Fairbairn it was secondary. The moral defense illustrates how each employed phantasy differently.

Klein conceived of idealization as a schizoid defense—not against the impingement of bad external objects (which is implicit in Fairbairn's moral defense), but against persecutory anxiety caused by internalized objects into whom the infant has projected his inherent destructiveness. Klein believed, first of all, that the infant creates his own objects—they are projective identificatory creations, which are projectively interposed onto external objects and then introjected and identified with. The Kleinian infant (and patient) must accept his own *sense* of responsibility for the putative badness of his objects, since that badness is a by-product of the infant's (or patient's) own greed, envy, and/or destructive hate upon them.

Klein's internal world, which consists of introjected (self-transformed) objects, is subsequently separated out from the real, non-self-created world in the depressive position. She assumed, as did Freud, that the infant can take in its experiences only with primary process because secondary process takes some time to develop (Freud, 1911). Thus, in Klein's scheme, phantasies (the mental representations of the instinctual drives) are primary, and reality, whether internal (needs, affects) or external (experiences with the real world of persons), merely selectively "releases" the primal (at first) phantasies that anticipate these reality impingements. These "released" phantasies become transformed over time into ever more complex phantasies (Isaacs, 1952).

The point of her psychology seems to be for the infant/patient to own and acknowledge the act of having created phantoms (internal objects), which become confused with real objects (persons). The advantage of her scheme is that it gives the infant/patient a sense of ownership of his own autobiographical scenario, a sense of being the creator of his own history by phantasmally ordering it. This sense seems to be lacking in all the other schemata based primarily on what the infant allegedly experienced from *outside* influences. This dilemma has been called the debate between "guilty man" and "tragic man" (Kohut, 1984). Fairbairn's predilection for "tragic man" over "guilty man" may have had a lot to do with his dissatisfaction with the strictures of his rigid upbringing, according to Sutherland (1989, see Chapter 2, this volume). A dual-track conception can contain both strands in parallel as an example of man's essential dialectical duality, the breakdown of which constitutes psychic conflict (Grotstein, 1978, 1980b, 1994c; Ogden, 1988).

Fairbairn took a different stance. He believed that infants confront and are confronted by an external reality that they realistically understand all too well. Fairbairn believed that children exchange their ambivalence about their objects for an unconditional badness and goodness, that become transformed into conditional badness and goodness by the introjection of the preambivalent object. They do this by splitting the image of the object into an accepted and a rejected object; they internalize the latter and identify with it, while preserving the relative goodness of the remaining aspect of the object as the IO. In this perspective, infants employ phantasy *secondarily* to alter the painfulness of and thus to tolerate the experience of reality. This burying or alteration of intolerable reality as endopsychic structure can be seen as the quintessential paradigm both for child abuse and molestation specifically and for post-traumatic stress disorder generally.

The interesting point of intersection between Fairbairn and Klein is this very assumption of a sense of responsibility for the creation of one's objects. A too-zealous Kleinian therapist would be in danger of colluding with the patient by assuming that the object's badness helps the patient maintain the object's goodness. The therapist would, in this case, be in danger of reinforcing the patient's hidden manic defense (omnipotence) that he indeed *is* responsible for the objects' deficits—with the forfeiture of the patient's own entitlement. The patient would have to foot the cost of the reparation out of his own scanty emotional resources, with a resultant ascetic, self-denigrating bitterness and everlasting envy. The collusion of the Fairbairnian approach would be the opposite: The infant/ patient would feel empathically understood in terms of his infantile helplessness, but would not be able to have "created the event" in order to separate out his own felt-to-be-*necessary* contribution from that reality.

Insofar as the infant or child takes over the parents' badness, introjects it, and identifies with it, he becomes a conscience to the parents and wields absolute moral authority over them—as one can see, for example, in the passive–aggressive manipulations of depressive patients that Freud (1917) and later Searles (1979) have brought to our attention. The symptomatology of one of my patients is also illustrative of this phenomenon:

The patient was a 35-year-old divorced advertising executive who characterologically proffered a "false-self" (Winnicott, 1960b) acquiescent goodness to all those whom she met and interacted with. As soon as the analysis was under way, she formed a positive idealizing transference to me, which was interrupted by periodic bursts of unaccountable (to her) anger and negativism. She mentioned that these nasty thoughts—seemingly innocent at first—seemed to originate in a part of her that was foreign to her, but one that "had her ear." She once mentioned that on her way to her analytic hour, she saw another analyst walking down the street (one for whom she had high regard), and found herself saying to herself, "Isn't Dr. C. pompous?"

The obvious transference aspects were explored, but the ultimate realization lay in another direction. First, it revealed the presence of an entombed and dissociated alter ego (second self). Second, the composition of this alter ego's personality seemed to include an introjective identification with the cruel and abusive aspects of her mother, as well as of her shameful and ignominious (to the mother and grandmother) biological father—in addition to a highlighting of her own underlying "mean" self. The patient seemed to have selectively incorporated and identified with the worst features of each parent (and one grandparent), so as to preserve the illusion of the goodness of her needed mother—as Fairbairn suggested. Once this negative alter ego had formed, it also became the repository for her own envy, greed, and hatred—the "Kleinian infant," as it were—and this composite self became banished to the catacombs of her psyche. She frequently became confused and disoriented as to who was the originator of the traits.

It became clear that her severe self-criticisms and provocative passive–aggressive behavior toward others were attempts to "bust" her internal objects, whose badness she had internalized and with whom she had identified. Thus was her way of bringing them "to justice."

The Schizoid Position versus the Paranoid–Schizoid Position, and the Differences between Klein's and Fairbairn's Depressive Positions

Important parallels and divergences between Klein and Fairbairn can also be seen in their views of infantile dependency. Fairbairn and Klein fundamentally revised the psychoanalytic conception of the infantile neurosis, as originally described in Freud's (1918 [1914]) case of the "Wolf Man" as the Oedipus complex. Fairbairn's and Klein's modification of the classical conception of the infantile neurosis was to render it properly "infantile" by returning to the binary relationship between mother and infant, in the period before the developmental advent of the tripartite parent–child relationship.

Fairbairn closely followed Abraham's (1924) conception of infantile dependency, which included an epigenetic parallel between autoerotic development and the conception of the associated part-objects. Fairbairn followed this protocol strictly, believing that Abraham's earlier oral (sucking) stage was preambivalent, although frustrating. Thus a frustrating breast/mother becomes unacceptable but not hated, whereas in the later oral (biting) stage, she becomes hated when frustrating.

According to Fairbairn, the preambivalent infant believes that it is his love that is rejected when his mother frustrates him. The rejection of his need results in futility, which is profounder and more absolute than the melancholic despair in the depressive position. Fairbairn's schizoid position is truly schizoid (not paranoid), and predicates alienation upon unaccepted love, neediness, and desire.

Klein's paranoid–schizoid position (which eschews preambivalence) is primarily paranoid and secondarily schizoid, because of hatred. Thus, Klein's paranoid–schizoid position includes Fairbairn's schizoid position (in part, but not his conception of alienation) and his depressive position, but Fairbairn's depressive position does not encompass all of Klein's. Fairbairn's conception does not include the almost spiritual transformation that characterizes Klein's depressive position—one that represents a reconciliation with (but not surrender to) external reality as the infant retracts his omnipotent phantoms from the images of his objects. The central task of the Kleinian infant is to acknowledge his own neediness, adapt to the individuality of the caretaker, and *appreciate* (not idealize) what it receives from the caretaker, which is truly vital for his own welfare. I believe that this aspect of Klein's depressive position is apposite for Fairbairn's endopsychic structure—to allow for the reintegration of subsidiary egos and split-off objects, so that they can become reunited with the original ego and the original object, a necessary integration suggested by Rinsley (1987 and Chapter 15, this volume).

Yet, in justice to Fairbairn, his schema strongly suggests the pre-eminence of the sense of shame that schizoid and depressive patients experience in regard to their objects, real or internalized; this fact accounts for the adhesive hold of bad objects (Malin, 1990). Klein's emphasis on projective identification misses Fairbairn's central point that infants can experience intense shame about objects that have failed in their task to proffer a sense of a "blessing" and a proud and caring entitlement—a notion that now is the headpiece of self psychology in the United States and that owes its origin to Fairbairn.

Although Fairbairn may have been short-sighted in making the consequences of sucking and biting the respective determinants of his schizoid and depressive positions, his conception of a schizoid position is to be differentiated from a paranoid position, insofar as the infant realistically perceives that his existence is endangered from without and that he has to make phantasmal accommodations for survival. Thus, in withdrawing, the infant becomes his own imaginary parent. In addition, the infant must exaggerate his need for inner grandiosity and exhibitionism (relating through showing), in order to compensate for the absence of special, meaningful parental confirmation. Furthermore, the infant must feel sufficiently bonded and attached by being "loved as a person in his own right," as Fairbairn advocates, in order to be able optimally to traverse Klein's paranoid–schizoid position on its way to her depressive position.

Whereas Fairbairn's schizoid position predicates a primary deficit theory, his depressive position predicates a melancholic theory—one that, like Klein's and Freud's, enfranchises the conflict theory and makes allowances for the results in phantasy for the child's putative aggression toward the breast. Unfortunately, Fairbairn's development of this aspect of his psychology was incomplete.

Finally, it seems that there is room for three positions: (1) Fairbairn's schizoid position; (2) Klein's paranoid–schizoid position (which can contain Fairbairn's depressive position), and (3) Klein's depressive position. More recently, Bick's (1968, 1986) and Meltzer's (1975) conception of "adhesive identification" ("identity") argues for a position earlier (or deeper) than Klein's paranoid–schizoid position, as do Marcelli's (1983) "autistic position" and Ogden's (1989) "autistic contiguous position." Although the work of Tustin (1980, 1981a, 1981b, 1986, 1987, 1988a, 1988b), based on the primitive, premature emotional separation of autistic children, seems to support these views, she opts for "states of infantile consciousness" rather than "positions" (personal communication, March 5, 1989).

Ogden (1989), building on the work of all the foregoing and especially of Tustin, proffers the conception of the "autistic contiguous position," by which term he captures the primacy of the functioning of the sensory apparatus in its capacity to mediate the "flow" of sensations between infant and mother. He also argues, as I have (Grotstein, 1980a, 1980b, 1990b), for a concept of simultaneity of positions from the very beginning, as currently Meltzer (1986) himself does. Bion (1970), in his concepts of "infantile catastrophe" and "emotional turbulence," may have anticipated this condition, and it may be fair to assign to him the putative concept of a "catastrophic position"—one prior to and profounder than the paranoid–schizoid position, where the hapless, uncontained infant falls into "the deep and formless infinite" (the "black hole"; Grotstein, 1990a).

One other significant difference between Klein's and Fairbairn's concepts of the depressive position is the *subjectivity* of the status (in contrast to the narcissistic status as *object*) that the Kleinian infant grants his objects once they are "released" from the constraints of infantile omnipotence characteristic of the paranoid–schizoid position.

Ultimately, the seeming contrasts between the perspectives of Fairbairn and Klein may be reconcilable when we realize that Fairbairn's schema is *intersubjective* (relational), whereas Klein's is *intrasubjective* (one person). Perhaps the two schemata are necessary complements to each other.

The Transitional Techniques

One of Fairbairn's unique contributions was to perceive neuroses as transitional techniques of regulating (maintaining) the splitting of egos and objects that originates in the period of infantile dependency. In conceiving of neuroses as techniques rather than as defaults, he assigned a heuristic role to them in a hierarchy that presupposes that splitting (and, by derivation, psychosis) is primary to neurosis, which modulates it. Here Fairbairn was even more specific than Klein in assigning primacy to psychosis and splitting.

Determining which neurotic technique to use is contingent upon internalization or externalization of the accepted or rejected object. Thus the paranoid technique internalizes the accepted object and externalizes the rejected object. The hysteric does the reverse. The obsessive compulsive neither internalizes nor externalizes either object, but the phobic externalizes both. Later Fairbairn divided the rejected object into the RO and EO of endopsychic structure. (I would "translate" Fairbairn's "externalization" as "projective identification" into external objects and/or into superego objects.)

It is important to distinguish two separate usages of the term "techniques of relating to objects" that Fairbairn has given us. For Fairbairn, the first and most important is that of the dynamic relationship between the internal objects of endopsychic structures. The second technique, which is implicit in his papers on the war neuroses (Fairbairn, 1943a, 1943b), is that of relating to external objects by virtue of one's inventory of internal objects. Thus a patient who is fixated in infantile (immature) dependency and who feels persecuted and limited by internal bad objects will tend to relate to his external objects in a number of maladaptive ways. In a wartime situation, he may project (externalize) his IO (and maybe even parts of his CE) into the group leader, and his RO and AE into the enemy; in a masochistic love affair he may treat the external object of desire as his EO (but secretly RO) and experience extremes of ambivalence about the object, who may feel controlled by the patient's disingenuous passivity.

We can also compare Fairbairn's conception of transitional techniques with Mahler's (1968) "differentiation" and "rapprochement" subphases of separation and individuation. Fairbairn's internal techniques correspond to Mahler's empirical observations. Brown (1987), in discussing the genetic factor in the borderline disorder, advances the idea of a "transitional position" that should normally be interposed between Klein's paranoid–schizoid and depressive positions.

The Relationship between Splitting and Repression

Fairbairn's conception of the relationship between these two defense mechanisms is interesting and unique. The earlier classical penchant for emphasizing the Oedipus complex over pre-Oedipal anxieties caused a corresponding emphasis on repression, with the superego emerging with the resolution of the Oedipus complex. Klein's (1928, 1933, 1945) conception of an earlier onset of the Oedipus complex allowed her to hypothesize a correspondingly earlier origin of the superego and thus of repression, but she too envisioned an epigenesis from splitting in the paranoid–schizoid position to repression in the depressive position.

Although he did not deal with the more archaic origins of repression, Fairbairn did emphasize the importance of the splitting of the ego and of its objects to an even greater extent than had Klein. However, he also emphasized the *reciprocal* relationship between splitting and repression—and their simultaneity. Thus to him, splitting of the ego, as manifested by the presence of endopsychic structure, requires repression so as to allow tentative cohesion of the ego. The more splitting the more repression, not the other way around.

GENERAL COMMENTS

Although many of Fairbairn's ideas are now in the mainstream of the psychoanalytic literature, others have been lamentably ignored. At the same time, many of his concepts deserve updating and integration with the ideas of other schools—particularly the Kleinian school, but also those of Winnicott, Jung, Kohut, Lacan, and ego psychology (the last of which Kernberg, in Chapter 4 of this volume, attempts). One initial emendation I should like to make was originally suggested by Hegel (1807, as quoted in Kojève, 1934–1935, p. 6): "Man does not desire an object. Man desires the object's desire." Today we would thus catalogue the spectrum of needs and desires that the object is to satisfy, and this would take us into the realm of differentiating between Winnicott's "object of usage" and the "holding object" (selfobject); between the part-object and the whole object; or, as I like to put it, between the "foreground presence" and the "background presence" (and, as a consequence, foreground and background transferences in analysis).

Would we now say that a CE, in relationship to its IO, represses subsidiary egos and objects, or instead would we now say that Fairbairn's dynamic formulation is a shorthand for a more complex dynamic—that of the repression of the *significance* and *meaning* of these unconscious relationships? I argue in Chapter 9 that Fairbairn's endopsychic structures are but a way station to an even profounder kind of repression—that of meaninglessness, chaos, and the phantasmagoria of the "black hole" (Grotstein, 1990a, 1991d).

Fairbairn's pivotal emphasis was on the relationship of libido to the object in the light of parental frustration, deprivation, and impingement; this emphasis prefigures the current interest in child molestation and abuse. Because the parent is *needed*, the moral defense (the defense of the superego) must be instituted so that the infant or child can preserve the intactness and goodness of his parental objects at his own expense. This expense is the projective arrogation of his own innocence and goodness to one aspect of the parent, while hiding the really bad parental object introjectively in his internal world. The fact that the avowed need for a bad parent has a libidinal bind confers upon the unconscious (and its internalized bad objects) enormous strategic power to keep large portions of the ego split off from the rest of the personality. Thus, Freud's (1915) original conception of the push of repression and its "afterpull" can now be adequately confirmed by Fairbairn's deployment of the personification of objects.

But the most important aspect of the Fairbairn legacy is his advocacy of the child—and his insistence that *entitlement* and *innocence* are minimum requirements for the development for a sense of self. One can view the concept of normal entitlement as consonant with the Biblical "blessing" or "birthright," and its absence with a "curse." Fairbairn, the would-be Scottish clergyman, could well have employed the terms "blessed" and "cursed" to capture the profound dynamics of the child's inner world.

ACKNOWLEDGMENT

I am grateful to Dr. Victoria Hamilton for her careful review and many helpful suggestions in this chapter and in Chapter 9.

REFERENCES

Abraham, K. (1924). A short study of the development of the libido. In *Selected Papers on Psycho-Analysis*. London: Hogarth Press, 1949, pp. 418–501.
Apprey, M. (1987). Projective identification and maternal misconception in disturbed mothers. *British Journal of Psychotherapy*, 4(1), 5–22.
Bacal, H. A. (1985).Object-relations in the group from the perspective of self psychology. *International Journal of Group Psychotherapy, 35,* 483–501.
Bacal, H. A. (1987). British object-relations theorists and self psychology. *International Journal of Psycho-Analysis, 68,* 81–98.
Bacal, H. A. (1990a). Does an object relations theory exist in self psychology? *Psychoanalytic Inquiry, 10*(2), 197–220.
Bacal, H. A. (1990b). W. R. D. Fairbairn. In H. A. Bacal & K. M. Newman, eds., *Theories of Object Relations: Bridges to Self Psychology*. New York: Columbia University Press, pp. 135–157.
Berman, E. (1974). Multiple personality: Theoretical approaches. *Journal of the Bronx State Hospital, 2*(2), 99–107.
Berman, E. (1981). Multiple personality: Psychoanalytic perspectives. *International Journal of Psycho-Analysis, 62*(3), 283–300.
Bick, E. (1968). The experience of the skin in early object relations. *International Journal of Psycho-Analysis, 49,* 484–486.
Bick, E. (1986). Further considerations on the function of the skin in early object relations. *British Journal of Psychotherapy, 2,* 292–299.
Bion, W. R. (1961). A psycho-analytic study of thinking. *International Journal of Psycho-Analysis, 43,* 306–310.
Bion, W. R. (1962). *Learning from Experience*. London: Heinemann.
Bion, W. R. (1970). *Attention and Interpretation*. London: Tavistock.
Blomfield, O. H. D. (1985). Parasitism, projective identification and the Faustian bargain. *International Review of Psycho-Analysis, 12,* 299–310.
Brandchaft, B. (1986). British object relations theory and self psychology. In A. Goldberg, ed., *Progress in Self Psychology*, Vol. 2. New York: Guilford Press, pp. 245–272.

Brooks, B. (1985). Sexually abused children and adolescent identity development. *American Journal of Psychotherapy*, 39(3), 401–410.

Brown, L. (1987). Borderline personality organization and the transition to the depressive position. In J. S. Grotstein, M. F. Solomon, & J. A. Lang, eds., *The Borderline Patient: Emerging Concepts in Diagnosis, Psychodynamics, and Treatment*, Vol. 1. Hillsdale, NJ: Analytic Press, pp. 147–180.

Cramer, B. (1982a). Interaction réele, interaction fantasmatique: Réflections au sujet des thérapies et des observations de nourrissons. *Psychothérapies*, 1, 39–47.

Cramer, B. (1982b). La psychiatrie du bébé: Une introduction. In M. Soulé, ed., *La Dynamique du Nourrisson*. Paris: ESF, pp. 28–83.

Cramer, B. (1984, September). Modèles psychoanalytiques, modèles interactifs: Recoupment possible? Paper presented at the International Symposium, "Psychiatry–Psychoanalysis," Montréal.

Cramer, B. (1985). Thérapies du nourrisson. In S. Lebovici, R. Diatkine, & M. Soulé, eds., *Traité de Psychiatrie de l'Enfant et de l'Adolescent II*. Paris: Presses Universitaires de France.

Cramer, B. (1986). Assessment of parent–infant relationship. In T. B. Brazelton & M. W. Yogman, eds., *Affective Development in Infancy*. Norwood, NJ: Ablex, pp. 27–38.

Cramer, B., & Stern, D. (1988). Evaluation of changes in mother–infant brief psychotherapy: A single case study. *Infant Mental Health Journal*, 9(1), 20–45.

Davies, J. M., & Frawley, M. G. (1992). Dissociative processes and transference–countertransference paradigms in the psychoanalytically oriented treatment of adult survivors of childhood sexual abuse. *Psychoanalytic Dialogues*, 2(1), 5–36.

Fairbairn, W. R. D. (1940). Schizoid factors in the personality. In *Psychoanalytic Studies of the Personality*. London: Tavistock, 1952, pp. 3–27.

Fairbairn, W. R. D. (1941). A revised psychopathology of the psychoses and psychoneuroses. In *Psychoanalytic Studies of the Personality*. London: Tavistock, 1952, pp. 28–58.

Fairbairn, W. R. D. (1943a). The repression and the return of bad objects (with special reference to the 'war neuroses'). In *Psychoanalytic Studies of the Personality*. London: Tavistock, 1952, pp. 59–81.

Fairbairn, W. R. D. (1943b). The war neuroses—their nature and significance. In *Psychoanalytic Studies of the Personality*. London: Tavistock, 1952, pp. 256–287.

Fairbairn, W. R. D. (1944). Endopsychic structure considered in terms of object-relationships. In *Psychoanalytic Studies of the Personality*. London: Tavistock, 1952, pp. 82–136.

Fairbairn, W. R. D. (1946). Object-relationships and dynamic structure. In *Psychoanalytic Studies of the Personality*. London: Tavistock, 1952, pp. 137–151.

Fairbairn, W. R. D. (1949). Steps in the development of an object-relations theory of the personality. In *Psychoanalytic Studies of the Personality*. London: Tavistock, 1952, pp. 152–161.

Fairbairn, W. R. D. (1951). A synopsis of the development of the author's views regarding the structure of the personality. In *Psychoanalytic Studies of the Personality*. London: Tavistock, 1952, pp. 162–182.

Fairbairn, W. R. D. (1952). *Psychoanalytic Studies of the Personality.* London: Tavistock.

Fairbairn, W. R. D. (1956). Considerations arising out of the Schreber case. *British Journal of Medical Psychology, 29*(2), 113–127.

Freud, S. (1905). Three essays on the theory of sexuality. *Standard Edition, 7,* 125–245.

Freud, S. (1910). The psychoanalytic view of psychogenic disturbance of vision. *Standard Edition, 11,* 209–218.

Freud, S. (1911). Formulations on the two principles of mental functioning. *Standard Edition, 12,* 213–226.

Freud, S. (1914). On narcissism: An introduction. *Standard Edition, 14,* 67–104.

Freud, S. (1915). Repression. *Standard Edition, 14,* 141–158.

Freud, S. (1917). Mourning and melancholia. *Standard Edition, 14,* 237–260.

Freud, S. (1918 [1914]). From the history of an infantile neurosis. *Standard Edition, 17,* 3–122.

Freud, S. (1919). Introduction to psycho-analysis and the war neuroses. *Standard Edition, 17,* 205–216.

Freud, S. (1920). Beyond the pleasure principle. *Standard Edition, 18,* 3–66.

Freud, S. (1921). Group psychology and the analysis of the ego. *Standard Edition, 18,* 67–144.

Freud, S. (1923 [1922]). A seventeenth-century demonological neurosis. *Standard Edition, 19,* 69–108.

Freud, S. (1923). The ego and the id. *Standard Edition, 19,* 3–66.

Gabbard, G. (1989). Two subtypes of narcissistic personality disorder. *Bulletin of the Menninger Clinic, 53*(6), 527–532.

Greenberg, J. R., & Mitchell, S. A. (1983). *Object Relations in Psychoanalytic Theory.* Cambridge, MA: Harvard University Press.

Grotstein, J. S. (1978). Inner space: Its dimensions and its coordinates. *International Journal of Psycho-Analysis, 59,* 55–61.

Grotstein, J. S. (1979a). Demoniacal possession, splitting, and the torment of joy. *Contemporary Psychoanalysis, 15*(3), 407–453.

Grotstein, J. S. (1979b). The soul in torment: A newer and older view of psychopathology. *Bulletin for Catholic Psychiatrists, 25,* 36–52.

Grotstein, J. S. (1980a). A proposed revision of the psychoanalytic concept of primitive mental states: I. An introduction to a newer psychoanalytic metapsychology. *Contemporary Psychoanalysis, 16*(4), 479–546.

Grotstein, J. S. (1980b). The significance of Kleinian contributions to psychoanalysis: II. A comparison between the Freudian and Kleinian conceptions of the development of early mental life. *International Journal of Psychoanalytic Psychotherapy, 8,* 393–428.

Grotstein, J. S. (1981). Who is the dreamer who dreams the dream and who is the dreamer who understands it?. In J. S. Grotstein, ed., *Do I Dare Disturb the Universe? A Memorial to Wilfred R. Bion.* Beverly Hills, CA: Caesura Press, pp. 357–416.

Grotstein, J. S. (1982). Newer perspectives in object relations theory. *Contemporary Psychoanalysis, 18,* 43–91.

Grotstein, J. S. (1990a). Nothingness, meaninglessness, chaos, and the "black hole": II. The "black hole." *Contemporary Psychoanalysis*, 26(3), 377–407.
Grotstein, J. S. (1990b). The mirror and the frame. *Bulletin of the Society for Psychoanalytic Psychotherapy*, 5(3), 21–34.
Grotstein, J. S. (1991a). An American view of the British psychoanalytic experience: I. Introduction: The Americanization of psychoanalysis. *Journal of Melanie Klein and Object Relations*, 9, 1–15.
Grotstein, J. S. (1991b). An American view of the British psychoanalytic experience: II. The Kleinian school. *Journal of Melanie Klein and Object Relations*, 9, 16–33.
Grotstein, J. S. (1991c). An American view of the British psychoanalytic experience: III. The British object relations school. *Journal of Melanie Klein and Object Relations*, 9, 34–62.
Grotstein, J. S. (1991d). Nothingness, meaninglessness, chaos, and the "black hole": III. Self-regulation and the background presence of primary identification. *Contemporary Psychoanalysis*, 27(1), 1–33.
Grotstein, J. S. (1994a). Why Oedipus and not Christ?: The importance of innocence, original sin, and human sacrifice in psychoanalytic theory and practice. I. A selected re-reading of the myth of Oedipus and Christ. Manuscript in preparation.
Grotstein, J. S. (1994b). Why Oedipus and not Christ?: The importance of innocence, original sin, and human sacrifice in psychoanalytic theory and practice. II. The transference/countertransference neurosis psychosis and their consummate expression in the crucifixion, the Pieta, and "therapeutic exorcism." Manuscript in preparation.
Grotstein, J. S. (1994c). The dual-track theorem: A newer paradigm for psychoanalytic theory and technique. Manuscript in preparation.
Grotstein, J. S. (in press). Object relations theory. In E. Nersessian & R. Kopff, eds., *Textbook of Psychoanalysis*. Washington, DC: American Psychiatric Press.
Hegel, G. W. F. (1807). *The Phenomenology of Spirit*, A. V. Miller, trans. London: Oxford University Press, 1977.
Hughes, J. M. (1989). Melanie Klein: The world of internal objects. In *Reshaping the Psychoanalytic Domain: The Work of Melanie Klein, W. R. D. Fairbairn, and D. W. Winnicott*. Berkeley: University of California Press, pp. 44– 88.
Isaacs, S. (1952). The nature and function of phantasy. In M. Klein, P. Heimann, S. Isaacs, & J. Riviere, eds, *Developments in Psycho-Analysis*. London: Hogarth Press, pp. 67–121.
Jacobson, E. (1964). *The Self and the Object World*. New York: International Universities Press.
Janet, P. (1889). *L'Automatisme Psychologique: Essai de Psychologie Expérimentale sur les Formes Inférieures de l'Activité Humaine*. Paris: Faylés Alcan.
Johnson, S. M. (1991). *The Symbiotic Character*. New York: Norton.
Kernberg, O. (1975). *Borderline Conditions and Pathological Narcissism*. New York: Jason Aronson.
Kernberg, O. (1976). *Object Relations Theory and Psychoanalysis*. New York: Jason Aronson.

Kernberg, O. (1980). Internal World and External Reality. New York: Jason Aronson.
Kernberg, O. (1984). Severe Personality Disorders. New Haven, CT: Yale University Press.
Klein, M. (1928). Early stages of the Oedipus conflict. In Contributions to Psycho-Analysis, 1921–1945. London: Hogarth Press, 1950, pp. 254–266.
Klein, M. (1933). The early development of conscience in the child. In Contributions to Psycho-Analysis, 1921–1945. London: Hogarth Press, 1950, pp. 267–277.
Klein, M. (1940). Mourning and its relation to manic–depressive states. In Contributions to Psycho-Analysis, 1921–1945. London: Hogarth Press, 1950, pp. 311–338.
Klein, M. (1945). The Oedipus complex in the light of early anxieties. In Contributions to Psycho-Analysis, 1921–1945. London: Hogarth Press, 1950, pp. 339–390.
Klein, M. (1946). Notes on some schizoid mechanisms. In M. Klein, P. Heimann, S. Isaacs, & J. Riviere, eds., Developments in Psycho-Analysis. London: Hogarth Press, 1952, pp. 292–320.
Klein, M. (1958). On the development of mental functioning. In The Writings of Melanie Klein: Vol. 3. Envy and Gratitude and Other Works, 1946–1963. New York: Free Press, 1975, pp. 236–246.
Kohut, H. (1971). The Analysis of the Self: A Systematic Approach to the Psychoanalytic Treatment of Narcissistic Personality Disorders. New York: International Universities Press.
Kohut, H. (1977). The Restoration of the Self. New York: International Universities Press.
Kohut, H. (1978). The Search for the Self, P. Ornstein, ed., Vols. 1 and 2. New York: International Universities Press.
Kohut, H. (1984). How Does Analysis Cure?, A. Goldberg, ed. Chicago: University of Chicago Press.
Kojève, A. (1934–1935). Introduction to the Reading of Hegel, J. H. Nichols, Jr., trans. Ithaca, NY: Cornell University Press.
Lacan, J. (1953). The function and field of speech and language in psychoanalysis. In Écrits: A Selection, A. Sheriden, trans. New York: Norton, 1977, pp. 30–113.
Mahler, M. (1968). On Human Symbiosis and the Vicissitudes of Individuation. New York: International Universities Press.
Malin, B. D. (1990). Shame and envy: A re-examination. Unpublished manuscript.
Marcelli, D. (1983). La position autistique: Hypothèses psychopathologiques et ontogénétiques. Psychiatrie Enfant, 24(1), 5–55.
Mason, A. (1985, March 15). A psychoanalytic view of a hypnotist. Lecture presented at the Topeka Psychoanalytic Society and the Menninger Foundation, Topeka, KS.
Masterson, J., & Rinsley, D. B. (1975). The borderline syndrome: The role of the mother in the genesis and psychic structure of the borderline personality. International Journal of Psycho-Analysis, 56, 163–177.

Meltzer, D. (1975). Adhesive identification. *Contemporary Psychoanalysis, 11,* 289–310.

Meltzer, D. (1986). *Studies in Extended Metapsychology: Clinical Applications of Bion's Ideas.* Strath Tay, Perthshire: Clunie Press.

Ogden, T. H. (1986). *The Matrix of the Mind.* Northvale, NJ: Jason Aronson.

Ogden, T. H. (1988). On the dialectical structure of experience. *Contemporary Psychoanalysis, 23*(4), 17–45.

Ogden, T. H. (1989). *The Primitive Edge of Experience.* Northvale, NJ: Jason Aronson.

Peebles, M. J. (1989). Post-traumatic stress disorder: A historical perspective on diagnosis and treatment. *Bulletin of the Menninger Clinic, 53,* 74–286.

Rapaport, D. (1959). A historical survey of psychoanalytic ego psychology. In E. H. Erikson, *Identity and the Life Cycle.* New York: International Universities Press, pp. 5–17.

Rinsley, D. B. (1987). Fairbairn's object-relations and classical concepts of dynamics and structure. In J. S. Grotstein, M. F. Solomon, & J. A. Lang, eds. *The Borderline Patient: Emerging Concepts in Diagnosis, Psychodynamics, and Treatment,* Vol. 1. Hillsdale, NJ: Analytic Press.

Robbins, M. (1980). Current controversy in object relations theory as outgrowth of a schism between Klein and Fairbairn. *International Journal of Psycho-Analysis, 61,* 477–492.

Rubens, R. L. (1984). The meaning of structure in Fairbairn. *International Review of Psycho-Analysis, 11,* 429–440.

Sandler, J. (1960). The background of safety. *International Journal of Psycho-Analysis, 41,* 352–356.

Searles, H. (1979). Jealousy involving an internal object. In J. LeBoit & A. Capponi, eds., *Advances in Psychotherapy of the Borderline Patient.* New York: Jason Aronson, pp. 347–404.

Stern, D. (1985). *The Interpersonal World of the Infant.* New York: Basic Books.

Stewart, H. (1979). The scientific importance of Ernest Jones. *International Journal of Psycho-Analysis, 60,* 397–404.

Sutherland, J. D. (1989). *Fairbairn's Journey into the Interior.* London: Free Association Books.

Suttie, I. (1935). *The Origins of Love and Hate.* New York: Matrix House, 1952.

Tuohy, A. L. (1987). Psychoanalytic perspectives on child abuse. *Child and Adolescent Social Work Journal, 4*(1), 25–40.

Tustin, F. (1980). Autistic objects. *International Review of Psycho-Analysis, 7,* 27–39.

Tustin, F. (1981a). Psychological birth and psychological catastrophe. In J. S. Grotstein, ed., *Do I Dare Disturb the Universe?: A Memorial to Wilfred R. Bion.* Beverly Hills, CA: Caesura Press, pp. 181–196.

Tustin, F. (1981b). *Autistic States in Children.* London: Routledge & Kegan Paul.

Tustin, F. (1986). *Autistic Barriers in Neurotic Patients.* New Haven, CT: Yale University Press.

Tustin, F. (1987). The rhythm of safety. *Winnicott's Studies: The Journal of the Squiggle Foundation, 2,* 19–31.

Tustin, F. (1988a). The "black hole"—a significant element in autism. *Free Associations*, *11*, 35–50.
Tustin, F. (1988b). To be or not to be: A study of autism. *Winnicott's Studies: The Journal of the Squiggle Foundation*, *3*, 15–31.
Winnicott, D. W. (1954). The depressive position in normal emotional development. In *Collected Papers: Through Pediatrics to Psycho-Analysis*. New York: Basic Books, 1958, pp. 262–277.
Winnicott, D. W. (1960a). The theory of the parent–infant relationship. In *The Maturational Processes and the Facilitating Environment: Studies in the Theory of Emotional Development*. New York: International Universities Press, 1965, pp. 37–55.
Winnicott, D. W. (1960b). Ego distortion in terms of true and false self. In *The Maturational Processes and the Facilitating Environment: Studies in the Theory of Emotional Development*. New York: International Universities Press, 1965, pp. 140–152.
Winnicott, D. W. (1971). *Playing and Reality*. London: Tavistock.

Section B

Fairbairn's Endopsychic Structure

8

Fairbairn's Structural Theory

RICHARD L. RUBENS

Beginning in the early 1940s, W. Ronald D. Fairbairn developed a unique psychoanalytic theory that anticipated and laid the groundwork for some of the most important current theoretical advancements in psychoanalysis. At the heart of Fairbairn's theory was a notion of endopsychic structure based directly on the vicissitudes of human object relatedness—in a way so radically different from other theories of his time that it is only now, a half-century later, that his ideas are finally having their appropriately profound influence on the general spectrum of psychoanalytic thinking.

In an earlier paper (Rubens, 1984), I advanced the position that Fairbairn had not been studied as widely and thoroughly as might be expected, because of the extent to which his ideas depart from classical analytic theory. Although psychoanalysts were increasingly drawn to Fairbairn's insights into the nature of human interactions and their implications for clinical practice, surprisingly few allowed themselves even to realize the extent to which these insights were based on a radically novel understanding of the human psyche—and fewer still could recognize and acknowledge the full implications of his departures.

It was my contention in 1984 that it was Fairbairn's complete rejection of Freud's structural theory (and the drive model it embodied) that explained this almost phobic avoidance of the deeper implications of Fairbairn's ideas. The theory of structure is the key issue in defining psychoanalysis in general, and in distinguishing among psychoanalytic theories in particular. Thus, to accept Fairbairn's theory in the fullness of its structural divergence from Freud was to abandon Freud in too radical a way for many psychoanalysts. Also, most psychoanalysts were so habitually attached to speaking in terms of Freud's tripartite division of the psyche into id, ego, and superego that they failed to notice that this structural theory was based on metapsychological assumptions that they themselves no longer adhered to.

In recent years there has been a growing awareness of the viability—and even necessity—of alternatives to the metapsychological assumptions embodied in Freud's structural theory. This change is expressed in the perspective developed by Greenberg and Mitchell (1983) that there are two very different basic models on which psychoanalytic theories are based:

> The most significant tension in the history of psychoanalytic ideas has been the dialectic between the original Freudian model, which takes as its starting point the instinctual drives, and a comprehensive model initiated in the works of Fairbairn and Sullivan, which evolve structure solely from the individual's relations with other people. Accordingly, we designate the original model the *drive/structure model* and the alternative perspective the *relational/structure model*. (p. 20)

Mitchell (1988, p. 18) describes Fairbairn as one of the "purest representatives" of this relational/structure model. Although a very large percentage of modern psychoanalysts actually have underlying assumptions far more consistent with those of the relational/structure model, there remains a tremendous inertia toward preserving a connection to the drive/structure model—or, at least, utilizing its terminology.

The typical use that has previously been made of Fairbairn's ideas has been to note their relevance to early development and to those conditions most directly deriving from these stages (i.e., schizoid, narcissistic, and borderline states), while maintaining that the later developments can still be satisfactorily described in terms of the traditional drive/structure model. Even British object relations theorists such as Winnicott (1965) have attempted to retain their connection to classical theory through just this sort of adherence to the importance of the drive/structure model in later development. Mitchell (1988) provides a brilliant discussion of the shortcomings of this maneuver, which he terms "developmental tilt" (pp. 136 ff.).

Fairbairn himself, while radically departing from Freud's metapsychological assumptions, was nevertheless guilty of employing terms taken too directly from the language of drive theory. He repeatedly utilized such terms as "ego" and "libidinal" in crucial positions in his theories, although they bear virtually no similarity to their original meanings in Freud's theories. Even his use of the term "object" is misleading, since it does not begin to convey how extensively it departs from the drive/structure model's concept of "object."[1] Although he was careful to redefine his use of such terms, Fairbairn's use of the language of drive theory introduced a great deal of confusion into the understanding of his work—and provided a considerable opportunity for avoiding the full impact of its novelty.

Nevertheless, Fairbairn did succeed in completely abandoning Freud's structural model. Moreover, in a still more radical way, he developed a new structural theory based on a very different notion of the psyche and of the underlying meaning and role of structure within it. It is only in recent years that psychoanalysis has finally begun to incorporate directly the full implications and novelty of Fairbairn's theoretical innovations.

This chapter is an attempt to explore the actual extent of Fairbairn's departure from traditional notions of psychic structure, through a detailed explication of his own theory of endopsychic structure in light of the assumptions out of which it was developed and the clinical implications that follow from it.

THE BASIC NATURE OF THE SELF

Fairbairn viewed people as being object-related by their very nature. As he saw it, the fundamental unit of consideration is that of a self in relation to an other—and the nature of the relationship in between. Personhood, in the external world, essentially and definitionally involves relationship with other people. Internally considered, the self therefore is to be understood as always existing in and defined in terms of the relationships it has, remembers, desires, or creates. In the relational/structure model of Fairbairn, the shape of the self grows and changes from its experience in relationships, while at the same time the nature of the relationships it has is being shaped and changed by that self.

Fairbairn's theory gives appropriately great weight to the significance of intrapsychic functioning. Unlike some interpersonal theories, it is no way guilty of naively reducing the study of the human psyche to a mere examination of external relationships. His relational/structure model provides room for the most extensive and rich of notions of inner world. Furthermore, as I discuss below, Fairbairn viewed the self not simply as the

---

[1]Although it is appropriate that Fairbairn used the term "object" in the sense that it conveys the fact that he was cognizant of its existence in the inner world, this usage does not convey the extent to which the quality of "other" is being suggested, even in inner experience. As will become obvious, nothing could be farther from Fairbairn's theory than the notion that an "object" is simply that toward which instinctual energy is directed; rather, it is the "other"—real or imagined, internal or external—with whom the self desires relationship.

result of experience, but rather as the precondition for it. In an irreducible way, the self is the pre-existent starting point for all experience and provides continuity in all that develops later—coloring and shaping all subsequent experience. On the other hand, Fairbairn firmly maintained that it is in relationship to others that the self expresses its selfhood and is shaped in the course of its development. Fairbairn's theory of self is therefore "relational" in precisely the way described by Mitchell (1988), in which "the interpersonal and the intrapsychic realms create, interpenetrate, and transform each other in a subtle and complex manner" (p. 9).

It is the self in its relationship to the other that constitutes the only meaningful unit of consideration for Fairbairn. This unit of self, other, and the relationship in between becomes the pattern for Fairbairn's understanding of the form of all subsystems within the self.

The Inseparability of Energy and Structure

Central to Freud's conception of the organization of the psyche is the primary existence of an energic, chaotic entity, the id. The fundamental principle of the id is the immediate and indiscriminate discharge of its stimulus-related and endogenous excitation, and the subsequent evolution of a highly structured ego, adaptively derived to mediate contact between the psyche's energic underpinnings in the id and the realities of the external world (Freud, 1900, 1923, 1933). In this way, Freud separated the structure for achieving self-expression from that energy within the self that strives to be expressed.

Fairbairn adopted as his most fundamental postulate the notion that structure and energy are inseparable: "both structure divorced from energy and energy divorced from structure are meaningless concepts" (Fairbairn, 1952, p. 149). The structure *is* that which gives form to the energy, and the energy does not exist without a particular form. For him, "impulses" (a term he characteristically set off in quotation marks, to indicate his discomfort with this notion of energy treated as through it possessed some independent and separate existence)

> cannot be considered apart from the endopsychic structures which they energize and the object relationships which they enable these structures to establish; and, equally, "instincts" cannot profitably be considered as anything more than forms of energy which constitute the dynamic of such endopsychic structures. (p. 85)

In Fairbairn's system, the structure for achieving self-expression is inextricably interrelated with that which strives for expression. The self is simultaneously structure and energy, inseparable and mutually interdefining.

The Object-Related Nature of the Self

Even in Freud's late description of the id (1933), he envisioned the reservoir of energy within the psyche as seeking at all times the reduction of tension through the immediate and indiscriminate discharge of its energy. This pattern was termed by Freud the "pleasure principle." In it, there is virtually no consideration of the object toward which this discharge takes place. The pleasure principle was seen by Freud as being developmentally prior to operation in accordance with the reality principle—a mode more coordinated with the specific nature of the world of external objects, and involving delay of gratification, planning, and purposive awareness of cause and effect and of future consequence.

Fairbairn (1952, pp. 149 ff.) understood Freud's position to be a direct consequence of his divorcing of energy from structure, for what goal could there be for structureless, directionless energy other than indiscriminate discharge for the purpose of homeostasis? For Fairbairn, having initially postulated the inseparability of energy and structure, it followed that the goal (or aim) of self-expression could no longer be viewed as mere tension reduction (the discharge of energy, ending the "unpleasure" of excitation and thereby definitionally resulting in pleasure), with little or no reference to the object by means of which this discharge is accomplished. Rather, he completely inverted Freud's position, maintaining that relationship with the object is itself the goal, and that the pleasure involved is a secondary consequence. Thus, he wrote that "The function of libidinal pleasure is essentially to provide a signpost to the object" (1952, p. 33), and that "The real libidinal aim is the establishment of satisfactory relationship with objects" (p. 138).

To Fairbairn, the pleasure principle, rather than being the universal first principle of self-expression, "represents a deterioration of behaviour" (1952, p. 139). The rightful mode of libidinal expression, at all developmental levels, is more closely related to that described by Freud as the "reality principle," at least insofar as this expression is seen as always purposively intending toward relationship with objects in some realistic way, rather than toward pleasure itself:

> Explicit pleasure-seeking has as its essential aim the relieving of the tension of libidinal need for the mere sake of relieving this tension. Such a process does, of course, occur commonly enough; but, since libidinal need is object need, simple tension-relieving implies some failure of object-relationships. (p. 140)

Central to this theory is the concept that human beings do not naturally operate with the goal of reducing tensions, but rather with the goal of self-expression in relationships with other human beings. This view of fundamental human motivation is one of Fairbairn's most important contributions to contemporary relational theory.

Unitary and Dynamic Origin of the Psyche

Fairbairn maintained that the genesis of the human psyche lay in "an original and single dynamic ego-structure present at the beginning" (1952, p. 148); or, as he wrote elsewhere, "The pristine personality of the child consists of a unitary dynamic ego" (1954, p. 107). The individual elements of these statements are important enough to the theory to merit expansion and explication.

It is first necessary to note again that Fairbairn's use of the term "ego" is in no way equivalent to Freud's structural use of the term. Rather, it refers to the entirety of the psychic self. In adopting this connotation of "ego," Fairbairn is closely paralleling Freud's use of the term prior to his writing *The Ego and the Id*. As Strachey (1961) points out, Freud in this period used the term to apply to the whole of a person's self. Nevertheless, it would have been better if Fairbairn had substituted "self" for "ego" to distinguish his usage from Freud's. To minimize any possibility for confusion, and to emphasize the differences inherent in Fairbairn's conception, I have utilized "self" rather than "ego" here wherever practical.

That Fairbairn referred to this primitive state as a "dynamic ego-structure" or "dynamic ego" followed directly from his postulate of the inseparability of energy and structure. He could not posit, as had Freud, an unstructured supply of energy out of which an adaptive structure would subsequently develop. Rather, he insisted on the innate structural integrity of the self: The self is a "singular" and "unitary" whole. Furthermore, this self is the *a priori* condition of life experience: "Original" and "pristine," it exists from the very outset and is not in any way dependent upon experience for its existence.

When these notions are combined with Fairbairn's idea that psychic energy is object-seeking, the resulting conception of the psyche is that of a self-generated, unitary center of definition and energy, with the potential for (and the drive toward) self-expression outward into the object world, and the potential for experiencing that world, its own self-expression, and the resulting interaction between the two.

THE NATURE OF ENDOPSYCHIC STRUCTURE

The self as it has been described above requires no further structural development. It begins in a condition of wholeness, already capable of and actively involved in the self-defining processes of self-expression and of experience. Although this assertion naturally does not imply that the capacities of this primitive self are fully matured, it does insist that they are all present, at least in seminal form.

Fairbairn acknowledged that structural differentiation in fact does occur within the psyche—and even that it is unavoidable and universal (1954, p. 107). He saw the substructures resulting from such differentiations as modeled after the self as a whole: Each is comprised of an element of self in an energic, affective relationship with an element of the object world. He termed these resultant substructures of the self "endopsychic structures."[2]

Fairbairn noted (1952, Chapter 4) that certain unavoidable features of early human experience lead universally to the establishment of two such endopsychic structures: the first formed around the experience of the self in intolerably exciting relationship, and the second formed around intolerably rejecting relationship.

He understood that each of these subsystems of the self represents a particular crystallization of what originally was the growing and continually self-defining process of the self as a whole. Whereas the original self is in ongoing and essentially unbounded relationship with the outside world as a whole, such an endopsychic structure is a particularized aspect of that self, in specific relationship with a particular aspect of the object world. Fairbairn eventually came to realize (1952, p. 158) that the entirety of such a subsystem is what constitutes the endopsychic structure set up within the self. The first of the two such endopsychic structures referred to in the preceding paragraph is here termed the "libidinal self," as Fairbairn never developed an explicit terminology to refer to the entirety of the subsystem composed of what he termed the "libidinal ego" in specific relationship to what he called the "exciting object." Similarly, the second subsystem is termed the "antilibidinal self" (following Fairbairn's later terminology for the "internal saboteur" and its "rejecting object").

The third element in Fairbairn's picture of the structurally differentiated psyche is here termed the "central self," consisting of Fairbairn's "central ego" in relationship with the "idealized object." This entity is what remains of the original self after the other two parts have been separated off. Because of this unique aspect of its origin, as well as for other differences discussed below, the central self is not an "endopsychic structure" in the same sense as the other two entities.

---

[2]Although at times he is inconsistent in his use of this term, applying it to the component parts of these substructures as well as to the entire substructure, it is clear that it is the complete unit, based on the model of the self as a whole, that properly deserves the designation "endopsychic structure."

The fact that Fairbairn's model of endopsychic structure is tripartite naturally invites comparisons to Freud's structural model. Of course, a certain congruence is to be expected, since both metapsychological models attempt to describe the same clinical phenomena. Nevertheless, Fairbairn repeatedly rejected such comparisons (1952, pp. 106–107, 148, etc.).

Freud's ego rather closely corresponds to the "ego" component of Fairbairn's central self, in that the ego is the organization of purposive self-expression and experience in relationship with the external world. It was viewed by Freud as a derivative structure, however, and not as the original structure Fairbairn saw as the source of all other endopsychic structures. It must be agreed that, as Kernberg (see Chapter 4, this volume) maintains, the ego psychologists' notion of an undifferentiated ego–id matrix existing prior to the emergence of either individual structure furthers the Freudian model in a direction more consonant with that of Fairbairn. Nevertheless, the ego-psychological viewpoint still posits the eventual developmental necessity of the progressive structural differentiation of the ego from the id. In so doing, it clearly differs from Fairbairn's understanding of structure. Furthermore, the metapsychological foundations of the ego-psychological view still rest on a drive/structure model— albeit one that recognizes the central importance of relationship in achieving this end—whereas Fairbairn's metapsychology is founded on the need for self-expression in relationship.

The differences become more striking in comparisons drawn with the other two endopsychic structures. The libidinal ego, although certainly id-like in many aspects of its functioning, is consistently viewed by Fairbairn as existing in dynamic relationship with the exciting object; and the libidinal self constituted by this relationship is a proper subsystem of the self, in that it is specifically object-related in a manner foreign to the concept of the id. The libidinal self represents a particularized relation of a specific aspect of the self in relationship with a specific aspect of the object world, and not the more generalized, freely displaceable, and mutable energic center that the id is conceived of as being. The superego is to some extent related to the rejecting object of the antilibidinal self, although not coterminous with it. The rejecting object does contain the more archaic elements of the superego, although the moral aspects of superego functioning are more closely related to the relationship with the idealized object that occurs in the central self, and to what Fairbairn discussed as the "mechanism of the moral defense." Moreover, the superego concept emphasizes the object component of the antilibidinal self, and not the antilibidinal ego component; it therefore becomes necessary to include the ego's relationship with the superego to make a more appropriate comparison.

The ego-psychological branch of object relations theory (most ably represented by Jacobson and Kernberg) has attempted, with considerable success, to transform Freud's metapsychology in a direction more consonant with the insights of Fairbairn. Yet it is not possible fully to incorporate Fairbairn's insights without abandoning central tenets of Freud's metapsychology, contrary to the claim to this effect made by Kernberg (Chapter 4, this volume).

Freud's structural model simply is not the same as Fairbairn's system of central, libidinal, and antilibidinal selves. Nor do the modifications introduced by ego psychology suffice to make Fairbairn's system subsumable under their revised drive/structure model. In the first place, the "self-component" of endopsychic structures is not the equivalent of "what we would now call a self-representation," as Kernberg claims (Chapter 4, p. 60). One of the most brilliant of Fairbairn's insights lies precisely in his recognition that the self—and not some ideational representation (for who, in that case, would be the one doing the representing?)— has as its primary, innate function active expression in the form of relationship with the object world, and not (until the intervention of some pathological process) with some ideational representation thereof. To alter this conception is to eschew the most essential thrust of Fairbairn's theory.

It is precisely Kernberg's refusal to acknowledge this difference that leads him to cite the criticism put forth by Winnicott and Khan (1953) of Fairbairn's concept of "primary identification" (which he described as a relationship between the self and an object that has not been differentiated from it):

> If the object is not differentiated it cannot operate as an object. What Fairbairn is referring to then is an infant with needs, but with no "mechanism" by which to implement them, an infant not "seeking" an object, but seeking de-tension, libido seeking satisfaction, instinct tension seeking a return to a state of rest or un-excitement; which brings us back to Freud. (p. 332)

The self in Fairbairn's theory is a living, growing, self-defining center that he viewed as the point of origin of human psychic process; it follows directly from this most basic of principles that it is possible for such a self to have relationships with other human beings, even though they have not yet representationally differentiated as objects separate from the self. Initially this self relates to the world with little basis in experience for self–object differentiation. Nevertheless, it does express itself and experience the world in a manner that is precisely the prototype for all later activities of the self. To assert that this brings Fairbairn's theory back to the pleasure principle of Freud is to miss his point completely.

It is an actual fragment of the self, and not a representation of it, that comprises the essence of an endopsychic structure in Fairbairn's theory. As a subsystem of the self, such a structure is a purposive entity with its own energy. It is not reducible, as Kernberg (Chapter 4, this volume) suggests it is, to self- and object representations energized by "an activation of affects reflecting . . . drives in the context of internal object relations" (pp. 59–60). Such a view is quite closely related to Freud's drive/structure model, modified to include the notion of the expression of drive derivatives in object-relational constellations—but is not at all the same as Fairbairn's relational/structure model.

The libidinal and antilibidinal selves differ from the original self in only two ways. The first difference is that each is a crystallization of what in the original self was a more freely developing potentiality. Whereas the original self (and later the central self, in a more limited way) was free to experience the world and express itself in relationships to that world, the subsidiary selves carry within them a pre-existing template (based on the experiences out of which they were formed) for particularized relationships with specific aspects of the world. As in the case of the central self, the libidinal and antilibidinal selves continue to seek experience and self-expression through relationship. In the case of the libidinal and antilibidinal selves, however, this process is sharply restricted by the fact that the particularized crystallization involved in the formation of each structure tends to permit only that experience and expression which is fundamentally consonant with the specific template involved. Thus, while there is a certain amount of growth within these subsidiary self systems, it is minimal. This limitation on the growth and change of the libidinal and antilibidinal selves is more potently enforced by the factor that is the second way in which they differ from the original self, and later from the central self: They were created in an act of repression and at all times continue under the pressure of this repression.

STRUCTURE AS PATHOLOGY

Virtually all psychoanalytic theories have accepted a metaphor for psychic growth that has been borrowed from biology: "Growth" is defined as movement through progressive levels of structural differentiation and complexity. This metaphor is manifested in Freud's notion that psychic growth (and health) involves the differentiation of an ego, structurally separate from the id, and later a superego, precipitated out from the ego. It also stands at the root of the generally accepted belief that the self–object differentiation implies structural differentiation within the psyche—and the unspoken underlying assumption that the process of self- and object representation is a structural one.

In his most radical departure from the mainstream of psychoanalytic thought, Fairbairn maintained that, far from being the necessary condition for psychic growth, structural differentiation is a defensive and pathological process in human development.

Fairbairn discussed at great length the process by which the psyche of the infant, because of some intolerable inability to cope with the unsatisfying aspects of experience, internalizes this experience in such a way as ultimately to eventuate in the establishment of certain endopsychic structures. The creation of such structures involves the splitting of the self and the repression of that part of the self that has been thus split off.

Repression is the key element in the creation of endopsychic structure, because it is the mechanism by which the self becomes split. Experience that is capable of being integrated into the self results simply in memory or in the gradual alteration of the nature of the self as a whole. It is only when such experience is not amenable to integration—when it is so intolerable as not to be permitted into consciousness (which, after all, is that which is "knowable together," or "capable of being integrated")—that it must be subjected to repression. When that which is thus in need of repressing is importantly a part of the self—in other words, when it is relationally so intrinsic to the life of that self that it is part of the definition of that self—then the act of repression must be understood as a splitting of the self. "Repression" and "splitting" in this structural sense are merely different perspectives on the identical operation. A particular aspect of the self, defined by its particular affective and purposive relationship with a particularized object, and reflecting a fundamental aspect of self-definition within the psyche, too intrinsic and powerful to be abandoned and too intolerable and unacceptable to be integrated into the whole—this fully functional, albeit crystallized, subsystem of the self is what becomes an endopsychic structure by virtue of the act of its repression. If it were not repressed, it would continue to exist within the conscious matrix of the self; there would be no splitting of that self, and consequently no formation of endopsychic structure.

Fairbairn came to this understanding in stages. At first, differing from what he viewed as Freud's mistaken notion that what is subject to repression must be either intolerably unpleasant memories or intolerably guilty impulses, Fairbairn (1952, p. 62) developed the idea that it is intolerably "bad" objects that are subject to repression. He later altered this view:

It becomes necessary to adopt the view that repression is exercised not only against internalized objects (which incidentally are only meaningful when regarded in the light of endopsychic structures) but also against ego-structures which seek relationships with these internal objects. This view implies that there must be a splitting of the ego to account for repression. (1952, p. 168)

Although Fairbairn repeatedly referred separately to the repression of objects and the splitting of the self, it is clear from this quotation that he understood the two to be inextricably bound together in a manner clearly justifying the use of the notion employed in this chapter that it is the entire subsystem of the self (including both the object and what he termed the "ego"—or self—element) that is repressed in the very act that creates its existence as endopsychic structure.

Thus it was that Fairbairn arrived at the notion that existence as a structure within the self means existence as a split-off subsystem of the self, created and maintained by repression, and owing its existence to the self's inability to deal with some important aspect of its experience that it found intolerable. He termed the process of establishing such structures "schizoid," because the splitting and repression by which it is constituted invariably diminish the self's capacity for growth and expression, and are therefore pathological.

The libidinal and antilibidinal selves, by their very existence, limit the range and depth of the conscious functioning open to the central self. Both of these endopsychic structures press continually for the recreation of experience of the sort that occasioned their creation. This experience always has two determining characteristics: It is equally experienced as intolerably "bad" (which, in Fairbairn's terminology, means "unsatisfying"), and it is equally experienced as being needed by the self absolutely for survival.

It is in this way that Fairbairn accounted for the clinically ubiquitous phenomenon of the repetition compulsion. There exists, at the very structural foundation of these subsidiary selves, an attachment to some negative aspect of experience that is felt as vital to the definition of the self (at least in the specific particularization thereof involved in each subsystem). The raison d'être of these endopsychic structures is to continue living out these "bad" relationships. Much as the original self sought to express psychic existence of the whole person, such a subsystem seeks at all times to express itself and to have experience in accordance with the template based on the formative intolerable experience that defines its existence. Thus the existence of such an endopsychic structure leads to the seeking of relationships that will be consonant with the specific neurotic paradigms of early experience; to the distortion of current relationships so that they can be experienced in accordance with such paradigms; and to the patterning of activity in the world so as to be expressive of such a relationship—and, as a result, to restrict the freer, more situationally appropriate expression of the self and experience of the world.

It is important to note that this theory is not only more parsimonious than Freud's appeals to explanations based on mastery, masochism, and finally a death instinct; it also provides a direct explanation for the clinically observed sense of loss that is involved when patients, as the result of a successful psychoanalytic process, begin to relinquish their tenacious adherence to such patterns. The loss is twofold: Most obviously, it involves the loss of the object component, which is felt as having made possible the particular internal relationship; and, perhaps more importantly, albeit less obviously, it involves a sense of loss of self, insofar as part of the self has been defined in the crystallization around the particular paradigm.

The fact that the libidinal and antilibidinal selves always exist under repression contributes further to their pathological nature. Although in Fairbairn's view these structures are at least minimally able to grow and evolve through progressive accretion and overlay of later experience (insofar as the experience is fundamentally consonant with the defining paradigm), the isolating effort of the repression results in an inertia that is not readily overcome. Central to the nature of this repression—and the resistance it subsequently offers to growth and change—is the attachment that has just been described. The self chooses to encapsulate and crystallize these aspects of itself and of its relationships, rather than to be at risk for their loss.[3] This maintenance of the internal world as a closed system is what Fairbairn (1958) ultimately described as "the greatest of all sources of resistance" (p. 380). Furthermore,

A real relationship with an external object is a relationship in an open system; but, in so far as the inner world assumes the form of a closed system, a relationship with an external object is only possible in terms of transference, viz., on condition that the external object is treated as an object within the closed system of inner reality. (p. 381)

The splits that create endopsychic structures are, of course, variable in their extent and depth, depending on the nature of the relationships out of which they have developed (which involve the specific strengths and weaknesses—constitutional and developmental—of the child, as well as those of the parent, and the vicissitudes of their interactions). The more profound the splits, and the more extensive and more deeply repressed the subsidiary selves that they engender, the greater the pathological effect on the central self. Just as this central self is what remains after the splitting off of the libidinal and antilibidinal selves, so too will the central self's

[3]A fuller exploration of this process and its central role in psychopathology is presented in my paper on tragedy (Rubens, 1992).

ongoing experience and expression be diminished by the tendency of the subsidiary selves to limit and to transform subsequent experience and expression according to the closed systems of their defining paradigms. The more extensive the portion of the self that has been repressed, the less that is available for open, ongoing interaction with the world.

Not only the quantity of the central self's experience and expression is diminished by the extent of the subsidiary selves; the quality of its relating to the world is similarly diminished. The more severe the tendency to experience the external world in accordance with the subsidiary selves, the more impoverished and idealized the nature of the objects with which the central self relates. It is in this light that the objects of the central self become the idealized object, rather than the actual objects of external reality—which is to say that all of the complexity and imperfection must be abstracted out and subsumed into the experience of the subsidiary selves. This position is fully in harmony with the clinical observation that all idealizations are invariably based on the denial of some experienced imperfection, inadequacy, or "badness."

The upshot of Fairbairn's theory is that healthy development is not dependent upon the establishment of endopsychic structures; rather, it is that such internal structural differentiation is a clearly pathological (albeit unavoidable) schizoid phenomenon, which, to varying extents, diminishes the functioning of all human beings. As Fairbairn (1952) concluded,

> Psychology may be said to resolve itself into a study of the relationships of the individual to his objects, whilst, in similar terms, psychopathology may be said to resolve itself more specifically into a study of the relationships of the ego to its internalized objects. (p. 60)

On the other hand "The chief aim of psychoanalytical treatment is to promote a maximum 'synthesis' of the structures into which the original ego has been split" (Fairbairn, 1958, p. 380).

NONSTRUCTURING INTERNALIZATION

Perhaps the most confused issue in Fairbairn's writings is the question of internalization. This confusion results from the fact that he used the concept of "internalization" in two distinctly different ways, while never acknowledging that the difference existed.

The first sense of "internalization" is the one that Fairbairn clearly delineated in his theory and that has been discussed in detail in the preceding two sections of this chapter. It is this form of internalization that eventuates in the formation of repressed endopsychic structures. For the purpose of clarifying the distinction that Fairbairn did not make explicit, this process is here called "structuring internalization."

As noted above, only intolerably "bad" experience gives rise to structuring internalization. It is to just such structuring internalization that Fairbairn was referring in his major theoretical disagreement with Melanie Klein. Klein posited the internalization of both good and bad objects. Fairbairn (1952, Chapters 3, 4, and 7) repeatedly disagreed, insisting that only bad objects are internalized: "It is difficult to find any adequate motive for the internalization of objects which are satisfying and "good" (Fairbairn, 1952, p. 93). Fairbairn's assertion here is that good objects are never *structurally* internalized, which follows directly from the fact that there would be no explanation for the repression (which is the essential ingredient of the formation of endopsychic structure), were it not for the intolerable "badness" of the experience with an object.

In apparent contradiction to this strongly propounded position, Fairbairn elsewhere (1952) writes of the internalization of "good" objects. He made it clear, however, that the internalized "good" object is the idealized object of the central self, which is a system in which none of the components is under structural repression. The apparent contradiction thus is easily resolved by the recognition that "good" objects, while they are internalized, are never subjected to structure generating repression. This process, in which there occurs no repression, and therefore no self-splitting and no formation of endopsychic structure, is here termed "non-structuring internalization." Thus, it can be true that only "bad" objects are involved in structuring internalization; it also can be true that "good" objects are internalized, but only in the nonstructuring sense.[4]

[4]Fairbairn specifically wrote about the existence of the early internalization of "good" objects as part of his revised notion of the process through which structuring internalization occurs (1952, pp. 134 ff.). According to this view, what is initially internalized is the "preambivalent object," which subsequently undergoes a tripartite split into exciting and rejecting "bad" objects, and an "accepted object" (which is what remains of the original preambivalent object after it has been divested of its "bad" components). This third internalized object, later identified by Fairbairn (1954) as the idealized object, does therefore constitute a "good" internalized object. Nevertheless, Fairbairn (1954, p. 107) makes very clear that the internalization of the preambivalent object must still be regarded as a defensive maneuver, motivated by the need to deal with the *unsatisfying* (i.e., "bad") components of that object. Furthermore, it is *only* these "bad" elements that are repressed and internalized in a way that generates structure-producing splits in the self. The "good" internalized object is in no way seen as subject to the same repression and splitting of the self, and therefore may appropriately be subsumed under the rubric of nonstructuring internalization.

It is obvious that a human being needs to be able to internalize aspects of his experience in the world in order to grow and thrive. There must be learning that takes place as the result of both positive and negative interactions, and this learning must be integrated into the self in some meaningful way. Although Fairbairn did not explicitly write about the nature of growth process, it is implicitly contained in the notion of nonstructuring internalization. To understand Fairbairn's position on the nature of the process of nonstructuring internalization, it is necessary to extrapolate from certain other of his previously discussed positions.

The most central principle, deriving from the definition of nonstructuring internalization, is that such a process cannot lead to repression. Clearly, there is no need for the self to repress segments of its experience that are "good," or even that are "bad" in a tolerable way. Rather, such experience must be capable of being integrated into the self in a manner that remains conscious and openly available.

Second, it should be clear that such a process cannot lead to the formation of endopsychic structure. Rather, nonstructuring internalization must be viewed as resulting in memory, or in the conscious organization of experience. The progressive development of a personal *Weltansicht*—viewed from any of what is an unlimited range of possible perspectives, be it that of Kant's categories of experience, Kohlberg's moral schema of development, or any other dimension of developmental progression—implies learning, memory, organization, and synthesis, but *not* structural differentiation. Even the all important development of self–object differentiation does not, of necessity, imply the structural differentiation *of* the self; rather, it implies the progressive recognition of the separateness of that self *from* the external world with which it interacts, and a progressive organization of the self's awareness of its own nature and potential.[5] In addition, it must be remembered that in Fairbairn's schema any fragmentation of the self cannot be viewed as a developmental arrest, but rather must be seen as some pathological miscarriage of development.

A further extrapolation can be made from another disagreement between Fairbairn and Klein. Fairbairn (1952) wrote:

> As it seems to me, Melanie Klein has never satisfactorily explained how phantasies of incorporating objects orally can give rise to the establishment of internal objects as endopsychic structures—and, unless they are such structures, they cannot be properly spoken of as internal objects at all, since otherwise they will remain mere figments of phantasy. (p. 154)

[5]This process, referred to by Fairbairn (1952, Chapter 2) as the progressive growth from infantile dependence to mature dependence, is discussed below in the section "The Growth of the Self."

It is clear from this position that nonstructuring internalization does not result in the establishment of any "entity" within the self, but rather results in an alteration of the integration of the self, or in the production of a thought, memory, or fantasy within the self.

Kernberg (1976) has presented a schema for the nature of internalization that is relevant to the present discussion. He writes:

> All processes of internalization of object relations refer to the internalization of units of affective state, object-representation, and self-representation. Following Erikson . . . I considered introjection, identification, and ego identity as a progressive sequence of such internalization processes. In the case of introjection, object- and self-representations are not yet fully differentiated from each other, and their affect is primitive, intense and diffuse. In the case of identification, not only is there a well-established separation between self- and object-representations, but there is an internalization of a role aspect of the relationship, that is, of a socially recognized function that is being actualized in the self–object interaction. The affective state is less intense, less diffuse, and . . . the spectrum of affect dispositions is broadened and deepened. . . . Ego identity may be thought of as the supraordinate integration of identifications into a dynamic, unified structure. (pp. 75–76)

Although in Fairbairn's theory the notion of structure is radically different, and a relational/structure model is employed rather than a drive/structure model, the phenomena being described in both theories are closely related. There is a high degree of correspondence between Fairbairn's nonstructuring internalization and Kernberg's concept of "ego identity." Both theories recognize that there is a continuity of self-experience and self-expression involved in such internalization, which results in progressively higher levels of synthesis and integration.

The opposite is true with respect to structuring internalization, which, like Kernberg's "introjection," refers to a level of functioning in which discontinuity and unintegrability result in a pathological form of internalization involving the splitting of the self and the radical formation of structure. Kernberg wrote of this process of introjection and the structures resulting from it: "The persistence of 'nonmetabolized' early introjections is the outcome of a pathological fixation of severely disturbed, early object relations, a fixation which is intimately related to the pathological development of splitting" (1976, p. 34).

Kernberg's intermediate mode of internalization, the important issue of "identification," is less obviously but just as certainly related to Fairbairn's nonstructuring internalization. Kernberg describes normal identification as follows:

(1) a partial modification of the total self-concept under the influence
of a new self-representation, (2) some degree of integration of both self-
and object-representations into autonomous ego functioning in the form
of neutralized character traits, and (3) some degree of reorganization of
the individual's behavior patterns under the influence of the newly introduced identificatory structure. (1976, p. 78)

Once again it is crucial to note the emphasis on continuity and integration within the larger unity of the self, as opposed to any sense of structural isolation within that whole. Even in what Kernberg termed
"pathological identification," it is clear that the correspondence is to nonstructuring internalization, although in this case the process takes place
largely in relation to either the libidinal or the antilibidinal self rather
than to the central self. This fact accounts for the rigidity and crystallization Kernberg observed to be characteristic of such internalizations:

> The final outcome of pathological identification processes is character
> pathology. The more rigid and neurotic the character traits are, the more
> they reveal that a past pathogenic internalized object relation (represent-
> ing a particular conflict) has become "frozen" into a character pattern.
> (1976, p. 79)

Although such identifications take place under the influence of pathological endopsychic structures and can slowly alter the nature of these
structures, they do not eventuate in any further formation of such structures.
    Kernberg (1976, 1980; see Chapter 4, this volume) is one of the first
important theorists who has explored and acknowledged the importance
of Fairbairn's theories, and it is clear that he has integrated into his theory
many valuable aspects of Fairbairn's thought. Most centrally, Kernberg
has accepted the notion that internalizations, on all levels, have the basic
form suggested by Fairbairn—an element of self, an element of object,
and the affective, purposive relationship between them. It is also clear
that Kernberg agrees that higher forms of internalization involve less
disjunction in the self and more integration and continuity. It remains as
a fundamental difference, however, that Kernberg integrates these insights
into a drive/structure model, whereas Fairbairn was intentionally departing from such a model. Moreover, Kernberg, like virtually every other
psychoanalytic theorist, maintains that the progressively higher levels of
internalization involve *increasing* levels of internal structure. In contradistinction, Fairbairn demonstrated that it is not necessary to view the
higher levels of internalization as creating structure *at all*. Rather, he

showed that there is a conceptual advantage to differentiating structuring internalization, which is invariably pathological, from nonstructuring internalization, which is defined by its continuity with and potential for integration into the self as a whole. Although Kernberg obviously agrees with Fairbairn's observations concerning the phenomenological differences involved in these different levels of internalization, he does not adopt Fairbairn's conclusions about the nature of structure itself. Thus, despite the similarities, there are profound differences between them when it comes to crucial issues such as the internalization of good experience and the metapsychological understanding of the self in which these questions occur.

The vicissitudes of these forms of internalization and their interrelationships are at the heart of Fairbairn's developmental notion of the movement from infantile to mature dependence, the central issue in which being the move away from primary identification (which, it is interesting to note, is the same issue of self–object differentiation that is central to Kernberg's hierarchy of forms of internalization).

THE GROWTH OF SELF[6]

Fairbairn chose to discuss the development of the self in terms of levels of dependency. In so doing, he was emphasizing his contention that all meaningful human activity—from its most primitive to its very highest expression—is at all times involved with relationship (be it with actual people in the external world or with the memory or fantasy of people in the inner world), and that the primary and ultimate goal of this activity, even in neonates, is self-expression in relationship.

Views of healthy adult development almost invariably include a positive notion of interdependence with significant others, and particularly of intense closeness and interrelatedness with loved ones. In such love relationships, it is clearly acknowledged that it is a virtue to be the sort of person who both can "be depended on" and can "depend on" a partner. Fairbairn, in labeling the highest level of development "mature dependence," was choosing to emphasize the importance of human interrelatedness and interdependence.

Dependency, in its pejorative sense, was associated by Fairbairn with the concept of infantile dependence. In doing so he was assigning the

---

[6]The material in this section is the subject of "Fairbairn's Developmental Theory" (Rubens, 1993), where they are discussed in greater detail.

pathology not to the dependency itself, but rather to its infantile character.

Central to Fairbairn's notion of infantile dependence, and almost synonymous with it (1952, p. 42), is his concept of "primary identification."
In primary identification, the infant relates to an other whom he does
not experience as separate or different from himself. It is clear that what
is taking place *does* represent a form of relating—complete with a sense
of intentionality and expression of the subject involved. Nevertheless, it
is equally apparent that the subject is not aware in any differentiated way
of the other person as being separate and apart from him. Fairbairn's
contention was that the reality of both sides of this situation needs to be
accepted: There is a relationship occurring, and self–object differentiation is not present (to a greater or lesser extent).

Although Fairbairn was completely insistent that the infant is object-
related from birth, he acknowledged that the infantile dependent relatedness of the earliest stages has specifically primitive characteristics: (1) It
is unconditional; (2) the quality of need is absolute (if the infant's needs
are not met, he will die); and (3) the infant is not aware of any sense of
option or choice of object (there is no experience of alternative, and the
failure of the relationship to meet the infant's needs is tantamount to death).

The process of psychological maturation, in Fairbairn's scheme of
the movement from infantile to mature dependence, consists of the gradual
"abandonment of relationships based on primary identification in favor
of relationships with differentiated objects" (1952, p. 42). The key element in this change is the progressive differentiation of the object from
the self: "The more mature a relationship is, the less it is characterized
by primary identification" (1952, p. 34 n.).

Fairbairn was clear that this process is a continuous one, ranging
through various levels of self–object differentiation. At its most infantile
level, there is no sense of separation between self and other—and thus
there can be no awareness of any concept of self or other. As the infant
has experience in the world, he gradually begins to organize an awareness of self and a concomitant awareness of other.

Although Fairbairn did not address the point, his system has obvious implications for the understanding of the highest levels of self–other
differentiation. This process does not cease with the establishment of the
notion that there is a discontinuity between one's self and others (physically as well as psychologically); rather, it involves progressive levels of
organization of the meaning of this differentiation and of the nature of
the objects being differentiated. Ultimately, it is possible to utilize this
schema to explore differences in the most mature levels of emotional
development. For example, it is possible to see even moral development
as an issue of learning to understand others as differentiated to the point

of being ends in themselves (cf. Kant, 1785) and having an equally valid claim on shaping and defining their own experience and meaning.

The state of mature dependence implies a recognition of the separateness of individuals, even while they are involved in the most intimate and interdependent of relationships. Separateness thus in no way implies isolation or even disconnection. Rather, separateness hinges on the recognition of the existence of the selfhood of the other, ultimately conceived of in a form that is not subsumable by one's own selfhood. It is the recognition that the other is a center of experience and intentionality, feeling and will, thought and purposiveness. In other words, it involves the acknowledgment of the unique individuality of the other in a way that is in no way diminished by the existence of the relationship between the self and that other. It should be clear that perhaps the most salient practical touchstones for this sort of separateness are the recognition and acceptance of individual responsibility.

Between the stages of infantile dependence and mature dependence, Fairbairn envisaged a stage that he termed "quasi-independence." It should be clear from what has been noted above that this term is designed, in part, as a negative comment on the traditional emphasis placed on independence in most developmental theories. Nevertheless, it is also designed to convey a sense of the struggle at this level to move out of the state of infantile dependence in a way that is still very much attached to that very state. (For this reason, Fairbairn also referred to this stage as "transitional.") The state of quasi-independence is ultimately doomed to failure, because it consists of an attempt to change an earlier state without relinquishing the essential tenets of that state. It is that state out of which neuroses, as classically conceived, arise; thus it is fitting that it be predicated on a situation of conflict between the preservation and abandonment, the expression and inhibition, of an infantile state of affairs.

It is essential to realize that Fairbairn's entire conception of how the self grows is in no way predicated upon the process of structural differentiation. The self's growing awareness of individuation and separateness is based on integrated development of the whole of that self. As the individual achieves progressively higher levels of organization and interpretation of his experience, he functions with an increasing level of self—object differentiation, and moves from operation in an infantile dependent mode toward a progressively more adult mode of mature dependence. This movement represents the growth of the self as a whole, proceeding through the process of nonstructuring internalization, and not through the establishment of divisions or structures within the self. This latter process of structuring internalization has been shown to be essential to the development of psychopathology, but not to the healthy development of the self.

CONCLUSION

It has been shown that Fairbairn's structural model of the psyche is in no way the same as Freud's drive/structure model. Fairbairn's theory is archetypally a relational/structure model. Based on the assumption that the fundamental human motivation is for self-expression in relationship, it is a theory that takes as the fundamental structural building block the constellation of self, other, and the relationship in between. Substructures of the self are naturally seen as conforming to this same pattern. Furthermore, the theory is predicated on a radically different notion of the nature of structure itself.

Fairbairn's insistence that structure implies pathology and that wholeness and integration imply health is unique among psychoanalytic theories. It presupposes a notion of the self that is in itself a radical departure. For Fairbairn, the self is not reducible to a self-concept, or a self-representation, or a system of reflected appraisals. It is a self-generating center of origin that, although it is shaped and changed in relation to its objects (or, more accurately, its "others") and does in part define itself in terms of those relationships, has an expressive, experiencing existence separate from and prior to these relationships.

There is room in Fairbairn's theory to accommodate identifications and representations of self and objects, as there is room to accommodate systems of reflected appraisals. These can be viewed as aspects of the self's experience of itself and its world. The major innovative insight of Fairbairn was that these phenomena do not in any way require structural differentiation of the self. Rather, he made a clear and crucially useful distinction between these nonstructuring internalizations, which are far more related to memory and the progressive organization of experience (and which do involve representations of self and object), and the internalizations that involve actual segments of the self (not representations thereof) and that therefore create real structures within the self-crystallized subsystems, which function within the self with a dissociated life of their own.

REFERENCES

Fairbairn, W. R. D. (1952). *Psychological Studies of the Personality*. London: Tavistock.

Fairbairn, W. R. D. (1954). Observations on the nature of hysterical states. *British Journal of Medical Psychology, 27*, 105–125.

Fairbairn, W. R. D. (1958). On the nature and aims of psycho-analytical treatment. *International Journal of Psycho-Analysis, 39*, 374–385.

Freud, S. (1900). The interpretation of dreams. *Standard Edition, 4*, 1–338; *5*, 339–627.

Freud, S. (1923). The ego and the id. *Standard Edition, 19,* 3–66.
Freud, S. (1933). New introductory lectures on psycho-analysis. *Standard Edition, 22,* 1–182.
Greenberg, J. R., & Mitchell, S. A. (1983). *Object Relations in Psychoanalytic Theory.* Cambridge, MA: Harvard University Press.
Kant, I. (1785). *Foundations of the Metaphysics of Morals,* L. W. Beck, trans. New York: Liberal Arts Press, 1959.
Kernberg, O. F. (1976). *Object Relations Theory and Clinical Psychoanalysis.* New York: Jason Aronson.
Kernberg, O. F. (1980). *Internal World and External Reality.* New York: Jason Aronson.
Mitchell, S. A. (1988). *Relational Concepts in Psychoanalysis: An Integration.* Cambridge, MA: Harvard University Press.
Rubens, R. L. (1984). The meaning of structure in Fairbairn. *International Review of Psycho-Analysis, 11,* 429–440.
Rubens, R. L. (1992). Psychoanalysis and the tragic sense of life. *New Issues in Psychology, 10*(3), 347–362.
Rubens, R. L. (1993). Fairbairn's developmental theory. Manuscript in preparation.
Strachey. J. (1961). Editor's introduction to "The ego and the id" by S. Freud. *Standard Edition, 19,* 3–11.
Winnicott, D. W. (1965). *The Maturational Processes and the Facilitating Environment.* New York: International Universities Press.
Winnicott, D. W., & Khan, M. M. R. (1953). Book review of *Psychological Studies of the Personality* by W. R. D. Fairbairn. *International Journal of Psycho-Analysis, 34,* 329–333.

9

Endopsychic Structure and the Cartography of the Internal World: Six Endopsychic Characters in Search of an Author

JAMES S. GROTSTEIN

INTRODUCTION

Fairbairn's central contribution to psychoanalytic theory—"endopsychic structure"—constitutes a radical revision of a fundamental tenet of Freudian theory, the primacy of the pleasure–unpleasure principle. Fairbairn maintained that the infant's need for object relatedness, not libidinal discharge, is the operating principle of emotional health and disease. To illustrate the primacy of object relatedness, Fairbairn fashioned a new understanding of the infant's internal world, one characterized by objects and egos in dynamic interplay. Fairbairn's model of mind reintroduced a phenomenon that had become all but lost to psychoanalysis—that of the "alter ego." The essence of Fairbairn's endopsychic structure—his diagrammatic sketching of the six psychical structures (three objects and three egos)—is captured in the title of one of Pirandello's (1921/1952) plays *Six Characters in Search of an Author*.[1] Fairbairn, like Pirandello, was intrigued by the complexity of endopsychic structure, and particularly the possibility of an alter ego or "second self." Once a cornerstone of

[1] I am grateful to John Padel for calling my attention to the analogy with Pirandello.

174

psychoanalytic theory, the alter ego phenomenon has since been rediscovered and documented by brain laterality research (Gazzaniga & LeDoux, 1975); it has also found a structural home in psychoanalysis, thanks to Fairbairn's unique architecture of the mind (Grotstein, 1991a, 1991b, 1991c, 1991d).

Fairbairn's concept of endopsychic structure was a psychoanalytic "Reformation," analogous to Martin Luther's posting of his 95 theses on the door of the cathedral at Wittenberg. It set forth an ego deficit model for the first time in psychoanalysis. In his reformulation, endopsychic structure is a statement both of the infant's loss of hope and trust in his primary caregivers, *and* of a need to internalize their bad or unsatisfying aspects. The incorporated (internal) objects constitute the infant's self-conception of "immorality" and become the counterparts to what Freud (1923) referred to as "the seething cauldron," the id. Repression consequently defends not against drives per se, but against the re-emergence into consciousness of bad objects (and egos identified with them). Thus, the infant resorts to internalizing the rejecting or disappointing objects to protect against the trauma of abandonment or loss.

In revising psychic structure, Fairbairn shifted the psychoanalytic emphasis from (horizontal) drive-based *repression* to a (vertical) *splitting* of internal objects and attached egos. He returned to an early view of hysteria (Janet, 1889, 1893) to help frame his new understanding of splitting. As Janet saw it, hysteria is a *maladie faiblesse*—a weakness of the organizing and integrating capacity of the mind that results in a splitting of consciousness. Although Janet's ideas became eclipsed by Freud's discovery of unconscious motive, Fairbairn took up Janet's notion of hysteria as a (vertical) splitting of consciousness; indeed, he regarded splitting as equivalent to, if not more important than, repression.

Fairbairn's belief that splitting results from a deficiency in the nurturing of the ego, rather than the intrinsic immorality of drives, heralded the ascendancy of infantile innocence (Grotstein, 1994a) over original sin. The infant's need to internalize bad objects constitutes a loss of "innocence" and a need to resort to a substitutive default mode of dissociated relating based upon the premise of expediency rather than basic trust and unconditional love (Grotstein, 1992, 1993, 1994a). One of the profoundest revelations of this revised structural scheme is our understanding that the presence of bad internal objects greatly impedes the infant's capacity to mature—and the patient's potential for progress.

The worse the object, the more it is internalized; the more it is internalized, the more tenaciously binding is the ego's identificatory relationship to it. Although Fairbairn maintained that good objects do not need to be internalized, he could have said that a good object leaves a good internal *legacy*, which allows for freedom and individuation.

BACKGROUND OF THE STRUCTURAL THEORY

The psychoanalytic conception of psychic structure has had few commentaries since Freud (1923) established the tripartite psychical organization of ego, id, and superego. Freud's related conceptions include the topographic theory (the conscious [Cs.], unconscious [Ucs.], and preconscious [Pcs.] systems; Freud, 1905); the ego ideal as a gradient in the ego (Freud, 1914); the concept of "internalized objects" in the ego and in the ego ideal (Freud, 1917), the concept of the "alter ego" or "second self" (Freud, 1919, but also adumbrated in Breuer & Freud, 1893–1895); the projective identification of the individual ego ideal into the leader of the group, and the concept of people in a group behaving as if they were a single organism (Freud, 1921, 1923); splitting of the ego (Freud, 1925, 1927); the concept of identification as a structure that forms "new psychical agencies" (Freud, 1940a); and a continuation of his earlier conception of splitting of the ego (Freud, 1940b). But these concepts have never been sufficiently integrated with the tripartite conception of psychic structure.

The classical (ego psychology) notion of the representational world[2], despite its adaptational modification of Freud's tripartite structural organization, is still rooted in the primacy of libido. Kernberg's (1980 and Chapter 4, this volume) formulation of primitive psychic structure as the product of a split between libidinal and aggressive selfobject representations attempts to unify aspects of Fairbairn's endopsychic structure and Klein's (1946) concept of splitting. Modell (Chapter 10, this volume) has also called attention to the failure of Fairbairn's failure in formulating endopsychic structure to deal adequately with affects.

In borderlines, Kernberg claims a polarized development of the split affect–selfobject representations. In the pathological grandiose self of the narcissist, he envisions a condensation of a real self, an ideal self, and the ideal object, the last of these being a term he has borrowed from Fairbairn.

Kohut (1971) has commented on two (horizontal and vertical) splits in the ego of narcissistic patients:

[2]It is of no small moment to recognize that there is less correspondence than meets the eye between British "internal objects" and American "object representations," as I have discussed in Chapter 7. The former are montages of parts of the self intermixed with images of objects from which separation has not yet been achieved, whereas representations are symbolic signifiers of external objects (in their absence) from which separation has *already* been achieved. Another rarely mentioned distinction between the internal object and the symbolic object representation is the self's investment of *subjectivity* in the latter. Thus, the term "object representation" is, from this standpoint, an oxymoron.

The acceptance by the analyst of the phase-appropriateness of the analysand's narcissistic demands counteracts the chronic tendency of the reality ego to wall itself off from the unrealistic narcissistic structures by such mechanisms as repression, isolation, or disavowal. Correlated with the last-named mechanism is a specific, chronic structural change to which I would refer, in modification of Freud's terminology (1927, 1937 . . .), as a *vertical split in the psyche*. The ideational and emotional manifestations of a vertical split in the psyche—in contrast to such *horizontal splits* as brought about on a deeper level by repression and on a higher level by negation (Freud, 1925)—are correlated to the side-by-side, conscious existence of otherwise incompatible psychological attitudes *in depth*. (pp. 176–177; emphasis in original)

It is striking how closely Kohut's vertical–horizontal considerations of psychic structure in narcissism correspond to Fairbairn's (1944) conception of the internal dynamics of endopsychic structure (Robbins, 1980 and Chapter 17, this volume). Rather than simply postulating that splitting is the primitive antecedent of repression, Fairbairn maintained further that splitting of the objects and egos requires repression to keep the awareness of the splits unconscious. Although Fairbairn did recognize that there is a reciprocal relationship between repression and splitting, he never reconciled his endopsychic structural theory with Freud's topographic theory.

The Importance of Freud's "Mourning and Melancholia" for Fairbairn's Endopsychic Structure

Fairbairn entered Freud's structural arena by taking up the latter's 1914 and 1917 hypotheses and radically altering the economic aspect of his metapsychology. Fairbairn saw that psychic structure is the personification of *failed experiences* with objects.[3]

Let us recall that Freud's (1894, 1896) first major hypothesis about the psyche was a topographic (subjective experiences of consciousnesses) rather than a purely structural one. The first simply designated a censorship of traumatic memories to the Ucs.[4] Later, when he discovered the importance of phantasy life and of its origins in the instinctual drives, he

---

[3]This should really be understood to mean that psychic structure represents the failure of relationships with *persons*, who then become repersonified as internal *demons* (objects).

[4]Fairbairn's endopsychic structure encompasses the topography for Freud's first theory of psychoanalysis, and yet accommodates his later ones as well!

believed that the contents of the primary repressed become *depersonified* into instinctual drives, to which traumatic memories (of relationships with persons) become only secondarily attached.

Freud's concept of internalized objects in the ego and the ego ideal, as set forth in "Mourning and Melancholia" (1917), was the primary stimulus in his work for Fairbairn and Klein. Freud (1917) stated that in melancholia, in contrast to mourning, there occurs a narcissistic regression in which the lost *external* object becomes reinstalled as an *internal* object through withdrawal of object cathexis, and identification in the ego with the lost object ("The shadow of the object falls on the ego"; Freud, 1917, p. 249). Freud hinted that the object is split upon internalization into two objects (actually part-objects), and becomes separately identified with two different aspects of the ego—the ego proper and a "gradient in the ego" known as the "ego ideal" (later the "superego").[5]

In the melancholic ego, Freud thus established a complex psychic structure composed of two dissociated egos relating to two dissociated part-objects, respectively. He demonstrated how the melancholic narcissist, unable to mourn, treats himself as if he *is* the lost object. At the same time he is the object treating himself as the subject—in the sadomasochistic *folie à deux* that causes his self-esteem to plummet.

The melancholic internal object restructuring of the internal world and the splitting of the ego became the point of departure for Fairbairn and Klein. Klein's concept of splitting was of an active splitting *by* the subject (ego) *of* the object. Fairbairn was more ambiguous on whether splitting by the ego is active or passive. He believed that it occurs by default: The ego's allegiance to an unaccepted object causes it to be pulled into a split; thus its experience of "being schizoid," of being alienated. Unlike Klein, Fairbairn believed that alienation, the deep anguish of self-isolation, is at the heart of the human condition.

Endopsychic Structure and the Alter Ego

Fairbairn's concept of alienation or dissociation (echoed by Laing, 1960; Winnicott, 1960; and Balint, 1968) evokes the phenomenon of the alter

---

[5]Freud (1917) implied but never made clear that the lost external object becomes *split* upon internalization. However, he did more strongly suggest that the ego ideal is a part of the ego and that it becomes identified with what amounts to a split-off ideal aspect of the object, whose debased counterpart finds its way into the lower portion of the ego gradient and becomes identified with it.

ego. The presence of semi-independent, dissociated, and alienated sub-personalities is evident in Fairbairn's first major clinical paper, "Notes on the Religious Phantasies of a Female Patient" (1927). He continued to develop this theme in "Features in the Analysis of a Patient with a Physical Genital Abnormality" (1931) and "The Effect of a King's Death upon Patients Undergoing Analysis" (1936).

Fairbairn envisioned the splitting of the ego as an organized series of split-off "half-selves," termed "introverted" after Jung (1934), which correspond to a preneurotic, preambivalent, premoral personality. Today, we see these dissociated structures more frankly manifested in the form of dissociative and multiple personality disorders. But it is my contention, following Fairbairn, that we are all comprised of discrete or quasi-discrete unconscious multiple selves.

Fairbairn uncovered a unique aspect of the infantile neurosis in postulating the schizoid (as well as depressive) position, and revealed a "true-self"–"false-self"[6] dichotomy of the personality. Although premoral, this early stage is *not* prepersonal. Fairbairn stated that from the beginning the infant–mother relationship is personal; it only becomes impersonal pathologically.

The ultimate significance of the alter ego phenomenon for psychoanalysis is not only in its immediate clinical application to dissociative and multiple personality disorders, but more generally to the concept of the lost selves that require psychoanalytic "exorcism" to rescue them from their incarceration by internal objects (and projected internal objects).

The "alienated self" or "alter ego" has had an intriguing history (Grotstein, 1994b). The concept appeared in the fiction of the 19th century, and was a subject of interest for psychologists and psychiatrists at that time. E. T. A. Hoffmann, Dostoyevsky, Melville, Poe, Stevenson, Mary Shelley, and others wrote about the "double" (*der Doppelganger*). In the mental sciences, the "second self" was evident in such phenomena as heautoscopy (the image of oneself as a double), hypnotism, and especially hysteria. Breuer and Freud (1893–1895) reported that virtually all their cases of hysteria suffered from "double conscience," by which they clearly meant "double consciousness."

When Freud (1900) first delineated his topographic approach, he postulated the existence of the Ucs. In Freud's usage it became thought of as a horizontal layer beneath the Cs.; in contrast, Charcot, Janet, and

---

[6]Furthermore, Fairbairn's libidinal ego, which can be correlated with Winnicott's "true self," is a dynamic structure in its own right, in contrast to the more static nature of the latter.

others saw the second self as situated *vertically* alongside the first self. Freud's later categorization, first of libido and then of the structural approach, departed further from the vertical second self. Once the id[7] was conceptualized as underneath the ego, the alter ego became eclipsed and was lost to psychoanalysis, only to be regarded as a minor contributor to dissociated states and multiple personalities, or as an accessory selfobject in Kohut's (1984) pantheon.

It is my understanding that psychoanalysis consistently focuses on the second self, insofar as *all* the objects in a patient's manifest or latent content can be thought of as projective aspects of the self that conform to concordant, complementary, and oppositional projective identifications. Thus every object and experience reported by a patient is to be deciphered by the analyst only in terms of what aspect (shadow) of the patient it reflects or illuminates. Psychoanalysis is ultimately "alter ego analysis," insofar as it facilitates the return of lost aspects of the self from their existential diaspora in objects.

By employing this perspective of the alter ego, I have begun to believe that the unconscious consists of the "undead" and the "unborn," the latter designating those emerging aspects of the self. I employ the term "undead" as a replacement for the term "object" (internal object), in order to designate a "dead-but-haunting" quality of unconscious existence.

The concept of the alter ego extends from the most normal to the most abnormal personality situations. The normal person may experience a "right-hemisphere" and a "left-hemisphere" personality differentiation (Gazzaniga & LeDoux, 1975; Gazzaniga, 1985), passivity and assertiveness, maleness and femaleness, or "hardness" and "softness" simply as different aspects of a single integrated self. As the sense of cohesiveness falters, the experience of multiple or fragmented selves is often encountered, particularly in borderlines and psychotics. Patients with multiple personalities seem to be unique insofar as their pathology predisposes them toward discrete splits of quasi-independent selves, some of which may not be in contact with other selves.

Dr. John Lundgren (personal communication, 1991) points out that the very discreteness of multiple personalities may lie in how (and when) the original traumata were encoded into memory. He cites Stone (1988) on the factors of state (traumatic) dependency of memory and the implications of procedural and/or evocative memory that remains in subcortical areas of the brain because it has not been processed by and thus en-

---

[7]Freud borrowed the term "id," actually *das Es*, from Groddeck (1923), who, in turn, borrowed it from Nietzsche in *Thus Spoke Zarathustra*. Groddeck and Nietzsche clearly meant by *das Es*—unlike Freud, who gave it a depersonified, "scientistic" significance—a strange–familiar "other," the personification of the hidden self.

coded in semantic memory. Interestingly, Salley (1988) has written of a case of 13 multiple personalities in which, for instance, one personality was able to predict dream themes in advance.[8]

Analysts who have dealt with primitive mental disorders, as well as with higher-level neurotic patients, frequently report sessions in which their patients experience a split or dissociation between a healthy self and an unhealthy, more infantile self, the latter of whom often constitutes the "saboteur" to the treatment.

One of the invariant characteristics of second selves is their independent and autonomous behavior. Each acts as if it is a separate personality with its own id, ego, and superego, but maintains a loose, "Siamese twin" connection to the other personality or personalities. When we say to a patient, "Part of you feels such and such a way, whereas another part of you feels another way", or when we say, "But on another level ...", we are addressing the alter ego phenomenon. The seeming independence, dissociation, alienation, and autonomy of these second selves—and their unique subjective perspective—are what has been ignored.

A REINTERPRETATION OF ENDOPSYCHIC STRUCTURE[9]

Fairbairn's depiction of the endopsychic situation as a closed system fails to envision that the personality (of any individual) can also function as if it were an *open* system. Although Fairbairn's system does not allow for the presence of a *normal* libidinal ego (LE), his metapsychology indicates that he believed in its existence. One could therefore postulate that there is a healthy personality beyond and independent of its endopsychic counterpart. This "normal" self could be experienced as "alter" to the endopsychic personality and could consist of an LE and a libidinal object, as well as a normally frustrating object, all of whose existences could be both conscious and unconscious.

In addition to the endopsychic personality, I should like to postulate two others—the "holographic personality," in which no separation of selves exists, but rather a sense of wholeness and at-one-ness; and a so-called "normal personality" that has particulate normal divisions corresponding to the pathological structures of the endopsychic situation, and

---

[8]The reader is referred to Seinfeld's (1990) *The Bad Object*, in which he correlates the work of Fairbairn, Searles, Kernberg, Kohut, and others in an integrative study of the symbiotic transference.

[9]In a later section of this chapter, I give clinical case vignettes that detail many aspects of endopsychic relationships.

can thus be called the "particulate personality." All three interact dialectically and can be conceptualized simultaneously from a holographic perspective.

I have developed my concept of these personality configurations mainly from my clinical experience with psychotic patients. When a patient has recovered from a psychotic break, he frequently reports that he experienced a normal, separate personality that impassively and helplessly observed the other personality experiencing its psychotic break. The "normal particulate personality" and "holistic personality" (which together comprise a "holographic personality") can each be considered a "Siamese twin" or an "alter ego" to the pathological personality; this corresponds to the dual-track principle (Grotstein, 1994c). Katan (1954) and Bion (1957) similarly conceived of a normal or neurotic personality conflicting with a psychotic personality in schizophrenics.

I believe that the mind is and has always been holographic, and can therefore, like the cerebral hemispheres, be thought of holistically and particulately (separately) at the same time. I further propose that Fairbairn's LE, one of his most valuable discoveries, is the link among all three putative personalities. It is itself holistic and particulate; it is also the prime agency of subjective experience.

Indeed, the holistic and particulate selves comprise the original innocence of the infant (Grotstein, 1992, 1993, 1994a). Any form of intrusion, abuse, neglect, or malattunement that causes irreparable trauma to the infant's or child's sense of feeling blessed and safe eventuates in a loss of innocence. As current childhood trauma research indicates, such a violation significantly disrupts the child's values, ideals, and expectations for environmental safety (Horowitz, 1976; van der Kolk, 1987). Traumatized children, as Fairbairn has so beautifully described, withdraw, become introverted, join up with their bad objects in a secretive nether world, and thus compromise themselves in their attempt to comply with survival needs. Fairbairn's endopsychic structure is a testimony to the loss of innocence, and thus to its Hellish nature: a forlorn self being excited by a tantalizing Devil and tormented by his sanctimonious double.[10]

To understand how endopsychic structure can function as a partially open system (the central ego [CE] and the ideal object [IO]), we need to acknowledge, as in cases of extreme dissociation such as those occurring in multiple personality disorder, that subpersonalities can be independent of each other. Let us now visualize that Fairbairn's structural image is in place. Let us then conceive of an original ego (OE) and original object (OO) (Rinsley, 1987 and Chapter 15, this volume), which hypothetically

---

[10]The reader is referred to Chapter 7 for an in-depth discussion of the demoniacal possession implicit within endopsychic structure.

antedate the splits into CE and so forth. I would envision this as a "Siamese twinship" relationship between the "background presence of primary identification" and the inchoate, subjective "I" (Grotstein, 1980, 1991d). By "Siamese twinship" I mean a relationship that is characterized by a sense of indivisible connectedness *and* separateness at the same time. Thus there is a whole "I" that can both experience its "I"-ness in parts (or selves), and represent this splitting in dreams and free associations.

Within each component of endopsychic structure, there is also a whole (subjective) self that can experience its internal condition. The antilibidinal ego (AE), for instance, has its own world view, sensitivities, sensibilities, and sense of entitlement. Its subjective perspective, however, is constrained by its history, fear for its own survival, and a sense of protective responsibility to the subordinated LE under its dominion. The AE, for instance, may hate the LE and the exciting object (EO), but its very hate can be thought of as protecting the LE against its own profligacy. The advent of the negative therapeutic reaction in the analysis of primitive mental disorders can be attributed not only to libidinal loyalty to bad objects, but also to the AE's need to protect the LE from danger of anticipated progress and separation.

The Dialectics of Endopsychic Relationships

The AE, as Fairbairn delineates it, exists only because of its dialectical adversary, the LE. In such a "twinship," an oppositional identification exists between them, for the disappearance of one would jeopardize the existence of the other.

Earlier, I have hypothesized that there is a normally particulate self that includes a normal id (loving, desiring self) and a normal counterbalancing self that embodies assertiveness and ambition. I believe that a tension exists between these selves (and their abnormal counterparts) in endopsychic structure. This holographic view suggests that each structure has its own autonomy, provenance, innocence, will (intentionality), rationale (*raison d'être*), birthright, blessing, or curse. Thus, each subsidiary ego (the CE, the AE, and the LE) has independent senses of subjective (normal and/or pathological) "I"-ness and may actually undertake cross-relations with estranged objects (the IO, the rejecting object [RO], and the EO).

The LE, for instance, may ignore its relationship with the EO and relate instead to the RO or to the IO. A direct cross-relationship between the LE and the RO would involve the experience of sadomasochism. A triangular competition of the LE with the AE for the affection of the RO (or a competition of the AE with the LE for the affection of the EO) would constitute the phenomenology of Klein's manic defense or of Kohut's and Kernberg's narcissistic grandiose self in relationship to slave selfobjects. All these possibilities are variants of a more fundamental relationship— that is, the atavistic prey–predator relationship,[11] which I believe consti- tutes one of the principal terrors of the primal scene (Grotstein, 1989).

In manic psychosis, as well as in schizophrenia, the LE is totally iden- tified with the EO (having incorporated it intact), and has taken over the agency of subjective "I"-ness. Thus, the LE behaves as if it were the sane ego repressing or splitting off the other egos and objects, which are all experienced as being entrapped in the manic's unconscious.

Fairbairn's endopsychic structure accounts for the nonpsychotic depres- sive. In depressive psychosis, however, one might postulate that the AE and the RO now occupy the position of the CE and the IO. The LE and the EO may be experienced as either repressed or split off and projected into others.

Davies and Frawley (1992) have recently studied the dissociative pro- cesses in adult survivors of child abuse and attempted an integrative syn- thesis with the work of Fairbairn. One of their findings is that these patients show an invariant dissociation between an "adult self" and a "child self," the latter of which can be further subdivided into the "good– perfect child", the "naughty–omnipotent child," and the "terrified–abused child." The "good–perfect child" may derive from a false central self (CE) repressing a victimized self (LE), which is simultaneously being abused by an abuser self (AE) while in a corrupt, collusive relationship with an "idealized omnipotent rescuer" (EO).

In Rinsley's (Chapter 15, this volume) epigenetic conceptualization of endopsychic structure, he envisions a progressive developmental agenda whereby, as identifications lessen, the subsidiary egos loosen their attach- ments to their respective objects and become reintegrated as a composite ego, a reminder of the OE before it became split. One can envision, for example, a relationship between the "libidinal self" (with or without the EO) and the CE being undermined by the internal saboteur (AE).

The belief system implicit within the libidinal self is that the EO will guarantee it omnipotent satisfaction. It is this belief that underlies addic- tive and symbiotic disorders in which issues of grandiosity and entitle- ment have not been resolved. With the "rejecting self," on the other hand, the belief seems to be a negative omnipotence, an identification with the hard power of hate that obliterates libidinal (needy) deficiencies.

Ultimately, in reviewing the *Weltanschauungen* of the endopsychic

[11]It is my contention that prey–predator anxiety, first elaborated by Bowlby (1969), is the constitutional template of Klein's concept of persecutory anxiety.

structures, it would seem that the pathological "libidinal self"[12] (the LE and EO) represents a licentious self that pursues wanton pleasure, tantalization, and frustration, whereas the "rejecting self" (the AE and RO) pursues a perversely destructive mode and becomes a tormenting self. I believe, and understand Fairbairn to have believed, that these four repressed endopsychic entities (LE, AE, EO, and RO) are created by default and represent the breakdown in a basic trust with the primal caretakers. The licentious self is what Freud meant by the id, and the rejecting self is what Klein meant by the operation of the death instinct. These four structures are victims of the "loss of innocence" (Grotstein, 1993, 1994a) and are condemned to having a hapless *fate* rather than a joyous *destiny* (Bollas, 1989).

My intention in this section has been to challenge Fairbairn's postulate that the "dynamic" relationships of endopsychic structures are actually *static* insofar as they occupy a closed system. The dynamics of a closed system are frequently referred to as "hydraulics" or "reciprocal relationships." I have been suggesting that a dialectic exists between the seeming absoluteness of the closed system and the myriad of possible relationships that can occur within its confines.

Since I postulate that there *can* be normal counterparts to endopsychic structures (normal *and* pathological LEs; a libidinal object *and* an EO; a disciplined and disciplining ego *and* an AE; and a normally disciplining "existential coach" object *and* an RO), there can also be an openness in the relationship between any one of the pathological entities and their normal counterparts.

The Spiritual and Diabolical Aspects of Endopsychic Structure

Fairbairn depicts a unidirectional relationship between the CE–IO structure and its subsidiary egos and objects. He depicts the denizens of endopsychic structure as angels (the IO) and demons (bad objects). The presence of religious imagery and of phantasies of the Crucifixion are replete in his paper "Notes on the Religious Phantasies of a Female Patient" (1927).

It is to the study of the Devil that I should now like to turn. A chance glimpse of a medieval portrait has suggested to me an alternative interpretation of the Devil and his origin. The Devil is consistently portrayed

[12]Recall that I, unlike Fairbairn, believe that there can be a normal LE as well as a pathological one, and that there can be a normal libidinal object (not an EO)—and likewise for the AE and the RO.

as having horns, a tail, and cloven feet. It has occurred to me that he is the Judeo-Christian transformation of the ancient lascivious god Pan, and thus represents the worship of sensuous (libidinal) excesses. If that is so, why do his excesses inspire the need for religious worship? The anatomical features of the Devil, I realized, are signifiers for the sacrificial lamb of the Old Testament. This sacrificial lamb (the "scapegoat") is the innocent part of us into which we project our sins (persecutory anxiety, guilt), and by which we transform the innocent lamb into the Devil. But if the lamb transforms and *transcends*, it becomes Christ, the Redeemer. Prior to the use of sacrificial lambs, ancient cultures chose innocent newborn children to appease the gods; apparently the Hebrews were no exception, as the synechdochic ritual of circumcision bears testimony (Grotstein, 1979a, 1979b, 1989, 1993, 1994a; Bergmann, 1992).

In contrast to Fairbairn's unidirectional view of endopsychic hierarchies, I suggest that the relationship (or series of relationships) exists between the LE (and AE) and the CE—*in a reverse direction*. One is spiritual and the other is diabolical. Fairbairn hints at this when he stated that in the moral defense, the schizoid modifies his view of the absolute badness of his objects into a conditional badness. The CE which undergoes this traduction, knows the truth![13] and must live in collusion with the supposedly "ideal" IO. This technique, of course, constitutes pathological idealization (Klein, 1946). The OE has, in effect, signed a Faustian bargain with the Devil—not for omnipotence per se (as in the case of Faust), but for safety and survival, at the cost of the soul (Blomfield, 1985; Grotstein, 1994a).

The LE, summarily banished by the CE into the wilderness of the unconscious, remains loyal to the object that betrayed it. Is this not virtuous? Thus the LE becomes the victim of sanctimonious foul play and always seeks to regain entry into its forfeited paradisiacal home. Scripture is replete with tales of God's arbitrary assignment of favoritism and entitlements. What does He do to make Lucifer envious? Why does He prefer Abel's gift of the sacrificial lamb to Cain's fruits of the field?

I am suggesting that the special relationship between the LE and the CE represents man's spiritual submission to God and His arbitrary ways. More than that, it represents man's hope for salvation through appeal. On the other hand, insofar as the LE is outraged over its banishment, its hostile counterpart, the AE, attacks the CE through diabolical threats. It seeks to re-enter the CE to purloin its goodness, to regain its lost entitlement, and to curse its traducer. Thus, the Devil reflects the discarded evil of the CE.

[13]See Vellacott (1971, 1978) and Steiner (1985) for the actualization of this phenomenon of "turning the blind eye" in the story of Oedipus.

What really is this evil of the CE? In addition to Melanie Klein's (1957) categories of greed, envy, rage, and the manic defense, I suggest that another sense of evil haunts the schizoid patient—that of self-abnegation and self-renunciation. Once rejected, the self becomes derelict, unclaimed, cast into the wilderness of futility. Remorseless diabolical revenge, paradoxically, becomes its only hope for redemption. The sense of innocence has long since been forfeited.

ENDOPSYCHIC STRUCTURE AS THE ULTIMATE DEFENSE AGAINST THE VOID: CASE EXAMPLES

All psychoanalytic theories can be understood as constituting a manic defense against an existential experience of nothingness, meaninglessness, randomness, chaos, and the void—the internal "black hole" (Grotstein, 1990a, 1990b, 1991d). It is a human compulsion to assign meaning and coherence to experiences. Whereas bonding and attachment with objects suspends our descent into the "black hole" of nothingness, the *absence* of that bonding accelerates it. In the following case examples, I describe how various patients negotiated their relations to objects, and how they tried to repair the splits that threatened to disrupt their personality and thrust them into psychic void and oblivion.

I begin with a dream segment from a female adult analytic case.[14] (In this and the following dream excerpts, I have inserted in brackets the components of endopsychic structure represented by various characters in the dreams.)

"I [CE] was observing children [AE plus LE]. One of the children [AE] was babysitting a younger child, a baby that was not being cared for. It was thin and grim-faced [LE]. The child seemed ill-disposed toward the baby. I felt the baby was me somehow. They all were children of homeless people [RO plus EO], and I [CE plus IO] thought I should take them home to live with me, but somebody said not to. It was my husband [EO]."

In this female analysand's past, emotional child abuse had been a significant feature. We can see that as the patient moved from immature dependency through a transitional stage toward mature dependency, her CE, fortified by its relationship with her IO, desired to repair the splits in her personality by allowing a return of her lost split-off selves and the

[14]I am grateful to Dr. Alan Bishop, who granted me permission to use this case example.

internalized objects with whom they were identified. The AE (internal saboteur) was seen as the sadistic "babysitter" for the abandoned LE. The homelessness of the children testified to a common heritage, despite their internecine warfare: All had experienced abandonment by an erstwhile CE and IO, which were now disposed to readmitting them back from exile. The EO, the "flip side" of the RO, importuned the LE (and its other compatriots) to remain in exile and to resist the attempts of the CE and IO to encourage liberation and reintegration.

The question arises as to why the EO resisted integration. The EO, while representing one aspect of the patient's husband in the manifest content of the dream, actually represented a split-off, Oedipally exciting aspect of the analyst on the other. The figure of her husband had been used virtually since the beginning of the analysis to represent both rejecting and exciting aspects of both her mother and her father, in successive dyadic analytic developments. Finally, it came to represent the Oedipal father. It had been difficult for the patient until recently to allow herself to experience the analyst in any of these nefarious roles. Instead, she kept him as the IO, but his interpretations showed her that she had been "protecting" him from personal involvement—that is, from becoming confused or commingled with the shameful, "homeless" phantom objects of her endopsychic structure.

The following is a dream segment from a single adult female patient who was the victim of child abuse by her hyperactive brother:

"I [LE] was in a bicycle race and people were in the way [AE plus RO]. Then I [LE] was in an airplane in tourist class. I [CE] had a first-class ticket, but because I had not signed in correctly, I [LE] could not get my seat, according to the stewardess [AE plus RO]. The seat, next to which a handsome man [EO] was sitting, was empty, however. I suddenly saw my mother [IO plus EO plus RO] there. She was alive! She took the seat. Apparently *she* was engaged to marry this man. I was surprised and delighted, not only that mother was alive, but was looking better, was even getting remarried, and I would be able to help her."

The patient chronically experienced victimization in her interpersonal and professional relationships. She had great difficulty in bonding with loving men. She idealized narcissistic types of men, whose interpersonal ruthlessness was admired for the illusion of protection it offered her against her physically abusive brother of childhood. She had only recently become aware that her victimized self (LE) was constantly being attacked by a portion of her (AE—the other bicycle racers, the stewardess) that was in an oppositional identification with her internal abusive brother. Although she was distant from her father while growing up, she was symbiotically close to her mother, who constituted both an IO and an EO.

Recently her mother had died from heart disease. The patient, who had suspended her career to nurse her mother during her illness, blamed herself for not being caring enough, and thus for being responsible for her death. This feeling had obvious Oedipal connections, which were magically repaired in the dream by restoring her mother to life, surrendering to her the first-class seat, and allowing her to have her boyfriend–father.

As in the preceding case, the role of the analyst was experienced as background, but actually can be seen in all the derivatives. The mother's return from the dead also had another meaning, that of the return of a bad object—bad insofar as the patient felt persecuted by her ghost for "allowing" her to die.

The endopsychic situation in psychosis is complex. In the state of acute psychotic disorganization one may see a plethora of internal objects and split-off egos, albeit in arcane or bizarre forms, rising to the surface of conscious experience. In the later stage of restitution one may see a quieter, more subdued picture—one where the CE may be repressed, while the formerly repressed internal objects and egos are conscious.

Here is a dream segment from a married female schizophrenic patient:

"I [CE] was in a large house with a strange tunnel doorway. I could see people outside. They were speaking normally to each other. As soon as they put their faces in the tunnel doorway of the house, they suddenly appeared bizarre [return of repressed bizarre objects and egos].

"Then I was in a resort where I was swimming in lots of different pools. The pools were carved out of sandstone. I liked being deep in the water and wanted to remain there. Then I walked around in this one pool and found two little girls [RO] who were playing in the water. A little distance from them, there was another little girl [LE] who was crouched under the water. I worried that she was drowning, but the other two children were apparently blithely ignoring her. I asked the two little girls about her, and they said, indifferently, 'We don't want to play with her any more.' I looked again at the little girl. She was beautiful. She had golden-colored skin. I was so sad that she was dead. Then all of a sudden she stood up and uttered, 'I don't want to do this any more!' I didn't know if she was dead and now a walking ghost or if she had just been under the water a little while and was still alive. I didn't feel comfortable with her. I was more compassionate when I thought she was dead. Alive, she was eerie, uncanny, scary!"

The patient associated as follows:

"From *her* point of view, she had been drowned for quite some time. From *my* point of view, her standing up rocked my perception of reality. Many times as a child, I would totally *immerse* myself [emphasis added] in reading books and would refuse to give myself the pleasure of going outside to play with other children. If I had done that, I would have been too real and stuck in the world of reality. I kept seeing dead animals on the drive here today—including several flying rats. I feel crazy. That little girl scared me. She reminds me of the me inside of me who is always trying to murder me. It was eerie seeing her face to face."

When I inquired into the first dream, I learned that the patient believed she had occupied an encapsulated existence all her life—that she had been in a schizoid cocoon or psychotic state, which seemed normal to the world because of her ability to dissemble. The outside objects appearing at the wall and entering the tunnel represented her "second birth" in the analysis, the cracking of her psychotic shell. She became confused as to whether she was psychotic in her schizoid cocoon, or whether becoming sane (by leaving the cocoon) was the same as going crazy. Thus her endopsychic structure was externalized, and she, psychotically identified with her LE and CE, was now afraid of persecution by her EO and RO, which had now become externalized.

I believe that the structural configuration explicit in this patient's dreams reveals a reversal of endopsychic structure, almost as if Fairbairn's paradigm were pulled inside out (or at least reversed); it brings to mind Freud's (1911) conception of psychotic restitution.

In another case, a 14-year-old adolescent girl, the 4th of 10 children of an alcoholic mother and father, had been abandoned at age 2 and sent to a series of foster homes, where she experienced love, abuse, and sexual molestation. Finally, at age 4 she was adopted by an upper-middle-class family. The patient reported that from age 3 to age 6, she had experienced "a voice of a woman inside my head who threatened me, told me that I was bad, and also ordered me to do bad things." The "voice," experienced as threatening at first, later became soothing, and the patient sought to remember this experience in later years in order to calm herself.

In her adoptive home, the patient became an incorrigible child. She was promiscuous, abused drugs (marijuana and alcohol), and was given to lying and manipulating her family and friends. She loved her adoptive parents but could not get along with them, so she frequently sought to leave home. She began having suicidal ideation, as if commanded by some inner voice; this resulted in her psychiatric referral.

The "inner voice" derived from her image of her biological mother (EO plus RO) infused with projective attributions from her own self (LE plus AE). She felt bonded with her family of origin, who became the denizens of her endopsychic structure but who also gave her a sense of authentic being. Their depravity "blessed" her, and thus became her lifetime "identity theme" (Lichtenstein, 1961) and her curse. Doomed to be the tantalized LE in search of her lost EO, she could only envy and reject the love offered her by her adoptive parents (and analyst), because accepting it put her in jeopardy of abandonment and depression. The fate that endopsychic inhabitants most fear is that of an abandonment in the deep and formless infinite.

GENERAL COMMENTS

Fairbairn's concept of endopsychic structure is the most elegant construct of the internal world yet conceived. It is readily inclusive of the two-person and three-person relationship epigenesis. And it is flexible enough to accommodate Freud's psychic apparatus and Klein's internalized persecutory objects.

Although Fairbairn makes little allowance for Klein's (1935, 1940) view of the transaction of phantasmal objects, I believe that a complementarity exists between Klein's internal world of phantoms and Fairbairn's endopsychic structures.[15] If we again employ the concept of a "Siamese twinship," a paradigmatic image of a dual phenomenon, Klein's "damaged object" can be seen as a phantasmal counterpart of the AE and the EO. It constitutes the phantasy relationship, whereas Fairbairn's AE and EO represent the realistic one. Similarly, Klein's "damaging object," or "primitive superego object," constitutes a phantasmal counterpart to the AE and the RO. In this sense, Klein's objects roughly approximate Fairbairn's endopsychic units.

Fairbairn's endopsychic structure in its essence designates the fact of psychopathology, both interpersonally and intrapersonally. It is a statement of the universality of the experience of being a "divided self." We have seen that this structural paradigm may be conceived of as a closed internal system wherein each unit depends on the other. But we can also conceive of such a system in terms of an overall holography, such that each element, ego and object, has its own autonomy.

REFERENCES

Balint, M. (1968). *The Basic Fault.* London: Tavistock.
Bergmann, M. (1992). *In the Shadow of Moloch: The Sacrifice of Children and Its Impact on Western Religions.* New York: Columbia University Press.

[15]The reader is referred to Mitchell's (Chapter 5, this volume) definitive treatise on the comparison of Klein's and Fairbairn's use of the term "object."

Bion, W. R. (1957). Differentiation of the psychotic from the non-psychotic personalities. *International Journal of Psycho-Analysis, 38*, 266–275.

Blomfield, O. H. D. (1985). Parasitism, projective identification and the Faustian bargain. *International Review of Psycho-Analysis, 12*, 299–310.

Bollas, C. (1989). *Forces of Destiny*. London: Free Association Books.

Bowlby, J. (1969). *Attachment and Loss: Vol. 1. Attachment*. New York: Basic Books.

Breuer, J., & Freud, S. (1893–1895). Studies on hysteria. *Standard Edition, 2*, 1–305.

Davies, J., & Frawley, M. (1992). Dissociative processes and transference–countertransference paradigms in the psychoanalytically oriented treatment of adult survivors of childhood sexual abuse. *Psychoanalytic Dialogues, 2*(1), 5–36.

Fairbairn, W. R. D. (1927). Notes on the religious phantasies of a female patient. In *Psychoanalytic Studies of the Personality*. London: Tavistock, 1952, pp. 183–196.

Fairbairn, W. R. D. (1931). Features in the analysis of a patient with a physical genital abnormality. In *Psychoanalytic Studies of the Personality*. London: Tavistock, 1952, pp. 197–222.

Fairbairn, W. R. D. (1936). The effect of a king's death upon patients undergoing analysis. In *Psychoanalytic Studies of the Personality*. London: Tavistock, 1952, pp. 223–229.

Fairbairn, W. R. D. (1944). Endopsychic structure considered in terms of object-relationships. In *Psychoanalytic Studies of the Personality*. London: Tavistock, 1952, pp. 82–136.

Freud, S. (1894). The neuro-psychoses of defence. *Standard Edition, 3*, 45–61.

Freud, S. (1896). The aetiology of hysteria. *Standard Edition, 3*, 189–224.

Freud, S. (1900). The interpretation of dreams. *Standard Edition, 4*, 1–338; *5*, 339–627.

Freud, S. (1905). Jokes and their relation to the unconscious. *Standard Edition, 8*, 3–239.

Freud, S. (1911). Psycho-analytic notes on an autobiographical account of a case of paranoia (dementia paranoides). *Standard Edition, 12*, 3–84.

Freud, S. (1914). On narcissism: An introduction. *Standard Edition, 14*, 67–104.

Freud, S. (1917). Mourning and melancholia. *Standard Edition, 14*, 237–260.

Freud, S. (1919). The 'uncanny.' *Standard Edition, 17*, 217–252.

Freud, S. (1921). Group psychology and the analysis of the ego. *Standard Edition, 18*, 67–144.

Freud, S. (1923). The ego and the id. *Standard Edition, 19*, 3–66.

Freud, S. (1925). Negation. *Standard Edition, 19*, 235–242.

Freud, S. (1927). Fetishism. *Standard Edition, 21*, 149–157.

Freud, S. (1937). Constructions in analysis. *Standard Edition, 23*, 255–269.

Freud, S. (1940a). An outline of psycho-analysis. *Standard Edition, 23*, 139–207.

Freud, S. (1940b). Splitting of the ego in the process of defence. *Standard Edition, 23*, 271–278.

Gazzaniga, M. S. (1985). *The Social Brain*. New York: Basic Books.

Gazzaniga, M. S., & LeDoux, J. E. (1975). *The Integrated Mind*. New York: Plenum Press.

Groddeck, G. (1923). *The Book of the It*, V. M. E. Collins, trans. London: Vision Press.

Grotstein, J. S. (1979a). Demoniacal possession, splitting, and the torment of joy. *Contemporary Psychoanalysis*, 15(3), 407–453.

Grotstein, J. S. (1979b). The soul in torment: A newer and older view of psychopathology. *Bulletin for Catholic Psychiatrists*, 25, 36–52.

Grotstein, J. S. (1980). A proposed revision of the psychoanalytic concept of primitive mental states: I. An introduction to a newer psychoanalytic metapsychology. *Contemporary Psychoanalysis*, 16(4): 479–546.

Grotstein, J. S. (1989). Some invariants in primitive emotional disorders. In L. B. Boyer & P. Giovacchini, eds., *Master Clinicians Working through Regression*. Northvale, NJ: Jason Aronson, pp. 131–155.

Grotstein, J. S. (1990a). Nothingness, meaninglessness, chaos, and the "black hole": I. Meaninglessness, nothingness, and chaos. *Contemporary Psychoanalysis*, 26(2), 257–290.

Grotstein, J. S. (1990b). Nothingness, meaninglessness, chaos, and the "black hole": II. The "black hole." *Contemporary Psychoanalysis*, 26(3), 377–407.

Grotstein, J. S. (1991a). An American view of the British psychoanalytic experience: I. Introduction: The Americanization of psychoanalysis. *Journal of Melanie Klein and Object Relations*, 9, 1–15.

Grotstein, J. S. (1991b). An American view of the British psychoanalytic experience: II. The Kleinian School. *Journal of Melanie Klein and Object Relations*, 9, 16–33.

Grotstein, J. S. (1991c) An American view of the British psychoanalytic experience: III: The British object relations school. *Journal of Melanie Klein and Object Relations*, 9, 34–62.

Grotstein, J. S. (1991d). Nothingness, meaninglessness, chaos, and the "black hole": III. Self-regulation and the background presence of primary identification. *Contemporary Psychoanalysis*, 27(1), 1–33.

Grotstein, J. S. (1993). Boundary difficulties in borderline patients. In L. B. Boyer & P. L. Giovacchini, eds., *Master Clinicians: Vol. II. On Treating the Regressed Patient in the Consultation Room and in the Residential Setting*. Northvale, NJ: Jason Aronson, pp. 107–141.

Grotstein, J. S. (1994a). Why Oedipus and not Christ?: The importance of innocence, original sin, and human sacrifice in psychoanalytic theory and practice. I. A selected re-reading of the myth of Oedipus and Christ. Manuscript in preparation.

Grotstein, J. S. (1994b). Why Oedipus and not Christ?: The importance of innocence, original sin, and human sacrifice in psychoanalytic theory and practice. II. The transference/countertransference neurosis psychosis and their consummate expression in the crucifixion, the Pieta, and "therapeutic exorcism." Manuscript in preparation.

Grotstein, J. S. (1994c). The dual-track theorem: A newer paradigm for psychoanalytic theory and technique. Manuscript in preparation.

Horowitz, M. (1976). *Stress Response Syndromes*. New York: Jason Aronson.

Janet, P. (1889). *L'Automatisme Psychologique: Essai de Psychologie Expérimentale sur les Formes Inférieures de l'Activité Humaine*. Paris: Faylés Alcan.

Janet, P. (1893). Quelques définitions récentes de l'hystérie. *Archives de Neurologie*, 25, 417–438; 26, 1–29.

Jung, C. G. (1934). Archetypes and the collective unconscious. In *Collected Works,* Vol. 9, 1, R. F. C. Hull, trans. New York: Bollinger Series, 1959.

Katan, M. (1954). The importance of the non-psychotic part of the personality in schizophrenia. *International Journal of Psycho-Analysis, 35,* 119–128.

Kernberg, O. (1980). *Internal World and External Reality.* New York: Jason Aronson.

Klein, M. (1935). A contribution to the psychogenesis of manic–depressive states. In *Contributions to Psycho-Analysis, 1921–1945.* London: Hogarth Press, 1950, pp. 282–310.

Klein, M. (1940). Mourning and its relation to manic–depressive states. In *Contributions to Psycho-Analysis, 1921–1945.* London: Hogarth Press, 1950, pp. 311–338.

Klein, M. (1946). Notes on some schizoid mechanisms. In M. Klein, P. Heimann, S. Isaacs, & J. Riviere, eds., *Developments in Psycho-Analysis.* London: Hogarth Press, 1952, pp. 292–320.

Klein, M. (1957). *Envy and Gratitude.* New York: Basic Books.

Kohut, H. (1971). *The Analysis of the Self.* New York: International Universities Press.

Laing, R. D. (1960). *The Divided Self.* London: Tavistock.

Lichtenstein, H. (1961). Identity and sexuality. *Journal of the American Psychoanalytic Association, 9,* 179–260.

Pirandello, L. (1921). Six characters in search of an author. In E. Bentley, ed., *Naked Masks: Five Plays.* New York: Dutton, 1952.

Rinsley, D. (1987). Fairbairn's object-relations and classical concepts of dynamics and structure. In J. S. Grotstein, M. F. Solomon, & J. A. Lang, eds., *The Borderline Patient: Emerging Concepts in Diagnosis, Psychodynamics, and Treatment,* Vol. 1. Hillsdale, NJ: Analytic Press.

Robbins, M. (1980). Current controversy in object relations theory as outgrowth of a schism between Klein and Fairbairn. *International Journal of Psycho-Analysis, 61,* 477–492.

Salley, R. D. (1988), Subpersonalities with dreaming functions in patients with multiple personalities. *Journal of Nervous and Mental Disease, 176*(2), 112–115.

Seinfeld, J. (1990). *The Bad Object.* Northvale, NJ: Jason Aronson.

Steiner, J. (1985). Turning a blind eye: The cover up for Oedipus. *International Review of Psycho-Analysis, 12*(6), 161–172.

Stone, M. H. (1988). Toward a psychobiological theory on borderline personality disorder: Is irritability the red thread that runs through borderline conditions? *Dissociations, 1*(2), 2–15.

van der Kolk, B. (1987). *Psychological Trauma.* Washington, DC: American Psychiatric Press.

Vellacott, P. (1971). *Sophocles and Oedipus: A Study of Oedipus Tyrannus with a New Translation.* London: Macmillan.

Vellacott, P. (1978). Sophocles at Colonus: An alternative view. Unpublished manuscript.

Winnicott, D. W. (1960). Ego distortion in terms of true and false self. In *The Maturational Processes and the Facilitating Environment.* New York: International Universities Press, 1965, pp. 140–152.

10

Fairbairn's Structural Theory and the Communication of Affects

ARNOLD H. MODELL

THE CONTRAST BETWEEN FREUD'S AND FAIRBAIRN'S THEORIES OF PSYCHIC STRUCTURE

The growing appreciation and understanding of Fairbairn's theory of endopsychic structure can be attributed in no small measure to several excellent exegeses of his work. I am thinking particularly about the work of Greenberg and Mitchell (1983), Rubens (1984), Hughes (1989), and most recently Sutherland (1989; see Chapter 2, this volume), who is perhaps the only surviving analyst to have had close contact with the man himself. These authors have helped both to clarify a very complex and subtle theory of endopsychic structure, and also to place Fairbairn's contribution in a historical perspective. Sutherland (Chapter 2, p. 195) puts it as follows:

> [Fairbairn] was the first to propose in a systematic manner the Copernican change of founding the psychoanalytic theory of the human personality on the experiences within social relationships instead of the discharge of instinctual tensions originating solely within the individual.

As Sutherland and many others have recognized, Fairbairn's theory was the first attempt to recast Freudian psychoanalysis—a predominantly (but not exclusively) one-person, intrapsychic theory—into a two-person, social theory.[1] In contrast to Freud's concept of primary narcissism, Fair-

[1]For a further discussion of psychoanalysis as a one-person psychology, see Modell (1984).

bairn viewed the self as a holistic, object-seeking entity from the beginning—a view that now finds support in infant research (Stern, 1985; for a review of 1980s infant observations, see Beebe & Lachman, 1988). Fairbairn's theory is radically different from that of Freud, so that Fairbairn's concept of psychic structure cannot be conflated with the structural concepts of ego psychology, as some authors (e.g., Kernberg, 1976) have attempted to do. Rubens (1984, p. 432) has noted:

> One of the most brilliant of Fairbairn's insights lies precisely in his recognition that the self—and not some ideational representation (for who, in that case, would be the one doing the representing?)—has as its primary, innate function active expression in the form of relationship with the object world—and not, until the intervention of some pathological process, with some ideational representation thereof!

A further divergence from Freud's conception of structural psychology was Fairbairn's belief that from an initially unitary, object-seeking self, dissociative splits develop as a result of traumatic *interactions* between the child and his caretaker. The nonacceptance of the self by the child's caretaker results in a split within the central ego (self), recreating this traumatic interaction within the ego (self). Fairbairn described this in endopsychic terms as a relation between the ego and its internalized objects. Perhaps the clearest exposition of this theory was provided by Fairbairn in response to criticism by a Jungian analyst, Abenheimer. Sutherland (1989, p. 147) quotes it as follows:

> [Fairbairn regards] the *developed* psyche as a multiplicity of structures of two classes, ego structures and internal objects. The latter are conceived of as introjected and structured as representations of emotionally significant aspects of persons upon whom the subject depended in early life. The internal object is an endopsychic structure, other than an ego structure, with which an ego structure has a relationship comparable to a relationship with a person in external reality. (emphasis added)

To find an analogous concept in Freud, one would have to turn to Freud's (1920) description of the child's game where the child adapts to the mother's departure by throwing and withdrawing a reel over the side of his cot. As Freud observed, the child stages, within his own world, those events in the external world that he cannot control. Winnicott (1960, p. 46) would later describe this as "impingements gathered into the infant's omnipotence." Freud, however, did not describe the child's internal representation of the mother's departure as a psychic structure. Instead, he viewed structure formation as something akin to an archeological or geological record, laid down as the consequence of both the loss of an object (as in mourning) and the renunciation of an instinctual desire, as illustrated in this oft-quoted passage:

> The broad general outcome of the sexual phase dominated by the Oedipus complex may, therefore, be taken to be the forming of a precipitate in the ego, consisting of these identifications in some way united with each other. This modification of the ego retains its special position: it confronts the other contents of the ego as an ego ideal or super-ego. (Freud, 1923, p. 34)

But Freud did describe something similar to internalized objects in the relation between the ego and superego, which he depicted as reminiscent of the power of a controlling parent and a submissive child (Freud, 1933a).[2] Unlike Fairbairn, however, Freud saw this internalized object relationship as resulting from an instinctual renunciation and did not attribute it to developmental trauma. Freud attributed the origin of the superego instead to phylogenetic trauma, a racial memory of the threat of punishment from the primordial father. In accordance with his acceptance of Haeckel's law, he held that the development of the individual recapitulates a phylogenetic trauma (Freud, 1933b). Freud continued to believe, for example, that the fear of castration that characterizes the relation between the ego and superego results from a racial memory of the murder of the father by the primal horde of sons (as described earlier in *Totem and Taboo*; Freud, 1913): "The super-ego, according to our hypothesis, actually originated from the experiences that led to totemism" (1923, p. 38).

In Fairbairn's theory structure is a record of traumatic *interactions*, whereas in Freud's theory psychic structure represents a mosaic of lost objects. This has enabled ego psychologists to make use of Freud's idea of unitary "object representations."

As Rubens (1984) has shown, Fairbairn's concept of psychic structure cannot be equated with the atomistic self- and object representations of ego psychology. I observed some years ago (Modell, 1968) that Freud's concept of the object representation can be traced to John Stuart Mill, whose concept of object representation was identical to that of the 17th-century philosopher John Locke. Freud, as an adolescent, was conversant with most major philosophical works, and as a university student

---

[2]Freud also suggested the idea of an internalized object in the following passage regarding the psychology of the psychoses. "Let us reflect that the ego now enters into the relation of an object to the ego ideal which has been developed out of it, and that all the interplay between an external object and the ego as a whole, with which our study of the neuroses has made us acquainted, may possibly be repeated upon this new scene of action within the ego" (1921, p. 130).

he translated John Stuart Mill into German. Freud never fully relinquished certain conventional philosophical assumptions that he acquired in adolescence, despite the fact that he was to revolutionize the Cartesian distinction between subject and object. Berlin (1956, p. 48) describes the Cartesian notion of mind,

> according to which the mind was something totally different in kind from the body which contained it like a box, in the part of itself called the brain. [This led to the idea of mental representation as follows:] particles emanating from material objects strike the human sense organs setting up a chain of effects in the nervous system, which somehow finally produces an entity different in kind from themselves—an idea in the mind.

Locke, who disagreed with Descartes regarding the existence of innate ideas, did not question Descartes's assumption that there is a discrete, encapsulated, atomistic entity in the mind that represents the corresponding object in the real world. Freud's acceptance of this particular philosophical tradition is most explicit in his early work on aphasia (Freud, 1891), which found its way into his paper "The Unconscious" (Freud, 1915). Freud quoted Mill as follows:

> The idea, or concept, of the object is itself another complex of associations composed of the most varied visual, auditory, tactile, kinesthetic, and other impressions. According to the philosophical teaching, the idea of the object contains nothing else; the appearance of a "thing", the "properties" of which are conveyed to us by our senses, originates only from the fact that in enumerating the sensory impressions received from an object we allow the possibility of a large series of new impressions being added to the chain of associations. (Freud, 1915, p. 213)

We have no indication that Freud altered this view of the object representation when he reformulated structural theory. Freud's concept of the "object representation" led Hartmann (1950) to suggest the complementary term "self-representation." This is the way the concept of the self entered into ego psychology. To trace the path further, the concept of self and object representation was used by Edith Jacobson (1964) in her description of the psychopathology of borderline and psychotic patients, which was later further elaborated by Kernberg (1976). He, in turn, as noted, attempted to conflate the term "self- and object representations" with Fairbairn's internalized object relationships. From the standpoint of ego psychology, one of the most influential and sophisticated uses of the concept of self- and object representations can be found in Sandler and Rosenblatt's (1962) paper "The Concept of the Representational

World." But here too, the self- and object representations are viewed as unitary elements shaped by energic (i.e., instinctual) forces.

As Fairbairn saw it, psychic structures comprise two broad classes: ego structures and internal objects. Ego structures, essentially conceived as portions of the self, have a relationship to internal objects that is comparable to relationships between the self and an external object. In this manner Fairbairn paired ego structures with corresponding objects: The "internal saboteur" is paired with the "rejecting object," and the "libidinal ego" is paired with the "exciting object." (For further discussion of the details of Fairbairn's schema, see Sutherland, 1989; Hughes, 1989; and Greenberg & Mitchell, 1983.)

THE LIMITATIONS OF FAIRBAIRN'S
MODEL OF THE MIND

As Gaarder (1965) has shown, there is an important distinction to be made between the representation of the object in the presence of the actual (external) object in current time, on the one hand, and the representation of the object in the absence of the actual object, on the other. This distinction has far-reaching implications, in that it corresponds to the difference between a one-person, intrapsychic psychology and a two-person, transactional psychology. In a one-person psychology, the representation of the object (and the corresponding psychic structure) is akin to a geological structure, inasmuch as it contains a record of past object relations; in a two-person psychology, the representation of the object is a template that organizes object relations in current time.

A one-person structural theory cannot easily be applied to the interactions that occur between the self and the object in current time. For example, we describe dependency, a process occurring between two people, as an event in the mind of only one person (Modell, 1984). On the other hand, it can be argued that Freud's structural theory has in fact illuminated the process of object choice and the perception of the object in current time. For example, transference can be understood as the reactivation of former identifications. But what is missing from this account is a kind of mental calculus that transforms the relatively fixed identifications of structural psychology into the rapidly fluctuating perceptions that characterize object relations in current time. The missing link is the communication of affects.

A reference to evolutionary biology provides a useful analogy (Modell, 1985). When investigating the case of bird migration, the biologist needs to consider not only the *ultimate* evolutionary cause (which traces the history of the species through millions of years), but also the *proximate* cause (which is in the realm of physiology, such as the bird's hormonal response to the shortening hours of daylight). Evolutionary thought and physiological thought occupy disparate conceptual realms; it took nearly a century for biologists first to recognize this disparity and then to reconcile both modes of thinking into what is now called the "modern synthesis" (Mayr, 1982). Both Freud's and Fairbairn's theories of endopsychic structure are essentially theories of ultimate causes. In psychoanalysis, we still await a new synthesis of proximate and ultimate causes such as we have seen in biology.

There is some irony in the observation that Fairbairn may have been the first Freudian analyst to offer a far-reaching alternative to the one-person context of Freud's structural theory (as illustrated in *The Ego and the Id*), and yet the model that Fairbairn proposed remains essentially an intrapsychic model. This is true, despite the fact that Fairbairn conceived the self to be object-seeking from the start. Fairbairn's theory can be considered, as has been noted earlier (Modell, 1968, 1975; Greenberg & Mitchell, 1983), as a response to an ongoing dialogue with Freud— Fairbairn's reply to *The Ego and the Id*. Unlike Freud's theory, Fairbairn's is a relational theory, but one that is translated back into a one-person psychology. The need to transpose transactional events into the mind of the subject can become a procrustean bed that leads to convoluted and ambiguous concepts. Elsewhere, I have criticized the concept of internalized object relations when used as a notational reference to "actual" object relationships in current time (Modell, 1984).

It can be said that every advance in psychoanalytic thinking receives its impetus from a specific clinical syndrome. For Freud, the study of depression illustrated the connection between identification and the loss of the object. His paper "Mourning and Melancholia" (1917) was a necessary precursor to *The Ego and the Id*. For Fairbairn, study of the schizoid personality performed a similar function; his paper "Schizoid Factors in the Personality" (1940) was a necessary precursor for his reformulation of psychic structure. The schizoid defense can be taken as a microcosm for his more general theory of endopsychic structure: Trauma can be controlled and assimilated through the transposition of the trauma of the real, external world into the internal world. This transposition results in a relationship between a sector of the self and an internalized object. Because these sectors of the self are observed to be noncommunicating, Fairbairn believed "splitting" to be a more accurate depiction of the dissociation that exists between states of consciousness and unconsciousness than Freud's concept of "repression." As I shall describe shortly, one can observe that in the process of projective identification, there are split-off sectors of the self that correspond to the two participants of the traumatic interactions of childhood. Like his model of the schizoid individual, who has become his own caretaker out of necessity, and who avoids transactional engagements with other people, Fairbairn's model of the mind is also a model of nonengagement; it is essentially a model of a defensive structure.

I believe that Sutherland (1989) is also aware of this limitation or unrealized potential in Fairbairn's theory, as indicated by his comments on Fairbairn's early paper "The Effect of a King's Death upon Patients Undergoing Analysis" (1936):

> In view of the interrelatedness of the internal objects and events in the outer world, . . . it is noteworthy that the theoretical implications of this are left aside. Fairbairn comments that Melanie Klein had early on in her observations noted the closeness of these interrelations, although he too did not pursue the issue. Most striking perhaps is that this relatedness points to a dynamic connection between "outer" and "inner" that requires a concept of the openness of the inner systems to the social field to maintain their stability by bringing supporting objects within their boundaries. It would seem that the ongoing existence in the external world of the King as its symbolic father-figure was needed against the inner destruction of the father, a presence in a supportive dynamic field even though an unconscious one. (Sutherland, 1989, p. 44)

SPLITTING OF THE SELF AND THE COMMUNICATION OF AFFECTIVE EXPERIENCES BY MEANS OF PROJECTIVE IDENTIFICATION

States of dissociated consciousness were known to psychological observers as early as the end of the 18th century (Ellenberger, 1970). This splitting of consciousness led in some cases to multiple personalities. If one could name a particular syndrome that dominated the attention and interest of psychologically minded psychiatrists in the 19th century, as borderline states do today, one would select the multiple personality. The phenomenology of splitting or dissociation was therefore known long before the advent of psychoanalysis. But it was not until Freud's invention of psychoanalytic theory that attention was paid to the *concept* of splitting.[3] The theory of splitting, as it developed within psychoanalysis, has several branches (for a history of the concept of splitting, see Grotstein, 1981). One such offshoot derives from Abraham's study of ambivalence

---

[3]An exception to this statement is Janet's contention that hysterical symptoms are related to split-off portions of the personality that are endowed with a certain autonomy (for further discussion, see Ellenberger, 1970).

in depression and mania, which led to Melanie Klein's theory of the splitting of the *object* into good and bad portions. Another division was
Freud's observation concerning the splitting of the *ego* as a defense in
cases of fetishism and in certain cases of psychosis. This was a new field
of observation that he uncovered in the last decades of his life. Freud's
concept of splitting differed from the more familiar intersystemic conflict between the ego and the superego, as "Freud's intention in speaking
of a splitting *of the ego* (intrasystemic) rather than a splitting *between
agencies* (between ego and id) is to bring out a process that is new in
comparison with the model of repression" (Laplanche & Pontalis, 1973,
p. 429; emphasis added). Fairbairn's concept of splitting represents a third
and different offshoot, in that he refered to a splitting within the *self.*
Unfortunately, he obscured the distinction between his concept and that
of Freud's by retaining the term "ego" rather than referring to the "self."
In summary, then, Klein described the splitting of the object; Freud, the
splitting of the ego; and Fairbairn the splitting of the self.

   I suspect that all major psychological discoveries appear first as intui-
tions gained through self-observation, and only later are verified by means
of more systematic observation. There is a long tradition of such self-
observation, extending from Saint Augustine to Freud and beyond. It is
well known that Freud discovered the Oedipus complex as a result of his
self-analysis. He told Wilhelm Fliess in a letter of October 15, 1897: "I
have found in my own case too, [the phenomenon of] being in love with
my mother and jealous of my father, and I now consider it a universal
event of early childhood" (Masson, 1985, p. 172). A similar piece of self-
observation led to Fairbairn's concept of the splitting of the self. Sutherland (1989) has described the interconnection between specific traumatic
events in Fairbairn's childhood and the content of his theory. We learn
of a particular episode in which Fairbairn as a boy saw some "blood-
stained diapers" [*sic*] in a pail at the back door and questioned his mother
about it, whereupon she flew into a furious rage.[4] Sutherland notes that
Fairbairn felt that there was something wrong with this kind of antisexual
atmosphere. Fairbairn had a marked sexual curiosity, which he experienced as both exciting and forbidden, and this characterized his relation
to his mother. As Freud viewed his own Oedipus complex as universal,
Fairbairn also elevated this self-observation into the status of a universal
theory of psychic structure, expressed in terms of sexually exciting and
prohibiting internalized objects. The details of this can be observed by
referring to Fairbairn's diagram of psychic structure (Fairbairn, 1952,
p. 105), where he portrayed a central ego and a libidinal ego with corre-

---

[4]This and other traumatic episodes in Fairbairn's childhood were reconstructed
through interviews with family members and close associates by Dawson (1985).

sponding rejecting and exciting internal objects. I question, however, whether Fairbairn's particular experience of his mother as an exciting and forbidding object, although not uncommon, is at the same level of universality as is the Oedipus complex. For this reason, I find it difficult to accept the specific content of the psychic structures that Fairbairn described. But what I do accept is the principle that traumatic relations with one's primary caretakers result in a splitting of the self into sectors that remain uncommunicative and hence unconscious.

As I have noted earlier, Fairbairn's model of the internalized object is one that can exist without the presence of the object in current time. What needs to be added to this theory is the process of the communication of affects that connects these internal structures with objects in present time. Fairbairn's aphorism that libido is not pleasure-seeking but object-seeking should be modified to state that *affects* are not pleasure-seeking but object-seeking (Modell, 1980). Affect is the missing dimension in Fairbairn's theory.

Kernberg (1976) has proposed the important idea, to which I fully subscribe, that affects are the organizers of internalized objects. However, I and others have had difficulty in accepting Kernberg's theoretical assumptions, in that he combines ego psychology with Fairbairn's theory of internalized objects. Fairbairn's importance in the history of psychoanalysis can be attributed in no small measure to the fact that he offered an alternative to Freud's instinct theory. Kernberg cannot accept both Freud's libido theory[5] and Fairbairn's theory of psychic structure. As Ghent (1989) remarks, Kernberg has performed a *trompe l'oeil* feat in changing the system while keeping it the same:

> . . . cathexes are, first if all, affective cathexes, that is, the qualitative element or economic factor involved in the intensity of primitive affect dispositions, which are activated in the context of primitive units of internalized object relations and constitute the organizers of such primitive units. (Kernberg, 1976, p. 113)

> In short, one might say that cathexes have a crucial function in organizing overall instincts as psychic drive systems: . . . From a different viewpoint, one may say that affects organize internalized object relations into the overall structures of the mind and, simultaneously, organize aggression and libido as major drives. (Kernberg, 1976, p. 114)

[5]Although I no longer believe in Freud's libido theory, and view the concept of instinct as obsolete, I am also unconvinced that Fairbairn's reformulation offers a fully satisfactory explanation for those phenomena formerly subsumed under the term "instinct" (Modell, 1968, 1975). Gregory Bateson (1972) has compared the term "instinct" to the term "gravity." Neither by itself explains anything, but denotes that which demands explanation and cannot be evaded.

We do have a concept that describes the affective interplay between psychic structure and objects in present time. I am referring to the theory of "projective identification." (For reviews of the concept of projective identification, see Grotstein, 1981, and Sandler, 1987.) I can confirm Grotstein's observation that splitting and projective identification work hand in hand. Projective identification can easily be incorporated into Fairbairn's theory of psychic structure. In turn, Fairbairn's theory requires what projective identification can provide—a means of conceptualizing the communication of affects. For what is split off and projected into the object, in the process of projective identification, corresponds to Fairbairn's internalized objects.

For example, a patient of mine during her childhood had repeated interactions with her father that proved to be traumatic: He would, for no apparent reason, and without any warning, become totally enraged at her. She accordingly distrusted her father's judgment and wondered whether he might be crazy. On one occasion during the course of her psychoanalysis with me (according to my best recollection), I informed her that I would be away for a single hour. She nevertheless arrived at that hour, firmly believed that I had not informed her of my absence, and wondered whether I might be going crazy. With this event in the background, she became increasingly condescending and critical of me. At first, I did not respond to her attacks upon me, but she perceived my anger in a change in my tone of voice. When I finally told her that I felt that she was harassing me, she was very surprised, for her aggressive behavior was completely unconscious to her. I believe that in this case the traumatic interaction with the father was mastered by means of an internalization whereby the attacking father and the attacked self became split-off sectors within the self. She experienced herself as a victim in relation to me inasmuch as her attack upon me was unconscious, so that when she observed my anger by noticing that my voice became somewhat more formal and stiff, she believed that this anger was unprovoked and came out of the blue as her father's attacks had done. It is clear, in this instance, that what was split off was an *affective* constellation corresponding to an internalized object.

My patient correctly perceived my anger, but she was unaware that another part of herself had provoked it. Accordingly, she felt that I was attacking her without any reason, as her father had done. In turn, I experienced her reaction to me as "paranoid," in that I knew that I was not initially angry at her but became angry in response to her provocations. The fact that certain affective sectors of the self remain unconscious contributes to the confusion that both participants experience when there is a projective identification. Furthermore, these split-off affective sectors explain why the experience of projective identifications can be uncanny.

I hope that this vignette illustrates that the concept of projective identification can be usefully joined with Fairbairn's endopsychic theory. Projective identification focuses on the affective experiences of the participants that provide the links between the representation of the object in past and present time. Freud considered this topic under the heading of the "repetition compulsion."[6] Freud's theory of the repetition compulsion required the postulation of a natural force that transcends the evident desire of all sentient beings to seek pleasure and to avoid pain; he viewed the death instinct as such a force. But contemporary biology offers no evidence that would support Freud's sweeping assertions. An alternative psychobiological explanation of the repetition compulsion has recently been proposed by Gerald Edelman (1987). (I have described Edelman's contribution in greater detail elsewhere; see Modell, 1990.) His theory of "neural Darwinism" revolutionizes the theory of memory. He believes that memory does not consist of a permanent record in the brain that is isomorphic with past experience; instead, he views memory as a dynamic reconstruction that is context-bound and established by means of categories. From this point of view, the internalized object as a carrier of affective experience may be thought of as a subclass of affect categories (Modell, 1990). But inasmuch as the repetition of painful affect categories is an essential mode of all cognition, not all affect categories are internalized objects. This leads to another problem concerning Fairbairn's theory of endopsychic structure. As unassimilated traumatic experiences reflect a certain degree of psychopathology, we are faced with the question: Is Fairbairn's theory valid as a general psychology? Fairbairn's theory can be best validated in our sicker patients, described as borderline or narcissistic personalities, but does his theory apply to healthier individuals as well? I tend to believe that we are all, to a certain extent, divided selves; however, whether such divisions in relative health correspond to Fairbairn's endopsychic splits within the self is a problem that awaits further investigation.

---

[6]Fairbairn made only passing reference to the problem of repetition in his theory. He noted that Freud's concept of the repetition compulsion is no longer necessary, as the libido is not pleasure-seeking, so that there is no pleasure principle to go beyond (Fairbairn, 1952, p. 78). Fairbairn explained the repetition of painful experiences by the fact that the individual is haunted by bad objects, ghosts in the mind.

REFERENCES

Bateson, G. (1972). A theory of play and fantasy. In *Steps to an Ecology of Mind.* New York: Ballantine, pp. 177–193.

Beebe, B., & Lachman, F. (1988). The contribution of mother–infant mutual influence to the origins of self- and object representations. *Psychoanalytic Psychology, 5*, 305–337.

Berlin, I. (1956). Locke. In *The Age of Enlightenment.* New York: Mentor.

Dawson, M. (1985). *W. R. D. Fairbairn: Relating His Work to His Life.* Unpublished master's thesis, Harvard University.

Edelman, G. (1987). *Neural Darwinism.* New York: Basic Books.

Ellenberger, H. (1970). *The Discovery of the Unconscious.* New York: Basic Books.

Fairbairn, W. R. D. (1936). The effect of a king's death upon patients undergoing psychoanalysis. In *Psychoanalytic Studies of the Personality.* London: Tavistock, 1952, pp. 223–229.

Fairbairn, W. R. D. (1940). Schizoid factors in the personality. In *Psychoanalytic Studies of the Personality.* London: Tavistock, 1952, pp. 3–27.

Fairbairn, W. R. D. (1952). *Psychoanalytic Studies of the Personality.* London: Tavistock.

Freud, S. (1891). *On Aphasia.* New York: International Universities Press, 1953.

Freud, S. (1913). Totem and taboo. *Standard Edition, 13,* 1–161.

Freud, S. (1915). The unconscious. *Standard Edition, 14,* 159–215.

Freud, S. (1917). Mourning and melancholia. *Standard Edition, 14,* 237–260.

Freud, S. (1920). Beyond the pleasure principle. *Standard Edition, 18,* 3–66.

Freud, S. (1921). Group psychology and the analysis of the ego. *Standard Edition, 18,* 67–144.

Freud, S. (1923). The ego and the id. *Standard Edition, 19,* 3–66.

Freud, S. (1933a). New introductory lectures on psycho-analysis. *Standard Edition, 22,* 1–182.

Freud, S. (1933b). *A Phylogenetic Fantasy.* Cambridge, MA: Harvard University Press/Belknap Press, 1987.

Gaarder, K. (1965). The internalized representation of the object in the presence and in the absence of the object. *International Journal of Psycho-Analysis, 46,* 297–302.

Ghent, E. (1989). Credo: The dialectics of one-person and two-person psychologies. *Contemporary Psychoanalysis, 25,* 169–211.

Greenberg, J. R., & Mitchell, S. A. (1983). *Object Relations in Psychoanalytic Theory.* Cambridge, MA: Harvard University Press.

Grotstein, J. S. (1981). *Splitting and Projective Identification.* New York: Jason Aronson.

Hartmann, H. (1950). Comments on the psychoanalytic theory of the ego. *Psychoanalytic Study of the Child, 5,* 74–96.

Hughes, J. (1989). *Reshaping the Psychoanalytic Domain.* Berkeley: University of California Press.

Jacobson, E. (1964). *The Self and the Object World.* New York: International Universities Press.

Kernberg, O. (1976). *Object Relations Theory and Clinical Psychoanalysis.* New York: Jason Aronson.

Laplanche, J., & Pontalis, J. B. (1973). *The Language of Psychoanalysis.* New York: Norton.

Masson, J., ed. (1985). *The Complete Letters of Sigmund Freud to Wilhelm Fliess.* Cambridge, MA: Harvard University Press/Belknap Press.

Mayr, E. (1982). *The Growth of Biological Thought.* Cambridge, MA: Harvard University Press/Belknap Press.

Modell, A. H. (1968). *Object Love and Reality.* New York: International Universities Press.

Modell, A. H. (1975). The ego and the id: Fifty years later. *International Journal of Psycho-Analysis, 56,* 57–68.

Modell, A. H. (1980). Affects and their non-communication. *International Journal of Psycho-Analysis, 61,* 259–267.

Modell, A. H. (1984). *Psychoanalysis in a New Context.* New York: International Universities Press.

Modell, A. H. (1985). Self preservation and the preservation of the self. *Annual of Psychoanalysis, 12–13,* 69–86.

Modell, A. H. (1990). *Other Times, Other Realities: Toward a Psychoanalytic Theory of Treatment.* Cambridge, MA: Harvard University Press.

Rubens, R. L. (1984). The meaning of structure in Fairbairn. *International Review of Psycho-Analysis, 11,* 429–440.

Sandler, J., ed. (1987). *Projection, Identification, Projective Identification.* Madison, CT: International Universities Press.

Sandler, J., & Rosenblatt, B. (1962). The concept of the representational world. *Psychoanalytic Study of the Child, 17,* 128–145.

Stern, D. (1985). *The Interpersonal World of the Infant.* New York: Basic Books.

Sutherland, J. D. (1989). *Fairbairn's Journey into the Interior.* London: Free Association Books.

Winnicott, D. W. (1960). The theory of the parent–infant relationship. In *The Maturational Processes and the Facilitating Environment.* New York: International Universities Press, 1965, pp. 37–55.

PART III

Clinical Formulations

11

The Tradition of Fairbairn

NEVILLE SYMINGTON

W. R. D. Fairbairn is one of the most striking figures within the psychoanalytic movement. He did not undergo a training analysis, yet he was accepted as a member of the British Psycho-Analytical Society long after it was mandatory to undergo such an analysis to become a member.[1] After having graduated from Edinburgh University with honors in philosophy, and then pursuing postgraduate studies in theology and Hellenistic studies, he decided while serving under Allenby in Palestine during World War I to become a psychotherapist. His decision meant starting again with graduate studies—this time in medicine, because this was necessary for someone wanting to become a psychotherapist. When he had qualified as a doctor and then as a psychiatrist, he worked as a psychoanalyst in Edinburgh for the next 40 years, essentially on his own.

Fairbairn showed no desire to found a "school," and yet he can be considered, together with Wilfred Bion, the most revolutionary thinker within psychoanalysis since Freud. The fact that he did not found a school has had the advantage that his clinical theories have remained uncontaminated by those disciples who give lip service to the words of their master, but misunderstand and misinterpret the content. Our knowledge of Fairbairn today comes from a direct reading of his papers, whereas it is quite possible for us to think we know the theories of Melanie Klein or Heinz Kohut through the practice of their followers. Fairbairn stands a solitary

[1]According to J. D. Sutherland (1989), Fairbairn underwent a personal analysis with E. H. Connell, an Edinburgh physician/psychotherapist who had had a personal analysis with Ernest Jones but who was not a training analyst.

beacon, with a few exponents of his views scattered here and there, but no organized school. The disadvantage of Fairbairn not having founded a school is that there has been little development of his theories, as there has been, for instance, among the followers of Melanie Klein. There has been no organized body of analysts working within the structure of his schemata, testing the different aspects of his theories against the phenomena thrown up by their clinical work.[2] So there has been no Fairbairnian tradition, no recognizable development. However, I want in this chapter to suggest one analyst who has, I believe (though perhaps unknowingly), worked within his orientation and framework and significantly developed his understanding. I am talking of the clinical work and theories of Frances Tustin—again, like Fairbairn, awarded membership in the British Psycho-Analytical Society for her exceptional clinical and theoretical contributions.

FAIRBAIRN'S DESCRIPTION
OF THE SCHIZOID PERSONALITY

Every psychoanalytic theory has been generated by a particular analyst in relation to a nonrandom group of patients. Consciously or unconsciously, patients with an identifiable symptomatology or character structure are referred to an individual analyst who also has a defined character. There is a developing process of mental growth in the patients as well as in the analyst. The patients have come to the analyst for assistance in overcoming their resistance to this development, and the analyst is challenged to develop a personal understanding in order to help them and himself in this endeavor. So every psychoanalytic theory is a structural mapping of a particular pathology. It is obvious, therefore, that the theory will not have general application to all patients; it will only be relevant to a discrete category. However, as understanding deepens, some elements in a theory will have a wider implication. Fairbairn focused his clinical attention on schizoid patients, and his theory represents his understanding of them.

The affect encountered in the schizoid patient is a sense of futility. Fairbairn stressed that this inner state is quite different from that of depression. Whereas depression is the affect accompanying a realization that the loved object has been damaged through the person's own unconscious

[2]A notable exception has been Donald Rinsley (1979, 1982, 1988; see also Chapter 15, this volume), who has critically examined and extended Fairbairn's concepts with particular application to personality disorders.

hatred and aggression, the sense of futility arises from the feeling that love has blown the object away. The schizoid patient has withdrawn from emotional relationships. He keeps his emotions and feelings in an inner sanctum, and defends himself against any contact with others that involves them. The schizoid patient hides what he feels—his pain, his disappointment, his happiness, his sadness—within an inner enclosure. According to Fairbairn, the analyst's task is to break through the outer defensive structure, and so establish contact with the inner emotional center. Fairbairn (1958) stated, "I have now come to regard as the greatest of all sources of resistance—viz. the maintenance of the patient's internal world as a closed system" (p. 380). A little later, he added, ". . . it becomes still another aim of psycho-analytical treatment to effect breaches of the closed system which constitutes the patient's inner world, and thus to make this world accessible to the influence of outer reality" (p. 380). These statements epitomize the sentiments that have more recently been expressed by analysts and therapists treating autistic patients,

Fairbairn said that this stage is similar to that described by Jung as "introverted." However, whereas Jung believed that this is a normal psychological type, Fairbairn viewed it as a pathological state that can be explained through early life experiences. It is the nature of libido, said Fairbairn, to be object-oriented. He repudiated Fechner's "theory of constancy," which Freud had adopted and which later, following W. B. Cannon, became known as the "homeostatic theory"; according to this theory, the aim of libido is the release of tension. Libido, according to Fairbairn, is that striving within each of us for emotional contact, and it is this that endows life with meaning. The person with a schizoid personality has, as a child, gone forth with love toward his loved one; on being repudiated, he has withdrawn into a shell and has remained there ever since, licking his wounds, so to speak. From then on, his emotional self is withdrawn and inaccessible to the outer world. His way of being in the world is now different from that of the emotionally confident person. This whole description is highly reminiscent of current clinical accounts of autistic patients.

The proper object of libido is the whole person of the other; therefore, when this is withdrawn the ego, libido, and object are split, and part of the ego attaches itself to part of the object. Instead of the emotional self (or "central ego," as Fairbairn called it) relating to the emotional center of another, there is an aspect of the ego attaching itself to a partial object. In the schizoid person, a split part of the ego attaches itself to a partial object, Often this is a bodily organ, but it may be the voice, the gait, some part of the person's clothing. This part-object attachment is well illustrated in Somerset Maugham's short story "The Consul" (1921). It is the story of a British consul in western China who tries to persuade an Englishwoman to return to Britain and leave her bigamous Chinese husband. At the last moment, she refuses:

> "But what on earth makes you stay with the man?" he cried. She hesitated for a moment and a curious look came into her eyes.
> "There's something in the way his hair grows on his forehead that I can't help liking," she answered. (p. 284)

So the withdrawn emotional state is frequently accompanied by fetishism or some perversion that assumes a compensatory function.

Another characteristic of the schizoid individual is the predominance of taking over giving. This is frequently conjoined with the attachment to a partial object. The partial object is always sought for the satisfaction of the self; it is taken for the pleasure of the split-off part of the ego. Freud's hedonistic theory, according to Fairbairn, is an expression of this schizoid pathology, and Fairbairn believed that it is a mistake to view it as a normal state of affairs. Hedonism is a deviant path taken by the libido following an experience of rejection from the mother.

Fairbairn discussed ways in which the schizoid individual manages his relations with people while keeping the emotional center withdrawn from contact. One is the way in which such a person stays within his role while maintaining emotional distance. I had a patient once of this sort. She was a secretary and felt safe when operating within this role, but got into a state of panic when a demand was put on her to mix socially, such as at a Christmas party. The adoption of an exhibitionistic mode is another means by which the schizoid individual manages to swap showing for giving.

The fundamental sense of the schizoid individual is that those close to him cannot reach him. Those who are close feel that they cannot reach the person and are somehow always in the presence of an absence. The central ego where the person resides is split off from those parts of the ego that are in contact with the outside world. With this splitting of the ego, the objects are also split and the libido as well. The subjective experience of this split libido is the dissociation of thinking from feeling, so that intellectualization becomes another defensive mode of someone with a schizoid character structure. When speaking to such a person, one becomes aware that the speech has a disembodied tone to it and that it is not expressive of the person. The speech is usually the expression of the ego's relation to an idealized object. The ego is in love with this object, as Fairbairn put it; I would prefer to say that the ego is hypnotized by the object in the service of repressing the bad objects to which the feelings are attached. Fairbairn (1940) stated:

Such a personality, when he is in love with an intellectual system, which he interprets rigidly and applies universally, has all the makings of a fanatic—which indeed he really is. When, further, such a fanatic has both the inclination and the capacity to take steps to impose his system ruthlessly upon others, the situation may become catastrophic. (p. 21)

The analyst trying to treat such a patient is frequently frustrated when he attempts to make contact with the self, which this ego–superego partnership is maintaining in a state of repression—in a "closed system," as Fairbairn called it.

Fairbairn believed that such a patient's experience of the outer world has been appalling, and so he has internalized this into the unconscious, where it exists as a bad object. The patient then defends himself against awareness. He has the illusion that the external world in which he was reared is good. According to Fairbairn (1943), it is preferable for him "to be a sinner in a world ruled by God than to live in a world ruled by the Devil" (p. 67).

What is this bad experience that the child has internalized? On this matter, Fairbairn's account is unsatisfactory because it is not specific enough. The bad situation that, via the internalization of bad objects, has created the schizoid structure is delineated only in a general sense. Fairbairn referred to homes in which there is drunkenness, quarreling, and physical violence. He did not say what the particular subjective experience of this is for the child. However, he stated that this situation is traumatic for the child because it connects him to an "internal bad object"; to avoid the experience of this, he is silent about being physically or sexually abused, since breaking the silence would then plug him into the internal bad object.

The child's earliest libidinal object is the breast, but this fairly soon expands to include the whole person of the mother. A bad consequence of civilization, however, is a larger degree of maternal absence than exists in a precivilized state. The mother's absence is experienced as bad, whereas her presence is experienced as good. To attribute both good and bad experiences to the same object is intolerable, so the object is split asunder, and this split is mirrored in the ego. Fairbairn did not specify the circumstances that lead to this. His conjecture came from some of the clinical formulations of Melanie Klein, but his view differed from hers. Whereas she believed that fear of annihilation is the primordial anxiety and that the projection of this intensifies the existing frustrations, Fairbairn thought that an actual bad situation has been internalized and that this explains the presence of the internal bad object. When we ask what that bad situation is, it seems to be the mother's absence, either physically or psychologically. The child's response to an emotionally rejecting mother is to turn inward and find gratification in autoerotic activities.

TUSTIN'S DESCRIPTION OF
THE AUTISTIC PERSONALITY

I now turn to the work of Frances Tustin, to see how it fits into this scheme of things. For Fairbairn, the bad experiences in a traumatic home environment establish a memory link with the internal bad object, but what this bad object is and how it originates remain unexplained. It is here, I believe, that Tustin fills in a gap. I think that Fairbairn's schizoid patients and Tustin's autistic patients are diagnostically the same. Fairbairn wrote most of his papers before Kanner (1944) wrote "Early Infantile Autism," and since that time the psychological state that Fairbairn describes as a "closed system" shut off from contact with the outer world has been called "autistic." Therefore, I believe that Fairbairn and Tustin have been concerned with the same group of patients. Fairbairn, however, only treated adults, whereas Tustin has mostly treated children. Although she has treated schizophrenic-type children, she has devoted her attention primarily to those who are autistic. I believe that Tustin, in these investigations, has both described the characteristics of the internal bad object and produced a coherent theory about its origins.

Problems with Fairbairn's Terminology

When we talk of an "internal bad object," it conjures up the image of a phenomenon that is entirely mental. This then leads us up a false trail. There is no doubt that a mental image which has a wrong pictorial coloring blocks the act of understanding. I would prefer to call the "internal bad object" a "repressed psychically active bad experience." This is a clumsy, awkward phrase, but I believe it to be more accurate than "internal bad object." Fairbairn's phrase is infelicitous on two counts: Both "internal" and "object" lead the investigator down a false trail. To take the word "object" first, an "object" conveys the sense of something that is inert, whereas the word "experience" incorporates the subjective participation as well. The bad thing is not only the something that has been done, but also the subject's interpretation of it and the subject's own active response to it. My criticism of the use of this word "object" is not confined to Fairbairn, but also refers to Melanie Klein and all those within the British object relations school. Bion broke away from this way of expressing things and mostly used the word "experience."

I do not mean to suggest that Fairbairn thought of the internal bad object as inert in itself; the problem is that the word "object" conjures up such an image for many. Fairbairn understood that there is a dynamic interplay between ego and object. I am here making a complaint about the mental images that are conjured up by language and the way a false image can block the act of understanding. I would prefer my readers to conceptualize Fairbairn's internal bad objects as bad experiences, because I think this will cue them in to the area that Frances Tustin has so elegantly illuminated. A reason for the repression is not only the bad memory, but guilt about the subject's own response. My clinical experience is that when a very good external experience is presented and the bad is heavily repressed, it is partly because what is unbearable is what the subject has done: It is extremely difficult to accept what "I have done" in the situation. Then the "I have done" is incorporated into the interpretation of the bad psychic happening.

The interpretation is the patient's active construction of events. I do not mean here an interpretation in words, such as that which the analyst gives, but rather the "domain assumption"—to invoke the phrase of the sociologist Alvin Gouldner (1971). By "domain assumption," Gouldner means the basic disposition that a person has about an aspect of mankind (e.g., that men are rational or basically good). The patient comes to the analyst with domain assumptions about his nuclear family, and these are partly unconscious and partly conscious. This bad experience is tenaciously held onto; to give it up requires an upheaval of the person's basic way of looking at things and his interpretation of the world.

Now it is true that the bad experience is held onto internally by the patient, but it is incorrect to think that as a psychic entity its existence is confined to the internal world, since it is psychically active in the external world as well. It is here that I believe that Melanie Klein's term "projective identification" comes in. This term is a description of the activity of this bad experience. Its activity is in an emotional pressure exerted upon objects in the outer world. The pressure is exerted in such a way as to try to force the outer objects to conform to internal configurations. The force of this pressure is enormous in patients who are psychotic or borderline. The term "internal" is therefore very misleading. That the configuration is inwardly held onto is true, but to think that its activity is maintained within that sphere can be misleading. As far as I can tell, Fairbairn was not aware of "projective identification," whereas Tustin is. I think this may explain why Fairbairn allowed the boundaries of the analytic setting to sag and be flexible, whereas Tustin holds them very firmly and in fact believes that the keeping of firm boundaries in itself begins to reverse the process whereby pathological autism has become established.

The Development of Autism: Tustin's View

So the "repressed psychically active bad experience" becomes deeply established in the personality. Fairbairn did not tell us specifically how this comes about, but he did say two things that set the stage for an explanation: (1) that the infant's first object is a partial object, the mother's breast; and (2) that if the child's love of the object is rejected, then he reverts to autoerotic activities such as thumb sucking, masturbation, or perverse gratifications. Fairbairn did not indicate exactly what this rejection consists of, but he implied that the mother is not emotionally contactable.

Frances Tustin suggests that there is an event filled with acute pain that occurs at a very early stage of development. The infant undergoes a violent separation from his primary love object before he is psychologically ready for this. The effect of this is to leave a great gaping "black hole" of emptiness at the center of the child's being, and this pain center is covered over with a protective shell that leaves the child impenetrable. The result is that the person cannot be reached emotionally by an outsider. At this early stage of development, when the infant is attached to the partial maternal object, no differentiation is felt to exist between the child and the object. This state has also been described by Mahler and others (Mahler, Pine, & Bergman, 1975). Infant and breast are one, with the result that when the breast is suddenly torn away, the child feels that parts of his insides have also been torn away. The result is described in the anodyne language of psychiatry as "psychotic depression," but as Tustin (1972) says, the child's own language—"black hole"—is much more descriptive. Bodily parts are felt to be torn away. I am sure we have all witnessed someone falling down some steps and hurting himself badly; as people rush toward the person, he desperately signals the philanthropists away. What happens is something akin to this. The child, following his intensely painful experience, signals all figures in the environment away and closes himself off from the surrounding world. The child turns inward to lick his wounds. The true object of libido, which is the emotional contact with another, is forsaken for a compensatory object, which is sensual. Tustin has described this as a "flowing over" of sensual elements.

The autistic child centers his activities upon sensations. His libido hones in on sensations per se, and these replace emotional contact. Because it is through effective contact that people develop emotionally, the autistic child remains closed off from the world of people and feeds his frustrated state with autosensuous sensations. In this early catastrophe the emotional being is torn away, and so the child has undergone not just the loss of the primary love object but part of himself also. Tustin came to this conclusion after treating a number of autistic children; more recently, she has demonstrated the existence of autistic areas in adult neurotic patients (Tustin, 1986). In this way she has supplied the missing link in Fairbairn's formulation. Inserting this discovery into Fairbairn's narrative of the origins of the schizoid state gives his formulation an authentic ring. It makes his theory more truly analytic.

Tustin's Technique versus Fairbairn's

The fact that Tustin has supplemented Fairbairn's account of the origin of the schizoid state raises some questions about the technique that he developed toward the end of his life and that he elaborated in some detail in his well-known 1958 paper. In her paper "Steps in Reversing Pathological Autism," Tustin (1981) emphasizes the need to hold all the treatment boundaries firm; she stresses this in other papers as well. She also says that the sensory state inside the autistic child is "soft," and that there is an inner experience of what she calls a "marshmallow mother." This is the hopelessly soft, gooey state of things inside the individual following the primordial catastrophe. Against this inner softness there is erected a hard shell or barrier. Tustin says that this inner soft, gooey state begins to develop "musculature" through encountering firm muscles in to the therapist. The experience of firm muscles is brought about through regular session times, firm boundaries, and not giving in to the patient. So, for instance, Tustin is firm about not allowing an autistic child patient to take a toy home. It is through coming up against a firm structure in this manner that "mental muscles" begin to develop in the child. Tustin says that this begins to reverse the autistic process, and implies that without it interpretation will be valueless. This contrasts with Fairbairn's 1958 paper, in which he described the way in which he modified classical analytic technique. He gave up the use of the couch and became free with time boundaries. He described the ways in which he became adaptable to his patients' needs in these regards. He implied that he crashed through the wall of the closed system through interpretation alone. So here is a crucial difference in technique.

Tustin speaks in the language of the tactile and of sensations, and therefore the reversal of the autistic (schizoid) state also needs to be thought of in these terms. By contrast, Fairbairn talked of the mind in strictly mental terms; he thought of the ego as split, and believed the work of psychoanalysis to be achieved through interpretations that mend the splits. Where Fairbairn talked of splits in the ego, Tustin speaks of a "soft, marshmallow" state. The latter way of talking corresponds more closely to the ways in which such patients actually describe themselves. For instance, when I finally managed to get through to a middle-aged patient with autistic features, she would subsequently describe herself as feeling in a state of collapse until she "flicked a switch" and managed to put her shell or wall up again. The advantage, it seems to me, of describing the inner state of affairs in a language of the senses is that it makes more evident the significance to the patient of minute changes in the psycho-analytical environment. My experience of patients with autistic or schiz-oid features is that they are ultrasensitive to the most minute changes in the analyst's tone of voice, deportment, dress, changes in time, arrange-ment of the room, and so on.

   Guntrip (1975) noted that when his analytic session with Fairbairn was over, he would then have a seminar with him in which they would discuss theory, clinical matters, and so on. What the effect of this on Guntrip was is unknown, but he indicates that in his interpretative work Fairbairn remained at the Oedipal level, which clearly was not effective for his patient. It would seem that although Fairbairn intellectually under-stood the pre-Oedipal level, he did not seem to connect with it emotion-ally and understand it at the sensory level; otherwise, he would not have seen Guntrip for a clinical seminar immediately after the analytic session. Tustin, however, clearly grasps the crucial significance of making such a connection, and I believe that if we understand that she is concerned with the same category of patients as Fairbairn was, we see that she has cor-rected an error in Fairbairn's technique. It is a correction that is of great importance for psychoanalysts and psychotherapists treating patients who are autistic or schizoid.

   Tustin was educated within the Kleinian tradition, and, it seems, was insulated from the work of analysts from other schools until she presented her first paper on autism in 1966, when someone pointed out to her that Winnicott and Mahler had described the very early type of depression that she was describing. This led her to read more widely both these authors and also Balint. She makes no mention of having read Fair-bairn, but I believe that when she made her conjecture about the psycho-logical origins of autism, she made a crucial theoretical move from Klein to Fairbairn. Klein posited that the inner state of disintegration is at-tributable to the inherent power of the death instinct and the infant's attempt to deal with it, whereas Fairbairn posited that it comes about through the infant's experience of an emotionally unresponsive mother. As I have tried to show in this chapter, Tustin fills out the picture here in detail—a picture of which Fairbairn only sketched the outline. Her explanatory model is in the tradition of Fairbairn, not of Klein. There-fore the place of Tustin is within the tradition of Fairbairn, and she emerges as a prime exponent of psychoanalytical treatment within that school.

CONCLUSION

I contend that the patients whom Fairbairn described as schizoid are diagnostically the same patients whom Tustin describes as autistic. Tustin has filled a gap left by Fairbairn by describing in detail the early traumatic experience that leads to autism. She has further corrected an error in Fairbairn's technique. The work of Tustin thus represents a development of psychoanalysis within the tradition of Fairbairn.

REFERENCES

Fairbairn, W. R. D. (1940). Schizoid factors in the personality. In *Psychoanalytic Studies of the Personality*. London: Tavistock, 1952, pp. 3–27.
Fairbairn, W. R. D. (1943). The repression and the return of bad objects (with special reference to the 'war neuroses'). In *Psychoanalytic Studies of the Personality*. London: Tavistock, 1952, pp. 59–81.
Fairbairn, W. R. D. (1958). On the nature and aims of psycho-analytical treatment. *International Journal of Psycho-Analysis, 39*, 374–385.
Gouldner, A. W. (1971). *The Coming Crisis of Western Sociology*. London: Heinemann.
Guntrip, H. (1975). My experience of analysis with Fairbairn and Winnicott (How complete a result does psycho-analytic therapy achieve?). *International Review of Psycho-Analysis, 2*, 145–156.
Kanner, L. (1944). Early infantile autism. *Journal of Paediatrics, 25*.
Mahler, M., Pine, F., & Bergman, A. (1975). *The Psychological Birth of the Human Infant*. New York: Basic Books.
Maugham, W. S. (1921). The consul. In *Collected Short Stories*, Vol. 2. Harmondsworth, England: Penguin Books, 1972.
Rinsley, D. B. (1979). Fairbairn's object-relations theory: A reconsideration in terms of newer knowledge. *Bulletin of the Menninger Clinic, 43*, 489–514.
Rinsley, D. B. (1982). Fairbairn's object relations and classical concepts of dynamics and structure. In *Borderline and Other Self Disorders: A Developmental and Object-Relations Perspective*. New York: Jason Aronson, pp. 251–270.
Rinsley, D. B. (1988). Fairbairn's basic endopsychic situation considered in terms of "classical" and "deficit" metapsychological models. *Journal of the American Academy of Psychoanalysis, 16*, 461–477.
Sutherland, J. D. (1989). *Fairbairn's Journey into the Interior*. London: Free Association Books.
Tustin, F. (1966). A significant element in the development of autism. *Journal of Child Psychology and Psychiatry, 7*, 53–67.
Tustin, F. (1972). *Autism and Childhood Psychosis*. London: Hogarth Press.
Tustin, F. (1981). Steps in reversing pathological autism. In *Autistic States in Children*. London: Routledge & Kegan Paul, pp. 173–183.
Tustin, F. (1986). *Autistic Barriers in Neurotic Patients*. New Haven, CT: Yale University Press.

12

The Allure of the Bad Object

ELEANORE M. ARMSTRONG-PERLMAN

Years ago, when working in a psychiatric hospital, I became aware that in many cases admission had been precipitated by the loss of a relationship. Such patients might be acutely regressed, or might present with a florid psychotic confusional state with manic grandiosity and paranoid and phobic features. Internal reality was superimposed on external reality. I was involved in interviewing members of the immediate family and any other relevant significant others. Slowly, in each case, a picture emerged of what might have been the emotionally salient features precipitating the breakdown. One breakdown might have been precipitated by the marriage of a sibling who had been *in loco parentis;* the patient could not tolerate the loss and the phantasies that it had aroused in him. Another might have been precipitated when the patient's long-separated wife finalized divorce proceedings so that she could remarry. Still another might have been precipitated by a more immediate and comprehensible loss, such as a current rejection in the patient's erotic life.

In this hospital, there was a policy of going through previous medical records with a fine-toothed comb and, in a case with a history of previous breakdowns, of looking for circumstances that might explain the periods of relative remission. Clinical features often varied, so that no neat classificatory diagnosis could be assigned. Such cases could be described as polyneurotic with intermittent psychotic episodes. "Borderline" was not then a fashionable term. In a Fairbairnian sense, it appeared that various forms of neurotic defenses had been utilized to stave off the collapse of the ego. Sometimes it appeared that a period of relative re-

222

mission had coincided with a period where the patient had been seen regularly by an interested senior registrar, and that the current episode had been precipitated by his leaving. The senior registrar had become a significant figure or good object for such a patient, and the patient's response to loss was fragmentation.

In private practice there are emergency referrals with similarities to the patients described above. The more acute of these referrals tend to come from psychodynamically minded general practitioners. Such a patient arrives complaining of fragmentation and often a fear of going mad. Again, on exploration, one often finds that there has been a loss or threatened loss of a relationship, which appears to function as a precipitant for the current subjective experience of a disintegrating, beleaguered, overwhelmed self. There are variations in the extent to which these patients have been able to establish "holding situations" for themselves—that is, their capacities to use friends or relatives to establish a containing environment. However, the presenting situation is that the loss or impending loss of a relationship is traumatizing, inasmuch as the anxiety or terror experienced has almost overwhelmed the self. An experience of loss or rejection has precipitated affects and fantasies that the patients cannot encompass.

With these patients, one often finds a history of detachment or even active rejection of others in their erotic relationships. Such people are often significantly high achievers, with an established history of being (for example) inspirational managers or teachers, but they have functioned as resources for others. They are often acutely perceptive and adaptive to the needs of other people, and have done well in careers where the use of these skills is maximized.

The currently lost, or about to be lost, others have been objects of desire for these patients. The patients have felt "real" in these relationships. Yet when they give a history of their relationships, one wonders at their blindness. Their object choices seem pathological or perverse. There are indications that the others were or are incapable of reciprocating, or loving, or accepting the patients in the way they desire. The patients have been pursuing alluring but rejecting objects—exciting yet frustrating objects. The objects may initially have offered the conditions of hope, but they have failed to satisfy. They have awakened an intensity of yearning, but have remained essentially elusive objects of desire—seemingly there but just out of reach.

These patients appear not to perceive or register how narcissistically damaged their others are. They assume that the rejecting response of the others can be attributed to the extent of their own needs, driving their others away. Or, if they do perceive their others more accurately, they have a fantasy that they can omnipotently repair them and then convert them into the loving, accepting objects or persons that they are so desperately and obsessively seeking.

Such patients often assume that if only they can repress the intensity of their own needs and adapt themselves to the needs of their others, their relationships offer hope, whatever the costs of personal submission. The rage consequent to the frustration and humiliation when this hope is not fulfilled may be totally repressed, or converted into anxiety or a somatic symptom, or deflected onto third parties, or turned against themselves for not being able (as they see it) to submit enough or wanting too much.

The judgment of the others becomes paramount. It is as if the others become the ego ideal, now externalized, who must be submitted to at all costs. The loss of these relationships, or rather the patients' hopes of relationships, cannot be borne. The frustrating aspects of the relationships are denied, as well as the consequent rage, hatred, and humiliation, and the shame regarding the humiliation. It is as if the patients tailor themselves, their behavior, their wishes, and their fantasies to the behest or assumed needs of their others.

The shame may lead to estrangement from friends, who withdraw their support. They are only aware of the self-destructive nature of these relationships—which, perceived at an everyday level, are perverse, masochistic, or addictive—and lose patience and sympathy with the patients as a result. But the individuals cannot let go, no matter how malign their experience. The need is compulsive, and the fantasy of loss is experienced as potentially catastrophic: The fear is that loss will lead either to the disintegration of the self, or to a reclusive emptiness to which any state of connectedness, no matter how infused with suffering, is preferable. Any anguish occasioned by these relationships is preferable to the feared anguish of the acceptance of the hopelessness of the relationships. The patients cannot acknowledge the hopelessness of their relationships, or admit that the satisfactions they provide are partial and illusory, for to give up that hope may lead to a collapse of the self. The patients cannot accept that their desired others perhaps cannot love them as they would wish to be loved. As Bowlby (1988) says, no child under 10 can tolerate the emotional realization that his parents do not love him. But these patients are not, at least superficially, children.

For Freud, a compulsive relationship is a mark of the unconscious; for Fairbairn, it is a mark of the infantile. For both, the issue is the adhesiveness of the libido. Such an individual is "fixated" to a particular form of object choice. As Freud saw it, this poses a problem, given his stress on the pleasure principle; for him it is a form of the repetition compulsion or a manifestation of the death instinct. Fairbairn, however, stressed that the basic need of the individual is the acceptance of the object, and that the maintenance of the relationship with the object is necessary for the psychic survival of the infant. I believe that Fairbairn's theoretical structure provides insight into understanding the compulsive, masochistic persistence of such relationships.

THE CHILD'S DEVELOPMENT IN RESPONSE
TO FRUSTRATION BY THE MOTHER

Fairbairn offerd a theory of the personality "conceived in terms of relationships between the ego and its objects, both external and internal" (1949, p. 153). In his theory, the self is reality-oriented from the start and therefore constrained by reality from the start. "The real libidinal aim is the establishment of satisfactory relationships with objects; and it is, accordingly, the object that constitutes the true libidinal goal" (Fairbairn, 1946, p. 138). This view would appear to be receiving increasing empirical validation from the work inspired by researchers in attachment theory, and also from the work of developmental psychologists (Stern, 1985).

The basic need of the child is for a satisfactory relationship with an object. There is a need to relate as a whole person to a whole person. Inasmuch as there is failure in the empathic responsiveness of the mother to her child, the child turns to other forms of substitutive satisfactions. According to Fairbairn, it is only then—if the basic needs have not been met—that the pleasure principle arises as a secondary and deteriorative principle because of this failure. Thus, in Fairbairn's theory, the self develops and is structured in the context of the relationship with the mother, and is affected by the actual vicissitudes of that relationship. Actual frustrations lead to the development of accentuated need and its consequent frustration. Because of this frustration, the infant develops an ambivalent attitude to his objects and is then confronted with an ambivalent object that he finds both exciting and rejecting. It tantalizes and is thus exciting, but inasmuch as it frustrates it is rejecting. If the mother is too frustrating, given the infant's absolute need of her, she becomes infinitely desirable but at the same time infinitely frustrating, which gives rise to hatred.

The mother has a duality of aspects. She represents both hope and hopelessness. This gives rise to ambivalence, in that the object is both desired and hated. For Fairbairn, the strength of this ambivalence is related to the actual frustrations experienced at the hands of the object: "Ambivalence is not itself a primal state, but one which arises as a reaction to deprivation and frustration" (1951a, p. 171). It is rooted in the subjective experience of the infant with his particularities, related to a particular mother's interaction pattern. Again there is empirical validation for this: Attachment patterns that have been established are related to the actual capacities of the mother to respond empathically to the needs of her child, as Ainsworth (1982) has shown. Frustration gives rise to aggression, which represents "a reaction on the part of the infant to deprivation and frustration in his libidinal relationships—and more particularly to the trauma of separation from his mother" (Fairbairn, 1951a, p. 172). The child's ambivalence is structured by the fear of the loss of the object, which, given his state of absolute dependence and need for acceptance, is necessary to his psychic and physical survival.

Given his absolute need for his parents, the child must somehow cope with and defend himself against this intolerable situation. His total need does not allow a recognition of his mother as a bad object—a strategy that would solve the ambivalence, but at an intolerable psychic cost. The first attempt at a solution is internalization. "With a view to controlling the unsatisfying object, [the child] employs the defensive process of internalization to remove it from outer reality, where it eludes his control, to the sphere of inner reality, where it offers prospects of being more amenable to control in the role of internal object" (Fairbairn, 1951a, p. 172). Internalization is viewed as a process to establish control by banishing the ambivalent aspects of the relationship. It arises surely from the primary helplessness of the infant, when the empathic responsiveness of the mother fails to meet the gesture of the child.

Fairbairn stresses the defensive use of internalization. If one considers that a defense always has a protective function, the protective function of internalization in this case is to preserve the image of the mother as a safe person that the child can safely love. By controlling the embodied expression of the child's emotional and physical needs, it also limits the risk of the experience of disappointment and rejection at the hands of his mother. It is clear from Fairbairn that what is internalized at this stage is the whole object, with all its contradictory and confusing features.

However, this first method of protection does not solve the problem, because the main body of the object is internalized, and "both the over-exciting and the over-frustrating elements in the internal (ambivalent) object are unacceptable to the original ego" (1951b, p. 135). The next step in the process of defense is to cope with this internalized object. This is done by splitting the internal whole object. There is conflict between the internalized object and the original ego. So the frustrating and the rejecting elements

> are both split off from the main body of the object and repressed in such a way as to give rise to 'the exciting object' and 'the rejecting object'. The libidinal cathexes of these two objects, persisting in spite of their rejection, will then give rise to a splitting of the ego. (1951b, p. 135)

This is the second step in the establishment of the child's endopsychic situation. But this step affects his ego, that part that relates, and in future will relate and filter his perceptions and responses to the external other, because the self splits in terms of its attachment to these internalized objects. The libidinal self is attached to the exciting object, and the anti-libidinal self is attached to the rejecting object. The successful maintenance of this endopsychic situation depends on both the strength of the infantile need and the persistence of the original ambivalence.

The child still needs his mother in external reality, however, and the reality still persists. He has coped with this by internalization and splitting, which means that he can no longer see his mother as bad. But all these strategies do not alter the reality of the mother, who may continue to be frustrating and rejecting in "reality." The child has altered only his perception; thus, when his mother is bad, he is left with the problem of rationalizing and explaining to himself *why* she is bad. How does he explain the situation to himself? Obviously, his mother is bad because *he* is bad. If she does not behave to him in a loving way, it is because he is bad or unlovable. His defense mechanisms to protect the relationship with his mother in external reality have left him totally unprotected, except for the illusion that if he behaves differently perhaps his mother might love him. Given his absolute dependence, he cannot afford to perceive the object he depends on as bad, so he must be bad. Given the threat of the loss of his mother, he cannot risk expressing his feelings lest he lose her as a good object. The blame for the badness is attributed to the self. The child can attempt to alter and control himself, rather than acknowledge his mother's confusing duality of aspects. Fairbairn put this very strongly:

It also becomes a dangerous procedure for the child to express his libidinal need, i.e. his nascent love, of his mother in face of rejection at her hands: for it is equivalent to discharging his libido into an emotional vacuum. Such a discharge is accompanied by an affective experience which is singularly devastating. In the older child this experience is one of intense humiliation over the depreciation of his love, which seems to be involved. At a somewhat deeper level (or at an earlier stage) the experience is one of shame over the display of needs that are disregarded or belittled. In virtue of these experiences of humiliation and shame he feels reduced to a state of worthlessness, destitution or beggardom. His sense of his own value is threatened; and he feels bad in the sense of 'inferior'. The intensity of these experiences is, of course, proportionate to the intensity of his need; and intensity of need itself increases his sense of badness by contributing to it the quality of 'demanding too much'. At the same time his sense of badness is further complicated by the sense of utter impotence which he also experiences. At a still deeper level (or at a still earlier stage) the child's experience is one of, so to speak, exploding ineffectively and being completely emptied of libido. It is thus an experience of disintegration and of imminent psychical death. (1944, p. 113)

The child is afraid of expressing his aggression lest he lose his good object, and afraid of expressing love lest he lose himself. A patient of mine once said that his subjective feeling when his mother failed to respond to a loving gesture was like falling down a cliff.

The steps in Fairbairn's argument can be briefly summarized. The frustrations of the actual, reality-based relationship with the mother lead to ambivalence. This leads in turn to internalization as an attempt at control. Internalization, however, does not work, because it merely banishes the intolerable situation to the inner world. The next step is the splitting of the whole object, which leads to the splitting of the self. All these stratagems, though they effectively protect the view of the mother, do not alter the frustrating situation of the mother's unresponsiveness. Since the child has successfully protected the object, the only way to cope with the reality is by attacking the self.

OBJECT CHOICE AS A REPETITION
OF THE MOTHER–CHILD RELATIONSHIP

The process I have described results in the establishment of an internal trinity within the child. The child has become split in relation to the whole object. This may put him on a path determined by the persistence of his infantile need of looking for an object to put him together again, so that he can regain the lost unity of the self. We can view the "perverse" or "addictive" object choice as an attempt to find an object that, through associative links, combines the duality of aspects of the internalized whole object. Its duality of aspects may offer the illusory hope of the reintegration of the self.

Though all the king's horses and all the king's men couldn't put Humpty Dumpty together again, perhaps if the individual finds an object or a person that resembles his mother in her duality of aspects but in another guise, this will provide a relationship that can re-establish the lost unity of the self. The seemingly "perverse," "addictive," object choice should be viewed as a libidinal manifestation—an attempt to restore the lost unity of the self. It is an attempt to repeat and work through, in a new relationship, the alluring and rejecting features that led to the establishment of the basic endopsychic situation, which structured the splitting of the self. This structuring was necessary for the emotional survival of the self, to stave off the terror and fragmentation induced by the fear of object loss, but it has led to a depletion of the central self. Perhaps the perverse object choice enables the individual to feel real. As one patient of mine said after he was able to mourn the loss of such a relationship, at least it had enabled him to feel real rather than frozen.

Sometimes a patient is able to give a clinically detached picture of the exceedingly disturbed mother he has emotionally repudiated—a picture based not only on childhood memories, but on the mother's grossly disturbed behavior in the present. The mother has continued to behave as an exciting and rejecting object. The exciting and rejecting aspects of the relationship have been internalized by the child/patient. But this defense can be continually threatened by an external relationship. The parent is not a safe object. (Some of the mothers of my patients, for example, thoughtlessly used their children for their own physical comfort until late in the children's pubescence; the patients were perhaps confused, excited, and disgusted by this, but could not acknowledge it.) Thus the original splitting is continually threatened, and increasing layering and fusion are probably superimposed upon the internal exciting and rejecting objects. The central ego must continually adopt fresh measures to strengthen the original repression.

But when such a patient begins to elaborate on his current fears of losing his wife, one has the sudden and growing realization that he has, like Oedipus, married her in ignorance. The parallels can be glaring, but the patient is blind to the fact that he is consumed by a desperate, desiring need for his mother—a need that is related to her alluring, rejecting features. The wife may behave with the patient in a tantalizing fashion, craving body contact but at the same time rejecting sexual contact, thus repeating the pattern of a relationship with the mother who used the child inappropriately for her own needs. The mother tantalized the child sexually and in some sense excited him, but always diminished him. Like Jocasta, she was not able to relate to her child as her son, and her boundaries were blurred. She offered him excitement. His need for her was and still is accentuated, and in conditions of stress he may turn to the only satisfactions he has known. Despair and desolation are denied, and the adult then seeks sexualized but rejective encounters; these again exacerbate the need and the frustration, but are necessary to stave off the object loss and the feared fragmentation of the self. Such a patient is an inveterate breast seeker at heart, but now the breast has become genitalized. He is seeking a relationship with a woman's body, perhaps out of despair and futility about the possibility of establishing a relationship with another as a whole person.

In such a case, the father has often been psychically unavailable to the child to help him out of this stifling bond with the mother. She has been essentially his only means of satisfaction. As one patient said, "My mother has colonized my sexuality." His mother had idealized him and had behaved sexually inappropriately in an arousing fashion, but she had responded to his emotional needs by shaming him. He went on to describe his later compulsive sexual re-enactments, after he had been able to let them go, as his "false comforters." His adult sexual needs were masking his infantile, clinging ones and a rapacious need for body contact, to maintain the partial satisfactions that he had known.

For Fairbairn, the eroticization of need is consequent to frustration and the resulting ambivalence arising in the original relation with the mother. And "the more satisfactory [is the child's] emotional relations with his parents, the less urgent are his physical needs for their genitals" (1944, p. 122).

A CASE HISTORY

I would like to present a case that combines the features I have been discussing. A young man sought therapy because of a psychotic break lasting 3 hours, during which he was delusionally convinced that there were voices on the radio accusing him of killing a prostitute. Occasionally he did—compulsively and with great shame—frequent prostitutes. When he looked in the mirror during his temporary psychotic episode, he also hallucinated the face of his girlfriend.

On exploration, the current regression appeared to have been precipitated by his girlfriend's announcing that their sexual relationship had ended because she had decided that she was a lesbian; however, she still wanted him to share the same bed on a nonsexual basis. She was alluring, frustrating, and rejecting.

His mother had intermittently had the patient in her bed until he was 12, while his father was away on business. At the same time he had memories from his preschool days of being isolated and alone in the house when his mother used to lock herself in her bedroom. His father was orphaned in early childhood and was a depressed, defeated man, who during the patient's childhood (as in the present) spent his time in isolation in the kitchen. His mother used her son collusively to air her contempt for his father as well as to express her sexual discontents. His father was emotionally unavailable to help him out of this collusive relationship with his mother.

He was an extremely gifted achiever in the same field in which his mother said she had sacrificed her career for him. She encouraged him to succeed, apart from phone calls when she would talk about how suicidal she felt and express the wish that he would take a job in the provinces, where they could live together. This would precipitate bouts of suicidal despair in him, but he did not make any emotional connection between these feelings and the phone calls.

The symptom of the furtive, shamed use of prostitutes disappeared quite early in the therapy, when it was interpreted in terms of a perverse excitement used to mask despair and desolation. Again, it related to breaches in the patient's empathic communication with either his mother or his girlfriend. His mother, though emotionally insensitive to his emotional needs, had used him physically to relieve her own desolation. She had also provided him with some satisfactions: She seemingly had a genuine capacity for humorous play. Externally he was capable of being "the life and soul of the party," no matter how desperate he felt. He had sung for his emotional supper, and thus had bought his mother's love.

Some years later, following his change of career—after he realized that he had compliantly lived out the aspirations of his mother—he wondered whether he genuinely loved the woman he later went on to marry. Though he desired her and felt genuine warmth for her, she was not an idealized object. He was aware of her neurotic anxieties and could behave assertively with her, but she did not obsess him like the girlfriend of his youth, who had wanted him in her bed but without sexual contact. She did not combine allure with rejection; She thus did not evoke his mother and was not totally fulfilling. His mother had been both exciting and rejecting, while blocking access to his father. He had related earlier to a woman who was like his mother.

There was one later near-psychotic episode when his mother telephoned him alleging that his father was a pederast. This reinstated her as a persecutory object, and I saw him on an emergency basis on a Sunday. In the session he focused on his feelings about his mother's lack of concern for him. This was a few weeks before he was due to marry; he was also anxious about his new career. He perceived the phone call as a destructive attack on both himself and his relationship with his father. The therapy obviously entailed working through ambivalence, murderous rage, and despair. I tended to be kept as a good object, the one place where he could be himself.

In the therapy, he later came to feel loving feelings for his father and to establish a relationship with him, after he came to perceive that underneath all his father's blocks there was a capacity for love and affection.

IMPLICATIONS FOR THERAPY

I have argued that the obsessive love for the exciting object is not a random choice, but a refinding of the bad object. The object has aspects that are similar to the frustrating and rejecting aspects of the original whole object. It has features related to the alluring but frustrating aspects of the original parents that have led to the construction of the basic endopsychic situation. The current interactions and reality mirror the initial trauma. As is so often true, the present gives us a clue to the past. By paying careful attention to the features of the relationship with frustrating objects, we can perhaps begin to reconstruct the conditions of failure that have led to the basic splitting of the self.

This externalization cannot be dismissed simply in terms of projection, inasmuch as there is a denial of the aspects of the object that are both frustrating and rejecting. Some of the men I have worked with were the children, not of depressed mothers, but of hysterics who had been genuinely exciting and rejecting with their sons. The sons had gone on to relate to hysterics, but hysterics with features similar to those of their mothers. Moreover, their mothers were hysterics who would not have satisfied the criteria for Zetzel's (1968) "good enough hysteric" who would be amenable to treatment; they were beyond repair.

The patient needs to understand what has happened and is happening, so that he can individuate and begin to distinguish what belongs to the self and what belongs to the other. He needs to feel and to work through his ambivalence, so that he can begin to dissolve the cathexis to the exciting object and accept that the wish for the loving acceptance of the object is hopeless. The patient also has to feel that this no longer means that there is no hope for the self. He has to feel that he can survive the trauma of loss with sadness, and can mourn for that which he did not receive and acknowledge the good in what he did receive. As Freud wrote, "a thing which has not been understood inevitably reappears; like an unlaid ghost, it cannot rest until the mystery has been solved and the spell broken" (1909, p. 122).

ACKNOWLEDGMENTS

This chapter was originally presented as a paper at the W. R. D. Fairbairn Centennial Conference organized by the Scottish Institute of Human Relations, September 14–16, 1989. I am grateful to the organizers and the participants of the conference for the stimulation they provided. I would also like to thank Frances Tustin and David Malan for their helpful comments.

REFERENCES

Ainsworth, M. D. S. (1982). Attachment: Retrospect and prospect. In C. M. Parkes & J. Stevenson-Hinde, eds., *The Place of Attachment in Human Behaviour.* London: Tavistock, pp. 3–30.

Bowlby, J. (1988). *A Secure Base: Clinical Applications of Attachment Theory.* London: Routledge & Kegan Paul.

Fairbairn W. R. D. (1944) Endopsychic structure considered in terms of object-relationships. In *Psychoanalytic Studies of the Personality.* London: Tavistock, 1952, pp. 82–132.

Fairbairn W. R. D. (1946) Object-relationships and dynamic structure. In *Psychoanalytic Studies of the Personality.* London: Tavistock, 1952, pp. 137–151.

Fairbairn W. R. D. (1949). Steps in the development of an object-relations theory of the personality. In *Psychoanalytic Studies of the Personality.* London: Tavistock, 1952, pp. 152–161.

Fairbairn W. R. D. (1951a) A synopsis of the development of the author's views regarding the structure of the personality. In *Psychoanalytic Studies of the Personality.* London: Tavistock, 1952, pp. 162–179.

Fairbairn W. R. D. (1951b) Addendum. In *Psychoanalytic Studies of the Personality.* London: Tavistock, 1952, pp. 133–136.

Freud, S. (1909) Analysis of a phobia in a five-year-old boy. *Standard Edition,* 10, 3–149.

Stern, D. N. (1985). *The Interpersonal World of the Infant.* New York: Basic Books.

Zetzel, E. R. (1968). The so-called good hysteric. In *The Capacity for Emotional Growth.* London: Hogarth Press, 1970, pp. 229–245.

13

Resistance to the Release of the Bad Object in the Psychotherapy of a Refugee

VICTORIA HAMILTON

W. Ronald D. Fairbairn lived in Edinburgh, an elegant, patrician city of imposing streets and winding hills, where the Kirk—the Church of Scotland—still dominates the conscience of its inhabitants. And his idiosyncratic concept of the "moral defense" seems a natural product of this stern culture where sinners derive their sense of security and hope of redemption from a world ruled by a God who is unconditionally good.

Ella Freeman Sharpe wrote that if she were arbiter of psychoanalytic training, she would insist that the following books were compulsory reading for analytical qualification: "*Nursery Rhymes*, the *Alice* books, *Grimm*, *Anderson*, the *Brer Rabbit* books, *Water Babies*, *Struwelpeter*, *Undine*, *Rumpelstiltskin*, *Greek Myths and Plays*, Shakespeare's Plays." In the examination for qualification, "the would-be analyst would stand or fall" if he could "quote in full a verse in which 'London Bridge is falling down' occurs, give briefly the story of three blind mice" and answer such questions as "If the mice were blind, how came they to run after the farmer's wife so purposely? Account for the cutting of their tails" (Sharpe, 1930, p. 14). I doubt whether many psychoanalytic institutes would give credibility to such a test! Sharpe believed that it is "the phantasies, the make-belief, the games played, the games not played" that will "be the main road leading to the unconscious life" (Sharpe, 1930, p. 14). In sympathy with Sharpe's spirit, I turned to Robert Louis Stevenson's famous rhymes

or jingles for children—*A Child's Garden of Verses* (Stevenson, 1896)—
as relevant background reading for Fairbairn's ideas. Stevenson's poems
were the first verses I learned as a child, as I expect they were for many
Scottish children who, like Fairbairn and Stevenson, grew up in the sort
of outwardly respectable though inwardly tormented households of civilized Edinburgh society. The repetitive imagery of the verses constitute
what the British analyst Christopher Bollas has called "a historical set"
of "image-memories" (Bollas, 1989, pp. 193–199) in the reconstruction
of a Scottish childhood.

Among the evocative and characteristic titles of Stevenson's verses—
"Bed in Summer," "Windy Nights," "The Land of Counterpane," "From
a Railway Carriage," "My Shadow"—there is one with the strange un-
childlike title of "System" (Stevenson, 1896, pp. 34–35). It goes like this:

> Every night my prayers I say,
> And get my dinner every day;
> And every day that I've been good,
> I get an orange after food.
>
> The child that is not clean and neat,
> With lots of toys and things to eat,
> He is a naughty child, I'm sure—
> Or else his dear papa is poor.

In the poem, the child tells us with conviction that the reason that he is
short of food and toys is that he is naughty. As an afterthought—punc-
tuated by a dash—he adds, "or else his dear papa is poor." You will recognize the logic of the child's mind in Fairbairn's paper on the repression
and return of bad objects (Fairbairn, 1943). In Fairbairn's system, the
child purchases outer security at the price of inner security. He achieves
this by employing the "moral defense" which protects him from the perception that the people upon whom he must depend are "bad objects."

> In becoming bad he is really taking upon himself the burden of badness
> which appears to reside in his objects. By this means he seeks to purge
> them of their badness; and, in proportion as he succeeds in doing so, he
> is rewarded by that sense of security which an environment of good
> objects so characteristically confers. (Fairbairn, 1943, p. 65)

In his work with cases of child assault, Fairbairn was puzzled both
by the great reluctance of the children to give any account of their experiences and by his observation that the more innocent the victim, the greater
the resistance to anamnesis. However, these children did not display an
equal reluctance to blame themselves, which led Fairbairn to conclude
that the children would rather be bad themselves than have bad objects.

Although Fairbairn stated categorically that "if a child feels bad, it implies that he has bad objects," he also believed that "internalised bad objects are present in the minds of all of us at the deeper levels" since it is impossible for anyone to pass through childhood without having internalized and repressed bad objects. "What are primarily repressed are neither intolerable guilty impulses nor intolerably unpleasant memories, but intolerably bad internalised objects" (Fairbairn, 1943, p. 62). Both the objects involved in memories and the objects with which the individual is impelled to have a relationship are bad objects from the standpoint of the ego. We turn away from these objects because *all* bad experiences are intolerable and, in particular, those relationships with bad objects *upon whom we depend and are controlled.* The crucial distinction between the universal and specifically pathogenic internalization of bad objects lies, therefore, in the qualifier "*in*tolerably bad." To me, "intolerably bad" is the reverse side of Winnicott's "good-enough." (In Scotland, the usual expression for a state of well-being is not a positive but a double negative: the answer to the question "How are you doing?" is not "Good enough" but "Not bad." In other words, *tolerably* bad.)

So what makes a bad internalized object intolerably bad? An intolerably bad object is one with whom the individual can establish no *satisfactory* relationship. Nevertheless, since, according to Fairbairn, the human being is primarily "object-seeking," the individual is impelled to seek out a relationship with this "bad" object, a relationship that he cannot give up without facing the threat of personal disintegration. Thus, the object excites as it rejects the subject's approaches. This is an intolerable situation for any human being.

Fairbairn's thesis in the paper "The Repression and the Return of Bad Objects (with Special Reference to the 'War Neuroses')" is that intolerably bad objects are subjected to massive repression and, in the therapeutic encounter, meet with massive resistance. This resistance is unusually strong and manifests itself in a particular form—in the moral defense of *guilt.* The observation that "guilt operates as a resistance in psychotherapy" (Fairbairn, 1943, p. 69) led Fairbairn to make specific technical recommendations concerning interpretations of guilt and aggression. Fairbairn was excited and influenced by the new ideas of Melanie Klein which were circulating in the British Society during the 1930s and 1940s. But, in his clinical practice, he found that interpretations of guilt and aggression easily played into the patient's resistance to the release of bad objects, since the therapist became a moralizing superego figure who supported the patient's moral defense. Moreover, Fairbairn observed, the patient deployed his resistance in order to preserve at all costs his tie to the bad object, since he could not face the consequences to himself of its loss.

Fairbairn's military experiences of two world wars gave him a particular interest in what were then called the "war neuroses." He contrasted the release of bad objects in the controlled analytic situation with the "spontaneous" traumatic release that occurs in military patients during wartime. Wartime provides ample opportunity for the activation of internalized bad objects against which the subject has little resistance. From his extensive work with military cases, Fairbairn concluded that the chief predisposing factor in determining the breakdown of a soldier is separation anxiety or an infantile dependence on internalized bad objects. This anxiety can be alleviated in a totalitarian system where the individual transfers his dependence from familial objects to the regime. The observation that dependence on familial ties is what constitutes the "degeneracy of democracies" in totalitarian eyes has been exploited in both military dictatorships and civilian "liberation" cults. However, if and when the army or state ceases to provide the superego function, the internal moral defense through which goodness is safeguarded in the hands of a powerful authority weakens. With the collapse of group morale, the individual is at the mercy of acute anxiety from the imminent return of vengeful bad objects. Totalitarian systems function just so long as they succeed. Under conditions of failure, however, the regime becomes a bad object to the individual and the socially disintegrating effects of separation anxiety begin to assert themselves.

CLINICAL ILLUSTRATION

To illustrate some of these observations on the link between the release of bad objects and the analyst's technical difficulties in interpreting guilt and aggression, I shall describe excerpts from sessions in the psychotherapy of a 48-year-old South American woman whom I saw twice weekly for 3 years—from 1985 to 1988—at the Tavistock Clinic. She had been twice exiled, a refugee from state terrorism and near civil war conditions in two South American countries. For reasons of confidentiality and for the personal security of my patient, I shall refer to these two countries as Country A and Country B. I also omit references to specific dates and details of career which might identify my patient.

Isabel, a short, plump, and vivacious woman, spent the early years of her life as an only child "with the full attention of a very authoritative father" and "plenty of good nannies" in a small rural village. Her father was a respectable, well-off civil servant and her mother was a school teacher. She enjoyed a companionable and intellectual relationship with her father, who took her with him on his tours of the province. Her mother, a tall, elegant, blond lady, taught at the local school that Isabel attended. When she was 10, they moved to a large city where her mother suffered some sort of depressive breakdown—"she thought she was running mad"—that resulted in the end of her teaching career. Isabel's relationship with her mother was rivalrous, taunting, and unsatisfying. Although Isabel was much admired by her father and others outside the home for her outstanding intelligence, humor, and understanding, she did not at all resemble the image of a sophisticated South American lady. During her adolescent and undergraduate years, Isabel was an avid reader; through reading, she formed intense relationships with Simone de Beauvoir and other literary, philosophical, and political figures.

At the age of 23, Isabel made her first determined attempt to separate herself from this bad relationship by moving into a flat of her own. But, a couple of weeks later, she was called home because her mother had become seriously ill; a day or two later, she died of a cerebral hemorrhage, aged 52. Isabel then stayed on with her father, but over the next 2 years, they began to quarrel more and more and their relationship turned bad too. Her father told her that, after her mother's death, Isabel had "changed into her mother,"—"a very difficult person who was mentally disturbed." Eventually, aged 25, Isabel left Country A to take a master's degree in a university in Country B. There she subsequently learned that her father had married a younger woman and that they had adopted a baby girl. She made a suicide threat by turning on the gas stove, but answered the telephone and told a friend. She then saw the first of many psychiatrists, toward most of whom she expressed feelings of warmth and gratitude. For the next 8 years, she held various senior research and lecturing posts.

At the age of 33, Isabel married one of her students, Luis, who was 12 years younger than she. Luis, also a radical, was the handsome and gifted eldest son of an established, aristocratic family. After a miscarriage and a complicated pregnancy, Isabel gave birth to a daughter, Juanita. Isabel suffered a severe postnatal depression. Eight months later, there was a military coup in Country B. Isabel and Luis were rounded up and sent to separate camps, while the baby girl was looked after by her grandparents. Through the intervention of Luis's father, the family were given 24 hours' notice to leave. They flew back to Country A, where Isabel and her father re-established the good relationship that had existed in her childhood. Isabel secured a government position. Over the next 2 years, she and Luis sought psychiatric help while resuming their involvement in left-wing university activities. On the day of his first therapy session, however, a coup took place in Country A and Luis disappeared. Isabel and Juanita were told he was dead; 4 months passed before he was found in a prison camp in an extremely debilitated state, having been starved and tortured. This time, with the help of Isabel's father, Isabel and the

3-year-old Juanita were given permission to leave the country. They went to the airport not knowing whether Luis would join them or whether, once outside the prison authority, he would be killed en route to the airport. In fact, he was repeatedly tortured by electric shocks and pulled out of the van to stand with a gun held at his head. Once inside the plane, they were reunited but they were not allowed to deplane at any of the stopovers. They landed in London and were put on a train to a small town in the north of England.

The family arrived in this northern town very early one winter morning and were met by a Marxist comrade who took them to a tenement flat in one of the city's most dangerous slums. Neither Isabel nor Luis could speak or understand English, let alone the local dialect. The next month, Isabel again became pregnant. Through the warm and generous support of Marxist colleagues at the University, they moved to a hall of residence in a peaceful suburb. Luis absented himself from the home and buried himself in the university library. Isabel was left alone with her 3-year-old daughter and, after the birth of her son, she again suffered a severe postnatal depression. Two years later, the family moved down to a London suburb, where they were given refugee housing through the Church of England. Both Isabel and Luis enrolled as postgraduate students and obtained government grants. Luis supplemented the family income by giving Spanish lessons. For 6 years they lived the meager, suspended existence of refugees, outwardly quiet and grateful to the host country, and inwardly in a state of ferment. They kept up their spirits by a constant stream of threatening and inciting telephone calls with comrades and exiles in Europe and the Americas.

What precipitated Isabel's search for help? Fairbairn noted that patients characteristically seek out therapy when their defenses prove inadequate to safeguard them against anxiety over a threatened release of repressed objects. It would be simplistic to suggest that, throughout these horrendous years, Isabel had repressed her relationship with internalized bad objects. Nevertheless, her suspended existence between past and present, Latin America and Britain, shielded her from the impact of her internal situation. In the section headed "Present Occupation" on the questionnaire that people are asked to fill in when they apply for treatment at the Tavistock Clinic, Isabel wrote: "to be at home, seeing how the time pass, unable to do nothing with life." Isabel spent much of the day waking up from the sleeping pills she had taken in the early hours of the morning. She had a long history of sleep disturbance, but had become acutely restless and anxious after the outbreak of another political crisis in South America. Dreams of police and persecution started to bother her again when she had to return suddenly to South America to visit her father, who was very ill. These dreams had become so insistent that she feared she would "lose touch with reality." On her way back to London, she was told at the airport that her papers were not in order. Nevertheless, she boarded the plane and during the journey she "enjoyed talking to other people and forgot about it." On arrival in London, however, she was told that she would have to go back to South America to get her visa. She "talked her way out of it" by talking until she knew the plane had taken off en route to Spain. She persuaded the officials that she was entitled to live in Britain. Five months later, her father died. Isabel was distraught and guilt-ridden that she was unable to see him as he was dying. Finally, after several extensions, the funds for the research grants came to a stop.

With the outbreak of renewed hostilities in South America, the death of her authoritarian father, the suspension of funds, and the increasing ineffectiveness of drugs in combatting her dreams, Isabel was besieged by returning internalized persecutory objects. Within this state, the Tavistock appeared as a beacon of safety. Isabel related to the interviewing consultant, Dr. X., as if he were the reincarnation of her father. The consultant described her as a very friendly, warm person who made good contact despite her very poor English, which was difficult to understand. She linked her English with her longing to return to South America and with a deep feeling of not being at home in England. She acknowledged that she had never felt at home since the move from the countryside to a large city when she was 10 years old. Dr. X. pointed out to her that her escape into manic overactivity and thinking was a serious handicap to her development since it stopped her from really attending to her own needs and consequently to those of her children. And he commented that it must be frightening for children to have a "mad" mother. At the time, she responded to this interpretation with guilty gratitude, praising him for his perceptiveness and blaming herself for being just like her own mad mother who had been unable to look after her as a child. Afterward, she fell into a persecuted panic, believing that she was mad and that her children would be taken away from her.

My first task was to interpret the burden of guilt that led Isabel to reidentify so readily with a mad and incompetent mother. She willingly supplied me with many examples from past and present that validated the consultant's interpretation about a mad mother. Since the time of her mother's death, Isabel had encountered formidable difficulties in her concentration and in bringing any project of her own to completion. Completion was a central theme in the 3 years of our work together since she had to complete her Ph.D. thesis. The thesis included sections on South American women. However, within a few weeks of starting therapy, Isabel was able to write the first two chapters and the conclusion.

The first holiday break aroused extreme anxieties about her mental and physical security. During our last session before the break, Isabel asked me, "Is this a hospital or a day clinic? Do people stay overnight?" I said that perhaps she wanted to stay overnight with me to feel safe, but this meant being mad. On the other hand, if she was sane, she would be separated from me and left alone with her fears. I felt that she returned to her identification with a mad mother as a way of protecting herself from the perception of me as bad and rejecting. She felt depressed and restless during the holidays but found comfort in reading R. D. Laing's *Sanity, Madness and the Family*, a central theme of which is the schizophrenic as the family scapegoat.

During the following months, the weeks took on some sort of rhythm, as she was able to work on the day before and the day after sessions, before lapsing into persecutory doubt about her safety. She began to relate to me as her "protector." She mapped out all the chapters of the thesis, working inward from the introduction and the conclusion until only the middle chapters remained. As she approached the central "missing" chapter on some influential South American women, she said, "I must include this very important figure." (The central important figure was a woman whom her mother had admired and followed.) I said to her, "Now you are able to contemplate the end of the thesis, you think that your life will go on after the thesis and that our relationship will continue too." I referred to her bad relationship with her mother, a figure she had tried to separate from by blotting out any leading associations. She said, "I was thinking that since October I have always been able to come every week, I have never missed an appointment, and I am nearly always on time. This is a great change for me." She set the date for the completion of her thesis on the anniversary of her mother's death. During our second break over Easter, she took her children for their first holiday to stay with an English friend in the countryside.

On reunion with me, Isabel commented, "It is nice to be with English people, not just South Americans talking about refugees." She noticed a big difference in herself during the holidays in that her worries about trains, which had made travel impossible in recent years, had receded, and she had managed the complicated journey to the countryside. She also made a trip alone to a conference at which she read a paper. There she met many people, both old friends from the north of England and new colleagues—in particular, a younger woman who had finished her Ph.D. and already obtained a job. This gave Isabel great hope. She had been asked out by three men, one of whom had asked her to dance. All her life she had loved to dance.

The following session (session 2 after the Easter holiday), however, Isabel returned in a very different mood. She was not feeling well and was having difficulty sleeping, waking every hour of the night. I said,

"When we met again last week, you were feeling very good about the holidays. Perhaps seeing me evoked other feelings—of depression and anger." She said, "I thought so—and in fact it bothered me, because I remember when I was going on the train, I thought, 'But I have been feeling so well, what shall I do with Victoria?' If I become well, I will not come here." She laughed. I said, "I think you are very frightened of losing the you that is getting better. You felt that you really could do things over the holidays which involved recovering parts of yourself that you had lost . . . you enjoyed taking the children for a holiday in the country, giving your paper, renewing old connections and meeting new friends, talking to men, even thinking of dancing . . . but you see this aspect of yourself in opposition to me. If you are well and functioning and successful, then you must discard me." Isabel replied, "Yes, in fact I was quite worried. I had been doing so well on my thesis, but the last 2 days I have done nothing, no excuse, just no energy." I suggested that she saw this well and successful part of herself as locked in a deadly struggle with me— as with her mother—and that one of us would die or would have to be got rid of. She said, "Yes, I have been very worried about my health this week." She went on to connect her feelings with a trip to Harrods with Juanita after the last session. Isabel had felt tired, in addition to which they had no money. But Juanita pleaded with her mother to go, saying, " . . . just to buy a pencil." Going to Harrods had upset Isabel because her parents had always bought their clothes at a large, traditional department store identical to the one in London.

I linked Isabel's feelings about going to Harrods with Juanita with what we had been talking about at the end of the previous session— namely, the struggle she felt she was in with me for her life, and the struggle now between herself and Juanita which was so like the one that had gone on between her own mother and herself. Isabel went on to talk about how disturbed she felt when I had talked about finishing her thesis and imagining life going on after it, "because if I think about it, it really means staying in this country and losing [Country A]." I said that seeing me last week was like a jolt and that it had brought up tremendous conflict, especially feelings of loss, and that maybe she had felt very disturbed in her sleep and in her work because she felt that I had created this disturbance and unbalanced the equilibrium she had reached during the holidays. She laughed and said, "Do you think so? Perhaps." She became serious again and said, "I really have been thinking of all these things. I have been here a long time now. I like this country, but I really know very little about it. I really do not *know* about this country." She then said that the trouble was Luis. *He* was still "in this limbo." He had been "*very* anxious during the whole holiday." He was in a terrible dilemma about whether to bury himself in his thesis or to apply for a full-time job.

I commented: "I think that you feel very alone and very resentful now that you are trying to face, and sort through, all these unresolved conflicts that have been in limbo for many years. And I think you look at me and think it is so easy for me, I am English, I am in my own country, everything fits, I do not need to worry about all these decisions. And perhaps I really do not understand at all what it is like to have to make such life decisions and to give up so much." She laughed, "Well, I do not think that any more, but Luis does. He said to me the other day, 'I think her father is a lord, she is the son of a lord' [she laughed], but I said no."

I wondered whether perhaps she did have feelings like this about me, and I referred to her earlier suspicions of me as a middle-class bourgeois person, involved neither in politics nor in the struggle of women in poor countries. I said, "If we are not the same, perhaps it feels as if I can't possibly experience your feelings; they would not be real to me." Isabel said, "I did think that, but now I don't. I feel you do understand me, that it is possible. But Luis persisted in this. He said he thinks your father is a Sir . . . Hamilton, an admiral in the navy: 'She is a very upper-class person.'" I said, "Even though Luis conjectures all these things about me, I really feel that when you got on the train to see me last week, you felt all the things *you* had during the holidays dwindling away and me having so much—wealth, a country—we just cannot both live and have good things. You feel that I am the lucky one." I linked these feelings to the visit to Harrods, suggesting that this had aroused strong feelings of injustice, hurt, and anger about all that she had lost. She agreed and spoke about the last time she had been to the large department store in Country A, when Luis was in prison. Her father had given her some money and she had gone with Juanita and bought a lot of clothes. She had felt terribly guilty. I said, "It is hard because the better you feel and the more you surface in to your present life here, the more loss you also feel." Isabel replied, "Yes, I think so, I think Luis cannot bear to think of it . . . he is not in therapy now; he was much better when he was before."

I suggested that if Isabel was getting something out of therapy and was able to do things that were inconceivable before, such as going on a train, then she felt she was taking something away from Luis, and that he became less. That her success was very frightening and made her feel very guilty about getting better. She said, "I do think so. Luis thinks I have everything, I have the Tavistock, the best place in the world, how I must have the best therapist, etc." As she left, she asked, "Do you think he should have therapy? I cannot bring it up as it is threatening to him."

Fairbairn observed that when the patient's resistance against the release of bad objects fails, "the world around the patient becomes peopled with devils which are too terrifying for him to face" (Fairbairn, 1943, p. 69). The most formidable part of the analyst's difficult task is "the overcoming of the patient's devotion to these bad objects." The onset of this phase in Isabel's therapy was marked by her coming to believe that she would have to discard me in order to feel well. As the relationship deepened, I could no longer protect her from the return of internal bad objects. From being Isabel's protector, I now became the instigator of depressive feelings because I "made her talk about her past." In the following weeks, she started to come late and to miss sessions, viewing therapy as an unwelcome interruption in her work on her thesis. She fought with Luis over the use of the typewriter that they had shared during their student years, seeing him as fiercely envious and competitive over her progress with her thesis and therapy. Since little headway was being made on the thesis, Isabel moved forward its completion date from the anniversary of her mother's death to her birthday.

Then three events occurring in rapid succession served to reinstate the persecutory world which was to pervade our therapy for the next 9 months. The three events were the Chernobyl disaster, the assassination of Olof Palme (the president of Sweden) by a suspected South American terrorist, and the failure of Isabel's local council to stop a massive housing development that was going to require the demolition of Isabel's little house.

One morning in June toward the end of the first year of therapy, the doorbell rang at ten in the morning when Isabel was still asleep. On the doorstep stood the developer, "a very aristocratic man, very rich, a millionaire." He questioned Isabel and Luis: Were they really refugees, because this was a house for refugees? How long had they been in the country? If x number of years, why did Luis still not have a job? Were they eligible for social benefits? Why, in this length of time, had they not improved their situation and, for instance, obtained council housing? Luis collapsed, terrified that they would have nowhere to go, and that he would be imprisoned for claiming social benefits when he had earned undeclared income by teaching Spanish.

Isabel came to her next session looking ill, grave, and tired; she was late because someone had thrown himself under the underground train. She had been up all night on the phone to three South American friends. Their homes had been broken into simultaneously, presumably, she said, by the secret police. The photos of their children had disappeared. Luis was in an extremely agitated state and, unable to sleep, had kept her awake by saying, "This is an external persecution. You think this is internal. My fear is right; yours is not right." Isabel felt guilty and angry, saying penitently, "We still don't have our own furniture," and then, reproachfully, "So it's no good to depend on the State just because it is your right." She was totally fed up with Luis, accusing him of "escaping into all this activity. . . . He always gets involved in external things when something is wrong at home." When she told him that she had had enough of "all this" and wanted to go to sleep, he remonstrated, "But our friends are in danger. We must help them. You can, because you know powerful people. You have given up, because you are sick, mentally ill. You have lost all your principles, your commitment. You are too weak to go on fighting." Isabel said to me, "I feel guilty, but maybe I am right. I am trying to be strong in another way. It was an effort to come today, but I had to."

After Isabel left the session, I felt great unease. For the first time, I felt afraid for her, her family, her home. The next day she wrote me a letter in which she said that although she felt "helped to realise the devastating effects of the events of the past 3 weeks on my mental balance, I feel that talking to you about them could overwhelm you with sadness. So I feel an enormous amount of remorse for doing that. I am really concerned—to what extent it is fair to talk to so nice and friendly person as you are about the problems of my life. Even though the therapy is very successful indeed, it does not provide a real substitute for the strong friendship I think I need." Clearly, her perception of my concern and apprehension had increased her sense of guilt and responsibility. She now turned her attentions to a neighbor, a married man. I thought that she did this because she was less willing to blame herself and to feel guilty. From a Fairbairnian perspective, this shift away from a guilt-arousing object toward a libidinal object could be seen as evidence of the weakening of the moral defense. Fairbairn observed that "the cathexis of the exciting object by the libidinal ego also constitutes a formidable source of resistance to therapy. . . . However, since the cathexis in question is libidinal, it cannot be regarded as itself a repressive phenomenon" (Fairbairn, 1944, p. 73).

During the next weeks, Isabel became more and more adamant about the necessity of separating from Luis, whom she now saw as pitiful, depressed, and dependent. She declared that he was harming her and her children. In despair, Luis, encouraged by Isabel, applied for help to the "world-famous" Tavistock Clinic with the "extremely powerful and well-known psychiatrist, Dr. X." After considerable deliberation, it was agreed that Luis should be seen, but by a different consultant than Dr. X. I felt uneasy, fearing further external disruptions in the already fragmented transference relationship between Isabel and myself. Nevertheless, for better or worse, by entering into the family system, the clinic now offered itself as the site for the release of the internalized bad objects.

Over the 3-month wait for Luis's appointment, Isabel became more and more excited, oscillating between seeing me as disapproving and obstructive on the one hand and, on the other, as an accomplice in her link to survival in the "outside" world against the persecuting and ill Luis inside her home. For a long time I felt caught in an impossible position since she responded in two diametrically opposite ways to my interpretations of her attempts to separate herself from me and Luis as the depressed obstructing person. On one occasion, for instance, she returned saying, "I followed exactly what you said. I insisted that Luis and I should sleep in separate beds. I telephoned him from downstairs in the clinic immediately after the session and told him to go out for the day, not to wait for me to come home." The next week, however, she was angry with me, saying, "I deeply disagree with your appreciation of my marriage. I don't know why for you it is not very clear that my husband is as a companion a disgrace. I feel such guiltiness of making other people unhappy with my new sense of achievement." I discussed my dilemma at a meeting of the unit to which I was attached at the Tavistock. The group interpreted Isabel's passionate romance with her neighbor, Noel, as a "manic" defense against feelings of depression and persecution. In principle, I agreed. But when I was with Isabel, I could not help feeling that I was having a constraining, moralizing influence on the analytic process.

Fairbairn described the bad object as split into a moralizing, primitive, judging object and an exciting, libidinal object. As the object of this divided relationship, I could be seen either as a secret, exciting person outside the prison of her refugee house or, in Fairbairn's words, as the "mother who rejects part of the libidinal self, the internal saboteur who is inevitably and permanently at war with the libidinal needs" (Fairbairn, 1944, p. 115). As she frantically begged me to help her to "achieve a divorce," Isabel felt more and more alone in the world. She wrote 40 to 50 letters over a weekend, 20 letters per night to friends in South America, to newspapers, to her local member of Parliament, to the vicar, and to the neighbor, Noel. To me she wrote of her isolation and suicidal thoughts: "Everyone is asleep except the hamster who keeps me company. He is sweet, gentle and living in a cage. . . . All your help has resulted in a labyrinth. . . . Luis's mere presence is a torture to me. He is my worst enemy." These letters of hatred and futility were followed by ones full of wild hope and love for me and the neighbor.

As the day for Luis's consultation approached—at the same time as one of Isabel's sessions—Isabel and Luis made elaborate plans for them to travel on separate trains and for the neighbour to meet her after the session at a pub. She told me, "I need to be protected from this terrible person who is not in my memories but in actual reality. Luis is an impostor and I have been his accomplice in this horrendous adventure which is his life for 18 years." Disbelieving the synchrony of their appointments, I checked with the consultant who told me that no letter of appointment had been sent out. The following session, however, Isabel described how terrible it had been for Luis to be seen in the opposite room to ours, where he could hear our voices, but not what we were saying. It was just like the cells in South America where they were interrogated simultaneously so that their stories could be checked. After listening, I said, "But Luis did not come." Isabel looked astounded. "I am sure that he did, I saw the letter," she said. However, because of their complicated plans to travel separately, she became doubtful and readily suspected that it was all her "madness." Again, I checked with the consultant and was assured that this was indeed her "fabrication." It seemed that it was I who underestimated the extent of her disturbance. Later that day, however, a colleague came up to me saying, "Oh, I saw the husband of your South American lady last week." Such was the disorder of the clinic that a letter had gone out without the knowledge of the consultant in charge.

This mix-up released enormous feelings of terror and persecution, with the Tavistock standing as the building in which such tortures and interrogations took place in secret. What Isabel and Luis feared most was that the consultant and I would get together, compare stories, and then name one of them as the guilty party. The trouble was, of course, that we had not collaborated at all! To my relief, Luis chose to be referred out to a counselor at the college where he was a student. After this, Isabel became much quieter and more dependent upon me—addressing her many letters to me—as she gave up any hope of becoming the neighbor's future lover. "I hope to become more normal and perhaps win a very good if boring new friend." She returned to work on her thesis saying, "I think my bad mother figure is somehow winning the game and playing for time in order to make me fail definitively in my thesis. But I am not strong enough to counter-attack. Obviously, I feel frustrated of being unable to love—or better to feel loved—for my husband or Noel. I no longer feel fear for my thesis, the end is so near . . . it is rather bored, lacking of excitement and mystery. But something real, I mean, it is not a mystery or a threat as it was." It seemed that after an intense struggle with an internal persecutory and provocative figure, Isabel had reached a more depressive, quiet, and thoughtful position.

Nevertheless, despite the relief that her more stable and continuous existence conferred upon our relationship, I could not help feeling that something was missing, and had gone underground. For several months, Isabel worked regularly on her thesis and in our sessions, despite abdominal pain because of a chronic urinary tract infection. One session in the middle of the second year, she reported Luis's concern because Juanita, a model student, wanted to give up "such an important subject as biology." Isabel declared that she did not mind about the subject; she was worried that Juanita looked at her parents as two well-known economists who still had not finished their Ph.D.s. As Isabel talked, I noticed that she put her hand across her stomach. I said to her that she was keeping going but actually she was in pain. She said, "I really am in pain, I feel dizzy and faint, usually I drink a lot of water." I offered to get her some water, which she drank. She said, "It's all right, it's sitting, in fact I was in agony by the end of the train ride." I said that she seemed to be in great pain but felt she must go on. She said, "I do feel very unwell, it is just the sitting. Usually I walk around." I asked her if she would like to get up and walk around. She said, "Yes, but I am dizzy." She lay down on the couch and told me that the pain was very sharp—but "what were we talking about?" I said that we were talking about Juanita's giving up biology and I wondered whether there was a connection with her ignoring her body. She said yes, and talked about her fear that if she took the time to go to the doctor, this might disrupt her work on her thesis and her therapy.

This session permitted Isabel to bring her body back into our work. I later learned that the anniversary of her mother's death fell on that day. The session after the one when she became ill, she told me that, on leaving me, she began to have romantic thoughts about Noel again. This time I did not interpret such thoughts as a diversion. Instead, I interpreted the way she kept her feelings for Luis and Noel, her mother and her father, very separate. She also tried to keep separate these two sets of feelings when she came to see me. This had led her to keep her body out, since she felt she could not tell me about her sexual thoughts and romantic dreams without arousing my disapproval. She agreed. She wrote to me after the session, saying, "Usually you have been rather reluctant to talk about my feelings towards Noel. I had tried to change my feelings towards him, I mean, repressing them (in your name perhaps?). It is much better this new other way, I think. I know you think it is wrong to love (or like) Noel, but you accept my feelings. It makes me feel much more connected to you. And, consequently, to associate that with one of the good things about my mother. She liked men a lot. I always loved her capacity for romanticising men–women relationship. And she felt very attractive to them."

In her next letter to me, Isabel wrote down a verbatim account of a phone conversation between herself and Noel that she had found very "strange." When she arrived for the following session, I had the letters on my table beside me. I said, "I think you want to show me this conversation word for word to let me know exactly what is going on so that you can sort out what is strange in your conversations with Noel." I suggested we go through the letter together. She said, "That is exactly what I hoped you would do." Together with me, she acknowledged that what was "strange" in the letter was that the object of her excitement was clearly cool and rejecting.

Looking at this exchange from the framework of Fairbairn's object relations theory, it seems to me that the shift in my alignment with the moralizing, rejecting object—the internal saboteur—against the libidinal ego previously aligned with the exciting object—the neighbor, Noel—enabled Isabel to see that these were not two separate objects, but rather aspects of the same object. Both maintained her tie with "an intolerably bad internalised object relationship." Fairbairn described the technique of "Divide et Impera" as a defense for the disposal of libido and agression. The risk involved in expressing both aggressive and libidinal feelings toward the mother in the role of a rejecting object is averted when the child "employs a maximum of his aggression to subdue a maximum of his libidinal need" (Fairbairn, 1951, p. 173). The difficulty for me at the time was to see that both the "moral" and the "romantic" aspects could serve the resistance against the release of the bad internalized objects. For instance, when Isabel worked well and steadily on her thesis and her therapy and thought less about the neighbor, it was easy to think that she was better than to think that she had achieved a balance through her old technique of "Divide and Rule."

REFERENCES

Bollas, C. (1989). *Forces of Destiny*, Chapter 11. London: Free Association Books.

Fairbairn, W. R. D. (1943). The repression and the return of bad objects (with special reference to the 'war neuroses'). In *Psychoanalytic Studies of the Personality*. London: Tavistock and Routledge & Kegan Paul, 1952.

Fairbairn, W. R. D. (1944). Endopsychic structure considered in terms of object-relationships. In *Psychoanalytic Studies of the Personality*. London: Tavistock and Routledge & Kegan Paul, 1952.

Fairbairn, W. R. D. (1951). A synopsis of the development of the author's views regarding the structure of the personality. In *Psychoanalytic Studies of the Personality*. London: Tavistock and Routledge & Kegan Paul.

Sharpe, E. F. (1930). The technique of psycho-analysis, lecture 1: The analyst. In *Collected Papers on Psycho-Analysis*. London: Hogarth Press and The Institute of Psycho-Analysis, 1978.

Stevenson, R. L. (1896). *A Child's Garden of Verses*. Yorkshire: The Scholar Press, 1979.

14

Fairbairn's Revision of Libido Theory: The Case of Harry Guntrip

JUDITH M. HUGHES

In Fairbairn's earliest paper one can already detect a note of dissatisfaction with classic libido theory.[1] Still it was not until the mid-1930s, not until he read Melanie Klein's work on manic–depressive states, that he ceased thinking along fairly conventional lines.[2] He quickly appreciated that Klein's concept of positions, by granting relations with internal objects a privileged status, called into question the explanatory power of libido theory. He also realized that Klein "failed to push her views to their logical conclusion."[3] For Fairbairn to push matters to their logical conclusion was his stock in trade, and what could be more logical than to reassess Freud's libido in the light of Klein's internal objects?

The operation which began as a mere tidying-up turned into a major revision of libido theory. In Fairbairn's view what mattered was not libidinal aims but object relations; what needed investigation was not infantile sexuality atomized into component instincts and erotogenic zones, but the relationship between child and caretakers in both external and internal reality.

*   *   *   *   *   *

"'You're always talking about my wanting this and that desire satisfied; but what I really want is a father,'" a patient protested. It was re-

From *Reshaping the Psychoanalytic Domain: The Work of Melanie Klein, W. R. D. Fairbairn, and D. W. Winnicott* (pp. 95–117) by Judith M. Hughes, 1989, Berkeley: University of California Press. Copyright 1989 by the Regents of the University of California. Reprinted by permission of the author, the publisher, and the Regents of the University of California.

flection upon such clinical phenomena that prompted Fairbairn to voice his own protest: the ultimate goal of libido was not pleasure; rather *"the ultimate goal of libido"* was *"the object."*

> The real libidinal aim is the establishment of satisfactory relationships with objects; and it is accordingly, the object that constitutes the true libidinal goal.[4]

Fairbairn's "libido" differed markedly from Freud's original notion of grossly sexual desire. Over the course of time the Freudian version had "developed into a properly mannered, barely sexual, almost mythical, hazy conception."[5] Fairbairn tried to dissipate the haze, and in the process, distanced himself from Freud. At his hands "libido" became *"the object-seeking principle."*[6]

Much more than semantics was involved. Fairbairn proposed a radical move: to replace libidinal development, understood as sexuality, by libidinal development, understood as dependency. In Freud's view sexual pleasure ranked as primary, and objects acquired importance only insofar as they provided gratification. In Fairbairn's opinion pleasure-seeking figured as a "secondary and deteriorative . . . principle of behavior."

> Explicit pleasure-seeking, [that is], . . . the relieving of . . . tension . . . for the mere sake of relieving this tension, . . . does, of course, occur commonly enough; but, since libidinal need is object-need, simple tension-relieving implies some failure of object-relationships. The fact is that simple tension-relieving is really a safety-valve process. It is thus, not a means of achieving libidinal aims, but a means of mitigating the failure of these aims.[7]

Like Freud, Fairbairn chose thumb-sucking as a concrete example. Freud considered such activity as evidence of a "need for repeating sexual satisfaction," a need that had gotten "detached from the need for taking nourishment;"[8] Fairbairn argued that Freud had missed the point. He had failed to ask the crucial question: Why the thumb? The answer was obvious: because there was "no breast to suck. Even the baby," Fairbairn claimed, "must have a libidinal object; and, if he is deprived of his natural object (the breast), he is driven to provide an object for himself. Thumb-sucking thus represents a technique for dealing with an unsatisfactory object-relationship; and the same may be said for masturbation."[9]

Fairbairn was on the verge of formulating his radical proposal, when, as Visiting Psychiatrist at Carstairs Hospital, a psychoneurosis unit in the Emergency Medical Service, he "began to see military cases in large numbers." During the early years of the Second World War, he treated something of an epidemic, a situation stressful to the therapist, yet potentially illuminating to the scientist. Fairbairn quickly realized that the size of the patient population might lend credence to hypotheses derived from the intensive study of a very few. Beyond that, the nature of the epidemic—Fairbairn described it as "homesickness"—was ideally suited to his interests: the patients he saw had been "suddenly removed from their normal environment, separated from their love-objects and isolated from all the accustomed props and supports upon which a dependent person would ordinarily rely. It was almost as if a laboratory experiment under controlled conditions had been gratuitously provided for testing" his views.[10] Here surely, dependency could be observed.

Observe it he did, and even though Fairbairn made no detailed statistical analysis, he came away convinced that his hypothesis had survived a preliminary trial. His civilian patient had wanted a father; the soldiers he encountered wanted their mothers or wives. One example stood out as paradigmatic, that of a twenty-four year old gunner who had been hospitalized three months after entering military service.

> He had felt 'depressed' from the day he entered the Army; and, in the absence of his wife, he felt completely 'alone'. It seemed to him that everything was against him; and he felt that his only hold on life resided in the hope of seeing his wife again—a fact in explanation of which he volunteered the remarks, 'She is like a mother to me', and 'She is all I have'.

Fairbairn's soldier had earlier been utterly dependent upon his maternal grandmother, with whom he had lived after his mother's premature death. He could scarcely be separated from her; he could venture out alone only if a speedy return was possible. What had saved him when his grandmother's health began to fail was meeting the young woman who eventually became his wife. Marriage, however, did not "provide an adequate solution to his problems."[11] Only after he had so arranged his affairs that his wife could remain constantly at his side was his separation anxiety allayed. And just at the point when those arrangements were complete, he was summoned for military service.

Why had this patient's infantile dependency persisted? What accounted for individual variation? Fairbairn confronted these questions; he did not answer them. With the data at his disposal, that is, clinical material from adult patients, he could merely discern the sketch of an answer. Nor for that matter could similar questions about infantile sexuality be resolved. Yet given a choice between Freud's sexual libido and the object-seeking variety, Fairbairn had grounds for preferring his own formulation. Still more, it had proved reasonable to pursue the revision of libido-theory—an enterprise based more on logic than on new facts.

*   *   *   *   *   *

To replace libidinal development understood as sexuality with libidinal development understood as dependence required grappling with Abraham's elaboration of Freudian oral, anal, and phallic stages. Criticism was crucial, yet by itself insufficient. Fairbairn did not expect either theoreticians or clinicians to cast aside what they regarded as a mainstay unless he offered them something in return. And he was intent on providing such an alternative sequence.

Recall that Freud's stages had derived in large part from the notion of erotogenic zones. Fairbairn demurred: instead of recognizing "that the function of libidinal pleasure" was "to provide a sign-post" to the object, Freud had made the object the "sign-post to libidinal pleasure."[12] What would happen to the stages if the object should be given precedence? At the very least the nomenclature would have to be altered: "oral" would give way to "breast"; "anal" would give way to "feces." It was at this point that a severe lack of comparability became apparent: the breast was a functioning biological object; feces were not. Anality seemed spurious: it could be reckoned an artifact. Yet deleting anality meant subverting Freud's sequence.

Fairbairn's alternative was simplicity itself. The earliest stage, which he called infantile dependence, contained within it Abraham's earlier and later oral phases; in similar fashion, "the stage of mature dependence" corresponded "to Abraham's 'final genital phase.'"

> Between these two stages of infantile and mature dependence is a transition stage characterized by an increasing tendency to abandon the attitude of infantile dependence and an increasing tendency to adopt the attitude of mature dependence. This transition stage corresponds to three of Abraham's phases—the two anal phases and the early genital (phallic) phase.[13]

"In infancy," Fairbairn noted, "owing to the constitution of the human organism, the path of least resistance to the object" happened "to lie almost exclusively through the mouth; and the mouth accordingly" became "the dominant libidinal organ." This dominant mouth shaped Fairbairn's conceptualization of infantile dependence: in his view such dependence and the "incorporation of the object" were "intimately associated." It followed, then, that the course taken by object-seeking turned on "*the extent to which objects are incorporated and the nature of the techniques which are employed to deal with incorporated objects.*"[14]

But not only did the infant incorporate the object; he also identified with it. Infantile dependence, oral incorporation, and a third notion, that of "primary identification," formed a cluster of linked concepts. "Oral incorporation" echoed the work of Melanie Klein. (So too did the notion of object relations from birth onwards.) "Primary identification" harked back to Freud.[15] Fairbairn spelled out more clearly than Freud what primary identification meant: non-differentiation of subject from object. In his words: *"the abandonment of infantile dependence"* involved *"an abandonment of relationships based upon primary identification in favour of relationships with differentiated objects."*[16] How was such differentiation to be accomplished? At this point the significance of equating primary identification with oral incorporation became apparent: differentiation *a fortiori* entailed expulsion.

By the time the child entered the transition stage, Fairbairn argued, he was no longer dealing with a solitary incorporated object. In line with Abraham, Fairbairn stressed the onset of ambivalence in the later oral phase: the original object had by now been replaced by two—*"an accepted object,* towards which love" was "directed, and *a rejected object,* towards which hate" was "directed."[17] (Fairbairn subsequently modified his views and wrote instead of an accepted object on the one hand and of exciting and rejecting objects on the other.) Acceptance and rejection—or retention and expulsion—furnished Fairbairn the requisite flexibility for reassessing the standard account of psychopathology. The variations he played on these themes, however, were less important than his having sketched an object relational version.

Was Fairbairn's sequence of infantile to mature dependence sturdy enough to replace orthodox libido theory? Clearly Abraham's stages had been found wanting. Even Freud's allegiance to a libidinal explanation of neurotic phenomena had been far from exclusive: he preferred the Oedipus complex, which, after all, emphasized object relations. To test the matter of his own theory, Fairbairn could not postpone confronting that complex.

* * * * * *

For Freud the Oedipus complex and libido theory were not alternative or incompatible accounts of neurosogenesis. On the contrary, the Oedipus complex and the phallic stage went hand in hand: in his view, the incestuous wishes that characterized the complex acquired their imperative force from instinctual drives. For Melanie Klein too, the Oedipus complex was fueled by sexual (and aggressive) instincts. Her departure from Freud concerned the question of dating. To make room for object relations, internal and external, from the moment of birth, without challenging the centrality of the Oedipus complex, she had simply pushed back both oedipal relations and the phallic stage (her term was "genital") to

the first year of life. In so doing she had tried to pour new wine into old bottles.
Fairbairn would have none of this:

> The Oedipus situation . . . is not . . . basic . . . , but the derivative of a situation which has priority over it not only in the logical, but also in the temporal sense. This prior situation is one which issues directly out of the physical and emotional dependence of the infant upon his mother, and which declares itself in the relationship of the infant to his mother long before his father becomes a significant object.[18]

For Fairbairn, with his understanding of development in terms of dependence, Freud's dictum that "every new arrival on this planet" was fated to become a little Oedipus obviously required emendation.

In emphasizing the mother–infant relationship, Fairbairn was once again following Melanie Klein. Yet he soon went beyond her. Not only did he deprive the father of his crucial status in the oedipal triangle; he relegated him to a derivative position.

> The chief novelty introduced into the child's world by the Oedipus situation, as this materializes in outer reality, is that he is now confronted with two distinct parental objects instead of . . . only one. . . . His relationship with his new object, viz., his father, is, of course, inevitably fraught with vicissitudes similar to those which he previously experienced in his relationship with his mother—and in particular, the vicissitudes of need, frustration and rejection. In view of these vicissitudes, his father becomes an ambivalent object to him, whilst at the same time he himself becomes ambivalent towards his father. In his relationship with his father he is thus faced with the same problem of adjustment as that with which he was originally faced in his relationship with his mother. The original situation is reinstated, albeit this time in relation to a fresh object; and, very naturally, he seeks to meet the difficulties of the reinstated situation by means of the same series of techniques which he learned to adopt in meeting the difficulties of the original situation.[19]

In the triangle the child appeared to be doing most of the work: indeed, Fairbairn argued, he constituted *"the Oedipus situation for himself."* The child confronted with a maternal object turned ambivalent—a situation he found intolerable—had responded by dividing it into an accepted object and a rejected object. To be called upon to deal with two ambivalent objects was still worse. In order to simplify the situation, and to make it more bearable, the child designated one parent the accepted object, and the other he rejected.[20]

What had happened to sexuality in Fairbairn's version of the oedipal drama? He assigned it a secondary role. The child's initial understanding of the difference between his parents had to do with breasts, not genitals: father was different from mother because he lacked breasts. (Unlike Melanie Klein, Fairbairn did not traffic in phylogenetically inherited knowledge of male and female organs.)

> When the child comes to appreciate, in some measure at least, the genital difference between his parents, and as, in the course of his own development, his physical need tends to flow increasingly (albeit in varying degrees) through genital channels, his need for his mother comes to include a need for her vagina. At the same time, his need for his father comes to include a need for his father's penis.[21]

Here Fairbairn introduced an important caveat: "The strength of these physical needs for his parents' genitals" varied "in inverse proportion to the satisfaction of his emotional needs. Thus, the more satisfactory his emotional relations with his parents, the less urgent" were "his physical needs for their genitals."[22]

This last point Fairbairn illuminated by a clinical vignette drawn from the case of a female patient:

> Owing to disagreements between her parents they occupied separate bedrooms. Between these bedrooms lay an inter-connecting dressing-room; and, to protect herself from her husband, my patient's mother made her sleep in this dressing-room. She obtained little display of affection from either parent. . . . Her father was of a detached and unapproachable personality; and she experienced greater difficulty in making emotional contact with him than with her mother. After her mother's death, which occurred in her teens, she made desperate attempts to establish contact with her father, but all in vain. It was then that the thought suddenly occurred to her one day: 'Surely it would appeal to him if I offered to go to bed with him!' Her incestuous wish thus represented a desperate attempt to make an emotional contact with her object—and, in so doing, both to elicit love and to prove that her own love was acceptable. . . . In the case of my patient the incestuous wish was, of course, renounced; and, as might be expected, it was followed by an intense guilt reaction.[23]

Fairbairn's own conclusions followed relentlessly:

> I venture to suggest that the deep analysis of a positive Oedipus situation may be regarded as taking place at three main levels. At the first level the picture is dominated by the Oedipus situation itself. At the next level it is dominated by ambivalence towards the heterosexual parent; and at the deepest level it is dominated by ambivalence towards the mother.[24]

Fairbairn did not discard the Oedipus complex; he did not reject outright Freud's "nucleus of the neuroses." He *did* transform it. And in the work of transformation his fundamental concept of libido and object-seeking emerged as a vigorous rival to the orthodox version.

Once again Fairbairn had insisted that psychopathology sprang from the infant's dependence on the maternal object. It remained for him to delineate what stemmed from that earliest stage.

*   *   *   *   *   *

When Melanie Klein had taken up what she had initially called the paranoid position, she found that her concerns intersected with those of Fairbairn. They were both attempting to chart the psychopathology which in their view—and Abraham's as well—germinated in the first year of life. Though their work overlapped, Klein took care to point out the differences in how she and Fairbairn conceived their enterprises: her approach, she noted, "was predominantly from the angle of anxieties and their vicissitudes," whereas Fairbairn's "was largely from the angle of ego-development in relation to objects."[25] What she failed to elucidate was the divergent conception of objects that prompted their respective approaches.

The point at issue was the status of external objects. In her early writings, when she had focused on aggression, Klein had suggested that "the first objects of the drives" were "created out of the drives themselves; their content" was "derived from the content of the child's own impulses which" were "experienced as directed towards him by the external object." With her papers on the depressive position, after she had shifted her attention to good objects, "the theory of the internal origins of early objects" receded "into the background;" instead Klein argued that "the real others in the infant's external world" were "constantly internalized, established as internal objects, and projected out onto external figures once again." This historical development resulted in a curious asymmetry: Klein had "a tendency to see bad objects as . . . derived . . . from the child's own drives, and good objects as derived largely from external others."[26] In contrast Fairbairn's views remained constant. As he saw it, the badness of an object was not a projection of the child's sadism; it was a reflection of a mother's unavailability. In short, the real mother, not some fantasy, now emerged as central to psychopathology.

What ranked as crucial for the child was the establishment of "a satisfactory object-relationship during the period of infantile dependence. . . . The traumatic situation," according to Fairbairn, was "one in which the child" felt he was "not really loved as a person, and that his own love" was "not accepted." (The critical nature of unsatisfactory object relationships, Fairbairn conceded, in part depended upon their continuing into "the succeeding years of early childhood.") That traumatic situation, and the ensuing psychopathology, he further differentiated in terms of whether it arose during the early or the late oral phase. His discussion of the latter amounted to a reiteration of Melanie Klein's depressive position.

> If . . . the phase in which infantile object-relationships have been pre-emi-
> nently unsatisfactory is the late oral phase, the reaction provoked in the
> child conforms to the idea that he is not loved because of the badness
> and destructiveness of his hate; and this reaction provides the basis for
> a subsequent depressive tendency. . . . Where [such] a . . . tendency is
> present, . . . the ultimate psychopathological disaster . . . follows from
> loss of the object.[27]

It was when Fairbairn got to the schizoid position that the difference between his approach and that of Melanie Klein began to tell. (It
should be recalled that her work on schizoid mechanisms appeared after
his.) Fairbairn concentrated on the child's first and failed love relationship with an external object: deprivation during the pre-ambivalent oral
phase provoked "in the child a reaction conforming to the idea that he"
was "not loved because his own love" was "bad and destructive." ("Bad"
in this context may be more than usually obscure.) Faced, then, with the
dilemma of whether to love or not—an infinitely less tolerable choice than
the one characteristic of the late oral phase between loving and hating—
the child might forsake object-seeking entirely. Given the child's unconditional dependence on his object, to renounce object-seeking would be
tantamount to psychic suicide. Hence Fairbairn's summary statement:
"loss of the ego" was "the ultimate psychopathological disaster" for those
with a schizoid tendency.[28]
    What became of such people? Fairbairn sketched out the conse-
quences of a chronic traumatic situation:

> (a) The child comes to regard his mother as a bad object in so far
> as she does not seem to love him.
> (b) The child comes to regard outward expression of his own love
> as bad, with the result that . . . he tends to retain his love inside him-
> self.
> (c) The child comes to feel that love relationships with external
> objects in general are bad, or at least precarious.
> The net result is that the child tends to transfer his relationships with
> his objects to the realm of inner reality. In the case of individuals with a
> schizoid component in their personality, accordingly, there is a great ten-
> dency for the outer world to derive its meaning too exclusively from the
> inner world. . . . Not only do their objects tend to belong to the inner
> rather than to the outer world, but they tend to identify themselves very

strongly with their internal objects. This fact contributes materially to the difficulty which they experience in giving emotionally.

The unloved child—unloved as a person in his own right, though perhaps valued as his mother's possession—"remained profoundly fixated" upon that mother as an internal object.[29] Once again Fairbairn had returned to the phenomenon of extreme dependence, as the paradoxical result of withdrawal from the external world.

Fairbairn appreciated full well that no child enjoyed "a perfect object-relationship during the impressionable period of infantile dependence, or for that matter during the transition period" which succeeded it. Maternal failure undoubtedly came in all shapes and sizes. It could be inferred (and this was Fairbairn's central point) that there was "present in every one either an underlying schizoid or an underlying depressive tendency."[30] What figured as decisive (and here Fairbairn returned to orthodox libido theory) was the relative strength of fixations and the degree of regression. Taken together, they would determine the mix of tendencies which might predominate.

In subsequent papers Fairbairn slighted the depressive position; the schizoid emerged as truly fundamental. It was this that he came to regard as the basis of all psychopathological development.

* * * * * *

What impact did Fairbairn's revision of libido theory have on his clinical practice? Analysts often claim that theory is of little importance—or intrudes little into their exchanges with their patients. Interpretations may rarely be framed in technical terms, yet it is naive to suppose that those interpretations are not informed by theory. Fairbairn was far from naive. His analysis of Harry Guntrip represented a not altogether successful attempt to bring his theory to bear on an individual case.

Guntrip was an unusual analytic patient. By the time he sought out Fairbairn—in 1949 at the age of 48—he had already established himself as a psychotherapist in Leeds. He chose Fairbairn with great deliberation: he had made a study of his articles (which had not yet appeared in book form) and had determined that "philosophically" he and Fairbairn stood "on the same ground and no actual intellectual disagreements would interfere with the analysis."[31] With equal deliberation he kept track of the analysis itself:

> Immediately after a session I would go straight to my rooms and write up my dreams (which I always pencilled down on getting up) and all that I remembered of my 'Free Associations' and Fairbairn's comments and interpretations. Fortunately for years I had a photographic memory for this kind of material. . . . I did not keep on refreshing my memory

of my analysis notes, once made, but left them to accumulate and kept
them with the vague idea that sometime I might find it interesting to look
back over them. To have studied them en route would have risked the
danger of 'intellectualizing' and disguising my 'resistance'.[32]

Shortly before his death Guntrip went back over those notes and, extract-
ing from them, wrote an account (never published) of his analysis with
Fairbairn. (In that document his "intellectualizing" is amply apparent.)
    In addition, Guntrip drafted a psychoanalytic autobiography, bas-
ing it, in part, on records of dreams he had meticulously kept for more
than a dozen years prior to starting analysis with Fairbairn. Here, as well
as in a brief published assessment, Guntrip dramatizes and simplifies the
story. He presents himself as having lived on top of a buried traumatic
event.

> At the age of 3½ years I went into our sitting room and there was con-
> fronted with the sight of my brother of 2 years lying naked and dead
> on my mother's lap. The effect of that shock on me was, so mother told
> me, so great that very quickly I was thought to be dying. I was revived,
> but all memory of that event was totally gone. I was left with an infan-
> tile traumatic amnesia for the rest of my life, which, from time to time
> (greatly to my mystification), when anything faintly comparable to it
> occurred in real life, would reinstate the original illness. Sometimes this
> outbreak was short-lived and not too severe and disappeared as suddenly
> as it had erupted. Once or twice, its eruption landed me with serious
> exhaustion illness, which lasted longer but would again fade out.[33]

    Neither of Guntrip's two analyses (the second with D. W. Winnicott),
which together took close to twenty years, succeeded in breaking through
his amnesia. (His expectations in this regard harked back to Breuer's treatment of Anna O., wherein the undoing of a repression, that is, the patient's
remembering the circumstances surrounding the formation of a symptom, had led to the disappearance of the symptom in question.) Guntrip's
dreams eventually broke through. At the age of seventy, roughly two years
after the end of his second analysis, he had a compelling dream sequence,
of several months duration, which he claimed led him so far back in time
that he was able to summon up his dead brother and his aloof, unresponsive mother. With his dream-apparition of his mother as "a woman who
had no face, arms or breasts," he thought he had reached bedrock.[34]
(Guntrip construed manifest content as a reliable rendering of the historical past!) He had found at last what he regarded as proof positive
that his mother had failed to relate to him. With that he seemed ready to
renounce his life-long quest for maternal recognition—by the crushing
verdict that he had had no mother at all.

The previous seventy years had in fact been dominated not by his brother's death, but by this quest. (The one obviously contributed to the other: the loss of his brother left Guntrip as an only child alone with his mother, thereby intensifying his need for and fear of her.) What was the matter with his mother? According to Guntrip she simply had no desire to be one. As the eldest daughter of eleven children she had borne heavy maternal responsibilities long before she bore children of her own; by the time she married "she had had her fill of mothering . . . and did not want any more." She preferred business to babies; she was far more interested in her clothing-shop than in her children. In her old age, living with Guntrip and his wife—she spent her last nine years in their house—she remarked: "I ought never to have married and had children. Nature did not make me to be a wife and mother, but a business woman" and "I don't think I ever understood children. I could never be bothered with them."[35]

In fact she did bother with her son—at least with his body. Two items stand out in his account. First, his mother tried to remake him into a girl. As a very small child he wore his hair long and dressed in female attire; in that garb he served as model in his mother's shop, until customers suggested that it was improper to display him in this fashion. Second, she fussed over his health. Until the age of five he suffered from a series of minor maladies that evoked maternal solicitude. After undergoing a painful circumcision (at his mother's insistence), he managed to stay well and tried to stay out of his mother's way. He did not succeed: he endured her temper and her beatings until the age of eight, when her business began at last to thrive and he began to grow away from her.

His brother's death may have left Guntrip alone with his mother, but he did not have only her: the household included his mother's sister and his father. It was his aunt's responsibility to look after him, and from Guntrip's account she emerges as gentle and kindly—yet a pallid invalid, which, in fact, she was, having been born with a defective heart and having been seriously ill when Guntrip was a child. His mother, he commented, adhered to "the neurotic pattern of identifying masculinity with strength and aggressiveness and femininity with weakness and passivity. Aunt Mary, who adored her, was her ideal female." She was Guntrip's as well. Yet it was something neither mother nor son wanted to be.[36]

As for Guntrip's father, under his wife's ministrations "he slowly but inevitably lost his active self" and gradually became wedded to an "unvarying routine."

> He came home from the City, lay on his black horse-hair sofa and read the paper . . . for half an hour, had his evening meal, and then went into the shop desk to spend the rest of the evening making up the books and

giving change. At week-ends, which then meant only Sundays, he went to Church in the morning, in the afternoon chaired a Men's Brotherhood meeting associated with the local Congregational Church, the one remaining relic of his active days, and went to Church again in the evening.[37]

This father deferred to his wife without a murmur, just as earlier he had deferred to his authoritarian mother. Notwithstanding his inability to oppose his wife or to shield his boy, his son insisted on his steadfast benevolence. In all his years of dreaming, Guntrip asserted, his father "never appeared as other than a supportive figure *vis-à-vis* mother, and in actual fact she *never* lost her temper in his presence."[38] The son might not want to be like the father, but he did not want to hit a man when he was down.

The son was determined to resist the mother, notably to resist her interference with his sex life. Her dislike of sex, as well as her puritanical views on the subject, had early been impressed upon Guntrip. Indeed his mother had been quite explicit:

> In one of her, to me, rather strange and at first somewhat embarrassing moments of confidential talking, she told me that she had once . . . gone . . . to have a long talk with an older female friend, who had told her that a man's health would suffer if he did not have a regular relationship. . . . I was in my late teens when she told me that and she must have felt uneasy for she added, seeking to shift responsibility off herself: "I don't know how we ever had any babies for often your father couldn't get in." I inferred that this was not true for the first three years, and after that was determined by herself. I several times heard her make the general remark "I don't like being touched" and she never showed any physical tenderness to me as a child.

Yet for Guntrip potency does not seem to have posed a major difficulty. "Variations," he commented, occurred during "periods of physical and mental strain and fatigue, or sinus attacks; and normal energy for sex . . . would return . . . after a good holiday or a rest." The one prolonged stretch of impotence he recorded, lasting two months, coincided with his mother's taking up permanent residence in his house.[39] Still, the problem of keeping her out of his bedroom, metaphorically that is, did not entirely vanish.

Guntrip's impotence may have been mild; his sinus attacks were not. Beginning in the mid-1930s, after his sinuses had become badly infected and surgical intervention had been required, he suffered from repeated attacks. In 1943 he submitted again to surgery, this time of a drastic kind:

> It was the time when the medical men were obsessed with the idea of 'focal infections'. This surgeon decided that I had a focal infection in

the soft alveolar tissue of my upper jaw, and ordered a 'radical alveolectomy. . . . All my top teeth were removed and the soft alveolar bone removed and the skin sewn back over the hard bone. Ever since I have had dentures which it is impossible to eat with, or even to wear for long, for the denture rapidly cuts through the skin on the hard bone, and my mouth becomes full of sores. The operation was a total failure, for my sinus attacks recurred each winter as usual, as soon as fogs or winter cold arrived. . . . It was in a social sense a 'castration' for I have never since been able to eat a meal in company with other people with comfort.[40]

Even after the advent of penicillin, Guntrip continued to be laid low by his sinuses. In the course of his analysis these attacks faded out. So too did his insomnia. At the very least analytic therapy notably improved his health.

It also, according to his own account, made him more appreciative of and open with his wife. From the start his marriage had stood in marked contrast to that of his parents: he and his wife, whom he had met in his early twenties, adhered to the conventions of gender stereotyping. He was a model of masculine drive and she of feminine self-sacrifice; he was constantly pushing himself; she smoothed the way and supported his morale. Her devoted nursing of his mother, who was tyrannical, critical, and bad-tempered, allowed Guntrip to remain at a safe distance during the old woman's final years. More than that, it freed him to travel to Edinburgh for analysis with Fairbairn.

It was not until 1946, when Guntrip was in his mid-forties, that he finally determined what he wanted to be and settled into a psychotherapeutic career. Before that he had been occupied with religion, first, in late adolescence, as an officer in the Salvation Army, and then, during the following two decades, as a Congregational minister. In both cases, as he put it, he "grew away from" the surrogate family which failed to nourish him (intellectually) and threatened to confine him. He did not grow away from psychotherapy. He did, however, grow away from his analyst: his own theoretical work, he claimed, took him "right beyond Fairbairn's halting point," and Fairbairn "with great courage . . . accepted that."[41]

*   *   *   *   *   *

According to Guntrip, by the time he began commuting to Edinburgh (two nights, four sessions per week), Fairbairn was already past his prime. With regard to his analyst's emotional and physical vigor, Guntrip's assessment was undoubtedly correct. Fairbairn's wife, after years of alcoholism, died in 1952, and though he remarried in 1959, it is clear that the intervening period had been difficult. (At one point he admitted as much to Guntrip.[42]) In that same decade Fairbairn's own health began to

deteriorate. In 1950 he suffered a first attack of viral influenza; such attacks became more and more severe as the years wore on. In the late 1950s
Fairbairn's health, or rather Guntrip's concern about it, became a central issue in the analysis—and crucial to the latter's decision to terminate.
     In Guntrip's view, Fairbairn was past his prime intellectually as well.
"After his experimental creative 1940s," the analysand commented, "his
conservatism slowly pushed through into his work."[43] By conservatism
Guntrip meant, above all, interpretations framed in terms of castration
anxiety and/or incestuous wishes—or more generally, the penis. During
the 300th session (May 23, 1951), the following exchange occurred, with
Guntrip leading off: "Maybe as a small boy I felt I could never grow as
big as father. He's a being of a different order." Fairbarin interpreted:
"You felt forbidden to have a penis of your own. It's not for little boys to
have a penis and be sexual." Guntrip subsequently added for his own
benefit:

> This is one of the points at which I now feel that Fairbairn's constant
> reiteration of interpretations in terms of penises, was a survival of clas-
> sic Freudian sexology that his theory had moved beyond. I feel that kept
> me stationary, whereas interpretations in terms of the penis ultimately
> standing for the 'whole personality' which mother did her best to restrict
> and dominate would have felt to me much more realistic. In effect, his
> analysis was a 'penis-analysis', not an 'ego-analysis'.

In session 512 (January 13, 1953), however, the analyst heeded the analysand's retrospective advice. "*Castration*," Fairbairn remarked, was "*really
symbolic of a total personality situation, feeling stopped from being oneself, fear of loss of individuality and personality.*"[44] With this pithy statement Guntrip had no quarrel.
     "Penis-analysis, not . . . ego-analysis" may have been closer to the
mark in late 1953. Fairbairn was hard at work on his article "Observations on the Nature of Hysterical States" in which he summarized his
revision of structural theory, illustrating that revision with clinical material. Guntrip, disguised as "Jack," was one of the patients pressed into
service. Fairbairn quoted a dream—a leopard sprawled out on the floor,
kept down by the dreamer's hand on his head—and interpreted. Jack
himself had understood the dream in terms of holding down his vital,
energetic side and adopting a passive attitude vis-à-vis his mother. What
he had not seen was how "keeping the leopard down" might represent
"keeping his penis down and preventing it erecting."[45] Guntrip was not
convinced, or at least not in retrospect:

> At a time when my life was overclouded with the gathering prospect of
> mother's death and real cause for anxiety about the strain that had been

growing on my wife, . . . it was a question, not of sexual potency, but of survival, a life or death matter. . . . In holding the leopard down I am in no doubt that I am keeping a tight hold by repression on my lifelong accumulated rage against her [i.e., his mother].[46]

At this point, with his mother on the verge of death, Guntrip felt the need to mobilize that rage.

Two years later, when Fairbairn was writing "Considerations Arising Out of the Schreber Case," the primal scene came to the fore. (Fairbairn was intent on substituting for Freud's libidinal explanation of paranoia, an explanation phrased in terms of object relations.[47]) Guntrip protested; he claimed he was simply being fitted into his analyst's "new twist of . . . theory." What is clear, however, is that Guntrip, not Fairbairn, was doing the fitting:

> I re-examined every activity of my life in terms of its being an unconscious expression of primal scene involvement; playing father's role in cricket, in preaching, in starting psychotherapy . . . , in writing and doing intellectual research, and much more detail to that effect, including psychosomatic symptoms as mother's role of sexual suffering. . . . I certainly did my best to co-operate and tried to find out what truth there was in this approach. . . .[48]

A less methodical patient would have sloughed off an inaccurate interpretation more readily.

Analyst and analysand alike were using the analysis to try out "new twists of theory." They also pursued these interests in extra-analytic sessions—infrequently, it would seem, possibly no more than ten times over the course of a decade. (In his article "Analysis with Fairbairn and Winnicott" Guntrip gives the impression that such sessions were regular occurrences.) That Guntrip found the discussions gratifying is clear: in talking "face to face," he claimed he found "the human Fairbairn," a Fairbairn who "realistically" became an "understanding good father."[49] What gratification a lonely and intellectually isolated Fairbairn derived from discussions with an obviously gifted analysand can only be surmised. So too the impact of this technical deviation, which was left unanalyzed, can only be guessed at. One suspects that, at the very least, it reinforced Guntrip's tendency to tidy-up and pigeon-hole feelings aroused in the analysis. In short, in indulging Guntrip, and possibly himself, in extra-analytic sessions, Fairbairn made his analytic task all the more difficult.

*   *   *   *   *   *

"The Oedipus complex is central for therapy, but not for theory." With this dictum, Fairbairn answered Guntrip's query about that complex—or so Guntrip claimed in his published account of his analysis.[50] If accurate, it would have been an extraordinary statement for his analyst to have made, all the more so since it is belied by the analysand's unpublished account. (Guntrip may have misrepresented Fairbairn because of how he himself used the term "oedipal." He extended it to cover *all* internalized bad-object relations, and then, rather illogically, complained that "oedipal" problems bulked too large.) To be sure, the unpublished document cannot be considered complete: it is not a verbatim transcript. Yet it provides evidence that at the end of his life Guntrip was still struggling with transference and that that struggle interfered with his full appreciation of what had gone on in the analysis.

The consulting room itself contributed to "the clear negative transference" which emerged at the outset. Here is Guntrip's description of the setting:

> I entered a large drawing room as waiting room, furnished with beautiful valuable antiques, and proceeded to the study as consulting room, also large with a big antique bookcase filling most of one wall. Fairbairn sat behind a large flat-topped desk, I used to think 'in state' in a high-backed plush-covered armchair. The patient's couch had its head to the front of the desk. At times I thought he could reach over the desk and hit me on the head. . . . Not for a long time did I realize that I had 'chosen' that couch position, and there was a small settee at the side of his desk at which I could sit if I wished and ultimately I did.[51]

"Before a word was spoken," Guntrip had cast Fairbairn "in the role of the mother who dominated" his "personality and crushed any initiative."[52]

Fairbairn consistently interpreted the negative transference. A few examples from early in the analysis follow:

> "You feel a struggle for power, for potency. A fundamental assumption is involved. You automatically, from a deep level, treat yourself as a little child, and automatically treat anyone like me as big, powerful, authoritative. You've never lost that assumption since childhood. Everyone else is a great big authority, in both sex and anti-sex and all matters."

> "You always feel a child vis-à-vis parent figures, a child over against a big dominating authoritative mother in both discipline and sex. Then you have to reverse that and be the big dominating man making the woman the child. But it's always a parent–child relationship, not two people 'on a level'. 'Being a man' came to mean to you 'dominating', 'turning the tables', not being grown up in the sense of being equal, but of being 'bigger'."

> "Your inner system demands that I take this role of the mother who is down on you. You justify it, or her, by making me do it."[53]

What was this "inner system"? Fairbairn was intent on finding out. (Keeping track of the transference, of Guntrip's oscillations between openness and reserve, of course, remained crucial.) The initial step was obvious: exploring Guntrip's attachment to his mother. Fairbairn interpreted:

> "You changed yourself from your natural desires into something else, to meet with approval from the puritanical crushing down self. *You changed into mother imposing restrictions on the child, on yourself.* When you were a child and mother imposed restrictions on you, you were helpless. When you identified with mother and imposed the restrictions, you were powerful, you exercised mastery."[54]

Guntrip was quite ready to acknowledge his identification with his mother and, still more, his perpetual struggle against it; he found it painful to recognize his continued longing for her:

> "She's not an attractive person now but I am conscious of wishing she were so that it could be a pleasure to come home and chat with her. It's harder to give up a bad mother than I realized. . . . I'm still unconsciously tied to the mother I hate and resent and regard as bad and a failure: depressing. She early roused a deep need and longing for her which she has never met."[55]

Guntrip remained tied, though he became more and more conscious of it. Four years into the analysis the following exchange took place:

> "When should I finish analysis? Why does it concern me? . . . I've made definite progress. Compared with five years ago, I was then depressed. . . , not sleeping too well, working feverishly, tense. Now I'm far better in health and freer in mind, and much more creative in my work and in writing. But *I'm up against a hidden core which I can't penetrate.* . . . I can't go on with analysis indefinitely, but must secure some further changes in myself. I still feel mother interferes with my freedom."

Fairbairn commented:

> "Tied to her by your needs."

Guntrip replied:

> "Yes. Ultimately I feel *I need mother deep down, it underlies my preoccupation with persisting anger and hate.* Some part of me can't give her up, so I keep hammering at her in my secret feelings to make her see how she neglects me, and make her change, I must settle accounts with mother. It's her I want love from and not make do with Aunt Mary. I feel I can't yet get out of this deep down dilemma. . . ."[56]

In his analysis with Fairbairn, Guntrip never did. A few months later the mother died at last; the son obtained little relief thereby. He was still hammering at her on the first anniversary of her death, or rather he was hammering at his analyst.

> "Towards the world outside me I'm feeling a sort of lifeless despair and rejection of it and fall back withdrawn into myself. I feel just now as if I've given up the outer world as hopeless, no one will ever understand. The child in me has only two choices, to create an internal fantasy world of fighting and suffering, . . . it's that or nothing, and I feel I don't understand what that means. On last Sunday morning I felt like a child of 1 year old and can't get them [adults] to understand what it is I need. I'm lonely, cut off, out of touch, because they are inaccessible and they don't understand. I'm puzzled, hopeless and helpless, can't find a way of opening their eyes to the fact and they haven't got the human intuition to see it. I don't even know what it is I need. If mother had been a real mother she would have met that need without my needing to know what it was."[57]

In Guntrip's eyes, Fairbairn was in the course of taking over the role of the parent who did not understand his needs as "child."

A graphic (albeit disguised) image of that child emerged in a dream whose clarity surprised the dreamer himself:

> "I was going home from Edinburgh by train and had a lifesize dummy of a man left with me, made of flesh, human but no bones in it. I put it in the Guard's van to get rid of it, and propped it up as it slumped limp. I hurried away so the Guard wouldn't know it was mine. Not that I was doing anything wrong but I didn't want him to know I had any connection with it. I met the Guard in the corridor and suddenly heard it shambling up after me, calling out. I felt a queer horror as if it was a sort of fleshly ghost, and said to the guard, 'Quick, let's get away. It's alive. It'll get us.'"

Guntrip gave the following associations:

> "This is my passive self that I am afraid will emerge into consciousness. I want to bring it to you. You are the guard. I want you to see it because I fear it. It's the part of me I've spent a lifetime trying to keep repressed. It would undermine me."

Fairbairn replied:

> "It's a good thing this is being uncovered and coming out now. That's what we're working for. A very interesting important dream."[58]

At this point the "passive self" became crucial. Fairbairn understood it in terms of "repression of the self mother crushed." Guntrip demurred: he insisted that it was the self which had never been evoked. Retrospectively he composed the lines he would have liked his analyst to have uttered:

> "There was no mother there. That's the part of you mother never saw, never related to, never called into life. Because she didn't you have now brought him to me so that I can recognize this inner you and call you to life."

If, according to Guntrip, Fairbairn had seen that it was "not being crushed, but being not noticed at all as a person," that was the problem, he would thereby have given his patient the relationship the mother had failed to provide.[59] From his demand that Fairbairn be to him a "good mother" in place of his "bad mother" Guntrip never retreated.

The analysis had reached a stalemate. By this time Guntrip had been in treatment for just under six years; he had had 777 sessions with Fairbairn. He was to keep at it for another five years, though with the frequency much reduced; in all he had 1014 sessions. His account of those last five years is thin; he complained repeatedly of ringing changes on old themes and of Fairbairn's continued off-the-mark interpretations. Yet he seemed tied to his analyst, no less than to his mother—as he himself appreciated full well: "I realize that my feeling unable either to go on or to stop analysis must involve a real transference of my rebellious bondage to mother. . . . Now I'm working hard at analysis and wanting to break free of it, from you."[60]

What brought the analysis to an end? By the seventh year it seemed destined to be interminable, with Guntrip oscillating between an effort to force his analyst to be the mother he wanted and anger at his own failure to control him. (Fairbairn at last confronted his patient with his compulsive and coercive note-taking, but to no avail.[61]) All the while Guntrip was toying with the idea of phasing out. Still it was not until Fairbairn's health began to fail that his patient became serious about ending the analysis.[62] Rather than deal with the fears—fear of abandonment among them—that his analyst's ill-health aroused, Guntrip abandoned Fairbairn, and he did so without a regular termination and without resolving his "rebellious bondage" to his analyst.

* * * * * *

The aim of "maintaining relationships with objects in the inner world at the expense of a realistic and therapeutic relationship with the analyst, viz., a movement having the aim of preserving internal reality as a closed system, . . . seems . . . to constitute the most formidable resistance encountered in psycho-analytical treatment." Fairbairn wrote these words at a point when Guntrip's analysis had stalled. He had not succeeded in effecting a breach in his patient's "closed system," he had not succeeded in inducing him "to accept the open system of outer reality."[63] At least he possessed the theoretical equipment for understanding his own lack of success.

ENDNOTES

1. W. R. D. Fairbairn, "Fundamental Principles of Psychoanalysis," *Edinburgh Medical Journal*, 36 (1929), 329–345.

2. Interview with John D. Sutherland, March 31, 1981.

3. W. Ronald D. Fairbairn, *Psychoanalytic Studies of the Personality* (London: Tavistock Publications and Routledge and Kegan Paul, 1952), p. 154.

4. Ibid., pp. 31, 137, 138 (emphasis in the original).

5. Michael Balint, "Pleasure, Object and Libido: Some Reflexions on Fairbairn's Modification of Psychoanalytic Theory," *The British Journal of Medical Psychology*, 29 (1956), 163.

6. W. Ronald D. Fairbairn, "Observations in Defence of the Object-Relations Theory of the Personality," *The British Journal of Medical Psychology*, 28 (1955), 145 (emphasis in the original).

7. Fairbairn, *Psychoanalytic Studies of the Personality*, pp. 140, 157.

8. Sigmund Freud, *Three Essays on the Theory of Sexuality* (1905), Standard Edition (London: Hogarth Press, 1953), VII: 182.

9. Fairbairn, *Psychoanalytic Studies of the Personality*, p. 33.

10. Ibid., pp. 80*n*, 260–261, 266.

11. Ibid., pp. 261–262, 264.

12. Ibid., p. 33.

13. Ibid., p. 32.

14. Ibid., pp. 34, 35 (emphasis in the original).

15. See Sigmund Freud, *The Ego and the Id* (1923), Standard Edition (London: Hogarth Press, 1961), XIX: 29.

16. Fairbairn, *Psychoanalytic Studies of the Personality*, p. 42 (emphasis in the original).

17. Ibid., p. 35 (emphasis in the original).

18. Ibid., p. 120.

19. Ibid., p. 121.

20. Ibid., p. 124 (emphasis in the original).

21. Ibid., p. 122.

22. Ibid., p. 122.

23. Ibid., p. 37.

24. Ibid., p. 124.

25. Melanie Klein, "Notes on Some Schizoid Mechanisms" (1946), in *The Writings of Melanie Klein*, III: *Envy and Gratitude and Other Works 1946–1963* (London: Hogarth Press, 1975), p. 3.

26. Stephen A. Mitchell, "The Origin and Nature of the 'Object' in the Theories of Klein and Fairbairn," *Contemporary Psychoanalysis*, 17 (1981), 379, 381, 384.

27. Fairbairn, *Psychoanalytic Studies of the Personality*, pp. 55–56.

28. Ibid., pp. 55, 56.

29. Ibid., pp. 17–18, 23.

30. Ibid., p. 56.

31. Harry Guntrip, "My Experience of Analysis with Fairbairn and Winnicott (How Complete a Result Does Psycho-Analytic Therapy Achieve?)," *The International Review of Psycho-Analysis*, 2 (1975), 146.

32. Harry Guntrip, "First Training Analysis, with W. R. D. Fairbairn" (unpublished manuscript: n. d.), p. 4.

33. Harry Guntrip, "Psychoanalytical Autobiography (A Study of the 'Dream Process' over Thirty-Six Years, Showing the Effects of an Amnesia for an Infancy Trauma)" (unpublished manuscript: n. d.), p. 1.

34. Guntrip, "Analysis with Fairbairn and Winnicott," p. 154.

35. Ibid., p. 149.

36. Guntrip, "Psychoanalytical Autobiography," p. 47.

37. Ibid., p. 38.

38. Guntrip, "Analysis with Fairbairn and Winnicott," p. 148 (emphasis in the original).

39. Guntrip, "Psychoanalytic Autobiography," pp. 39, 294, 342–343.

40. Ibid., pp. 340–341.

41. Guntrip, "Analysis with Fairbairn and Winnicott," pp. 148, 151.

42. Guntrip, "Training Analysis," p. 284; see also Fairbairn to Guntrip, June 27, 1956 (unpublished).

43. Guntrip, "Analysis with Fairbairn and Winnicott," p. 147.

44. Guntrip, "Training Analysis," pp. 138, 234 (emphasis in the original).

45. W. Ronald D. Fairbairn, "Observations on the Nature of Hysterical States," *The British Journal of Medical Psychology*, 27 (1954), 114.

46. Guntrip, "Training Analysis," pp. 263–264.

47. W. Ronald D. Fairbairn, "Considerations Arising Out of the Schreber Case," *The British Journal of Medical Psychology*, 29 (1956), 113–127.

48. Guntrip, "Training Analysis," pp. 364, 366.

49. Guntrip, "Analysis with Fairbairn and Winnicott," pp. 146–147. See also Henriette T. Glatzer and William N. Evans, "On Guntrip's Analysis with Fairbairn and Winnicott," *International Journal of Psychoanalytic Psychotherapy*, 6 (1977), 95, and Otto F. Kernberg, *Internal World and External Reality: Object Relations Theory Applied* (New York and London: Jason Aronson, 1980), p. 59.

50. Guntrip, "Analysis with Fairbairn and Winnicott," p. 147.

51. Ibid., p. 148.

52. Guntrip, "Training Analysis," p. 16.

53. Ibid., pp. 38, 43, 101.

54. Ibid., p. 79 (emphasis in the original).

55. Ibid., p. 80.

56. Ibid., p. 245 (emphasis in the original).

57. Ibid., p. 322.

58. Ibid., p. 337.

59. Ibid., pp. 337, 338.

60. Ibid., p. 349.

61. See ibid., pp. 334–335, 344.

62. In Guntrip's view, losing Fairbairn would represent the death of his brother, and he "would be left with a full scale eruption of that traumatic event, and no one to help" him with it. Guntrip, "Analysis with Fairbairn and Winnicott," p. 151; see also Guntrip, "Training Analysis," p. 402.

63. W. Ronald D. Fairbairn, "On the Nature and Aims of Psycho-Analytical Treatment," *The International Journal of Psycho-Analysis*, 39 (1958), 381, 385.

PART IV

Fairbairn's Contributions to Understanding Disorders of the Self

15

A Reconsideration of Fairbairn's "Original Object" and "Original Ego" in Relation to Borderline and Other Self Disorders

DONALD B. RINSLEY

Fairbairn's contributions to an elucidation of endopsychic structure are receiving increasing if belated recognition, particularly in view of their relevance to an understanding of borderline and related disorders of the self (Sullivan, 1963; Kernberg, 1980; Grotstein, 1981; Rinsley, 1982; Greenberg and Mitchell, 1983). His findings, long outside the psychoanalytic mainstream, afford us profound glimpses into the origins of mental life, most importantly into its prerepresentational and representational components and how they function in the pathogenesis of the characterologic or personality disorders.

In his final published work, Fairbairn (1963) referred to what he termed an *original object* (O.O.) and an *original ego* (O.E.):

> Internalization of the object is a defensive measure originally adopted by the child to deal with his original object (the mother and her breast) in so far as it is unsatisfying.

From *The Borderline Patient: Emerging Concepts in Diagnosis, Psychodynamics, and Treatment*, Vol. 1 (pp. 219–232), edited by James S. Grotstein, Marion F. Solomon, and Joan A. Lang, 1987, Hillsdale, NJ: Analytic Press. Copyright 1987 by The Analytic Press. Reprinted by permission of Mrs. Charlotte Rinsley and the publisher.

The original ego is split into three egos—a central (conscious) ego attached to the ideal object (ego-ideal), a repressed libidinal ego attached to the exciting (or libidinal) object, and a repressed antilibidinal ego attached to the rejecting (or antilibidinal) object.

Throughout his writings, Fairbairn appears to refer to the O.O. in a variety of ways. Thus, in his "Schizoid Factors" paper (1940) he differentiates between the mother as the child's "libidinal object . . . as a whole" and the child's "libidinal interest . . . focused upon her breast . . ." (p. 11). He further develops this theme in his "Revised Psychopathology" paper (1941) where, in reference to his postulated late oral stage of infantile dependence, he specifies the mother-with-the-breast (whole-object treated as part-object) as the focus of the child's libidinal interest and attachment. Again, in that paper Fairbairn describes the mother's breast as the child's "natural object" during the early oral stage of infantile dependence, and in his "Endopsychic Structure" paper (1944) he uses the term "first libidinal object" as synonymous with "natural object." The term "natural object" reappears in his "Object Relationships and Dynamic Structure" paper (1946) within the same context in which it appeared in the 1941 paper. Again, in his discussion of indirect repression and the "Oedipus situation" in his "Synopsis" paper (1951), Fairbairn employs the phrase "only significant object" in reference to the child's relationship to the mother during infancy. In the 1944 paper, Fairbairn also appears to refer to the O.O. as "the figure of (the child's) mother." The term *original object* as such is not to be found elsewhere in his writings except for the final, 1963, paper.

Although Fairbairn makes considerable reference to the O.O. in his writings, references to the O.E. are few.[1] A number of considerations may be put forward to account for the discrepancy. First, the then extant terminology favored the use of the term "object" as inclusive of aspects of both self and non-self; indeed, Kleinian writers are wont to write of objects as condensates of both. Second, Fairbairn's writings antedate the appearance of a theory of mental representations as embodied in the contributions of Edith Jacobson (1954a,b,c, 1957, 1964, 1971), further elaborated by Kernberg (1966, 1972) and in various degrees by others (Mahler, 1968, 1971, 1972; Mahler, Pine, and Bergman, 1975; Masterson, 1975,

---

[1]The term *Original Ego* makes its appearance in the 1963 paper. The concept of O.E. appears earlier, however, in Fairbairn's 1944 paper, where he adumbrates it as "the undivided ego" by reference to the Central Ego as its "residue." In his 1951 paper, however, he uses the term "undivided ego" in reference to the Central Ego. In this paper I shall adhere to Fairbairn's 1944 use of the term.

1976; Masterson and Rinsley, 1975; Rinsley, 1977, 1978, 1982).[2] Third, there is the salient fact that Fairbairn never grasped the important, equally idiosyncratic contributions of Federn (1952) to the metapsychology and phenomenology of self-experience, most of which continue to languish outside the psychoanalytic mainstream or have long been incorporated into it without due and proper acknowledgment of their author.

It should be noted, moreover, that Grotstein's (1981) concept of what he terms the "background object of primary identification" clearly encompasses Fairbairn's O.O. as well as Sandler's (1960) concept of the "background of safety," Winnicott's (1965) "environmental mother," Erikson's (1959) "objects of tradition," and Bion's (1962) "inherent preconceptions." A proper consideration of the subtlety and inclusiveness of Grotstein's formulation is beyond the scope of this chapter and the reader is accordingly referred to his 1981 treatise on splitting and projective identification for an extended discussion of the subject.

EARLY ENDOPSYCHIC STRUCTURE

My inferences concerning the nature of the O.O. go beyond Fairbairn's view of it in terms of the infant's mother and her breast. I consider it, moreover, to constitute a dimly perceived proto-object associated with the infant's similarly perceived, coenesthetic complex of self-representations that together comprise the O.E. (Rinsley, 1982). My further inferences regarding these two pristine representational complexes must, of course, remain highly speculative. There is reason to believe, however, that they come into existence as derivatives of the infant's global perception of its autonomic–visceral vicissitudes very soon after birth or even before. Inasmuch as drive states underlie the formation of representations (Freud, 1895), we may infer that the exigencies of hunger and of distended bowels and bladder cause a congeries of vague yet cogent representations of these tension-related states to be raised to a certain degree of conscious awareness; and, further, that these unpleasant representations come to be disowned by the infant just as he needs to eliminate their physical counterparts—feces and urine—by means of normal excretory mechanisms (Rinsley, 1968). The disowning mechanism is *primal projection*, by means of which the infant splits them off as quasi-object-representations in the

[2]In keeping with Hartmann's (1950) and Jacobson's (1964) usage, I here employ the term "representation" to apply to unconscious, preconscious, and conscious endopsychic perceptions or awareness of bodily and mental content irrespective of degree of perceptual clarity or organization.

form of *internal* percepts, a process that precedes their external projection into the "container" provided by the mother (Bion, 1957). Integral to this conception of the earliest object relations are several important insights developed by Melanie Klein and Margaret Mahler:

First, inasmuch as these unpleasant quasi-object-representations arise from the infant's own autonomic–visceral tensions (primitive self-representations), they come to serve as the earliest internal persecutors responsible for the origin of paranoid anxiety (Klein, 1935). Again, in her 1952 paper devoted to the mutual development of the ego and the id, Melanie Klein explicates her concept of the death instinct in terms of the infant's fear of annihilation, based in turn on the experience of internal persecutors derived from the "instinctual reservoir" of the id (Freud, 1923).

Second, in her classic paper devoted to early infantile psychosis, Mahler (1965) draws attention to the affectomotor storm–rage reactions of early infancy as discharge phenomena derived from the tension of unrelieved instinctual needs.

From these considerations it is possible to conclude that the infant generates internal persecutors in the form of defensively quasi-objectified, internally sequestered self-representations derived from autonomic–visceral tensions and attendant affectomotor discharges. It would appear that these instinctually derived representational phenomena, indigenous to the infant, are sufficient to account for Freud's and Melanie Klein's death instinct, for whatever heuristic purposes that concept might serve.

We may now conclude that these pristine quasi-object-representations comprise nothing less than the anlagen of the O.O., the self-representational components of which comprise nothing less than the anlagen of the O.E. From these will later differentiate Fairbairn's postulated Ideal Object ("I.O."), Exciting Object ("E.O.") and Libidinal Ego ("L.E."), and Central Ego ("C.E."), Rejecting Object ("R.O.") and Anti-Libidinal Ego ("Anti-L.E."), respectively, We may schematize these various endopsychic components as follows:

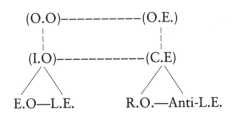

The parentheses are intended to convey the very early, minimally differentiated nature of the O.O. and the O.E. as well as the early, unformed nature of the I.O and the C.E.; the I.O. will later emerge as the ethical–

moral component of the (classical) superego while the C.E. will later emerge as the (classical) reality ego (Rinsley, 1982). The broken line connecting the I.O. and the C.E. is intended to convey the fact that until related depressive-position and Oedipal issues are worked through, self- and object-representations remain split from each other, and the child's internalized object relations are based on part-representations, viz., the E.O., R.O; L.E. and Anti-L.E. It should be noted that this internal state of affairs constitutes the essence of Fairbairn's (1944) basic *endopsychic situation,* which becomes egregiously evident among individuals who suffer from the borderline spectrum disorders (Rinsley, 1982; Meissner, 1984).

As I have elsewhere noted (Rinsley, 1982), the evolution of the I.O.–C.E. alliance forms the basis for the inception of whole-object relations. As integral to this development, the E.O.–L.E. and R.O.–Anti-L.E. alliances undergo rearrangement such that their self-representational and object-representational components come into respective association. We may schematize these structural rearrangements as follows:

Thus, a whole-self complex (C.E.–L.E.–Anti-L.E.) and a whole-object complex (I.O.–R.O.–E.O.) begin to form and differentiate from each other in earnest during the rapprochement subphase of separation–individuation (Kernberg, 1972). Among the signal results of this endopsychic restructuralization are the establishment of increasingly firm ego boundaries (Federn, 1952) and the enhancement of the individual's growing sense of self.

The significance of the object-relations postulate that object assumes primacy over aim now takes on added meaning. It may be said that the pristine O.O. that the pristine O.E. "seeks" is a condensate of the infant's internally projected, sequestered autonomic–visceral percepts, which are split off from the remainder of his endopsychic structure, the latter constituting the elements of the O.E. It follows that the O.O., as Fairbairn has variously defined it in terms of a libidinalized breast–mother figure, comes into existence secondarily, as a result of the infant's projection of his autonomic–visceral, affectomotoric (pristine O.O.) elements into the maternal container (Bion, 1957); in turn, these elements undergo repetitive reinternalization and re-externalization, thereby modeling and remodeling the persecutory internal objects, topical of the paranoid–schizoid position, which these elements had come to represent.

To summarize, the infant early generates an internally projected repository of split-off perceptual elements that function as quasi-objectified self-representations and serve as the infant's primal persecutors—these comprise the (pristine) O.O. In turn, these quasi-objects undergo secondary (external) projection into the breast–mother, the maternal container (Bion, 1957), from and by which they are repetitively remodeled by means of circular mother–infant reintrojection–reprojection (cf. Kohut's [1971, 1977] process of "transmuting internalization"). By virtue of this remodeling or transmuting process, the infant's persecutory quasi-objects, the pristine O.O., undergo assimilative metabolization, or depersonification (Kernberg, 1966), their "raw" affect charges deintensified and the affectomotor storms associated with them eased. In the case of the psychoses and the major personality disorders, the maternal container-transmuting function has proven inadequate, with the result that the repository of infantile internal projects, the pristine O.O., remains a disruptive core within the child's evolving mental structure. Evidently from the beginning as well as resulting from the circular remodeling–transmuting process, the pristine self-representational elements associated with the O.E. come to be intimately associated with the elements of the pristine O.O. In addition, the infant's body of internal persecutors incorporates introjected and reintrojected elements of the maternal container per se. Thus, the entire assemblage of internal persecutors is comprised of the following:

The sequestered, internally (primally) projected autonomic–visceral percepts, here termed the pristine O.O., which are quasi-objectified.

The self-representational (pristine O.E.) elements associated with the pristine O.O.

The reintrojected components of the "later" O.O., that is, the maternal container, into which the infant had previously projected them.

And, finally, those components indigenous to the maternal container which the infant has introjected by virtue of their frustrating aspect.

In the 48th hour of treatment, a gifted borderline–narcissistic professional woman in her early thirties said, "I always felt that I was full of shit—that I had taken it in from all the crap my parents had handed out to me—my mother was depressed and couldn't nurse me—but I always knew somehow that I'd put the shit there myself, hidden away—I remember my mother saying to me 'Don't give me any of your shit, girl!'"

This young woman's utterances concerning her sequestered excrement reflected her feeling of being "bad," of being filled up with bad objects (feces), and of being empty (of good objects); they gave arresting expression to Melanie Klein's (1935) equation of what she termed the dead internal object with feces and flatus and to Abraham's original inferences regarding melancholia. In his 1911 paper, Abraham described the melancholic's feelings of inner impoverishment, of the inability to love, and the need to project hate into others. In his 1916 paper he described the phenomenon of regression to oral cannibalism, with its devouring of the (lost) object. His 1924 paper described the mechanism of anal expulsion with subsequent annihilation of the lost object. The origin of the harsh, sadistic (classical) superego is associated with these related phenomena: (1) the self-derived, endopsychically sequestered (primally projected, hence split-off), untransmuted representational equivalents of excremental products that require elimination, the core of bad objects comprising the pristine O.O. with its associated O.E.; (2) the feelings of inner impoverishment and inability to love that result from failure of maternal nurturance; and (3) the mechanism of anal expulsion that further impoverishes the self through unremitting efforts to get rid of the plethora of O.O.–O.E.-related bad objects that persist as untransmuted representations of the powerfully cathected feces. The endopsychic situation reflective of these phenomena becomes established during the late oral (oral aggressive, oral devouring) and early anal (anal aggressive) stages, coincident with the differentiation and practicing subphases (Mahler, et al., 1975). The regression to oral cannibalism in particular represents a defensive effort to wrest supplies (good objects) from what the infant perceives as an essentially withholding, rejecting breast.

The ubiquity of depression among psychotics and borderline–narcissistic personalities underscores this pathogenic timetable. Thus, the core of sequestered bad objects, the pristine O.O.–O.E., accounts for Fairbairn's schizoid condition, the universality of which among those who have failed to achieve whole-object relations cannot be disputed. Finally, Abraham's cited anal-expulsive mechanism, together with the mechanism of oral cannibalism, underlies the infant's failure to negotiate the depressive position in view of the everpresent threat they pose for the annihilation of the potential whole object. In particular, the anal-expulsive mechanism forms the anlage of the projective component of the manic defense of identification with the superego (Klein, 1935), by means of which manic–depressives and borderline and narcissistic personalities proceed to devalue and hate others (Rinsley, 1985).

The persistence of the pristine O.O.–O.E. likewise accounts for the persistence of primary narcissism in these cases. As these split-off internalized projects are indeed of one's own making, as it were, they are ever prone to become overvalued; as such, they assume the characteristics of Fairbairn's (1941) retained good and bad objects in accordance with his obsessional transitional mechanism. This apparently paradoxical endo-psychic situation reaches its peak of development among obsessionals, in whom both good and bad objects are retained as a defense against pow-erful annihilative propensities.

I have elsewhere discussed the process of premature ego development as found in narcissistic personalities (Rinsley, 1984, 1985) in whom there occurs a dissociation of the individuation subprocess from the separa-tion subprocess, leading to the pathological persistence of obsessional and manic defenses.

A COMMENT ON MOURNING
AND ENDOPSYCHIC STRUCTURE

In an earlier publication (1968), I put forward the view that the (classi-cal) ego relates to the Ucs [the unconscious] and the "outside" as foreign territories into which it banishes its contents, as it were, by means of repression in the case of the Ucs and projection in the case of the outside. As a corollary to this view, the ego was considered as striving to get back its repressed and projected contents, banishment of which in sufficient measure leads to an endopsychic condition of impoverishment or empti-ness. It is generally recognized that the development of a dynamic Ucs can occur only as a result of a shift from reliance on splitting to reliance on repression, and that this momentous shift takes place as the child negotiates the depressive position, associated with which is the develop-ment of the ability to mourn. Melanie Klein's (1940, 1945) insight into these developmental achievements led her to conclude that the work of the depressive position and the formation of the Oedipus complex are intimately related and that the oedipal child relates to the parents as whole objects.

Basic to the mourning process is the ability to call to mind a series of mental representations of the "lost" object and of the situations with which that object had been associated. For such working-through to occur, the prospective mourner much have achieved object constancy (Fraiberg, 1969; Rinsley, 1982). Obviously, the mourning process involves an exten-sive remodeling of the representations of "lost" objects such that they undergo depersonification, assimilation, or metabolization (Kernberg, 1966). The mourning process has its origin in the mother's capacity to transmute the infant's projected bad objects derived from the previously sequestered O.O.–O.E., to attenuate their traumatic impact on the child's developing endopsychic structure. *It is concluded that the failure of the maternal container function (Bion, 1957) brings about an arrest of the child's potential for the depersonification of metabolization of the child's repository of autonomic–visceral internal projects, that is, the O.O.–O.E.* The pristine O.O.–O.E. thus remains inordinately vivid for the child, splitting continues, and the capacity to mourn remains undeveloped.

Kernberg's (1966) conceptualization of the process of depersonification (metabolization) of representations has its roots in Edith Jacobson's seminal studies (1954a,b,c, 1957, 1964, 1971). Their work leads to the conclusion that what is undepersonified (unmetabolized) is unrepressed; thus, when the ego "takes back" what is unrepressed, it reinternalizes split-off, willy-nilly projected and reintrojected representations with their associated "raw" or unneutralized affect charges. In regressed states, with failure of repression, Ucs content undergoes various degrees of vivid repersonification. When this is the case, the reinternalized representations continue to be split into "all good" and "all bad" entities; as a consequence, the endopsychic structure is riven by ambivalence and mourning cannot take place. Given these considerations, Fairbairn's view of repression and splitting as essentially the same assumes greater clarity.

The importance of Fairbairn's 1940 paper, "Schizoid Factors in the Personality," becomes [all] the more evident when it is recognized that he was applying the term "schizoid" to a range of symptomatic and characterologic disturbances that later clinicians would classify within the borderline–narcissistic spectrum (Stone, 1980; Rinsley, 1982; Meissner, 1981; Adler, 1985). The pathogenesis of these cases is fundamentally developmental and not regressive, is therefore preoedipal in nature, and reflects the failure of endopsychic metabolization that results from very early deficiency of the maternal container.

THE RELATION OF STRUCTURES (REPRESENTATIONS) TO BOUNDARIES

In a 1968 paper, I emphasized the importance of "good" internal objects for the maintenance of the ego boundaries. Federn (1952) postulated the existence of two of these, namely, an internal ego boundary delimiting the content of the Ucs from the territory of the ego and an external ego boundary delimiting the "inside" from the "outside." Federn considered that the integrity of these boundaries is maintained by a specific ego boundary cathexis, deficiency of which forms the basis for abnormal modes of experience. Thus:

Deficient cathexis of the external ego boundary leads to its progressive contraction so that more and more ego content crosses and falls outside it and is then perceived as "real"—the result is hallucination and illusion (failure of reality testing).

Deficient cathexis of the telereceptors embedded in the external ego boundary causes distorted perception of outside objects and events—the result is estrangement (impairment of the sense of reality).

Failure of cathexis of the internal ego boundary, that is, the barriers separating the unconscious from the conscious, leads to the irruption of unconscious mental content into the conscious ego, with resultant psychotic symptomatology.

Deficient cathexis of what Federn termed the core of the ego leads to depersonalization (impairment of the sense of reality).

Federn considered the ego core to be the locale of function of what he called "medial ego feeling," the ineffable, prereflective awareness of *one's being as such* (Rinsley, 1962). The core percepts integral to this medial mode of self-experience reflect one's mere existence or extension in time and space, hence are quasi-objectless; by the same token, their impairment leads to depersonalization, in which the sufferer perceives himself as oddly, strangely, or peculiarly self-unfamiliar or, in the extreme, even lifeless. It may be inferred that these medial percepts, including their distortion in cases of depersonalization, are associated with the pristine autonomic–visceral and vestibulo-cerebellar processes that serve as anlagen of one's bodily image (Schilder, 1935, 1953; Frick, 1982). Accordingly,

Basic self- and body images, that is, one's personified sense of self, have their origin in these autonomic–visceral and vestibulo-cerebellar processes, that is, the pristine O.O.–O.E.

If ineffectively modulated by the maternal container, these processes, particularly those associated with autonomic-visceral functions, lead to a condition of heightened inner tension, with its proneness to affectomotor discharges with their associated impairment of one's (medial) sense of self.

Fairbairn's O.O.–O.E. may be conceptualized as the very earliest representations associated with these processes, *the prototypical self-object,* as it were.

Modulation of these processes involves the depersonification, or metabolization, of their associated representations. In turn, such "metabolic remodeling" promotes the development of object constancy through repetitive projection and introjection as these occur between the child and the maternal container. Again, the repetitive projection and introjection serve as anlagen of the mourning process that is, in turn, integral to the work of the depressive position with its resulting generation of oedipal whole-object relations. By the same token, the failure of such modulation–depersonification underlies the development of psychotic and borderline pathology in which the pristine percepts function as horrifically bad objects.

SUMMARY

One of Fairbairn's less pellucid formulations concerns his notion of a whole, or unitary, original object (O.O.) and a whole, or unitary, original ego (O.E.) supposedly existing *a priori* (Rinsley, 1982, pp. 85–88, 256; Greenberg and Mitchell, 1983, pp. 163–164, 180). The view developed here, that these entities are derived from very early, dimly perceived autonomic–visceral and vestibulo-cerebellar processes, allows for the retention of the object as foremost in relation to aim and suggests a somatic substrate for the range of self- and object-representations. It further links representations, in the sense of Jacobson and Kernberg, to more pervasive experiences of body image and self-awareness as described by Federn and Schilder. Finally, it accounts for the globality of the infant's pristine representational experiences without the necessity of postulating aprioristic whole-self and whole-object representations of which the infant is obviously incapable. Rather, the O.O. (or, better, the O.O.–O.E.) postulated by Fairbairn is considered as a secondary derivative resulting from later projection and introjection.

In the end, we may speculate whether the sequestered, internally (primally) projected, split-off autonomic–visceral and vestibulo-cerebellar percepts comprise the anlage of what will later emerge as the (classical) Ucs concomitant with the development of normal repression. I conclude that they do. The metabolization of these percepts causes them to fall below the level of conscious awareness, and the "internal rearrangement" of "egos" and "objects" (*v. sup.*) generates whole-objects from previously split-off "all good–all bad" part-representations, thereby bringing them under the hegemony of the I.O.–C.E. (Rinsley, 1982, pp. 265–268). With the inception of these interrelated processes, the child is on the way toward healthy separation–individuation and the development of libidinal object constancy.

REFERENCES

Abraham. K. (1911), Notes on the psycho-analytical investigation and treatment of manic–depressive insanity and allied conditions. In: *Selected Papers of Karl Abraham.* London: Hogarth Press, 1927, pp. 137–156.

——— (1916), The first pregenital stage of the libido. In: *Selected Papers of Karl Abraham.* London: Hogarth Press, 1927, pp. 248–279.

——— (1924), A short study of the development of the libido, viewed in the light of mental disorders. In: *Selected Papers of Karl Abraham.* London: Hogarth Press, 1927, pp. 418–501.

Adler, G. (1985), *Borderline Psychopathology and Its Treatment.* New York: Aronson.

Bion, W. R. (1957), Differentiation of the psychotic from the nonpsychotic personalities. In: *Second Thoughts.* New York: Aronson, 1967, pp. 43–64.

——— (1962), Learning from experience. In: *Seven Servants: Four Works by Wilfred R. Bion.* New York: Aronson, pp. 1–111.

Erikson, E. H. (1959), *Identity and the Life Cycle.* New York: International Universities Press.

Fairbairn, W. R. D. (1940), Schizoid factors in the personality. In: *An Object-Relations Theory of the Personality.* New York: Basic Books, 1954, pp. 3–27.

——— (1941), A revised psychopathology of the psychoses and the psychoneuroses. In: *An Object-Relations Theory of the Personality.* New York: Basic Books, 1954, pp. 28–58.

——— (1944), Endopsychic structure considered in terms of object-relationships. In: *An Object-Relations Theory of the Personality.* New York: Basic Books, 1954, pp. 82–136.

——— (1946), Object-relationships and dynamic structure. In: *An Object-Relations Theory of the Personality.* New York: Basic Books, 1954, pp. 137–151.

——— (1951), A synopsis of the development of the author's views regarding the structure of the personality. In: *An Object-Relations Theory of the Personality.* New York: Basic Books, 1954, pp. 162–179.

——— (1963), Synopsis of an object-relations theory of the personality. *Internat. J. Psycho-Anal.,* 44:224–225.

Federn, P. (1952), *Ego Psychology and the Psychoses,* ed. E. Weiss. New York: Basic Books.

Fraiberg, S. (1969), Libidinal object constancy and mental representation. *The Psychoanalytic Study of the Child,* 24:9–47. New York: International Universities Press.

Freud, S. (1895), Project for a scientific psychology. *Standard Edition,* 1:283–397. London: Hogarth Press, 1966.

——— (1923), The ego and the id. *Standard Edition,* 19:3–66. London: Hogarth Press, 1961.

Frick, R. B. (1982), The ego and the vestibulocerebellar system: Some theoretical perspectives. *Psychoanal. Quart.,* 51:93–122.

Greenberg, J. R., & Mitchell, S. A. (1983), *Object Relations in Psychoanalytic Theory.* Cambridge, MA: Harvard University Press.

Grotstein, J. S. (1981), *Splitting and Projective Identification.* New York: Aronson.

Hartmann, H. (1950), Comments on the psychoanalytic theory of the ego. In: *Essays on Ego Psychology.* New York: International Universities Press, 1964, pp. 113–141.

Jacobson, E. (1954a), Contribution to the metapsychology of psychotic identifications. *J. Amer. Psychoanal. Assn.,* 2:239–262.

——— (1954b), On psychotic identifications. *Internat. J. Psycho-Anal.,* 35:102–108.

——— (1954c), The self and the object world: Vicissitudes of their infantile cathexes and their influence on ideational and affective development. *The Psychoanalytic Study of the Child,* 9:75–127. New York: International Universities Press.

——— (1957), Denial and repression. *J. Amer. Psychoanal. Assn.,* 5:61–92.

────── (1964), *The Self and the Object World*. New York: International Universities Press.

────── (1971), *Depression*. New York: International Universities Press.

Kernberg, O. F. (1966), Structural derivatives of object relationships. *Internat. J. Psycho-Anal.*, 47:236–253.

────── (1972), Early ego integration and object relations. *Ann. New York Acad. Scis.*, 193:233–247.

────── (1980), Fairbairn's theory and challenge. In: *Internal World and External Reality*. New York: Aronson, pp. 57–84.

Klein, M. (1935), A contribution to the psychogenesis of manic–depressive states. In: *Melanie Klein: Love, Guilt and Reparation & Other Works, 1921–1945*. New York: Delacorte Press/Seymour Lawrence, 1975, pp. 57–60.

────── (1940), Mourning and its relation to manic–depressive states. In: *Melanie Klein: Love, Guilt and Reparation & Other Works, 1921–1945*. New York: Delacorte Press/Seymour Lawrence, 1975, pp. 344–369.

────── (1945), The Oedipus complex in the light of early anxieties. In: *Melanie Klein: Love, Guilt and Reparation & Other Works, 1921–1945*. New York: Delacorte Press/Seymour Lawrence, 1975, pp. 370–419.

────── (1952), The mutual influences in the development of ego and id. In: *Melanie Klein: Envy and Gratitude & Other Works, 1946–1963*. New York: Delacorte Press/Seymour Lawrence, 1975, pp. 57–60.

Kohut, H. (1971), *The Analysis of the Self*. New York: International Universities Press.

────── (1977), *The Restoration of the Self*. New York: International Universities Press.

Mahler, M. S. (1965), On early infantile psychosis: The symbiotic and autistic syndromes. In: *The Selected Papers of Margaret S. Mahler*, Vol. 1. New York: Aronson, 1979, pp. 155–168.

────── (1968), *On Human Symbiosis and the Vicissitudes of Individuation, Vol. 1: Infantile Psychosis*. New York: International Universities Press.

────── (1971), A study of the separation-individuation process and its possible application to borderline phenomena in the psychoanalytic situation. In: *The Selected Papers of Margaret S. Mahler*, Vol. 2. New York: Aronson, 1979, pp. 169–187.

────── (1972), On the first three subphases of the separation-individuation process. In: *The Selected Papers of Margaret S. Mahler*, Vol. 2. New York: Aronson, 1979, pp. 119–130.

──────, Pine, F., & Bergman, A. (1975), *The Psychological Birth of the Human Infant: Symbiosis and Individuation*. New York: Basic Books.

Masterson, J. F. (1975), The splitting defense mechanism of the borderline adolescent: Developmental and clinical aspects. In: *Borderline States in Psychiatry*, ed. J. E. Mack. New York: Grune & Stratton, pp. 93–101.

────── (1976), *Psychotherapy of the Borderline Adult*. New York: Brunner/Mazel.

Masterson, J. F., and Rinsley, D. B. (1975), The borderline syndrome: The role of the mother in the genesis and psychic structure of the borderline personality. *Internat. J. Psycho-Anal.*, 56:163–177.

Meissner, W. W. (1984), *The Borderline Spectrum*. New York: Aronson.

Rinsley, D. B. (1962), A contribution to the theory of ego and self. *Psychiat. Quart.*, 36:96–120.

———— (1968), Economic aspects of object relations. *Internat. J. Psycho-Anal.*, 49:38–48.

———— (1977), An object relations view of borderline personality. In: *Borderline Personality Disorders*, ed. P. Hartocollis. New York: International Universities Press, pp. 47–70.

———— (1978), Borderline psychopathology: A review of aetiology, diagnosis and treatment. *Internat. Rev. Psycho-Anal.*, 5:45–54.

———— (1982), *Borderline and Other Self Disorders*. New York: Aronson.

———— (1984), A comparison of borderline and narcissistic personality disorders. *Bull. Menn. Clin.*, 48:1–9.

———— (1985), Notes on the pathogenesis and nosology of borderline and narcissistic personality disorders. *J. Amer. Acad. Psychoanal.*, 13:317–328.

Sandler, J. (1960), The background of safety. *Internat. J. Psycho-Anal.*, 41:352–356.

Schilder, P. (1935), *The Image and Appearance of the Human Body*. London: Paul, Trench, Trubner.

———— (1953), *Medical Psychology*. New York: International Universities Press.

Stone, M. H. (1980), *The Borderline Syndromes*. New York: McGraw-Hill.

Sullivan, C. T. (1963), *Freud and Fairbairn: Two Theories of Ego Psychology*. Doylestown, PA: The Doylestown Foundation.

Winnicott, D. W. (1965), *The Maturational Processes and the Facilitating Environment*. New York: International Universities Press.

16

'Narcissism' in Fairbairn's Theory of Personality Structure

JOHN PADEL

Fairbairn lived and worked in Edinburgh, and only rarely was present to take part in discussions of the British Psycho-Analytical Society, always held in London. So the influence that his ideas had on other thinkers during the 1940s and 1950s came about almost entirely through his writings. Probably for that reason, theorists like Melanie Klein, Michael Balint, and Donald Winnicott did not often relate their thought to his. Yet his theories transcended the 'one-person psychology' that Balint and Rickman felt had long restricted classical psychoanalytic thinking (Balint 1949). Winnicott had not consciously realised that the term 'transitional', of which he made much use from 1951 on, had already, ten years earlier, been an important term in Fairbairn's account of personal development; and he never overtly related the gap between what he called 'the true self' and 'the false self' to the splitting processes, which Fairbairn had shown to be of central importance in human development and psychopathology.

In 1940 Fairbairn had maintained (1952, p. 8) that 'some measure of splitting of the ego is invariably present at the deepest mental level' (splitting of the ego is, of course, the primary postulate of narcissism) and that *'the basic position in the psyche is invariably a schizoid position'* (his italics). Four years later he arrived at a statement of 'endopsychic structure considered in terms of object-relationships' (p. 82), in which the

Modified and slightly amplified by the author from "Narcissism—A Fairbairnian View" by John Padel, *British Journal of Psychotherapy*, 1986, 3, 256–264. Copyright 1986 by John Padel. Adapted by permission of the publisher.

schizoid processes he had described before (and had found at work much earlier, according to his clinical papers of 1927, 1931, and 1936) were shown to lead to, and to account for, the structured development of the psyche, both normal and pathological.

Fairbairn's paper of 1944, according to Phyllis Grosskurth's biography of Melanie Klein, 'initiated what was to be the last major creative period of Klein's life. [It] forced her to trace life from its very first moments rather than select later critical events in infantile development' (1986, p. 371). So Fairbairn is with reason regarded in the USA as the founder of an object-relations theory of the personality, which was the title chosen for the publication of his book there (p. 325 n.). In the second publication of her paper on schizoid mechanisms (1946) Klein acknowledged some debt to Fairbairn and, 'combining his term with hers' in developing her theory of the earliest weeks and months of life, adumbrated a 'paranoid–schizoid' position more basic than the depressive one which she had hitherto regarded as central.

'Narcissism' and 'narcissistic' were terms that Fairbairn used only rarely, so at first sight the concept does not appear to play a part in his theoretical thought; but he had used it twice in his clinical paper of 1931 (followers of Kohut will be interested to note that in one passage the word *grandiose* occurs: 'in this case the patient's narcissism achieved a more grandiose expression') and in his theoretical papers of 1940 and 1941 he uses it to make a link between his account of the schizoid individual and Freud's theoretical and clinical ideas. In describing how, for the depressive individual, loss of the object provokes the depressive state, Fairbairn asks how it is that physical injury or illness may also provoke it, and answers that for the individual who still remains in a marked degree in a state of infantile identification with his object bodily loss is functionally equivalent to loss of the object: 'this equivalence is reinforced by the presence of an internalised object, which, so to speak, suffuses the individual's body and imparts to it a narcissistic value' (1941, in 1952, p. 54). The year before, Fairbairn had pointed to the way in which individuals with a schizoid tendency always evince a sense of inner superiority (which may be revealed in psychoanalysis only after considerable resistance, and its sources after even more formidable resistance). However, Fairbairn had clearly succeeded clinically in uncovering the sources of this sense of superiority, which is 'based upon: (1) a general *secret* over-valuation of personal contents, mental as well as physical; and (2) a narcissistic inflation of the ego arising out of *secret* possession of, and considerable identification with, internalised libidinal objects (e.g. the maternal breast and the paternal penis)' (1952, p. 22; his italics).

So, in his paper 'A revised psychopathology of the psychoses and psycho-neuroses' (1941), Fairbairn can write of 'the merging of emotional identification with oral incorporation, that confers upon the stage of infantile dependence its most distinctive features . . . based upon the fundamental equivalence for the infant of being held in his mother's arms and incorporating the contents of her breast'. He continues:

> The phenomenon of narcissism, which is one of the most prominent characteristics of infantile dependence, is an attitude arising out of identification with the object. Indeed *primary narcissism* may be simply defined as just such *a state of identification with the object, secondary narcissism* being *a state of identification with an object which is internalised.* (1952, p. 48; his italics)

Fairbairn argues that narcissism is common to both the early (sucking) and the late (biting) oral phases of development, but the infant in the early phase is bound to react to object-loss as if his own love is bad and, being so identified with the external object, to experience object-loss as loss of his ego. The infant in the later stage is in not quite so parlous a case: following object-loss he can direct his ambivalence towards his internalised object. He can cope with life as long as his needs, especially his need for love, are met, but he will remain subject to attacks of depression as long as his intense ambivalence is liable to be mobilised by loss of the external object (or, of course, by any such situation or event as he, narcissistically, equates with its loss).

It is therefore justifiable to think of Fairbairn's whole exposition of object-relationships (certainly internal, and external as long as they are influenced by the internal) as a detailed account of narcissism, unless one decides as he probably did that the term 'narcissism' is not really useful for explanatory purposes, being too coloured by its descriptive uses, its meaning too biased towards the pathological and too derogatory for use as a scientific term.

To grasp the main features of Fairbairn's theories and their reconcilability or otherwise with Freud's, it is useful to review an article by Rubens (1984), which brings out both the strengths and a deficiency in Fairbairn's thought and has an interesting but, I think, mistaken suggestion for supplementing the deficiency. But first of all a couple of pieces of clinical material are worth keeping in mind to give life to the theory; they both come from Fairbairn's own work.

The first is an historic dream since it led Fairbairn immediately to formulate his schema of psychic structure.

> The dream consisted of a brief scene in which the dreamer saw the figure of herself being viciously attacked by a well-known actress in a venerable building which had belonged to her family for generations. Her husband was looking on but seemed quite helpless and quite incapable

of protecting her. After delivering the attack the actress turned away and resumed playing a stage-part which, as seemed to be implied, she had momentarily set aside in order to deliver the attack by way of interlude. The dreamer then found herself gazing at the figure of herself lying bleeding on the floor; but, as she gazed, she noticed that this figure turned for an instant into that of a man. Thereafter the figure alternated between herself and this man until eventually she awoke in a state of acute anxiety. (1952, p. 95)

The dozen pages (1952, pp. 95–107) in which Fairbairn cautiously yet thoroughly analyses this dream deserve study from all concerned with psychotherapy, and paraphrase would not do justice to them. He saw almost at once that he could interpret the dream in three ways, all valid and potentially useful. One was that it was a thinly-veiled picture of the patient's marriage and personal life: she acted a part, pretended privately to be gratified in sex with her husband and publicly to ignore his affairs, especially one with a young woman by whom he had been accompanied to his tailor's to order the suit worn by the bleeding man in the dream, and maintained against him a strong though unconscious aggression. The second way was to deepen the patient's understanding of her oedipal relationships: she was strongly identified with her libidinally exciting but rejecting father, killed in war when she was six, yet also with her emotionally cold mother, whom the description of 'actress' had fitted even better than it did the patient. The third way of interpreting the dream was to find in it a structural pattern, the model or 'paradigm of all endopsychic situations'; that structure was of a central ego bound to an idealised object and of two detached subsidiary egos, libidinal and antilibidinal, each firmly bound to an appropriate, repressed object, respectively exciting and rejecting, and each opposed to the other because of the antilibidinal hostility to the exciting object.

So by 1944 Fairbairn had established the tripartite structure of a dream and of the personality, linking it (with reservations) to Freud's Id, Ego, and Superego and defining the differences. In 1954 he published a paper, 'Observations on the nature of hysterical states', in the *British Journal of Medical Psychology*; it showed the clinical application of his theory in a number of cases, using vignettes of patients mostly by means of their typical dreams. One such was of a narcissistically masochistic young woman: she dreamed that she was half-way along a short corridor, next to a window through which she could see a number of couples strolling in a garden; she was facing her father who was holding between his legs a stick that pointed at her like a phallus; she turned round and at the other end saw her father again but with the stick raised as if to strike her. This dream has a structural resemblance to the former dream, except that the patient uses the same parental figure as both libidinal and antilibidinal. She has knowledge of the possibility of sexual harmony (cf. the couples outside) but cannot progress to it because of her attachment to an ambivalent object. (I would add, 'probably also because of her attachment to a libidinally good but forbidden object—her mother, whose genital was symbolised by a short corridor and was the appropriate place for encountering the sexually potent father'. A feature of this case requiring analysis would then have been the girl's identification with the phallus, a potent source of bodily narcissism.)

In 1924 Karl Abraham, whose schematic phase-theory of infantile development was acceptable to Fairbairn only for its account of the first two (the oral) phases, had described a striking dream recalled by a depressive patient from his childhood. Structurally it resembled the first of the dreams related above. It was a dream of standing before the door of his parents' house and of observing three horse-drawn carts with high sides ascending the hill past his home. Each cart had, slung underneath it, a man dragged by a rope around his neck and barely able to breathe. The driver of each cart walked beside it, beating the horses. The feeling had been as of a scene from hell. Abraham had pointed out that the dreamer's ego appeared in three places—once as the observing self, once by identification with the horses as the beaten child, and once by identification with the suffocating man as the choking child. But, unlike Fairbairn, Abraham did not examine the relationship of these three subsidiary egos to each other. If he had done so, he might have lighted upon the same three kinds of *relationship* in his patient's dream that Fairbairn was to find just twenty years later. Both Abraham and Fairbairn operated easily with the notion of identification alternating with object-relationship, but Fairbairn was more alert to the structure of an experience, to the ways in which the various elements of it related to each other.

In his article Rubens emphasises Fairbairn's radically new ideas on mental structure. In the first place Fairbairn had maintained the inseparability of energy and structure and therefore would not accept the presence in the mind of unstructured energy (Freud's Id) in contradistinction to the structured (and relatively unenergised) Ego. He had therefore rejected the notion of 'discharge' as an account of libidinal and emotional satisfaction; he had insisted that the individual ego is object-related from the start and therefore seeks an emotionally satisfying *relationship* with another person (an 'object').

Fairbairn's use of 'ego' was, in Rubens's view, equivalent to 'self' because it signified the whole person, capable of self-expression and of experiencing all three—the world, his self-expression towards the world, and the interaction between the world and himself. In this sense the psyche had a unitary and dynamic origin. However, for Fairbairn, every individual's psyche had three substructures, two of them relatively split off from the third, the central self ('central' because consciousness is located there). A 'self', in Rubens's view, deserves this name because it consists of 'ego' closely linked with 'object' and each subsidiary ego-plus-object is treated as a unit by the other 'selves'. The three subsidiary 'selves' are all modelled in the same way and the object-relations of each are characteristic. The libidinal self has been split off from the central self because the excessive excitement of the libidinal relationship had threatened the integrity of the whole psyche; the antilibidinal self has been split off because, in its relationship with the rejecting object (necessary for stability and security), it has by its enslavement to it forgone or impaired the possibility of deeply satisfying experience. These split-off selves (i.e., aspects of the self which are primarily repressed) nevertheless keep up a fundamental opposition to one another—at least the antilibidinal self maintains persistent hostility towards and domination over the libidinal self (secondary repression). The libidinal self, structured as it is—with ego- and object-elements—is of course not to be equated with the classical Id (though Fairbairn did accept some correspondence), nor is the antilibidinal self the same as the Superego (though I think Fairbairn did allow that 'superego' could be understood as antilibidinal ego plus rejecting object along with aspects of the central self plus aspects of idealised objects; it played a crucial part in his theory of the 'moral defence' and of guilt). Rubens calls the libidinal and antilibidinal selves 'crystallisations'; they carry templates for self-repetition and are therefore capable of only minimal growth. They have been created by repression and continue under its pressure.

Rubens next points out that psychic structure, according to Fairbairn's account of it, is pathological. Almost all psychoanalytic theories have a metaphor for psychic growth, the metaphor being 'movement through progressive levels of structural differentiation and complexity'. For Fairbairn, however, the differentiated structures had been created by internalisation as a defensive act against intolerably bad object-relations: this had led to the creation of the two split-off selves, a schizoid state. These repressed structures are experienced both as intolerably bad and as absolutely needed; hence the repetition-compulsion, according to which the absolutely needed is sought and found again and again, and is as often rejected as soon as its intolerable badness is recognised. The very movement implied here means of course that the central self, indeed the total self, does have an on-going interaction with the external world, albeit in relationships limited by the extent and depth of repression of the subsidiary selves. Fairbairn had described the neurotic's world as a closed system (1958) but with the possibility of its being breached and so being slowly transformed into a (relatively) open system, if the psychoanalyst managed to deal successfully with the patient's transference (i.e. with the patient's sustained attempts to treat him simply as an object in his closed system).

Rubens then argues that if *all* internalisation were pathological (i.e. undertaken only to dispose of libidinally bad objects), there would be no growth of the personality, no memory, no learning, no conscious organisation of experience. But as these are real features of the healthy psyche, there must be internalisation which is not pathological, internalisation of good objects. Fairbairn had realised this and had added a corrected account of the motives for internalising before he republished his papers as his book; yet it remains true that he gave an inadequate account of what Rubens calls 'non-structuring internalisation', i.e. of internalisation that does not lead to repression or to further fragmentation of the self. Rubens' own account, which he finds implied in Fairbairn, is of the internalisation of good objects which are absorbed into the central self and are therefore not subjected to repression and so not productive of further endopsychic structure. From this point on Rubens speaks of 'structuring' and 'non-structuring internalisation' as if these were Fairbairn's own terms (which they were not) to describe two different 'forms of internalisation.' In a footnote, however, he concedes that Fairbairn spoke of early internalisation of an object which *subsequently* undergoes a tripartite split into exciting and rejecting 'bad' objects and an 'accepted object' [my italics]. *Pace* Rubens, my inference is that Fairbairn came to regard any act of internalisation as preceding the splitting of the object into good and bad elements, which are only then disposed of by acceptance (of 'good') in the central self or by repression (of 'bad') into the libidinal–antilibidinal system. However Rubens quotes with approval Kernberg's acceptance of 'the notion that internalisations, on all levels, have the basic form which Fairbairn suggested—an element of self, an element of object, and the affective, purposive relationship between them'.

This last point is very important for the understanding of narcissism. If, as Fairbairn held, the very dynamic of the self (*he* spoke of the 'ego') is its object-seeking and object-attachment, it is impossible to internalise an object without internalising an aspect of the self affectively and purposively attached to that object; also, it is impossible to split off versions of the already internalised object without splitting off the appropriate versions of the self along with them. Therefore every internalised object would have been, for Fairbairn, a Kohutian 'selfobject' (though he might not have approved the term). The purpose of internalising objects is twofold: first, to control and refashion them as required; secondly, to use them in projective–introjective exchange as a basis for external relationships. Clearly the repressed elements are less available for this purpose than those in the central self, but clinical experience shows that it is inevitable, once therapy gets under way, for the repressed elements, both libidinal and antilibidinal, sooner or later to devolve upon the relationship of therapist and patient.

All this was sketched (however lightly) in a short paragraph in Freud's paper 'On Narcissism': 'A human being has originally two sexual objects—himself and the women who nurses him—and so we are postulating a primary narcissism in everyone, which may in some cases manifest itself in a dominating fashion in his object-choice' (Freud 1914, p. 88). As I understand this, each one of us has internalised from the first the nursing couple of which he was part along with its affective, purposive relationship, and in forming any later love-relationship finds elements of that original couple in his partner: if the elements found in the other belong more to the self-side of the original couple, the object-choice will be 'narcissistic'; if more to the side of the nursing mother, the object-choice will be more of the attachment type; but no object-choice will be purely one or the other.

If this can be taken as the model of all internalisation, it follows that all relationships have a narcissistic aspect, although of course that aspect is more obvious when it is the projected elements of self that preponderate or when the relationship is not personalised (e.g. in the possession of 'the best'—car, clothes, address, or analyst—or of things to show off) or when it remains within the self. The term 'narcissism' applies to the affective, purposive bond between the self and the object with which the self is identified (or, after the nursing period, between self and 'selfobject' in the Kohutian term); so we can ask where its energy is to be thought of in the psyche. The answer is, wherever there is a bond between two or more aspects of the self, or between any of them and any internalised objects. A positive bond means attachment to a good or to a bad internalised object (the bad objects account for negative narcissism—low self-esteem, compulsion to fail, or the need for punishment); a negative bond means repression of an object (along with whatever aspect of self is attached to it by a positive bond). In behaviour narcissism will become obvious only when repressed or split-off internal relationships powerfully affect external relationships, but it is reasonable to regard the self as getting 'narcissistic supplies' from any good ongoing relationship and from any successful achievement.

Without doubt Rubens has pointed to an important incompleteness in Fairbairn's theory of psychic structure: although Fairbairn insisted on 'dynamic structure', he has no image for psychic growth and gives no account of the ongoing interchange which there must be between the central ego and the split-off libidinal and antilibidinal selves. Also, his formulas for cure do not go beyond diminishing the splitting, reconciling the split-off elements of the self, and accepting a more open relationship with the world. If Rubens's solution of two different forms of internalisation seems incompatible with Fairbairn's account of splitting into good and bad *after* internalising, it is necessary to suggest a different way of describing the process of growth.

My first point would be that 'structuring internalisation' is not necessarily pathological, certainly not according to Fairbairn's later thought. To create an internal system for disposal of the unwanted (and the not-yet accepted) seems good psychic physiology. My second point is that the accepted good object and the repressed bad objects are not to be thought of in a simple binary way—white and black. The exciting and the rejecting or controlling objects *are not bad at the same time*; and each seems at times to be absolutely needed. Partly because of that good aspect they each tend to appear in dreams and other experiences (e.g. particularly in transferences); partly also because the ego does not tolerate the inevitability of the schizoid state. The natural conclusion is that the categories of libidinal and antilibidinal, strongly related to each other by the negative bond of secondary repression, contain ego–object relations which are at first only provisionally sorted as well as those which are more deeply repressed. During each night the day's ego–object relations will be worked over and, unless incompatible or otherwise unsuitable, will be established in the central ego by means of associative bonds. The new ego–object relations so accepted are likely to have the tripartite structure of libidinal, neutral, and antilibidinal aspects acquired during the provisional sorting; so that the whole of the central ego will have been, and will continue to be, built up in a mosaic of more or less closely integrated ego–object relations. Any mosaic is liable to have lines of potential cleavage under stress; those lines of cleavage, which account for break-down, indicate areas in which identifications that have been formed in relationships are still unstable or have remained in potential conflict with other earlier-made identifications. A 'false self,' for instance, will be an individual who early in life over-emphasised certain antilibidinal identifications at the expense of the libidinal, and may even have taken a spurious libidinal pleasure in doing so; a psychopath will have over-emphasised the libidinal at the expense of the antilibidinal.

It is worthwhile to consider briefly how it was that Fairbairn's theory was left with the incompleteness it has and, in spite of his insistence upon 'no energy without structure,' with a rather static picture of the psyche in which structured energy seems to be in equilibrium rather than operatively mobile.

Fairbairn was first (1940) preoccupied with severely schizoid states in which, because of gross defects in early parenting, the individuals had engaged in massive internalising; he contrasted these with cases where there had been no such massive internalisations thanks to good early mothering. Then (1941) he had seen his way to describe a splitting of the object into good and bad, the acceptance of the good and the rejection of such bad as had been unavoidable, by means of repression. He realised that he could account for the four main neurotic syndromes by permutation of the inside/outside *loci* of the good and the bad (in phobias and obsessions good and bad are kept together—outside for phobias, inside for obsessions; in paranoias and hysterias good and bad are kept separate—for paranoias good is inside with bad outside, for hysterias *vice versa*), but he did not as yet ask further about the nature of the 'bad' nor about the relations of the 'inside/outside space' to the internal space of internalisation and repression.

He embarked upon the latter problem when he investigated war-neuroses and thought further about 'repression and the return of bad objects' (1943). At last (1944) he saw his way to write about psychic structure, yet still making the assumption that 'bad' meant simply 'libidinally bad' and not asking about the point of view from which it was accounted bad (given the tripartite ego-structure there must be at least three points of view).

In 1946 Melanie Klein queried the motive Fairbairn had assigned for internalisation. Preoccupied herself with internal badness, she naturally assumed (with Freud) that the only motive at first for internalising was to get the good inside. Fairbairn, assuming goodness inside, had found no motive for internalising unless it was to remove the bad encountered in the earliest object-relationships of infancy. So, according to his earlier view, splitting into good and bad seems to have been a matter of perception before internalising. In 1951, when preparing his papers for his forthcoming book, he tried to remedy two defects: firstly he accepted the rightness of the criticism that he had not allowed for internalisation of the good, and decided that it was the *ambivalent* (good but potentially defective) object that was internalised. So splitting of the object into good and bad was done *after* internalisation. (Of course the consequent ego-splitting was entirely secondary to the object-splitting.) Secondly he saw that 'libidinally bad' must have two different meanings: in the experience of essential needs not being met, the antilibidinal object or 'rejecting' object appeared bad to the central ego; when libidinal excitement imperilled the central ego and its good object-relationship (biting the nipple would be a case in point), the libidinal object-relationship became 'bad' and the controlling side 'good'.

In writing the 'Addendum' to his 1944 paper Fairbairn did not ask how this double nature of the 'rejected object' affected his structural theory. So we are left with a rather static picture of the internal situation in neurosis, and, if we consider it in terms of narcissism, we can see a libidinal narcissism in which identification with the spoiling mother and the spoiled child predominates, and a negative narcissism in which identification with the depriving mother and the deprived child is to the fore. The healthy narcissism of the good and accepted ego–object relationships, by internalising which the central ego has grown, is not examined: apparently it does not require examination.

Yet by asking about the conditions upon which a good ego–object relationship is centrally internalised or an ambivalent ego–object relationship, having been internalised, is made good enough for acceptance by the central ego, it may be possible here to remedy the incompleteness to which Rubens has pointed.

The short paragraph in Freud's 'On Narcissism' from which a sentence was quoted earlier shows Freud's conception of the flexibility in normal development: a self–other 'emotional and purposive relationship' is reflected upon, unconsciously as well as consciously; either element can be regarded and loved from the point of view of the other but the two elements are not distinct; they are mixed so that later, in a new-found object of love, there may be more or less of the original self, and so the love may be more or less narcissistic. The original 'two sexual objects' which each of us carries internally (i.e. two in an affective, purposive relationship with each other) form the nucleus of the central ego which, thanks to its capacity to reflect upon them unconsciously, can also use that internal relationship to form and develop relations with other people, who are also capable of reflecting upon and using their own internal relationships to meet and respond to our individual approaches. Not only love-experiences but every meaningful encounter with another person may modify, slightly or radically, the primary nucleus with all the transformations it has undergone since it was first formed by internalisation of the nursing couple.

The conditions for acceptance of a newly internalised relationship into the central ego and for its integration there will be positive and negative. The positive condition is that we have been able to reflect upon it and to regard each of its elements from the point of view of the other. (The regarding of the self-element will account for the healthy narcissism.) Such reflection and regard may be long-drawn-out or even momentary. Adopting this point of view of the other person implies a longer or shorter identification with that other, but it cannot be a lasting identification before the relationship has been accepted and integrated.

The negative condition for acceptance of a new relationship into the central ego is the judgement that there are no obstacles to reflection upon it, no elements in it that conflict with the ego's established nature, and nothing to prevent regard of each element from the point of view of the other or to prevent free identification with each element. If any unacceptable elements are found, the relationship may be filed for working over or may be relegated to join the repressed libidinal–antilibidinal systems. Reflection, regard, and judgement are according to this account the central activities which maintain growth of the self. We turn these powers upon other selves which have the same capacities but different identities. When asleep we turn our reflection upon the ego–object relationships we have internalised in the course of the day and also upon those previously repressed; this can lead not only to our acceptance of the new but also to modification and acceptance of items previously rejected and repressed; if this does happen our narcissism also is modified in the direction from pathology to health. To employ our powers of reflection, regard, and judgement in waking life, we need as well the capacity to perceive, recall, and anticipate and to act in ways suited to a situation, but especially to apprehend, survey and respond to others similarly capable of reflection and of apprehending and responding to us.

Something particularly creative occurs when two people are each unusually aware of the other's reflective activity. This can happen in playing music together, in acting a scene, in conversation, and in love-making; it can happen between teacher and pupil and between psychotherapist and patient. Much depends at these times upon acceptance of the other's narcissism, which can be an obstacle if it is not a facilitator of the joint activity on which they are engaged. When a mutual relationship is marked by asymmetry there is a special opportunity for transformation, perhaps for both participants but certainly for the one who has so far been the less free to reflect and to respond. He can find in the relationship with the other what Christopher Bollas (1979) has called 'the transformational object' and can use it to change his closed narcissistic system to an open system. As he succeeds in that, instead of rejecting the new he will begin to welcome it and to discover new pattern and new possibilities of pattern in the long-familiar.

REFERENCES

Abraham, K. (1924). A short study of the development of the libido. In *Selected Papers on Psycho-Analysis*. London: Hogarth Press, 1949, pp. 418–501.

Balint, M. (1949). Changing theoretical aims and techniques of psychoanalysis. In *Primary Love and Analytic Technique*. London: Tavistock, 1965, pp. 202–222.

Bollas, C. (1979). The transformational object. *International Journal of Psycho-Analysis*, 60, 97–107.

Fairbairn, W. R. D. (1952). *Psychoanalytic Studies of the Personality*. London: Tavistock.

Fairbairn, W. R. D. (1954). Observations on the nature of hysterical states. *British Journal of Medical Psychology, 27,* 105–125.

Fairbairn, W. R. D. (1958). On the nature and aims of psycho-analytical treatment. *International Journal of Psycho-Analysis, 39,* 374–385.

Freud S. (1914). On narcissism. *Standard Edition, 14,* 67–104.

Grosskurth, P. (1986). *Melanie Klein.* London: Hodder & Stoughton.

Klein, M. (1946). Notes on some schizoid mechanisms. In M. Klein, P. Heimann, S. Isaacs, & J. Riviere, eds., *Developments in Psycho-Analysis.* London: Hogarth Press, 1952, pp. 292–320. (Also in *The Writings of Melanie Klein,* Vol. 3. London: Hogarth Press, 1975, pp. 1–24.)

Rubens, R. L. (1984). The meaning of structure in Fairbairn. *International Review of Psycho-Analysis, 11,* 429–440.

17

A Fairbairnian Object Relations
Perspective on Self Psychology

MICHAEL ROBBINS

INTRODUCTION

Psychoanalytic theorists who trace the roots of their ideas are much like those of us who research our genealogies in quest of distinguished ancestors, hoping not to encounter illegitimate or disreputable connections en route and perhaps even trying to deny that any might exist. Most analysts tend to forget, repress, or deny the existence of theoretically fruitful but politically unacceptable forebears, at the same time that they are ready and eager to claim as ideational ancestors Freud and his acknowledged disciples and successors. Although I do not mean to suggest any correlation between the quality or importance of a person's work and that person's sociopolitical status within the psychoanalytic movement, it is not uncommon that at least some of the contributions of these politically disreputable or illegitimate analytic ancestors—for example, Ferenczi, Rank, Tausk, Reich, Horney, and Alexander, and to a lesser extent Klein and Fairbairn—may undergo decades of neglect and suppression, only to re-enter and enrich the corpus of legitimate theory cloaked as more or less "original" contributions of more "acceptable" analysts from a newer generation.

Adapted from *American Journal of Psychoanalysis*, 1992, 52, 247–263. Copyright 1992 by the Association for the Advancement of Psychoanalysis. Adapted by permission of the author and the Association for the Advancement of Psychoanalysis.

An example of this phenomenon is encountered in tracing the roots of two of the important and apparently trail-breaking theorists of our time, Kernberg and Kohut. In 1980 I pointed out that Kernberg's basic ideas bear a powerful resemblance to those of Melanie Klein, although he manifestly disagrees with most of her theory. Curiously, in relation to the subject of this chapter, Kernberg *does* acknowledge a theoretical debt to Fairbairn with regard to his concept of developmental building blocks or internal object relations units (representations consisting of part-self, part-object, and linking affect). But, as Rubens (1984) notes, Kernberg's use of conventional drive and structural theory makes his definition of these units so fundamentally different from Fairbairn's that the claim of familial linkage is moot.

I have also noted the almost uncanny resemblance of much of Kohut's self psychology to Fairbairn's object relations theory (Robbins, 1980). It is of interest in this regard that Fairbairn is nowhere cited as a reference in Kohut's two major books (1971, 1977). The correspondence of these two theories has since also been noted by Bacal (1987), who speculates that Kohut, like other American analysts with classical training, may not have studied the work of the British object relations group.

The problem of acknowledging sources is not simply one of scientific veracity and academic ethics, however. It is part of a more fundamental requirement that if a discipline aspires to be scientifically respectable, new ideas must be tested against old ones as well as against data, and those ideas that survive must be selectively amalgamated into an ever-growing body of knowledge, while the dross is discarded. The alternative is a field comprised of noncumulative knowledge, whose content shifts with the winds of fad and fashion, discovered, forgotten, and rediscovered. Whether one considers this process from the perspective of Santayana's comment that those who do not learn from history are doomed to repeat it, or Freud's insights about the unconscious and the repetition compulsion, the conclusion is inescapable that full examination of legitimate sources is bound to raise new questions, yield new insights, and result in more sophisticated and comprehensive theory.

Some theories are so incompatible in their basic assumptions, however, that no matter how one may try to amalgamate phenomenal data from one with apparently or superficially related data from the other, the outcome is as sterile as efforts to breed a giraffe with an elephant. So it is with the many efforts that have been made to reconcile the ideas of Klein and her followers with Kohut's self psychology, in the hope that such a mating might produce a single more powerful theory. In contrast, Fairbairn's theory shares an impressive number of theoretical genes with self psychology. For this reason, a Fairbairnian perspective on self psychology may suggest fruitful areas for revision and expansion, which might make self psychology a more comprehensive and valid theory. Such an undertaking is fraught with irony, as it is one of those quirks of psychoanalytic history that Kohut's unacknowledged reincarnation of Fairbairn seems to have found a permanent place in mainstream psychoanalysis, whereas Fairbairn's more original ideas are unlikely ever to become widely known in their own right.

In the spirit of shedding new light on self psychology and giving long-overdue credit to Fairbairn, I propose to examine the areas of correspondence and divergence of the two theories. In the review that follows, Fairbairn's object relations theory is abstracted from his own work (1952, 1958; see also Chapter 3, this volume) and from reviews by Guntrip (1961) and Wisdom (1963), which I synthesized in my 1980 paper on Klein, Kernberg, Fairbairn, and Kohut. Since then there have been some interesting additions to the literature on Fairbairn. The same year (1980), Sutherland summarized his impressions of the British object relations theorists. Rubens (1984) and Bacal (1987) have elaborated some of my ideas and added insights of their own. Kohut's self psychology is summarized from his own work (1971, 1977), that of Kohut and Wolff (1978), and previous work of my own (Robbins, 1980, 1982). I do not consider the interesting question of where Fairbairn got *his* ideas; the bibliography in his 1952 book is a small and unrevealing one. Sutherland, a friend and colleague of Fairbairn, has pointed out the remarkable similarity of some of Fairbairn's basic doctrine with that of Ian Suttie (1935), a central figure in the Tavistock group of which Fairbairn was a member (Bacal, 1987).

SELF PSYCHOLOGIES

The most significant similarity between object relations theory (Fairbairn) and self psychology (Kohut) is that they are *both* self psychologies. That is, the basic conceptual unit is an intact self—a seamless, cohesive, dynamic entity with libidinal and aggressive *aspects* (not components), which "exists" in relation to and with the facilitation of objects, both actual (Fairbairn's "primary identification," by which he referred to cathexis of the original undifferentiated object, and Kohut's "selfobject") and intrapsychic (or to use Fairbairn's term, "endopsychic"). Fairbairn's "intact ego" (used as Freud employed *das Ich* in his prestructural writings to designate the self) exists and functions from birth, can test reality, has innate libidinal and aggressive *qualities* (not components), and has an undeveloped capacity to give and to love. Fairbairn stated that "structure divorced from energy and energy divorced from structure are meaningless concepts" (1952, p. 149). He called the initial state of self a "primary identification" and characterized it very much as Kohut did: as dependent on and undifferentiated from the loving object (Kohut's "selfobject"), while simultaneously being an intact self structure. It is worthy of note that "structure" used in this sense is a hypothetical state, a theoretical fiction—a virtual image presumed to exist in the neonate, rather than something to be inferred from stable processes one may encounter in an actual clinical experience.

Kohut defined the self "in the broad sense" as the center of inquiry, and the primary psychological configuration as the merged relationship between the self and the empathic selfobject. He stated, "Nondestructive aggressiveness is a part of the assertiveness of the demands of the rudimentary self" (1977, pp. 120–121). Although he maintained in his 1971 book that the self is cathected with narcissistic libido (and therefore he implicitly retained drive theory), in his later work Kohut abandoned this idea and simply defined the self as Fairbairn did—as a dynamic entity. The archaic self in Kohut's theory is at once cohesive and dissociated, or, to use Kohut's term, "bipolar." Whereas the birth of the self in primary identification with the object in Fairbairn's theory is coincident with physical birth, in Kohut's theory the emergence of a cohesive self in relation to an empathic selfobject, and the first psychologically meaningful events (which are deemed equivalent to the child's central subjective experience), occur during the second year of life (Kohut & Wolff, 1978). Previous mental events are deemed psychologically meaningless!

It should be noted that both Fairbairn and Kohut repudiated drive or instinct theory and the related notion that mental activity is regulated by a pleasure principle and/or a death instinct. Instead, the self structure in each theory has an integral dynamic aspect. Aggressive and pleasure-seeking behaviors that are not part of the self's efforts to relate to the object are looked upon as disintegration products reflective of the self's failure to negotiate a satisfying connection with the object.

DEVELOPMENT OF OBJECT RELATIONS AND NARCISSISM

Both Kohut and Fairbairn held that development occurs in the context of an undifferentiated or merged relationship between the self and a caring parent. Kohut called this a "selfobject" relationship, and saw the crucial nutrient as empathy, whereas Fairbairn referred to it as a "primary identification," based on love. Both believed that the central task of development is to achieve a mature state of differentiation within the dyad, not to resolve an Oedipal triangle. Both maintained that satisfactory relationships and not instinctual gratification are what promote growth. They conceptualized a mother of love, empathy, and holding, or else one of frustration, rejection, and failure of attunement, rather than a mother of libidinal gratification or prohibition. This is consistent with clinical experience that although patients often insist that they will be cured by experiences of pleasure or gratification of impulses, neither normal infant development nor therapeutic efficacy seems to depend on these things as much as on good relationships.

Fairbairn's developmental theory emphasizes the viscissitudes of dependence from immaturity to maturity. He conceived of this as a process of progressive differentiation of self from object; a process of relinquishing narcissistic or self-centered attitudes in favor of loving and caring ones; and a process of more or less successful actualization of one's ideals in a relationship. Fairbairn's central self seeks an ideal object, which is modeled after realistic qualities of the primal identification. Pleasure is a signpost to the object, and the erogenous zones are the routes to the object, but the purpose of the relationship is love and not impulse gratification. In the state of mature dependence, the capacity to give and to love is fully developed (1952, p. 39).

Kohut's archaic cohesive self is in fact bipolar or dissociated. The opportunity to merge with the empathic selfobject, followed by well-timed or optimal frustrations or disillusionments, leads to progressive internalization and structuralization of the two poles of the self—beginning with archaic grandiosity in relation to a mirroring object and idealization of an accepting one, and ending with nuclear ambitions and ideals, the poles of mature narcissism. It should be noted that these aspects of what Kohut called a cohesive self never integrate.

Because Fairbairn and Kohut focused on different aspects of self-development, there is considerable potential for their theories to enrich each other. Fairbairn's primary interest was in the development of object relations and in the formation of the schizoid personality as a consequence of the inevitably frustrating nature of the primary identification, whereas Kohut was concerned with normal and pathological narcissistic development. Fairbairn stated that

> ... the greatest need of a child is to obtain conclusive assurance (a) that he is genuinely loved as a person by his parents, and (b) that his parents genuinely accept his love. ... Frustration of his desire to be loved as a person and to have his love accepted is the greatest trauma that a child can experience. ... (1952, p. 41)

Fairbairn outlined the consequent process of endopsychic structuralization, which he considered to be a pathological splitting of the self— resulting in unintegrated internal object relations and crystallization of various personality disorders as well as the neuroses, each of which involves repetitive enactments of projected endopsychic dramas. Kohut, in contrast, articulated the evolution of narcissism or self-development when the selfobject connection is optimal, and he studied the consequences of insufficiently empathic parenting (narcissistic personality development). But he maintained that when the primary relationship is very frustrating and fails to sustain a developmentally necessary merger, the self becomes hopelessly fragmented and unable to enter into a cohesive relationship or transference, so that resultant mental events are meaningless.

In summary, Kohut's theory elaborates narcissistic development, both normal and pathological, and the transferences characteristic of pathological narcissism. He did not study the conditions characterized by extreme splitting and fragmentation, such as borderline personality and schizophrenia, as he considered such patients incapable of forming stable transference relationships. Fairbairn concentrated on the fate of object relations, both normal and pathological, and on what he called the "schizoid personality" (a stable configuration related to extreme splitting and fragmentation, and characterized by specific transference configurations), as well as on "schizoid states" (which are transient regressive episodes characterized by splitting). Most likely Fairbairn's schizoid personality would today be called borderline or sicker, and deemed by Kohut beyond the pale of psychological meaning, transference relationship, and psychoanalysis; however, Fairbairn did describe characteristic transferences formed by his schizoid patients. To confuse matters further, the three salient features of the schizoid personality—omnipotence or grandiosity (though this latter term must be inferred from Fairbairn's descriptions, as he himself did not employ it), isolation and detachment, and self-preoccupation—sound very much like characteristics of Kohut's narcissistic personalities.

Fairbairn's ideas about normal development and the maturation of the self and of object relations seem quite different from those of classical analysis. He maintained that endopsychic structuralization arises from frustration, is more or less synonymous with splitting or fragmentation, and is entirely a pathological process. He did not believe that maturation is characterized by internalization and progressive complexity of psychic structure. Good experiences of loving and being loved, in contrast to frustrating ones, are integrated into the self system (1952, p. 9), contribute to what Fairbairn describes as the central self's relationship with the ideal object, and do not necessitate repression or mental representation. They result in accretions to the pre-existing self rather than structuralization or fragmentation of it, and somehow (Fairbairn did not make this process clear) involve progressive differentiation of self from object. During what Fairbairn called the "transitional period," primary identification evolves into mature dependence and the capacity to care for others: "... *the more mature a relationship is, the less it is characterized by primary identification*; for what such identification essentially represents is failure to differentiate the object" (1952, p. 42; emphasis in original). Once again, there are common-sense observations that fit Fairbairn's theory: We have all observed how some people who seem naturally to feel good about themselves and others, and to live happy and productive lives, appear not to have to reflect about themselves deeply and analyze what they do.

Kohut described the development of healthy narcissism, defined as ambitions and ideals, from the poles of the archaic grandiose self (a concept similar to Freud's [1915] "purified pleasure ego") and the idealized parent imago or archaic idealizing self, respectively, in the course of relationships with empathic selfobjects. Phase-appropriate mergers of the aggressive grandiose self with the mirroring selfobject, and of the idealizing self with the idealized parent imago, followed by more or less optimally timed frustration of the wish to merge with the selfobject, induce "transmuting internalizations" and evolution of narcissistic structures. Intrapsychic structuralization, according to Kohut, is not only a normal but a developmentally necessary process, and one very different from self-fragmentation. The grandiose self evolves during the first few years of life into a mature ego, characterized by self-esteem, initiative, nuclear ambitions, and the capacity for pleasure; this process occurs mostly in relation to the mother. The idealized parent imago evolves at about 4–6 years of age, through interactions with both parents, into an "idealized superego" that performs functions related to ideals and values. Once the selfobject has been metabolized into structure, and the self has a sense of continuity based on the tension between nuclear ambitions and ideals, the individual is self-directed and self-sustaining, and separations from the selfobject no longer have disastrous intrapsychic consequences.

One respect in which the developmental pathways of the two theories are quite different is in their implicit goals; in Kohut's theory the end is not an object relationship (love or mature dependency), as in Fairbairn's theory, but achievement of the capacity to function more or less (though never entirely) independently of others. Kohut's theory, unlike Fairbairn's, maintains the analytically traditional equation of mental development with internalization of structure. Just as it is difficult to imagine Fairbairn's ideally mature but structureless personality, so it is difficult to envision how Kohut, who focused so exclusively on self-development, might account for the developmental transformation of an archaic "self" from self-centeredness to the remarkable empathic capacity he described as being a requisite of the selfobject. In these states of selflessness, which sound much more like the states of mature dependency described by Fairbairn than they do narcissistic states, the selfobject appears to have no thoughts beyond optimal attunement to children, spouses, and patients. Can such activity be merely a guise for mature self-centeredness? That is, is mature empathy simply a realization of one's ambitions and ideals, or is one required to postulate a developmental line of object love as Fairbairn did?

PATHOLOGICAL DEVELOPMENT AND ITS CONSEQUENCES

Both Fairbairn and Kohut maintained that frustration or significant empathic failure and disappointment in the primary identification or selfobject relationship leads to horizontal splitting (repression) and vertical splitting (fragmentation). Fairbairn maintained that frustration of any degree is the stimulus for development of endopsychic structuralization, which he equated with splitting or fission of the self, and which he believed leads to the adult schizoid personality. He viewed schizoid phenomena as universal and believed that we are all schizoid, more or less. In other words, it may be ideal to be structureless, but such an ideal is virtual and unattainable, whereas the norm is to be psychically structured or schizoid. Kohut maintained that intrapsychic structuralization consequent to frustration is not always pathological, and that phase-appropriate object-related frustration is necessary if mature and autonomous forms of narcissism and normal structuralization of the psyche are to evolve. He differentiated these growth-promoting frustrations from failures of empathic attunement which are destructive to the self because they occur at times when empathy is necessary for growth of the self. In Kohut's theory, the pathological failures or frustrations are what lead to fragmentation or loss of self-cohesion.

In other words, both Kohut and Fairbairn believed that frustration leads to the emergence of phenomena that appear to be drive-related, such as rage, autoerotic or hedonistic behavior, and states of excitement, as well as to states of detachment and apathy. However, Kohut maintained that such pathological consequences ensue only if the frustration is sufficiently severe and occurs at critical developmental phases, whereas Fairbairn maintained that schizoid phenomena are the norm. And both believed that the emergence of these phenomena reflects breakdown or splitting of the self, not emergence of its component parts. As Kohut put it:

Nondestructive aggressiveness is . . . a part of the assertiveness of the demands of the rudimentary self. . . . Destructiveness (rage) and its . . . companion . . . conviction that the environment is essentially inimical—

M. Klein's 'paranoid position' . . . are disintegration products—reactions to failures of traumatic degree in the empathic responsiveness of the selfobject. . . . [These] tenets . . . also apply to the libidinal drives. . . . The primary psychological configuration (of which the drive is only a constituent) is the experience of the relation between the self and the empathic selfobject. . . . If the self is seriously damaged . . . then the drives become powerful constellations in their own right. (1977, pp. 120–122)

Fairbairn described autoeroticism as "a deterioration of behavior . . . since libidinal need is object need, simple tension-relieving implies some failure of object relations" (1952, pp. 139–140).

One important implication of these ideas, which differentiates both Fairbairn's and Kohut's schemata from most other object relations theories, is that regression is not looked upon as a retracing of a developmental route already taken, but a new and pathological pathway characterized by fission of the nuclear self. This is consistent with my own observations (Robbins, 1981, 1983, 1989) that there tend to be significant differences between so-called regressive states in adults and the superficially similar states of normal infancy. Fairbairn and Kohut would agree not only that unmodulated drive behavior in disturbed adults does not imply regression to a normal but arrested state in infancy, but that it cannot be used to "reconstruct" infant development (e.g., a primary autoerotic state or a primary death instinct). According to these authors, such "normal" states do not ordinarily exist. In a way such reasoning leaves both Fairbairn and Kohut caught in a contradiction of their own making: Like so many analysts of adults, both reconstructed or constructed normal infant development from analysis of pathological patients, while simultaneously maintaining that adult pathology represents a deviant developmental pathway and not a normal developmental process.

PATHOLOGICAL SYNDROMES: SCHIZOID AND NARCISSISTIC PERSONALITIES

According to Fairbairn, the unempathic or unsatisfying object simultaneously arouses overexcitement because the infant needs it, and anger and frustration because it is rejecting of the infant's quest to love and be loved. To deal with the resulting conflicts, repression ensues, as well as a splitting of the self (what Fairbairn called a "schizoid process"). What are repressed are not wishes or drives, but bad objects—or, as we would now say, representations of these unsatisfying objects—and the parts of the ego that seek relationships with them. The results are Fairbairn's three self subsystems: the unconscious libidinal and antilibidinal selves, and the conscious central self. Repression of the attracting or exciting aspect of the relationship produces an unconscious libidinal or needy self, comprising libidinal ego in relation to an exciting object. Repression of the rejecting aspect of the relationship creates an unconscious antilibidinal ego in relation to a rejecting object. The libidinal and antilibidinal selves are not integrated. Later the libidinal and antilibidinal configurations are projected into salient relationships. As Rubens has put it, "these press for re-enactments . . . an attachment to some negative aspect of current experience which is felt as vital to the definition of the self" (1984, p. 434).

According to Fairbairn,

> A real relationship with an external object is a relationship in an open system; but, in so far as the inner world assumes the form of a closed system, a relationship with an external object is only possible in terms of transference, viz., on condition that the external object is treated as an object within the closed system of inner reality. (1958, p. 381)

The major consequences of internal mastery of disappointing relationships are schizoid withdrawal and depression; attitudes of isolation, omnipotence, or grandiosity; and self-preoccupation, followed by distortion of subsequent relationships by projective identification. The details comprise Fairbairn's schizoid and depressive positions, as well as the neuroses.

The third element of self in Fairbairn's system, the central self in relation to the ideal object, is a conscious residue of the primary identification. Over time the ideal object is modified by accretion of positive experience and evacuation via repression of frustrating elements. Thus, Fairbairn's concept of the development of idealization is the reverse of that held by most analysts. It is initially thought to be a realistic process, but has the potential to become quite unrealistic if actual experiences are sufficiently unsatisfying.

In Kohut's theory the response to frustration or failure of caretaker empathy is not so clear-cut, and depends on the nature, timing, and intensity of the experience. Kohut distinguished himself from Fairbairn, and placed himself more in the mainstream of psychoanalytic tradition, by maintaining that frustration is an essential aspect of normal development—or, to put it differently, that there is a normal adult state and not simply gradients of pathology. People do not thrive on love alone, and optimal phase-appropriate frustration of the wish to merge is necessary for transmuting internalization of structure and narcissistic maturation. At the other extreme of Kohut's schema, extreme and chronic frustration of the wish to merge with a selfobject yields the chronically fragmented or shattered personality, borderline or schizophrenic, whose self is incapable of being coherently contained even when an empathic mirroring relationship such as therapy is eventually provided. Such individuals manifest naked drive derivatives and defensive operations: rage, autoerotic preoccupations, splitting and projection, and delusional restitution—states Kohut looked upon as psychologically meaningless. Kohut might well have written that "masturbation and anal erotism . . . [are encountered] where relationships with outer objects are unsatisfactory, [and] we also encounter such phenomena as exhibitionism, homosexuality, sadism, and masochism," but in fact the author was Fairbairn (1952, p. 40). The difference is that Kohut adhered to Freud's no longer tenable position that schizophrenics are incapable of forming transferences, and added borderlines to this group; by contrast, Fairbairn believed that these fragmentary phenomena reflect compensatory relationships with internal objects, which are susceptible to reprojection and are the basis for transference re-enactments.

If the frustration is midway in intensity and timing between optimal and shattering, according to Kohut, then development will be arrested at the level of the normal but archaic bipolar self structures, grandiose and idealizing. This is Kohut's "narcissistic personality organization." Kohut implied that more than simple developmental arrest is involved in such organization. The grandiose self may be horizontally split off (repressed), in which case symptoms of depletion (including lack of initiative and of a sense of meaning, as well as depression and hypochondriasis) will be prominent; or it may be vertically split off, in which case episodic grandiose thinking (as well as such symptoms as excitement, shame, and embarrassment) will alternate in ascendency with more normal behavior and with idealizing configurations. Such individuals are capable of forming archaic selfobject transferences, but under stress (e.g., breach of the selfobject relationship), each of the bipolar configurations may transiently and regressively be transformed into fragmentary perverse and autoerotic fantasies and activities and into restitutive delusional thinking. This description is certainly not very different from Fairbairn's account of the schizoid personality, and one gets the impression that Kohut and Fairbairn viewed pathology in very similar ways, although they drew markedly different conclusions about structure, object relatedness, and analyzability from their observations.

In Fairbairn's schema, it is the intensity of the splitting process that determines the existence and significance of Oedipal conflicts; if there is not a powerful separation between exciting and rejecting aspects, then there should be little conflict over heterosexual longings. If there is, then the child "comes to equate one parental object with the exciting object and the other with the rejecting object; and by so doing *the child constitutes the Oedipus situation for himself*" (1952, p. 124; emphasis in original). In this Fairbairn also anticipated Kohut; both believed that it is only in pathological situations, not in normal development, that the Oedipal conflicts assume particular importance. Both of their theories are concerned primarily with dyadic and not triangular relationships.

NARCISSISM

Fairbairn and Kohut viewed so-called drive-related phenomena similarly—as pathological breakdown products. However, Fairbairn viewed the result of the breakdown as a disorder of object relations, whereas Kohut viewed it as a disorder of narcissism in its milder forms, and a state of meaninglessness and unrelatedness of any kind in its extreme form. Both of them traced the evolution of primary narcissism, which both related to undifferentiation from primary objects. But there are important differences in their viewpoints about object relations development and in their understanding of idealization, and hence their respective positions about narcissistic phenomena. Fairbairn defined narcissism as "a state in which the ego is identified with objects" (1952, p. 83). He believed that there is a gradual maturation of dependency, which "is identical with Freud's distinction between the narcissistic and anaclitic choice of objects" (1952, p. 42). The relinquishment of primary identification for more differentiated relationships entails a related relinquishment of personal grandiosity and omnipotent feelings. This is similar to Kohut's belief that optimal frustration of the wish to merge leads to evolution of grandiosity, except that in Fairbairn's view the maturational process is triggered by love, and leads to relinquishment of narcissism and development of object relations; in Kohut's view, by contrast, frustration is also required for development to occur, and archaic narcissism is replaced by more mature forms. Kohut did not conceptualize an object relations line of development.

Fairbairn's ideal object, comprising what Kohut would call the other pole of archaic narcissism, includes real qualities of the primary object and accretions from subsequent good relationships, impoverished by repression of frustrating and exciting aspects. The ideal object, evacuated of disturbing qualities by repression, is the nucleus of the ego ideal in Fairbairn's theory—a concept he related to superego but believed to be more important. Fairbairn believed that initial infantile idealization is realistic, and that unrealistic or pathological narcissistic idealization (as well as what appear to be isolated drive configurations) is a response to frustration. The greater the primary frustration, then the more unrealistic the subsequent idealization of the objects of the central self, and the more impoverished and unsatisfying the actual object relations. In these instances, according to Rubens, "all of the complexity and imperfection must be abstracted out and subsumed into the experience of the subsidiary selves" (1984, p. 435). Kohut, by contrast, believed that the normal archaic idealized parent imago is quite unrealistic, and that in normal development it evolves into ideals that are progressively more realistic.

In Fairbairn's theory, narcissistic and object relations development are closely and reciprocally interwoven, and object relations gradually replace narcissistic ones. He maintained that the more profound the failure of the primary object relationship, then the more serious the splitting and the more profound the pathology, including development of grandiosity and unrealistic idealization. Kohut articulated a normal narcissistic line of development, and saw no apparent need for separate concepts of object relations. He believed that an unrealistic idealization reflects one pole of normal archaic narcissism and selfobject relations, and a profound grandiosity the other. In this regard, I wonder whether Fairbairn's position is more compatible with clinical experience.

CONCLUSION

I have noted some of the similarities and strengths of Fairbairn's object relations theory and Kohut's self psychology. I conclude with a brief critique of Fairbairn's theory, mostly but not entirely from a self-psychological perspective, and then with some suggestions about some of the ways in which a Fairbairnian view of the self may enrich self psychology.

Fairbairn's theory, interesting as it is, has relatively little to say about normal and narcissistic development. It allows no normal developmental role for limits, controls, frustration, and aggression. But it does allow for and interrelate narcissistic and object relations development. What is most curious about Fairbairn's theory, however, is his apparent belief that there is no such thing as normal endopsychic structuralization. He equated structure with fission of the psyche and schizoid pathology, which he claimed is present in all of us, more or less. For Fairbairn pathology is the norm, and the ideal state of development—which is synonymous with a kind of integration that leads to a seamless, unstructured entity with no parts or divisions—is unattainable; it is a modern parable of the Garden of Eden.

Whereas I look upon "parts" of the psychic apparatus as products of differentiation, and the capacity to experience intrapsychic conflict as an achievement involving integration (so that discrete entities can simultaneously be held in mind), Fairbairn viewed these as indicative of psychic splitting. Although this problem may simply be a matter of semantics, it is my opinion that a theory that defines everyday ordinary human functioning as pathological, and that makes no provision for development and expression of healthy mental structure and function, is limited. Possibly the problem of structure in Fairbairn's theory is one of confusion of "differentiation" with "splitting," and "*de*struction" with "*con*struction." Structuralization defined as differentiation and construction may be viewed as part of a process of integration, whereas structuralization defined as destruction is truly a process of fission or splitting. One cannot build a structure without differentiating components and then articulating them in novel ways. It would appear that Fairbairn confused "disintegration" with "structuralization," or perhaps failed to appreciate that the pathological psyche may be integrated by a different set of principles. He seems to have been similarly confused about the process of normal development, which he claimed is not a process of endopsychic structuralization. From his description it sounds like a process of accretion, in which the result is not a differentiated or articulated whole so much as an undifferentiated mass, although he also claimed that this process leads to differentiation of self from object. A definition of structure that encompasses differentiation and integration as well as splitting, disintegration, and dedifferentiation might better reflect Fairbairn's idea of the growth process, and at the same time make better provision for both normal and pathological development and function.

As for self psychology, I think it has much to learn from its as-yet-undiscovered ancestor W. R. D. Fairbairn. One of the major criticisms of self psychology is that it slights object relations development. How do people develop the capacity for love and caring? Are these things simply narcissistic by-products? How does the narcissistically mature individual become the empathic selfobject a developing child needs? Fairbairn demonstrated that it is possible to construct a model that considers narcissistic and object relations development as reciprocal and interrelated processes.

Are the grandiose and idealizing transferences Kohut described so closely related to normal arrested development, as he maintained? Fairbairn suggested that both grandiosity and unrealistic idealization are pathological products of severe frustration and structural disorganization, and not part of a developmentally normal configuration. It is true that normal children idealize their good-enough parents, but is this process unrealistic? Or would it be more accurate to say that it is quite realistic, given the limited experience that children have with humankind in general and their parents in particular?

It seems a major deficiency of self psychology that it dismisses developments before nearly 2 years of age, as well as the poorly integrated borderline personality and schizophrenic, as psychologically meaningless; and that it maintains that such individuals are incapable of entering into selfobject (or symbiotic) relationships. This proposition was disproven with regard to schizophrenia decades ago, and it has been demonstrated by numerous authors—including Kleinians, Kernberg (1966, 1967), and myself (Robbins, 1980, 1983, 1989)—that borderlines form transferences. In fact, the symbiotic transferences of narcissistic personalities and borderlines are not all that dissimilar, and narcissistic personality structure is also unintegrated (Robbins, 1982, 1989). Kohut's belief that narcissistic personalities may be distinguished from borderlines by the presence of internal integration or coherence even seems internally inconsistent with some of his other beliefs: He made it clear that the archaic self is bipolar (unintegrated), and that the consequent mature narcissistic structures remain so.

In conclusion, if Fairbairn's ideas about normal development and the relationship between narcissism and object relations, as well as his theory of endopsychic structuralization in response to frustration of primary identification, were modified to differentiate construction from destruction more clearly, they could fill a significant gap in self-psychological theory and make it a more comprehensive and useful model of the mind.

REFERENCES

Bacal, H. A. (1987). British object relations theorists and self-psychology: Some critical reflections. *International Journal of Psycho-Analysis, 68*, 81–98.

Fairbairn, W. R. D. (1952). *Psychoanalytic Studies of the Personality.* London: Tavistock.

Fairbairn, W. R. D. (1958). On the nature and aims of psycho-analytical treatment. *International Journal of Psycho-Analysis, 34*, 374–383.

Freud, S. (1915). Instincts and their viscissitudes. *Standard Edition, 14*, 109–140.

Guntrip, H. (1961). *Personality Structure and Human Interaction.* New York: International Universities Press.

Kernberg, O. (1966). Structural derivatives of object relationships. *International Journal of Psycho-Analysis, 47*, 236–253.

Kernberg, O. (1967). Borderline personality organization. *Journal of the American Psychoanalytic Association, 15*, 641–685.

Kohut, H. (1971). *The Analysis of the Self.* New York: International Universities Press.

Kohut, H. (1977). *The Restoration of the Self.* New York: International Universities Press.

Kohut, H., & Wolff, E. (1978). The disorders of the self and their treatment: An outline. *International Journal of Psycho-Analysis, 59*, 413–426.

Robbins, M. (1980). Current controversy in object relations theory as outgrowth of a schism between Klein and Fairbairn. *International Journal of Psycho-Analysis, 61*, 477–492.

Robbins, M. (1981). The symbiosis concept and the commencement of normal and pathological ego functioning and object relations: II. Developments subsequent to infancy and pathological processes. *International Review of Psycho-Analysis, 8,* 379–391.

Robbins, M. (1982). Narcissistic personality as a symbiotic character disorder. *International Journal of Psycho-Analysis, 63,* 457–473.

Robbins, M. (1983). Toward a new mind model for the primitive personalities. *International Journal of Psycho-Analysis, 64,* 127–148.

Robbins, M. (1989). Primitive personality organization as an interpersonally adaptive modification of cognition and affect. *International Journal of Psycho-Analysis, 70,* 443–459.

Rubens, R. L. (1984). The meaning of structure in Fairbairn. *International Review of Psycho-Analysis, 11,* 429–440.

Sutherland, J. D. (1980). The British object relations theorists: Balint, Winnicott, Fairbairn, Guntrip. *Journal of the American Psychoanalytic Association, 28,* 829–860.

Suttie, I. D. (1935). *The Origins of Love and Hate.* London: Kegan Paul, Trench, Trubner.

Wisdom, J. O. (1963). Fairbairn's contribution on object-relationship, splitting, and ego structure. *British Journal of Medical Psychology, 36,* 145–159.

Epilogue: The Fairbairn Legacy

JAMES S. GROTSTEIN

By introducing the primacy of object relations, Fairbairn inaugurated and all but formalized the existential (ontological) perspective in psychoanalytic thinking. His emphasis on the primary relational aspects of instinctual drives as dynamic aspects of egos directed toward objects, which led him to abandon Freud's concept of the id, differentiated Fairbairn and later object relations theorists from orthodox/classical and Kleinian analysts, whose theories still depended on the primacy of the drives. In stressing the fundamental importance of the object's (caretaking person's) meeting the infant's needs, he became, along with Ian Suttie, the first "infant advocate" in psychoanalysis—and, as a consequence, one of the first formulators of the principle of "infantile innocence" and "entitlement." In this regard, he also anticipated Bowlby's work on bonding and attachment.

His emphasis on the relational rather than the hedonic aspects of the object-seeking drives challenged the primacy of Freud's pleasure principle and substituted for it the primacy of the reality principle—a concept that has been affirmed by infant developmental research. He thus introduced and formalized the interactional perspective of psychoanalysis and anticipated the intersubjective dimension, which has been the subject of inquiry of other authors, such as Binswanger (1963), Trevarthen and Hubley (1978), Stern (1985), and Stolorow and Atwood (1992; Atwood & Stolorow, 1984).

When we compare the Freudian, Kleinian, and Fairbairnian views of the infant, we see that the orthodox Freudian infant is libidinally hedonic, the classical one libidinally hedonic and aggressively peremp-

319

tory, the Kleinian one ruthless and maniacal, and the Fairbairnian one
loving and "civilized." Defense mechanisms are, from Fairbairn's point
of view, always constructed against internalized objects and their relationships, not against "uncivilized" drives. In some ways, Fairbairn's
psychopathology reminds one of Freud's (1894) first theory of psycho-
analysis, the censorship of traumatic reality.

Whereas unconscious phantasy plays a fundamentally more important role than external reality in the Kleinian system (the latter modifying the former), Fairbairn believed the reverse. As he saw it, the reality of
the caretaking person is always the most important element. *Persons become internalized objects*[1] *only when they fail as parents.* For Fairbairn,
phantasies regulate (modify) the reality of failed persons and transform
them into objects for protection and control.

Side by side with Klein, however, he helped to establish the importance of orality—not as a regressive autoerotic psychosexual zone, but
as the most important initial channel of communication between the infant
and his mother. Autoerotic psychosexuality constitutes a default (failure)
of the mother–infant relationship. By establishing orality as the prime
relationship and as the determiner of all later stages and positions of
development ("the principle of genetic continuity"; Isaacs, 1952), Fairbairn (1941) reduced the importance of the phallic/Oedipal phase, placing it under the rubric of a "transitional technique" for resolving split
attitudes toward the mother as well as toward the father. Like Klein, he
subordinated infantile sexuality to Freud's earlier (and later discarded)
life-preservative instincts, as opposed to libido, which Freud associated
with the preservation of the race.

By illuminating and expanding on the role of splitting (as had Klein,
1946, in a somewhat different way), he cast new light on its reciprocal,
rather than sequential, relationship to repression. He uncovered the archaic origins of repression and ambivalence, and thereby restored the
importance of vertical splitting (dissociation), which had been discarded
by Freud (1896) after *Studies on Hysteria* (Breuer & Freud, 1893–1895)
and only infrequently revived when he discussed splitting per se (Fairbairn,
1943a). Fairbairn's concept of horizontal–vertical splitting was later to
appear as a pivotal concept in Kohut's (1984) formulation of the defensive structure of the narcissistic personality disorder. Fairbairn's understanding of the relationship between repression and splitting offered a

---

[1]The reader is reminded that the internalized object is the subject's *experience*
(i.e., phantasy) of the object and occupies, according to Ogden (Chapter 6, this volume), two positions: the experience of identification with the object, and identification with the self aspect of the object.

valuable and hitherto missing perspective. Whereas orthodox/classical contributors postulated that repression is the successor to splitting, suggesting an epigenesis between them, he suggested that repression is made necessary by the very existence of splitting—to keep awareness of the splits conscious.

Fairbairn's (1940, 1941) concept of the schizoid personality, both as a specific entity in its own right and as a universal generalization for all personalities, added a missing dimension to psychoanalytic psychopathology. It opened up a vast "premoral" subcontinent whose nature and laws differ considerably from the traditional psychopathological considerations of Freud and Klein—the melancholic disorders, putatively caused by guilt (or persecutory anxiety) resulting from instinctual drive excesses. Fairbairn, following in the footsteps of Ferenczi and Federn, was claiming that disorders due to *deficit* were antecedent to, and more important than, those due to *conflict*. His pioneering work on the schizoid personality and schizoid states set the stage for the current interest in the narcissistic and borderline disorders.

By envisioning that splitting in the schizoid position occurs between accepted and unaccepted objects where one's love is bad (destructive), and in the depressive position where one's hate is bad, Fairbairn (1941, 1944, 1946, 1949, 1951) suggested that the individual finds refuge from these catastrophic splits in the form of transitional "neurotic techniques" (paranoid, obsessional, hysteric, and phobic). Each technique differs in how it handles the self-and-object splits (e.g., which object is internalized and which is projected). As a corollary of these techniques, he recast the autoerotic zones as channels for relating to the object.

By his probing into the war neuroses, Fairbairn (1943a, 1943b) uncovered the soldier's attempted regression to an archaic object relationship based on primary identification, which was the basis for yet another personality disorder, the symbiotic (though he did not call it this). He referred to this disorder as one of a class of personality disorders that is fixated in "immature dependency." Fairbairn's concept of psychology was based on the primacy of dependency and its epigenesis from infantile dependency to mature dependency, thus eschewing the classical analytic "requirement" of becoming "genital." He implied, but did not fully explicate, "interdependency".

Both Klein (1946) and Fairbairn (1941) proposed a psychopathology based on the vicissitudes of splitting and projective identification. Fairbairn, however, believed that splitting and pathological introjective identification involve incorporation. For Klein (1955), the "demonic" aspects of the infant transform the external object into omnipotent, preternatural internal objects (projective transformations). For Fairbairn

(1941), the infant who incorporates the object is simultaneously incorporated by it, and thus by default regressively returns to primary identification with the object. His formulation of the nature of endopsychic structure appears to be the best format for understanding the development of the post-traumatic consequences (internalizations and identifications with the aggressor) of infant and childhood neglect and of child abuse (including molestation) (Fairbairn, 1943a, 1943b, 1944). The more abusive the parent(s), the more loyal the child is to them, in order to obtain the conditional (exciting, forbidden) love. In the war neuroses, the soldier, following demoralization, turns away from the abusive metaphoric "parent of battle" and returns to the primary caretaking object at home (usually his wife or mother), in order to reconnect to the original object of primary identification.

Fairbairn's (1943b) concept of trauma has never been fully explicated. As I read his work, he envisioned trauma in the following object-related terms: The traumatic event is personified as an object that incorporates ("swallows") the victim in the same moment he incorporates the traumatizing object. Thus, the victim is inside the object, which is also inside him. In contrast to Klein's conception of projective identification of bad internal objects into external objects, Fairbairn held that the schizoid patient, if victimized, believes that he deserves it.

His differentiation between the primal experiences of the "badness of one's hate" for depression, and the "badness of one's love" for schizoid phenomena, is of great phenomenological importance in understanding some polarities between the narcissistic and schizoid personality disorders (Fairbairn, 1940, 1944). The narcissistic patient is often characterized as possessing a stabilized manic defense against both the importance of the needed object and the awareness of his dependent self. He employs grandiosity to further this denial, but also employs triumph, contempt, and control—all aggressive mechanisms. The schizoid patient, on the other hand, feels futile about the goodness of his love and thus withdraws by default. The latter comes to believe that his needy love is predatory.

The concept that one's love is bad is far-reaching. Victims of rape, war, and other tormenting events often feel guilty *after* the event, and also ashamed—as if they have unwittingly demonstrated a "scarlet letter" revealing that they deserve to be victimized. Their identification with bad internal objects, instead of protecting or blessing them, condemns them either by default or curse to ostracism and victimization. This is one of Fairbairn's most important insights: that the impact of personal experience is retrospectively processed in terms of the content of one's endopsychic world, and that it is vitally important whether that world is peopled by good, blessing objects or bad, deserting, cursing ones.

REFERENCES

Atwood, G., & Stolorow, R. (1984). *Structures of Subjectivity*. Hillsdale, NJ: Lawrence Erlbaum Associates.

Binswanger, L. (1963). *Being-in-the-World*. New York: Basic Books.

Breuer, J., & Freud, S. (1893–1895). Studies on hysteria. *Standard Edition*, 2, pp. 1–305.

Fairbairn, W. R. D. (1940). Schizoid factors in the personality. In *Psychoanalytic Studies of the Personality*. London: Tavistock, 1952, pp. 3–27.

Fairbairn, W. R. D. (1941). A revised psychopathology of the psychoses and psycho-neuroses. In *Psychoanalytic Studies of the Personality*. London: Tavistock, 1952, pp. 28–58.

Fairbairn, W. R. D. (1943a). The war neuroses—their nature and significance. In *Psychoanalytic Studies of the Personality*. London: Tavistock, 1952, pp. 256–287.

Fairbairn, W. R. D. (1943b). The repression and the return of bad objects (with special reference to the 'war neuroses'). In *Psychoanalytic Studies of the Personality*. London: Tavistock, 1952, pp. 59–81.

Fairbairn, W. R. D. (1944). Endopsychic structure considered in terms of object-relationships. In *Psychoanalytic Studies of the Personality*. London: Tavistock, 1952, pp. 82–136.

Fairbairn, W. R. D. (1946). Object-relationships and dynamic structure. In *Psychoanalytic Studies of the Personality*. London: Tavistock, 1952, pp. 137–151.

Fairbairn, W. R. D. (1949). Steps in the development of an object-relations theory of the personality. In *Psychoanalytic Studies of the Personality*. London: Tavistock, 1952, pp. 152–161.

Fairbairn, W. R. D. (1951). A synopsis of the development of the author's views regarding the structure of the personality. In *Psychoanalytic Studies of the Personality*. London: Tavistock, 1952, pp. 162–182.

Freud, S. (1894). The neuro-psychoses of defence. *Standard Edition*, 3, pp. 45–61.

Freud, S. (1896). The aetiology of hysteria. *Standard Edition*, 3, pp. 159–185.

Isaacs, S. (1952). The nature and function of phantasy. In M. Klein, P. Heimann, S. Isaacs, & J. Riviere, eds., *Developments in Psycho-Analysis*. London: Hogarth Press, pp. 67–121.

Klein, M. (1946). Notes on some schizoid mechanisms. In M. Klein, P. Heimann, S. Isaacs, & J. Riviere, eds., *Developments in Psycho-Analysis*. London: Hogarth Press, 1952, pp. 292–320.

Klein, M. (1955). On identification. In M. Klein, P. Heimann, & R. E. Money-Kyrle, eds., *New Directions in Psycho-Analysis*. London: Tavistock, pp. 309–345.

Kohut, H. (1984). *How Does Analysis Cure?*, A. Goldberg, ed. Chicago: University of Chicago Press.

Stern, D. (1985). *The Interpersonal World of the Infant*. New York: Basic Books.

Stolorow, R., & Atwood, G. (1992). *Contexts of Being*. Hillsdale, NJ: Analytic Press.

Trevarthen, C., & Hubley, P. (1978). Secondary intersubjectivity: Confidence, confiding, and acts of meaning in the first year. In A. Lock, ed., *Action, Gesture and Symbol: The Emergence of Language*. London: Academic Press, pp. 183– 229.

Appendix I

Fairbairn's Main Papers

JOHN D. SUTHERLAND

1927   Notes on the religious phantasies of a female patient. In *Psychoanalytic Studies of the Personality*. London: Tavistock, pp. 183–196.

1929   *The Relationship of Dissociation and Repression, Considered from the Point of View of Medical Psychology*. Unpublished M.D. thesis, Edinburgh University.

Fundamental principles of psychoanalysis. *Edinburgh Medical Journal*, 36, 329–345.

1930   Some points of importance in the psychology of anxiety. *British Journal of Medical Psychology*, 9, 303–313.

1931   Features in the analysis of a patient with a physical genital abnormality. In *Psychoanalytic Studies of the Personality*. London: Tavistock, pp. 197–222.

1933   Psychological aspects of dentistry. *The Dental Record*, 53(10), 465–476.

1935   The sociological significance of Communism considered in the light of psycho-analysis. *British Journal of Psychology* 15(3), 218–229. In *Psychoanalytic Studies of the Personality*. London: Tavistock, pp. 233–246.

Medico-psychological aspects of child assault. *Mental Hygiene*, 13, 1–16.

Adapted from *Fairbairn's Journey into the Interior* (pp. 179–181) by John D. Sutherland, 1989, London: Free Association Books. Copyright 1989 by John D. Sutherland. Adapted by permission of the author and publisher.

1936   The effect of a king's death upon patients undergoing analysis. *International Journal of Psycho-Analysis, 17*(3) pp. 278–284. In *Psychoanalytic Studies of the Personality*. London: Tavistock, pp. 223–229.

1937   Arms and the child. *Liverpool Quarterly, 5,* 27–34.

        Communism as an anthropological phenomenon. *Edinburgh Medical Journal, 44,* 433–445.

1938   Prolegomena to a psychology of art. *British Journal of Psycho-Analysis, 28,* 288–303.

        The ultimate basis of aesthetic experience. *British Journal of Psycho-Analysis, 29,* 167–181.

1939   Is aggression an irreducible factor? *British Journal of Psycho-Analysis, 18,* 163–170.

        Psychology as a proscribed and a prescribed subject. In *Psychoanalytic Studies of the Personality*. London: Tavistock, pp. 247–255.

        The psychological factor in sexual delinquency. *Mental Hygiene, 5,* 44–50.

1940   Schizoid factors in the personality. In *Psychoanalytic Studies of the Personality*. London: Tavistock, pp. 3–27.

1941   A revised psychopathology of the psychoses and psycho-neuroses. *International Journal of Psycho-Analysis, 22,* 250–279. In *Psychoanalytic Studies of the Personality*. London: Tavistock, pp. 28–58.

1943   The war neuroses—their nature and significance. *British Medical Journal, 10,* 183–186. In *Psychoanalytic Studies of the Personality*. London: Tavistock, pp. 256–287.

        The repression and the return of bad objects (with special reference to the 'war neuroses'). *British Journal of Medical Psychology, 19,* 327–341. In *Psychoanalytic Studies of the Personality*. London: Tavistock, pp. 59–81.

1944   Endopsychic structure considered in terms of object-relationships. *International Journal of Psycho-Analysis, 25,* 70–73. In *Psychoanalytic Studies of the Personality*. London: Tavistock, pp. 82–136.

1946   The treatment and rehabilitation of sexual offenders. In *Psychoanalytic Studies of the Personality*. London: Tavistock, pp. 289–296.

        Object-relationships and dynamic structure. *International Journal of Psycho-Analysis, 27,* 30–37. In *Psychoanalytic Studies of the Personality*. London: Tavistock, pp. 137–151.

1947   Revicion de la psicopatologia de los psicosis y psiconeurosis. *Revista de Psicoanalisis*, 4(4). [Spanish translation of "A revised psychopathology of the psychoses and psycho-neuroses" (1941).]

La respresion y el retorno de los objetos malos. *Revista de Psicoanalisis*, 5(2). [Spanish translation of "The repression and the return of bad objects" (1943).]

Las estructuras endopsiquicas consideradas en terminos de relaciones de objetos. *Revista de Psicoanalisis*, 5(2). [Spanish translation of "Endopsychic structure considered in terms of object-relationships" (1944).]

1949   Steps in the development of an object-relations theory of the personality. *British Journal of Medical Psychology*, 22, 26–31. In *Psychoanalytic Studies of the Personality*. London: Tavistock, pp. 152–161.

Critical notice: *On Not Being Able to Paint*. *British Journal of Medical Psychology*, 24, 69–72.

1951   A synopsis of the development of the author's views regarding the structure of the personality. In *Psychoanalytic Studies of the Personality*. London: Tavistock, pp. 162–182.

1952   Theoretical and experimental aspects of psycho-analysis. *British Journal of Medical Psychology*, 25, 122–127.

Psychoanalytic Studies of the Personality. London: Tavistock. (Published in the United States as *An Object-Relations Theory of the Personality*. New York: Basic Books, 1954.)

1953   Critical notice: *Psychoanalytic Explorations in Art*. *British Journal of Medical Psychology*, 26, 164–169.

1954   Observations on the nature of hysterical states. *British Journal of Medical Psychology*, 27, 105–125.

Review of *The Unconscious Origins of Berkeley's Philosophy* by John Oulton Wisdom. *British Journal of Medical Psychology*, 27, 253–256.

1955   Observations in defence of the object-relations theory of the personality (a reply to Abenheimer). *British Journal of Medical Psychology*, 28, 144–156.

1956   Considerations arising out of the Schreber case. *British Journal of Medical Psychology*, 29, 113–127.

A critical evaluation of certain basic psycho-analytical conceptions. *British Journal for the Philosophy of Science*, 7, 49–60.

Critical notice on *The Techniques of Psycho-Analysis* by Edward Glover. *British Journal of Psychology*, 47, 65–66.

1957   Freud: The psycho-analytical method and mental health. *British Journal of Medical Psychology, 30,* 53–62.

Fairbairn's reply to the comments of Balint, Foulkes and Sutherland. *British Journal of Medical Psychology, 30,* 53–62.

1958   On the nature and aims of psycho-analytical treatment. *International Journal of Psycho-Analysis, 39,* 374–383.

1963   Synopsis of an object-relations theory of the personality. *International Journal of Psycho-Analysis, 44,* 224–225.

Autobiographical note. *British Journal of Medical Psychology, 36,* 107.

Appendix II

Contributions Related to Fairbairn

JAMES S. GROTSTEIN

Abenheimer, K. M. (1955). Critical observations on Fairbairn's theory of object relations. *British Journal of Medical Psychology, 28*, 29–41.

Akhtar, S. (1987). Schizoid personality disorder: A synthesis of developmental, dynamic, and descriptive features. *American Journal of Psychotherapy, 41*(4), 499–518.

Albiston, R. K. (1984). The advent of object representation: A Piagetian critique of the British school theorists: Klein, Fairbairn, Winnicott and Guntrip. *Dissertation Abstracts International, 44*(10), 3185B.

Bacal, H. A. (1987). British object-relations theorists and self-psychology: Some critical reflections. *International Journal of Psycho-Analysis, 68*, 87–98.

Balint, M. (1956). Pleasure, object and libido: Some reflexions on Fairbairn's modification of psychoanalytic theory. *British Journal of Medical Psychology, 29*, 162–167.

Berman, E. (1974). Multiple personality: Theoretical approaches. *Journal of the Bronx State Hospital, 2*(2), 99–107.

Berman, E. (1981). Multiple personality: Psychoanalytic perspectives. *International Journal of Psycho-Analysis, 62*(3), 283–300.

Berman, E. (1983). "Collective figures" and the representational world. *Psychoanalytic Review, 70*(4), 553–557.

Bowlby, J. (1960). Grief and mourning in infancy and early childhood. *Psychoanalytic Study of the Child, 15*, 43–52.

Brooks, B. (1985). Sexually abused children and adolescent identity development. *American Journal of Psychotherapy, 39*(3), 401–410.

Buckley, P. (1985). *Essential Papers on Object Relations.* New York: New York University Press.

Callea, G., & Rubino, I. A. (1980). Appunti sull'incidenza e la struttera dei disturbi della personalita. *Lavoro Neuropsichiatrico, 67*(3), 255–263.

Capponi, A. (1979). Origins and evolution of the borderline patient. In J. Leboit & A. Capponi, eds., *Advances in Psychotherapy of the Borderline Patient.* New York: Jason Aronson, pp. 63–148.

Celani, D. P. (1993). *The Treatment of the Borderline Patient: Applying Fairbairn's Object Relations Theory in the Clinical Setting.* Madison, CT: International Universities Press.

Chrzanowski, G. (1984). Can psychoanalysis be taught? In L. Caligor et al., eds., *Clinical Perspectives on the Supervision of Psychoanalysis and Psychotherapy.* New York: Plenum Press, pp. 45–58.

Cutchins, C. B. (1975). The use of marital treatment with homosexual couples. *Smith College Studies in Social Work,* 46(1), 56–57.

Dawson, M. (1985). *W. R. D. Fairbairn: Relating His Work to His Life.* Unpublished master's thesis, Harvard University.

Dicks, H. V. (1963). Object relations theory and marital studies. *British Journal of Medical Psychology,* 36, 125–129.

Doeff, A. M. (1977). Early childhood intervention with disadvantaged, developmentally disordered preschool children: A case study. *Dissertation Abstracts International.*

Eagle, M. N. (1981). Interests as object relations. *Psychoanalysis and Contemporary Thought,* 4, 527–565.

Eagle, M. N. (1984a). The pursuit of superordinate motives. In *Recent Developments in Psychoanalysis: A Critical Evaluation.* New York: McGraw-Hill, pp. 197–202.

Eagle, M. N. (1984b). Object-seeking and object relations. In *Recent Developments in Psychoanalysis: A Critical Evaluation.* New York: McGraw-Hill, pp. 190–196.

Eagle, M. N. (1984c). Individuation and self-differentiation. In *Recent Developments in Psychoanalysis: A Critical Evaluation.* New York: McGraw-Hill, pp. 185–189.

Eagle, M. N. (1984d). Replacement of instinct theory by object relations theory: The work of Fairbairn. In *Recent Developments in Psychoanalysis: A Critical Evaluation.* New York: McGraw-Hill, pp. 75–86.

Eigen, M. (1981). Guntrip's analysis with Winnicott: A critique of Glatzer and Evans. *Contemporary Psychoanalysis,* 17, 103–117.

Finkelstein, L. (1987). Toward an object-relations approach in psychoanalytic marital therapy. *Journal of Marital and Family Therapy,* 13(3), 287–298.

Forrester, R. (1974). Why we have to say good-bye: A psychological examination of a social custom. *Canadian Psychiatric Association Journal,* 19(5), 517–522.

Forti, L. (1966). Theoretical problems about the genesis of object relations. *Revista di Psicoanalisis,* 12(2), 199–211.

Friedman, L. J. (1975). Current psychoanalytic object relations theory and its clinical implications. *International Journal of Psycho-Analysis,* 56, 137–146.

Giovacchini, P. L. (1987). *A Narrative Textbook of Psychoanalysis.* Northvale, NJ: Jason Aronson.

Glatzer, H. T., & Evans, W. N. (1977). On Guntrip's analysis with Fairbairn and Winnicott. *International Journal of Psychoanalytic Psychology,* 6, 81–98.

Goldberg, R. W. (1974, February 15). Synthesis and reformulation of some views of Piaget and Fairbairn on object relations. In G. I. Lubin, J. S. Magary, & M. K. Poulsen, eds., *Proceedings of the Fourth Interdisciplinary Seminar:*

Piagetian Theory and Its Implications for the Helping Professions. Los Angeles: University of Southern California, 1975, pp. 129–139.

Gordon, R. (1972). Moral values and analytical insights: Some reflections. *Bulletin of the British Psychological Society, 25*(89), 319–320.

Greenberg, J. R. (1981). Prescription or description: The therapeutic action of psychoanalysis. *Contemporary Psychoanalysis, 17*(2), 239–257.

Greenberg, J. R., & Mitchell, S. A. (1983). *Object Relations in Psychoanalytic Theory.* Cambridge, MA: Harvard University Press.

Grotstein, J. S. (1979). The psychoanalytic concept of the borderline organization. In J. LeBoit & A. Capponi, eds., *Advances in Psychotherapy of the Borderline Patient.* New York: Jason Aronson, pp. 149–186.

Grotstein, J. S. (1982). Newer perspectives in object relations theory. *Contemporary Psychoanalysis, 18*(1), 43–91.

Grotstein, J. S. (1983). Some perspectives on self psychology. In A. Goldberg, ed., *The Future of Psychoanalysis.* New York: International Universities Press, pp. 165–202.

Guntrip, H. (1961). *Personality Structure and Human Interaction.* London: Hogarth Press.

Guntrip, H. (1963). Psychodynamic theory and the problem of psychotherapy. *British Journal of Medical Psychology, 36,* 161–172.

Guntrip, H. (1968). *Schizoid Phenomena, Object-Relations and the Self.* London: Hogarth Press.

Guntrip, H. (1971). *Psychoanalytic Theory, Therapy, and the Self.* New York: Basic Books.

Guntrip, H. (1975). My experience of analysis with Fairbairn and Winnicott (How complete a result does psycho-analytic therapy achieve?). *International Review of Psycho-Analysis, 2,* 145–156.

Guntrip, H. (N.D.-a). Fairbairn re-examined in historical perspective (The development of personal "object-relations" theory). Unpublished manuscript, The Menninger Foundation.

Guntrip, H. (N.D.-b). First training analysis, with W. R. D. Fairbairn. Unpublished manuscript, The Menninger Foundation.

Guntrip, H. (N.D.-c). Psychoanalytic autobiography (A study of the "dream process" over thirty-six years, showing the effects of an amnesia for an infancy trauma). Unpublished manuscript, The Menninger Foundation.

Holbrook, D. (1971). *Human Hope and the Death Instinct: An Exploration of Psychoanalytical Theories of Human Nature and Their Implications for Culture and Education.* Oxford: Pergamon Press.

Holm, K., & Hundevadt, E. (1981). Borderline states: Prognosis and psychotherapy. *British Journal of Medical Psychology, 54*(4), 335–340

Iwasaki, T. (1973). A historical background and recent development of psychoanalytic object relations theory. *Japanese Journal of Psychoanalysis, 18*(2), 41–54.

Karon, B. P. (1970). An experimental study of parental castration phantasies. *British Journal of Psychiatry, 117,* 69–73.

Kayton, L. (1972). The relationship of the vampire legend to schizophrenia. *Journal of Youth and Adolescence, 1*(4), 303–314.

Kernberg, O. F. (1963). Discussion of J. D. Sutherland's paper. *British Journal of Medical Psychology*, 36(2), 121–124.

Kernberg, O. F. (1976). *Object Relations Theory and Clinical Psychoanalysis.* New York: Jason Aronson.

Kernberg, O. F. (1980a). The object relations theory of W. Ronald D. Fairbairn. *Bulletin of the Association of Psychoanalytic Medicine*, 19(4), 131–135.

Kernberg, O. F. (1980b). *Internal World and External Reality: Object Relations Theory Applied.* New York: Jason Aronson.

Kohon, G., ed. (1986). *The British School of Psychoanalysis: The Independent Tradition.* London: Free Association Books.

Kwawer, J. S. (1981). Object relations and interpersonal theories. *Contemporary Psychoanalysis*, 17(2), 276–289.

LeBoit, J. (1979). The technical problem with the borderline patient. In J. LeBoit & A. Capponi, eds., *Advances in Psychotherapy of the Borderline Patient.* New York: Jason Aronson, pp. 3–62.

Luzes, P. (1980). The contribution of child psychoanalysis to psychoanalytic theory. *Revue Française de Psychoanalyse*, 44(5–6), 962–968.

Macdiarmid, D. (1989). Self-cathexis and other-cathexis: Vicissitudes in the history of an observation. *British Journal of Psychiatry*, 154, 844–852.

Markillie, R. E. D. (1963). Observations on early ego development. *British Journal of Medical Psychology*, 36, 131–140.

Mendez, A. M., & Fine, H. J. (1976). A short history of the British school of object relations and ego psychology: With comments by Harry Guntrip. *Bulletin of the Menninger Clinic*, 40, 357–382.

Modell, A. H (1968). *Object Love and Reality: An Introduction to a Psychoanalytic Theory of Object Relations.* New York: International Universities Press.

Morse, S. J. (1972). Structure and reconstruction: A critical comparison of Michael Balint and D. W. Winnicott. *International Journal of Psycho-Analysis*, 53(4), 487–500.

Nelson, M. C. (1968). Narcissistic and borderline states. In M. C. Nelson et al., eds., *Roles and Paradigms in Psychotherapy.* New York: Grune & Stratton.

Ogden, T. H. (1986). *The Matrix of the Mind: Object Relations and the Psychoanalytic Dialogue.* Northvale, NJ: Jason Aronson.

Ogura, K. (1969). Little Hans. *Japanese Journal of Psychoanalysis*, 15(3), 15–17.

Padel, J. (1973). The contributions of W. R. D. Fairbairn (1889–1964) to psychoanalytic theory and practice. *Bulletin of the European Psycho-Analytic Federation*, 2.

Padel, J. (1985). Ego in current thinking. *International Review of Psycho-Analysis*, 12(3), 273–283.

Pao, P.-N. (1979). *Schizophrenic Disorders: Theory and Treatment from a Psychodynamic Point of View.* New York: International Universities Press.

Pave, J. F. (1963). A multi-ego theory of libido–destrudo dynamics and mental illness. *British Journal of Medical Psychology*, 36(2), 173–198.

Pruyser, P. W. (1975). What splits in "splitting"?: A scrutiny of the concept of splitting in psychoanalysis and psychiatry. *Bulletin of the Menninger Clinic*, 39(1), 1–46.

Rinsley, D. B. (1979). Fairbairn's object-relations theory: A reconsideration in terms of newer knowledge. *Bulletin of the Menninger Clinic, 43,* 489–514.

Rinsley, D. B. (1982a). Fairbairn's object-relations and classical concepts of dynamics and structure. In *Borderline and Other Self Disorders: A Developmental and Object-Relations Perspective.* New York: Jason Aronson, pp. 251–270.

Rinsley, D. B. (1982b). Object relations theory and psychotherapy with particular reference to the self-disordered patient. In P. Giovacchini & L. B. Boyer, eds., *Technical Factors in the Treatment of the Severely Disturbed Patient.* New York: Jason Aronson, pp. 187–216.

Rinsley, D. B. (1988). Fairbairn's basic endopsychic situation considered in terms of "classical" and "deficit" metapsychological models. *Journal of the American Academy of Psychoanalysis, 16*(4), 461–477.

Robbins, M. (1980). Current controversy in object relations theory as outgrowth of a schism between Klein and Fairbairn. *International Journal of Psycho-Analysis, 61,* 477–492.

Robertiello, R. C. (1974). Physical techniques with schizoid patients. *Journal of the American Academy of Psychoanalysis, 2*(4), 361–367.

Robertiello, R. C. (1979). Critique of Kernberg and Langs. *Journal of Contemporary Psychotherapy, 10*(2), 151–157.

Rodriguez Sutil, C. (1984). Algunas indagaciones sobre el caracter en la histeria: Aspectos vinculares. *Clinica y Analisis Grupal, 8*(34), 514–524.

Rubens, R. L. (1984). The meaning of structure in Fairbairn. *International Review of Psycho-Analysis, 11,* 429–440.

Searles, H. F. (1979). Jealousy involving an internal object. In J. LeBoit & A. Capponi, eds., *Advances in Psychotherapy of the Borderline Patient.* New York: Jason Aronson, pp. 347–404.

Seinfeld, J. (1990). *The Bad Object; Handling the Negative Therapeutic Reaction in Psychotherapy.* Northvale, NJ: Jason Aronson.

Seinfeld, J. (1991). *The Empty Core.* Northvale, NJ: Jason Aronson.

Seinfeld, J. (1993). *Interpreting and Holding: The Paternal and Maternal Functions of a Psychotherapist.* Northvale, NJ: Jason Aronson.

Silverman, D. K. (1986). A multi-model approach: Looking at clinical data from three theoretical perspectives. *Psychoanalytic Psychology, 3*(2), 121–132.

Stern, D. N. (1977). *The First Relationship: Mother and Infant.* Cambridge, MA: Harvard University Press.

Stierlin, (1971). The function of inner objects. *Psyche, 25*(2), 81–99.

Sugarman, A. (1977). Object-relations theory: A reconciliation of phenomenology and ego psychology. *Bulletin of the Menninger Clinic, 41,* 113–130.

Sullivan, C. T. (1963). *Freud and Fairbairn: Two Theories of Ego Psychology.* Doylestown, PA: Doylestown Foundation.

Sutherland, J. D. (1963). Object-relations theory and the conceptual model of psychoanalysis. *British Journal of Medical Psychology, 36,* 109–124.

Sutherland, J. D. (1965). W. R. D. Fairbairn: Obituary. *International Journal of Psycho-Analysis, 46,* 245–247.

Sutherland, J. D. (1979). The British object relations theorists. *Bulletin of the Association of Pyschoanalytic Medicine, 19*(1), 21–31.

Sutherland, J. D. (1980). The British object relations theorists: Balint, Winnicott, Fairbairn, Guntrip. *Journal of the American Psychoanalytic Association, 28,* 829–860.

Sutherland, J. D. (1989). *Fairbairn's Journey into the Interior.* London: Free Association Books.

Sym, J. C. B. (1963). Derivatives of anal erotism. *British Journal of Medical Psychology, 36*(2), 141–144.

Symington, N. (1986). Fairbairn. In *The Analytic Experience.* London: Free Association Books, pp. 236–253.

Thornton, K. E. (1980). Ego boundaries and psychoneurosis. *Dissertation Abstracts International, 42*(2–B), 753.

Tuohy, A. L. (1987). Psychoanalytic perspectives on child abuse. *Child and Adolescent Social Work Journal, 4*(1), 25–40.

Tuttman, S. (1980). An historical review of psychoanalytic concepts leading to the British schools of object relations. *Issues in Ego Psychology, 3*(2), 5–17.

Tuttman, S. (1988). Psychoanalytic concepts of "the self." *Journal of the American Academy of Psychoanalysis, 16*(2), 209–219.

von Minden, G. (1978). The schizoid personality structure and the theory of object relations. *Zeitschrift für Psychosomatische Medizin und Psychoanalyse, 24*(4), 328–354.

Wassell-Kuriloff, E., & Rappaport, D. M. (1987). Eating disorders and hostility towards the inner-life. *Contemporary Psychotherapy Review, 4,* 96–104.

Wibisono, S. (1972). Reviewing some theories about schizophrenia: A look at literature. *Indonesian Psychiatric Quarterly, 5*(4), 71–80.

Wilcoxin, S. A. (1987). Perspectives in intergenerational concepts. *Family Therapy Collections, 21,* 1–10.

Winnicott, D. W., & Khan, M. R. (1953). Review of *Psychoanalytic Studies of the Personality,* by W. R. D. Fairbairn. *International Journal of Psycho-Analysis, 34,* 329–333.

Wisdom, J. O. (1963). Fairbairn's contribution on object relationship, splitting, and ego structure. *British Journal of Medical Psychology, 36,* 145–159.

Yankelovich, D., & Barrett, W. (1970). *Ego and Instinct: The Psychoanalytic View of Human Nature—Revised.* New York: Random House.

Zetzel, E. (1955). Recent British approaches to problems of early mental development. *Journal of the American Psychoanalytic Association, 3,* 534–543.

Appendix III

Fairbairn's Concepts and Terminology

DONALD B. RINSLEY

FOREWORD

The growing importance of W. R. D. Fairbairn's ideas for psychoanalysis is attested to by the inclusion of his terms in the forthcoming revised edition of the American Psychoanalytic Association's official *Glossary of Psychoanalytic Terms and Concepts*. The Association has asked me to provide definitions for a number of these terms, specifically those required for an understanding of Fairbairn's concepts and, of course, of his theory of endopsychic structure.

I have, of course, found Fairbairn's concepts of immense usefulness in both my more theoretical writings and my clinical work. Although his vocabulary appears strange to beginning students of object-relations theory, and even to knowledgeable and mature analysts, his writings, if very sedulously studied, will provide rich rewards for those who desire a subtle, in-depth grasp of human psychological structure and functioning.

The twenty-two terms defined here constitute, in my opinion, a minimum number required for a beginning understanding of Fairbairn's concepts. Of course, they are intended as a basis for an in-depth study of his writings and not as a substitute for them.

The reader will note that I have not included references to Guntrip's writings among the citations at the end of the definitions; although a rich expositor of Fairbairn's ideas, Guntrip managed often and subtly to alter, emend or even distort their original meaning and significance, such that Guntrip's work demands its own study in addition to but apart from that of his mentor and analyst.

Finally, this small glossary of Fairbairn's terms is warmly and appreciatively dedicated to him and to Dr. John Sutherland, his profound student and the executor of his estate.

CONCEPTS AND TERMINOLOGY

ACCEPTED OBJECT. The component of the Original Object that receives the infant's love and is internalized as the Ideal Object.

ANTILIBIDINAL EGO. The split-off and repressed part of the Original Ego that comes into libidinal relationship with the Rejecting Object. In his earlier writings, Fairbairn called it the Internal Saboteur and analogized it to the classical Superego.

BASIC ENDOPSYCHIC SITUATION. Equivalent to Fairbairn's definition of the Schizoid Position, which he regarded as the basis of his theory of mental structure. It arises from the Central Ego's "aggressive attitude" toward the Libidinal Ego and the Antilibidinal Ego, which it splits off from itself and represses. Integral to Fairbairn's formulation of the Basic Endopsychic Situation are the following: the dynamic of repression is aggression; hysterical symptomatology results from splitting; splitting and repression are essentially similar; the Central Ego's "aggressive attitude" toward the Libidinal Ego and the Antilibidinal Ego results from an excess of aggression; and the Central Ego's repression of the Libidinal and Antilibidinal Egos is secondary to its repression of "bad objects," i.e., the Exciting Object and the Rejecting Object.

CENTRAL EGO. The "residue of the undivided ego" (that is, of the Original Ego) that serves as the agent of repression of the Exciting Object and the Rejecting Object, and secondarily of their respectively affiliated Libidinal Ego and Antilibidinal Ego. Fairbairn called it the "I" and considered that it was comprised of conscious, preconscious and unconscious elements, although he emphasized its conscious nature. Rinsley additionally considers the Central Ego as analogous to Freud's Reality Ego and emphasizes its whole-object-like nature in its relationship to the Ideal Object.

EXCITING OBJECT. The split-off and repressed alluring, seductive component of the Split Internalized Bad Object. Pre-Oedipally it represents the breast (the maternal part-object) while Oedipally it represents the penis (the Oedipal father regressively treated as a part-object).

IDEAL OBJECT. Also called the Ego Ideal, the nucleus of the internalized Original Object that remains after the Exciting Object and the Rejecting Object have been split off and repressed. It is originally internalized as the comforting, gratifying aspect of the breast (mother) and becomes idealized and desexualized after the Central Ego has divested itself of the Libidinal Ego and the Antilibidinal Ego. In his earlier writings, Fairbairn termed it the Accepted Object and considered that it constituted the "nucleus of the Superego." Rinsley considers it to be a whole-object in its relationship to the Central Ego.

INTERNAL SABOTEUR. Fairbairn's earlier term for the Antilibidinal Ego.

LIBIDINAL EGO. The split-off and repressed part of the Original Ego that comes into relationship with the Exciting Object. Fairbairn considered it to be analogous to the classical Id, while Rinsley analogizes it to Freud's Purified Pleasure Ego.

MORAL DEFENSE. The effort by the Central Ego to live up to the ideals of the Ideal Object, [and] thereby to achieve contact with and relationship to others; the effort also serves as a defense against the cathexis of "bad internal objects," that is, the Libidinal Ego–Exciting Object relationship and the Antilibidnal Ego–Rejecting Object relationship.

OBJECT-RELATIONSHIPS, THEORY OF. Fairbairn's concept of mental ("endopsychic") structure differs radically from the classical concept. He dispenses with the Id and reformulates the Ego and the Superego as "dynamic structures" in the nature of libidinally and aggressively energized mental representations. He elaborates his scheme for the development of object-relationships in terms of the evolution of dependent needs, postulating three stages of this development: *Stage I*—Infantile Dependence, divided into Early Oral (Preambivalent) in relation to the maternal breast (part-object) and Late Oral (Ambivalent) in relation to mother-with-the-breast, i.e., whole-object treated as part-object; this stage reflects object-relationships based upon *primary identification*, i.e., lack of differentiation of self and objects. *Stage II*—Quasi-Independence, transitional between infantile and mature dependence, i.e., whole-object treated as bodily contents; this stage reflects the beginning differentiation of self from objects with efforts to "exteriorize" (externalize) the objects, akin to the elimination of fecal content, hence becoming perceivable as *real*. *Stage III*—Mature Dependence, reflects the achievement of full self–objects differentiation, hence of genitality and whole-object relationships. Cf. Transitional Stage Techniques.

ORIGINAL EGO. A precursory "undivided" self-representational structure from which the Central Ego, Libidinal Ego and Antilibidinal Ego are derived as secondary to the derivation of the Ideal Object, Exciting Object and Rejecting Object from the Original Object.

ORIGINAL OBJECT. A precursory "undivided" object-representational structure variously defined by Fairbairn as: the "first libidinal object"; the "only significant object"; the "natural object"; and "the figure of the child's mother." In part-object terms it represents the breast. Fairbairn considered that the Original Object receives both the infant's love and hate, later becoming dichotomized into the Ideal Object (which he earlier called the Accepted Object) that receives the infant's love and the Rejected Object that receives the infant's hate; in turn, the Rejected Object, which Fairbairn also called the Split Internalized Bad Object, splits into the Exciting Object and the Rejecting Object that are held in repression by the Central Ego.

REJECTED OBJECT. The component of the Original Object that receives the infant's hate and is internalized as the Split Internalized Bad Object that is subsequently split off and repressed by the Central Ego.

REJECTING OBJECT. The split-off and repressed frustrating, withholding, persecutory component of the Split Internalized Bad Object. Pre-Oedipally it represents the breast (the maternal part-object) while Oedipally it represents the penis (the Oedipal father regressively treated as a part-object).

REPRESSION. Fairbairn defines repression as either *direct* or *indirect*: the former consists of "an attitude of rejection" on the part of the Central Ego toward the Exciting Object and the Rejecting Object and secondarily toward their respectively associated Libidinal Ego and Antilibidinal Ego; the latter is defined as the Antilibidinal Ego's "uncompromisingly hostile attitude" toward the Libidinal Ego and its associated Exciting Object, which furthers the Central Ego's direct repression. In both cases, aggression serves as the energy of repression and in both cases splitting is the result—the Exciting Object from the Rejecting Object in the case of direct repression, and the Libidinal Ego from the Antilibidinal Ego in the case of indirect repression. Accordingly, splitting and repression are essentially the same process. Although Fairbairn refers to "the unconscious mind," he nowhere attempts to account for how repressed (i.e., split-off) mental contents, specifically the "subsidiary" egos and objects, become unconscious.

SPLIT INTERNALIZED BAD OBJECT. Also called the Rejected Object, which, see.

SUBSIDIARY EGOS. Fairbairn's inclusive term for the Libidinal Ego and the Antilibidinal Ego.

SUBSIDIARY OBJECTS. Fairbairn's inclusive term for the Exciting Object and the Rejecting Object, to which he also inclusively refers simply as "bad objects." Again, Fairbairn at times uses the term "bad objects" to apply, not only to the Exciting and Rejecting Objects, but also to their associated Libidinal and Antilibidinal Egos.

SUPEREGO. Fairbairn's concept of the Superego, like that of Freud, evolved over time. He found uncongenial Freud's view of the Superego as resulting from object-introjection; rather, he viewed it as a complex "dynamic structure" which he early considered to be the Antilibidinal Ego; later, he considered it to be the associated Antilibidinal Ego and Rejecting Object. However, he found it impossible to attribute the origin of guilt to either of these, claiming instead that the Superego originates at a "higher level" of mental organization, not further explained. Rinsley's analysis of Fairbairn's writings on the Superego led him to conclude that the associated Antilibidinal Ego–Rejecting Object constitutes the harsh, sadistic, persecutory component of the Superego, while its ethical–moral component is the associated Central Ego–Ideal Object; this analysis was based upon Fairbairn's view of the Ideal Object as the Central Ego's "Accepted Object" and his conclusion that the associated Central Ego–Ideal Object is not repressed.

TRANSITIONAL STAGE TECHNIQUES. During the Quasi-Independent or Transitional Stage (Fairbairn's Stage II), the Original Object becomes "dichotomized" into the Accepted Object and the Rejected Object. As this occurs, four "techniques" or "methods" come into play by which the child attempts to regulate or "deal with" these two objects as to renounce Stage I (oral) relationships based upon primary identification in favor of relationships based upon differentiated objects. Fairbairn emphasized that these techniques persist into later life as pathologic mechanisms for warding off regression to schizoid (early oral) and depressive (late oral) states. *Phobic Technique*: both the Accepted and the Rejected Objects are externalized in an effort to resolve conflict over separation from and reunion with the Original Object; *Obsessional Technique*: both the Accepted and the Rejected Objects are internalized in an effort to resolve conflict over the urge to retain or expel the Original Object as (fecal) contents; *Hysterical Technique*: the Accepted Object is externalized as an overvalued or idealized, genital symbolic of an overvalued or idealized breast, while the Rejected Object is internalized as one's own devalued genital symbolic of a devalued breast; *Paranoid Technique*: the Accepted Object is internalized and ideally overvalued, while the Rejected Object is externalized as a congeries of persecutors.

UNDIVIDED EGO. Alternate term for the Original Ego.

UNDIVIDED OBJECT. Alternate term for the Original Object.

BIBLIOGRAPHY

Fairbairn, W. R. D. (1954), *An Object-Relations Theory of the Personality*. New York: Basic Books. (*Psychoanalytic Studies of the Personality*. London: Tavistock Publications, 1952.)

Greenberg, J. R., and S. A. Mitchell (1983), W. R. D. Fairbairn. In: *Object Relations in Psychoanalytic Theory*, pp. 157–187. Cambridge, MA: Harvard University Press.

Kerberg, O. F. (1980). Fairbairn's theory and challenge. In: *Internal World and External Reality: Object Relations Theory Applied*, pp. 57–84. New York: Jason Aronson.

Rinsley, D. B. (1979), Fairbairn's object-relations theory: A reconsideration in terms of newer knowledge. *Bull. Menninger Clin.*, 43:489–514. *Reprinted as*: Fairbairn's object-relations theory. In: Rinsley, D. B. (1982), *Borderline and Other Self Disorders: A Developmental and Object-Relations Perspective*, pp. 75–95. New York: Jason Aronson.

Rinsley, D. B. (1982), Fairbairn's object relations and classical concepts of dynamics and structure. In: *Borderline and Other Self Disorders: A Developmental and Object-Relations Perspective*, pp. 251–270. New York: Jason Aronson.

Sullivan, C. T. (1963), *Freud and Fairbairn: Two Theories of Ego Psychology*, with Preface by W. R. D. Fairbairn. Doylestown, PA: The Doylestown Foundation.

Index

341